Rupert B. Vance

University of North Carolina

1 9 3 2

AMERICAN GEOGRAPHICAL SOCIETY
SPECIAL PUBLICATION NO. 14
Edited by W. L. G. JOERG

PIONEER SETTLEMENT

COÖPERATIVE STUDIES

BY

TWENTY-SIX AUTHORS

AMERICAN GEOGRAPHICAL SOCIETY
BROADWAY AT 156TH STREET
NEW YORK

1932

COPYRIGHT, 1932

BY

THE AMERICAN GEOGRAPHICAL SOCIETY

THE COMMONWEALTH PRESS, WORCESTER, MASS.

CONTENTS

PREFACE

Throughout the world new lands are being opened up to settlement. In the Prairie Provinces of Canada, in the eastern foothills of the Patagonian Andes, on the cool subtropical highlands of southern Africa, along the southern edge of the Siberian forest belt, in the great lowland plain of Manchuria, and on the inner side of the fertile crescent of Australia virgin soil is being put under the plow, houses are being built to shelter pioneer families, and the web of frontier civilization is being woven. But conditions have changed since the heroic age of American pioneering in the nineteenth century. In all but a few regions of the world the best land has been taken up, and, to occupy what remains, special agricultural methods such as dry farming or the introduction of frost- or drought-resistant cereals must be employed. Then, too, the spirit of the pioneer has altered. While he is willing to work hard to attain his goal he does not expect to have to undergo the hardships of the earlier age of colonizing. He tries to take civilization with him and to maintain the relatively high standard of living to which he has been accustomed.

To study and if possible solve the complex problems of pioneer settlement brought about by these new conditions the scientific approach is necessary. What is needed is a "science of settlement." It is the purpose of the present book and its companion volume in the same series, "The Pioneer Fringe," by Isaiah Bowman, to lay the groundwork of such a discipline. In "The Pioneer Fringe" are discussed the general principles of pioneer settlement, illustrated by regional examples; the present volume constitutes a world survey of pioneer problems by specialists who have an intimate personal knowledge of the regions they discuss.

The two volumes are an outgrowth of a program of research undertaken by the American Geographical Society, a program which received the approval of the National Research Council and the Social Science Research Council as well as the financial support of the latter organization, as set forth in the introduction to "The Pioneer Fringe." The Social Science Research Council has gen-

v

erously shared with the American Geographical Society the cost of producing the present volume. It is also fitting to record grateful appreciation for the time and thought that have been given by the contributors of the papers in this volume and for their willingness to coöperate with the Society in the present undertaking. In fairness to them it should be stated that their papers were submitted on different dates over a period of three years, time being necessarily involved in a coöperative undertaking of such wide scope and drawing upon specialists in different fields residing in countries far apart.

PIONEER SETTLEMENT

THE PIONEER PROBLEMS OF THE PRAIRIE PROVINCES OF CANADA: GENERAL OUTLINE

W. A. MACKINTOSH

AFTER the "great emigrations" of 1826 to 1832 settlement in Canada proceeded mainly in subordination to other industries than agriculture—chiefly lumbering—and in dependence on such small local markets as had been built up. In the Northwest agricultural settlement had been dependent on the fur trade for markets. The creation of British Columbia in 1858 and the purchase by Canada of the territories of the Hudson's Bay Company in 1870 indicated the decisions of the Governments of Canada and of Great Britain that agricultural settlement could be established with direct rather than indirect contact with the expanding world market.

These decisions and their necessary complement, the undertaking to build the Canadian Pacific Railway, were reached after extensive inquiries had been made into the physical basis for settlement in the region between the Red River and the Rocky Mountains. While the agricultural settlements of the Canadian Northwest were, from a continental point of view, merely the pushing of the frontier beyond the northwestern states of the United States into Canadian territory, yet, since a fur-trading company was in supreme control north of the forty-ninth parallel, a definite decision as to the suitability of the southern part of Rupert's Land for settlement was made before the area became a part of the Dominion. The settlement of Western Canada, therefore, may fairly be looked on as an experiment in colonization permitted only after official expeditions had made extensive exploratory surveys of the country.

EARLY EXPLORATIONS TO DETERMINE AGRICULTURAL VALUE OF CANADIAN NORTHWEST

In 1857–1860 Captain John Palliser conducted, under commission from the British Government, explorations primarily in the valleys of the North and South Saskatchewan. In 1857–1858 Professor Henry Youle Hind explored the country as far as the headwaters of the Qu'Appelle. Between 1870 and 1880 further extensive surveys were carried out for the purpose of determining a satisfactory route for the Canadian Pacific Railway.

Palliser drew striking contrasts between the wooded or burned-over regions drained by the North Saskatchewan and the true prairies in the valley of the South Saskatchewan. "Palliser's triangle" was the extension of the "Great American Desert" into British territory.

The existence of a general law regulating the distribution of the woods in this portion of the continent suggested itself to us during our first summer's explorations, and subsequent experience during the seasons of 1858–9 fully confirmed it.

The fertile savannahs and valuable woodlands of the Atlantic United States are succeeded, as has been previously alluded to, on the west by a more or less arid desert, occupying a region on both sides of the Rocky Mountains, which presents a barrier to the continuous growth of settlements between the Mississippi Valley and the States on the Pacific coast. This central desert extends, however, but a short way into the British territory, forming a triangle, having for its base the 49th parallel from longitude 100° to 114° W., with its apex reaching to the 52nd parallel of latitude.

The northern forests, which in former times descended more nearly to the frontier of this central desert, have been greatly encroached upon and, as it were, pushed backwards to the north through the effect of frequent fires.

Thus a large portion of fertile country, denuded of timber, separates the arid region from the forest lands to the north, and the habit which the Indian tribes have of burning the vegetation has, in fact, gradually improved the country for the purpose of settlement by clearing off the heavy timber, to remove which is generally the first and most arduous labour of the colonist.[1]

It was the true prairie, as distinguished from the park or grove region, which Palliser dismissed as worthless. From the absence of trees he deduced lack of soil fertility and moisture. In the valley of the North Saskatchewan he found fish, grass for grazing, land already cleared, and fuel—great advantages in pioneer agriculture.

H. Y. Hind reached similar conclusions. "Other visionaries have converted the four hundred thousand square miles drained by the Saskatchewan into a region of unbounded fertility and inexhaustible resources. Whereas, a proper appreciation and use

[1] Journals, Detailed Reports, and Observations Relative to the Exploration by Captain Palliser of That Portion of British North America Which in Latitude Lies Between the British Boundary Line and the Height of Land or Watershed of the Northern or Frozen Ocean Respectively and in Longitude Between the Western Shore of Lake Superior and the Pacific Ocean, During the Years 1857, 1858, 1859, and 1860, British Parliamentary Paper, London, 1863; reference on p. 7.

of facts will convince the most sanguine that the larger portion of this area is, in its present state, unfit for the permanent habitation of man both on account of climate, soil, and absence of fuel."[2] Hind estimated that between the Red River and the Moose Woods on the South Branch of the Saskatchewan there were available 11,100,000 acres of land of first quality. The 1926 census records 22,000,000 acres of improved land in this area (assuming that one-half the improved land in Saskatchewan lies east of the Moose Woods).

More enlightened and thorough surveys were made under the direction of Sandford Fleming, the engineer-in-chief of the Canadian Pacific Railway, prior to the completion of that road. A map accompanying his report for 1880[3] sets out the information derived from these surveys and also from the records of earlier explorers.

Professor John Macoun, the botanist attached to the staff of the chief engineer, was much more optimistic than preceding explorers had been. He asserted that recurring fires, and not aridity as Palliser inferred, were the cause of the treelessness of the true prairie. Fire spread most easily in those areas where the grass was thickest, and hence trees were most likely to be found in "bluffs" or on sandy hills where the scanty vegetation of inferior soils did not provide sufficient fuel for frequent fires.[4] Macoun allowed only about 20,000 square miles for the "arid" region of Palliser's triangle. He estimated 150,000,000 acres of land suitable for agriculture and stock-raising between the western boundary of Manitoba and the Rocky Mountains.[5] The census of 1926 reports in this area 75,000,000 acres of occupied land, of which 41,000,000 acres are improved.[6] In 1921 it was estimated that there were in this area 191,000,000 acres of agricultural land, of which 117,000,000 acres were then unoccupied.[7]

[2] H. Y. Hind: Reports of Progress Together with a Preliminary and General Report on the Assiniboine and Saskatchewan Exploring Expedition Made under Instructions from the Provincial Secretary, Canada; Printed by order of the Legislative Assembly, Toronto, 1859; reference on p. 131. See also Hind's "Narrative of the Canadian Red River Exploring Expedition of 1857 and of the Assiniboine and Saskatchewan Exploring Expedition of 1858," 2 vols., London, 1860; reference in Vol. 2, p. 377.

[3] Report and Documents in Reference to the Canadian Pacific Railway, Sandford Fleming, Engineer-in-Chief, 1880, Ottawa, 1880, Pl. 7, 1: 3,000,000. On it the belts of land along the network of explorers' routes from Winnipeg to the Peace River District are differentiated as (1) soil of rich quality and pasture land more or less fertile, (2) pasture land of questionable value, not sterile, (3) marshy land, much of it producing hay, (4) muskeg, (5) rocky or sterile land.

[4] John Macoun: General Remarks on the Land, Wood, and Water of the North-West Territories from the 102nd to the 115th Meridian and Between the 51st and 53rd Parallels of Latitude, ibid., pp. 235–245 (Appendix 14); reference on pp. 238–239.

[5] Ibid., p. 245.

[6] Canada Year Book, 1929, Dominion Bureau of Statistics, Ottawa, 1929, p. 272.

[7] Ibid., p. 36.

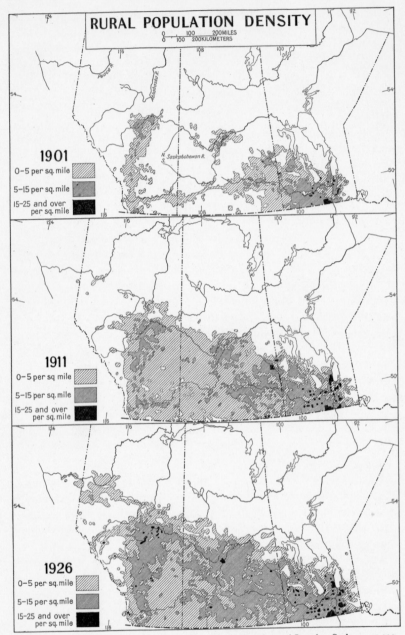

Figs. 1–3—The growth of rural population in the Prairie Provinces of Canada. Scale, 1 : 22,000,-
000. (Based on manuscript maps prepared by the Canadian Pioneer Problems Committee.)

MAVOR'S ESTIMATES OF THE AMOUNT OF POTENTIAL WHEAT LAND

In 1904 the report of Professor James Mavor to the British Board of Trade on the Northwest of Canada made public five independent estimates of the amount of good land and the probable export surplus of wheat, of which the three most important were as follows:[8]

The first estimate gave the acreage of land suitable for settlement and cultivation as 92,000,000, of which 13,750,000 might be devoted annually to wheat, producing 254,000,000 bushels, of which two-thirds, 169,000,000, would be available for export.

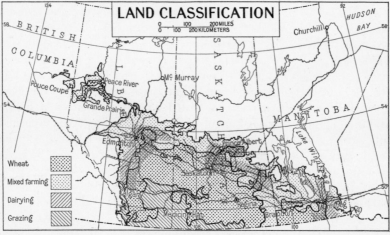

FIG. 4—Land utilization in the Prairie Provinces (approximately status of 1930). Scale, 1:22,-000,000. (Based on map by National Development Bureau, Ottawa.)

By the second estimate, land suitable for settlement was placed at 101,000,000 acres, of which 22,000,000 might be devoted annually to wheat, producing a crop of 357,000,000 bushels. The census of 1926 reports 90,000,000 acres in farms, 22,000,000 acres in wheat, and a production of 381,000,000 bushels.

Dr. William Saunders, the originator of Marquis wheat, made the third estimate and was clearly overoptimistic or at least visualized a much more distant future. Of a total area of 232,000,000 acres, he estimated 171,000,000 acres as suitable for settlement and capable of producing 812,000,000 bushels of wheat.

[8] James Mavor: Report to the Board of Trade on the North West of Canada, With Special Reference to Wheat Production for Export, British Parliamentary Papers, Cmd. 2628, London, 1904, pp. 68–77 and 116–123 (Appendixes A, B, C).

Settlement of the Prairie Provinces

The Canadian Northwest contained in 1870, 48,000 people; in 1926 it supported a population of slightly over 2,000,000. In the decade 1901–1911 population was multiplied by four, and since 1911 it has increased by 75 per cent (Figs. 1–3).

The settlement of the Canadian West has exceeded all but the most optimistic estimates. Settlers have invaded Palliser's triangle; country long designated as grazing country has been homesteaded; the northern forest has been attacked in some areas. Settlers with tractors are as far north as the 58th parallel, while the discovery of rich mining areas in northern Saskatchewan and Manitoba will undoubtedly attract subsidiary agricultural settlement (Fig. 4).

All this has not been done, however, without grave human wastage. To the hardships of those pioneers who have succeeded we must add the losses of those who have failed. The invasion of the "dry belt" was turned into a retreat in the abandonment, recorded in 1926, of 55 per cent of the farms in Census District No. 3 in Alberta (approximately the area enclosed by the Red Deer, Bow, and South Saskatchewan Rivers northwest of Medicine Hat). The post-war settlement of the Peace River Valley turned into an exodus of settlers in 1924 and 1925. Settlement of the bush country between Lakes Winnipeg and Manitoba brought undesirably low standards of living.[9]

By 1928 the tide had turned, and the pioneers were once more pushing into unoccupied areas. The motor car, the truck, and the tractor, Reward and Garnet wheat, four successive years of good crops and good prices (1925–1928), the airplane and the radio—these combined with the old lure of virgin prairie to move back still farther the margin of settlement. The squatter reappeared as a problem in the province of Alberta. At the moment three years of low prices and disastrous drought in southern Saskatchewan have brought another period of abandonment of farms, coupled in this instance with a marked movement into the sub-humid and wooded north.

At the moment also the control of available land has passed from the Dominion Government to the three provinces of Manitoba, Saskatchewan, and Alberta. These governments must perforce establish policies, and the record of experience has already led

[9] Unused Lands of Manitoba: Report of Survey Conducted by R. W. Murchie and H. C. Grant, 1926, 191 pp., Manitoba Department of Agriculture and Immigration, Winnipeg, 1927. Second edit., with additional chapter, "The Correlation of Physical, Economic and Social Factors," 206 pp., 1927.

them to decide against the traditional policy of free land. With further mechanization of farming it is possible that the settled area may contract rather than expand. No time could be more opportune for making a scientific study of settlement in Western Canada. The records of the period of rapid settlement are available for study: new policies of settlement must be framed.

THE CANADIAN PIONEER PROBLEMS COMMITTEE

It is at this juncture that has taken place the establishment of the Canadian Pioneer Problems Committee to undertake such a scientific study.[10] In formulating its program the Committee was guided by the following general analysis of the situation in pioneer regions.

In the process of agricultural settlement people enter a new area and adjust the art and business of farming to certain physical and economic controls. With inadequate knowledge of those controls the adjustment will be faulty and perhaps disastrous; accurate knowledge might preclude settlement altogether. The art and practice of living must be adjusted perchance to a new freedom but also to that lack of social institutions characteristic of the pioneer fringe. Such institutions as are built up are limited and modified by sparseness of population and inadequacy of communication. Assuming successful settlement, it is the social lacks of the frontier that constitute the most significant item in the costs of settlement. Only as those social deficiencies are filled does the successful settlement pass out of the pioneer into the mature stage.

The problems to be investigated by the Committee have been divided into five sections: 1, physical conditions; 2, agricultural economics; 3, history; 4, general economics; 5, social structure.

[10] In connection with the American Geographical Society's research program relating to problems of settlement in the pioneer regions of the world, of which the present symposium and its companion volume, "The Pioneer Fringe," are an outgrowth, the interest of the Social Science Research Council in New York was secured for an intensive study of the pioneer regions of Canada, mainly in the Prairie Provinces. Through the generous donation of funds by the Council a program covering a period of five years (1929–1933), including field work in the summers, was decided upon. The members of the Canadian Pioneer Problems Committee are: D. A. McArthur, Professor of History, Queen's University, vice-chairman; C. A. Dawson, Professor of Sociology, McGill University; Chester Martin, Professor of History, University of Toronto; R. C. Wallace, President of the University of Alberta (in place of D. A. MacGibbon, Professor of Economics, University of Alberta, who resigned on being appointed to the Board of Grain Commissioners of Canada); and W. A. Mackintosh, Professor of Political and Economic Science, Queen's University, director of research. The Committee was deprived through his death in May, 1930, of the services of its chairman, W. J. Rutherford, Dean of the School of Agriculture, University of Saskatchewan, who had been closely associated with the undertaking from the first presentation of the project to the Social Science Research Council at Hanover, N. H., in August, 1927, through the preliminary organization of the Canadian committee at Ottawa in May, 1928, to its final organization in May, 1929.

The separation of agricultural economics from general economics, though illogical, was dictated by the specialization of individual economists in one or the other branch.

In what follows the main problems of each section are briefly outlined and some reference is made to the work already accomplished. In the next five papers the setting of these problems is dealt with by the members of the Committee in charge of the respective sections and by others. It has been possible to dispense with an article on the physical conditions in view of a recent presentation of this topic, to which the reader is referred.[11]

ITS PROGRAM OF RESEARCH: PHYSICAL CONDITIONS

Where is there unsettled land? Is it suitable for settlement? What kind of soil is there? Is precipitation sparse or abundant? Are the summers hot and dry or cool and moist? How long is the growing season? How variable are climatic conditions? These are questions which the prospective settler should ask concerning the physical controls in the area in which settlement is in prospect.

Much study of these problems has been carried on and is being carried on by the Provincial and Dominion governments. The aerial and horizontal control maps of the Topographical Survey of Canada (Department of the Interior) give ordinary topographic information, while the surveyors' reports give a general characterization of the areas surveyed. During the period when the settlement of returned soldiers was a pressing problem definite land classification surveys were made by this branch and are still being conducted on a reduced scale. The governments of the three Prairie Provinces through the agricultural colleges are conducting soil surveys differing in the degree of detail studied according to the degree of variation in the different provinces.

With the coöperation of these agencies this information is being brought together, and work in the unsettled areas is being pushed in the expectation that by the completion of the project there will be available three degrees of soil information, the approximation to detailed accuracy becoming rougher as one proceeds from the settled to the unsettled area. Maps based on soil surveys will cover the settled area; land classification and reconnaissance soil maps, the fringe of settlement; "potential agricultural land maps," areas remote from settlement.

[11] L. Rodwell Jones: Some Physical Controls in the Economic Development of the Prairie Provinces, *Geography* (formerly *The Geographical Teacher*), Vol. 14, 1927–28, pp. 284–302.

Only a small part of the records of the Meteorological Service of Canada has been published in map form, and a considerable part has not been published at all. In coöperation with the service and with the Dominion Bureau of Statistics a series of maps has been prepared for publication in a comprehensive atlas entitled "Agriculture, Climate, and Population of the Prairie Provinces of Canada." These maps will provide the basis for studies on the relation of climate to agriculture.

AGRICULTURAL ECONOMICS

From Palliser's day till now many have expressed opinions based on little or much knowledge as to the proper utilization of the various natural regions of Western Canada. How in fact have they been utilized? How has utilization varied between one area and another? between one race and another? between one farmer and another? At what rate have original settlers made business progress? What proportion of original homesteaders have remained to become successful farmers? How do those who are ultimately successful get a start on the fringe? What are the economic rewards of pioneering?

Answers to these and many related questions are being sought, first, by compiling and mapping all the information that is available in the quinquennial census of the Prairie Provinces and other public sources and, secondly, by a series of surveys in selected areas.

These surveys will be carried on partly in mature communities and partly in distinctively pioneer areas. They will be directed toward ascertaining settlers' progress and types of farming. In general they will record in detail for selected areas the business results of farming.

These surveys, which were begun in the summer of 1930, are directed by Dr. R. W. Murchie, lately of the Manitoba Agricultural College, now of the Department of Agriculture of the University of Minnesota, assisted by Dr. William Allen of the University of Saskatchewan.

HISTORY

While many problems are being approached historically, certain definite tasks have been assigned to the historians under the direction of Professor Chester Martin of the University of Toronto. They will provide an historical background for the whole period of settlement in Western Canada and in general will study move-

ments of population up to the point of settlement.   Professor
Martin himself is extending his studies in the history of land policy,
and Professor D. A. McArthur of Queen's University has undertaken an intensive study of immigration policy.   Professor A. S.
Morton of the University of Saskatchewan is continuing studies
he has been carrying on for some years on the early history of
settlement.   Special historical studies will be made of particular
racial and religious groups, such as the Icelanders, the Mennonites,
the Ukrainians, the Scandinavians, and others.

General Economics

Economic institutions that serve all regions but are less available
to the pioneer than to the mature community are frequently temporary or permanent controls determining the economic limits
of settlement.   Banking and credit institutions, railways and roads,
marketing organizations and taxation present the chief problems
of this sort.   To what extent is the pioneer community deficient
in the services of these institutions?   To what extent does it pay
more heavily for them?   To what extent are the older communities
taxed in order to provide these services to the scattered population
of the fringe?

Four special studies dealing with credit, transportation, marketing, and taxation have been planned.   Each study will be directed
to the problem of the pioneer, not of the institution as such.

Social Structure of the Pioneer Society

As suggested by Dr. C. A. Dawson, who is directing the sociological studies of the project, the distinguishing characteristics
of the pioneer fringe are social.   The lack of social institutions
and the modified standard of living are often more distinctive than
the types of farming or the sparseness of population.

A series of surveys carried out in coöperation with the agricultural surveys will be directed toward the measurement of these
deficiencies and modifications.   Necessarily, mature and evidently
satisfactory communities will also be studied in order that standards may be determined for measuring the deficiencies of the pioneer
areas.

The results of detailed surveys will be supplemented by studies
of basic institutions throughout the three provinces.   The family,
the church, the school, health organization, social work, and

interest-group organization, recreational facilities, and the machinery of local government and the administration of justice are all
important objects of scientific study.

CONCLUSION

Ideally certain objectives may be set up for study:

> The area—the physical controls of settlement.
> The people—racial and ethnological characteristics.
> The process of settlement.
> The life history of the pioneer community of the Cana-
> dian West.
> The results of settlement.
>   A scientific appraisal of policy.

In practice so comprehensive a social and economic study will
not be possible. With the data acquired and available, ideal objectives can be only partially attained. Even incomplete results will,
however, be highly significant and useful.

AGRICULTURAL LAND UTILIZATION IN WESTERN CANADA

R. W. MURCHIE

IN the past there has been in Canada a considerable amount of good land open for settlement under the Homestead Act and a considerable amount of good land available for purchase at low prices. Neither the Dominion government nor the Provincial governments, however, felt the necessity of assisting the settler to choose his land, nor was advice given as to the methods of development. The policy was rather to allow the greatest freedom of choice and of method on the assumption that any one who had natural ability for farming, whether experienced or not, would eventually succeed, as indeed the great majority actually did. In the early days of settlement it was quite true that almost any tract of 160 acres that an intelligent settler would on inspection select could be developed into a farm home.

As the best of the land began to be picked over, and as the great influx of immigrants at the beginning of this century rushed to take up land, it soon became evident that some of the land on which they settled was decidedly inferior, at least so far as its suitability for growing grain was concerned. It was, nevertheless, true that many of these immigrants had come from countries where much poorer land had been farmed for generations, and the farms they chose seemed to suit them well enough. What they neglected to take into account was the difference in climatic and economic conditions. Land of a quality that could be economically developed under European conditions turned out to be submarginal under Western Canadian conditions. Then arose the necessity for the close examination of the soil characteristics and of the economic factors bearing on the successful utilization of the land.

The problem of land utilization in Canada is twofold: first, the more intensive development of land within areas now settled and, second, the extension of the boundaries of present settlement northward.

More Intensive Development of Areas Already Settled

The more settled areas are of course in the east and, in passing, this part of the country may be referred to for a moment. In the Maritime Provinces, of a total area of land supposed to be of agricultural value and estimated[1] at approximately 20,000,000 acres, 10,000,000 acres are found to be actually farmed. Soil conditions and topography are here the chief limiting factors. In Ontario and Quebec both types of problem are to be found. In many of the settled areas there is considerable acreage undeveloped, and in the northern portion of these provinces there is the great Clay Belt, in which a sparse settlement now exists and which gives promise of further agricultural development. These two provinces have more than 40,000,000 acres of unoccupied land rated as agricultural, most of it being in the Clay Belt.

In the main area of inquiry, the Prairie Provinces, the underlying factors relating to both problems can readily be appreciated from a glance at the two accompanying maps showing the percentage of the total land area occupied (Fig. 1) and the percentage of the total land area improved (Fig. 2). It will be seen that the occupied land lies south of a line drawn from the southeast corner of the Province of Manitoba in a northwesterly direction, crossing Saskatchewan just north of Prince Albert and passing north of Edmonton to meet the Rocky Mountains. Within the area south of this line, however, considerable portions of the land are very thinly settled. With the exception of the southern portion of Manitoba and the south-central region of Saskatchewan, only a small percentage of the available land is actually improved.

Several of the areas now represented as sparsely settled were previously homesteaded and after a series of failures were evacuated. Climatic conditions and the physical composition of the soil are the limiting factors, but the chief cause of failure was in the system of land utilization. Much intensive work in soil mapping and in the development of agricultural programs will be necessary before a successful agricultural use can be found for this land. The Dominion government and the Provincial governments are now carrying on soil surveys, and new developments are already taking place in some of the areas covered.

The introduction of power farming, especially the introduction of the "combine" (harvester-thresher), is bringing about a revolution

[1] Canada Year Book, 1929, Dominion Bureau of Statistics, Ottawa, 1929, p. 36.

in prairie agriculture that will be far-reaching in its effect on the utilization of land within this area.

Southwestern Saskatchewan and southeastern Alberta are popularly known as the dry belt. Here only by advanced methods of dry farming and by the building of expensive irrigation works can the land be put to any intensive agricultural use, and grazing

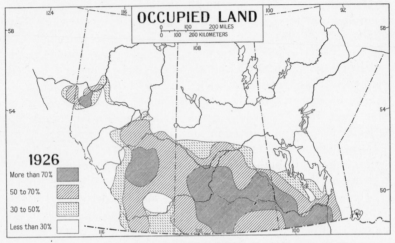

Fig. 1—Occupied land in the Prairie Provinces, 1926. Scale, 1 : 22,000,000.

is likely to continue to be its chief utilization. Within the remainder of the settled portion of Alberta the thickening up of settlement is proceeding rapidly.

Northward Extension of Present Limit of Settlement

In the Prairie Provinces, it is estimated, there are about 215,000,-000 acres of agricultural land. Of this only about 90,000,000 acres are at present occupied and 50,000,000 acres improved.[2] If the estimate is correct, there are still 125,000,000 acres of unoccupied land that could be turned into farms. Much of this land, however, lies north of the southeastern Manitoba-Edmonton line described above.

In Manitoba, owing to the extent in this province of the vast soil-denuded rocky area known as the Precambrian Shield, which covers all of northern Manitoba and the strip east of Lake Winnipeg, very little of this agricultural land is to be found. The Provincial

[2] Canada Year Book, 1929, p. 36.

government of Manitoba recently had a survey made covering approximately 9,000,000 acres on the fringe of settlement, and the report[3] would seem to indicate that less than 1,000,000 acres are available for settlement under present economic and technological conditions. Beyond this fringe, however, there are considerable patches of clays and clayey loams within the Precambrian Shield.

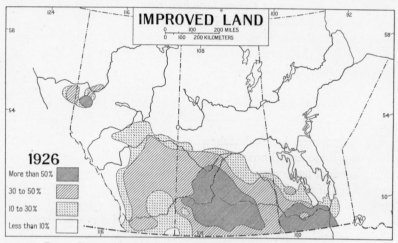

FIG. 2—Improved land in the Prairie Provinces, 1926. Scale, 1 : 22,000,000.

Their development for agricultural purposes will probably be as subsidiaries to the development of other natural resources such as minerals, timber, water power, and fisheries.

The problem so far as these patches are concerned will be to devise a system of agriculture that in its earliest stages will be chiefly suited to supplying the local needs of those engaged in the above-mentioned primary industries but which, when the mines are worked out and the timber cut down, will provide a self-sufficing or else a commercial agriculture. Little is known of the actual areas of these patches or concerning their real agricultural value, but the growing season is known to be short. The new development of mineral resources in the north and the recent completion of the Hudson Bay Railway will no doubt bring these small areas into prominence, and there is urgent need for detailed scientific information on which to base a sane policy of settlement and development.

[3] Unused Lands of Manitoba: Report of Survey Conducted by R. W. Murchie and H. C. Grant, 1926, 191 pp., Manitoba Department of Agriculture and Immigration, Winnipeg, 1927. Second edit., with additional chapter, "The Correlation of Physical, Economic, and Social Factors," 206 pp., 1927.

The Topographical Survey of Canada has since 1918 been carrying on land classification surveys, whose chief purpose is to assist
the intending settler to choose a desirable farm.   This work, which
is carried on under the direction of F. H. Peters, the director of the
Topographical Survey, is defined as "the systematic survey or
examination of the land in order to obtain complete and authentic
information concerning the surface covering, the nature of the soil,
and the extent of the surface improvements."   The work already
done by the Dominion government includes some 27,000,000 acres
of land along the northern edge of the settled parts of Manitoba,
Saskatchewan, and Alberta.[4]

The Carrot River and Peace River Districts
As Examples

On the fringe in Saskatchewan, northeast of Prince Albert,
there is a large area known as the Carrot River district into which
many settlers have gone in recent years but regarding which very
little scientific information is actually available at the present
time.   Much of this area is low land and will require drainage
before being settled, but whether this would be an economic
project is still undetermined.   Macoun comments[5] very favorably
on the fertility of the soil of this region, but the extent of agricultural land and the rapidity with which it ought to be settled are
unknown.

In Alberta interest centers in the now famous Peace River valley
concerning which we hear so much but know so little.   The available
agricultural land in this area is variously estimated by the con-
servatives as 47,000,000 acres and by the optimists as 100,000,000.
Macoun as early as 1882 noted the luxuriance of the natural
vegetation[6] in this area as indicating not only the fertility of the
soil but the occurrence of sufficient rainfall.

Into this region a very large migration has taken place, and,
while the boosters are enthusiastic, there are many authorities
who hold that settlement should not be encouraged until much
more has been found out concerning the true economic possibilities
and limiting factors of this area.   The questions of transportation

[4] For a conspectus of the areas covered by these surveys see Index [Map] to Land Classification
and Soil Maps, 1 : 3,801,600, Topographical Survey of Canada, Ottawa, 1927.   In addition the
Colleges of Agriculture of the Universities of Saskatchewan and Alberta have published reports
with soil maps of numerous scattered areas in these two provinces (about nine areas in Saskatchewan and four in Alberta).

[5] John Macoun: Manitoba and the Great North-West, Guelph, Ontario, 1882, p. 95.

[6] Ibid., p. 126.

and water supply and soil characteristics all require immediate investigation. The Provincial government and the University of Alberta have been trying to keep just a little ahead of settlement and have been warning intending settlers against establishing themselves in some of the areas, but when a settlement rush is on little can be done to control the location of homesteaders or to prevent them from locating on any piece of land that has been opened for settlement.

DANGER OF COLONIZATION OF MARGINAL LAND BY SETTLERS WITH A LOW STANDARD OF LIVING

The present state of information would lead one to conclude that much of the land beyond the southeastern Manitoba-Edmonton line described above is marginal land in the economic as well as in the geographic sense, and that, if settled at all, it is likely to be colonized only by those who will be content with a standard of living lower than that demanded by the average English-speaking settlers in Western Canada. If this be true it is highly probable that, beyond the present fringe, agricultural settlement will largely be made by Central and Southeastern Europeans, who have shown in the past a lower rate of assimilability.[7]

This may start a vicious circle, for, if non-assimilable, illiterate people are placed on marginal lands where they cannot hope to have a high standard of living, the difference between their standards and the accepted standards of the country will be accentuated and perpetuated. Herein may lie many problems for the sociologist and administrator of the future. Only by a scientific survey, by fearless facing of the facts, and by carefully prepared programs of administration and development based on these facts can these problems be met.

Consideration must therefore be given, first, to the need for new land to be brought into cultivation and the rate of development most desirable; second, to the scientific classification of land from the point of view of its physical characteristics; third, to the clear enunciation of the agricultural programs for each type; and, fourth, to the selection of the best type of settler to place on it.

[7] Origin, Birthplace, Nationality, and Language of the Canadian People (A Census Study Based on the Census of 1921 and Supplementary Data), Dominion Bureau of Statistics, Ottawa, 1929.

EARLY HISTORY AND LAND SETTLEMENT OF THE PRAIRIE PROVINCES OF CANADA

CHESTER MARTIN

THE physical controls in the recent economic development of the Prairie Provinces have been admirably outlined by Professor L. Rodwell Jones.[1] A prefatory note may be added for the earlier period in which the major problems of early settlement have their beginning.

Glacial Lake Agassiz, larger at one time than all the Great Lakes put together, was drained at first southward into the Mississippi and finally northward through the receding ice wall. Lake Winnipeg, which is left of this vast reservoir, still gathers the streams of three vast watersheds, the Winnipeg River, the Red, and the Saskatchewan, before pouring them forth by the Nelson River into Hudson Bay. In these facts of geography lies the key to many of the problems of early settlement.

THE HISTORIC ROUTES OF ACCESS TO THE WEST

There have been no fewer than four historic routes of access to the West, each charged with a distinctive destiny. The first, by way of Hudson Bay, was the route by which the fur trade of the Hudson's Bay Company was carried on for two centuries, and under their auspices, during a single decade, from 1812, settlement was begun at Red River. The second, the long canoe route from Canada, through no fewer than sixty lakes and over more than three hundred portages, enabled the North-West Company to cut athwart the Hudson Bay route, intercept the furs on the way to the bay, and precipitate at the point of intersection the bitterest conflict in the history of the country—a conflict which nearly exterminated the Red River Settlement and led through sheer exhaustion to the coalition of the two fur companies in 1821. Governor Simpson promptly closed this "back door" from Canada, and the long water route to the east appears again only spasmodically in the Dawson route or in combination with the railways of a later date. Had the Red River region been united to Canada

[1] L. Rodwell Jones: Some Physical Controls in the Economic Development of the Prairie Provinces, *Geography* (formerly *The Geographical Teacher*), Vol. 14, 1927–28, pp. 284–302.

in 1821 or in 1840 instead of 1870 many historic problems of early settlement could scarcely have arisen.

The third route of access, by way of the United States, developed in a single generation, until annexation was regarded in many quarters—by the Governor of Rupert's Land himself in 1869—as inevitable. The contrast between the Red River Settlement and Oregon, however, held momentous consequences for the future of Canada and the personnel of settlement. The first railway nevertheless reached Manitoba from the south in 1879, the precursor of the boom of 1880–1881 and one of the chief incentives, both direct and indirect, to the building of a fourth route of access, a transcontinental railway on Canadian territory. It was against this southern approach that the "monopoly clause" of the Canadian Pacific Railway charter was directed in 1881; and indeed it may be said that not only the first transcontinental Canadian railway but the original design of a transcontinental Canadian dominion was discerningly projected in defiance of nature and the barriers of physical geography.

The Red River Settlement

One of the most distinctive features of the Canadian West has thus been the spirit of the Western Canadian people: a feature determined only partially by normal physical or economic controls. Many of the historical problems of motive and of personnel are of this nature. The beginning of settlement in this vast region was the work of one man. In defiance of the purely trading interests of both fur companies Selkirk carried the Hudson's Bay directorate into his project of settlement at Red River in 1811. The North-West Company, convinced that colonization would "strike at the very existence of our trade," twice destroyed the Red River Settlement and consented only against their will to its survival at the coalition with the Hudson's Bay Company in 1821. The Hudson's Bay directors themselves, won for a time to grudging acquiescence by Selkirk's promises of supplying provisions and apprentices for the trade as well as grants of land for retiring servants of the Company, were equally skeptical in 1821. One of Selkirk's own relatives wished the Red River Settlement "at the bottom of the Red Sea twenty years ago."

This fundamental conflict of interest between fur trade and settlement is a recurring problem for half a century. It dominated the policy of the British government, first in favor of the trade and

of the native Indian population in the monopolistic licenses granted
to the new Hudson's Bay Company in 1821 and 1838, and finally in
favor of settlement by the creation of British Columbia in 1858
and by the transfer of the rest of the vast Hudson's Bay Territories—
a quarter of the entire continent—to Canada in 1870. The policy
of the company towards the settlement, paternal but upon the
whole benevolent, can only be interpreted by bearing in mind their
legal rights and trading interests to the contrary. In dealing, too,
with the Indian there has been no fairer record than that of the
Hudson's Bay Company, a tradition unbroken for two centuries
by a single major conflict.

Developments of the Seventies and Eighties

The transfer to Canada in 1870 was the triumph of settlement
over the fur trade, but the rest of the century was still dominated
by problems that survived from the earlier period. The demands
of the primitive French métis for "some breakwater" against the
deluge of immigration occasioned an insurrection at Red River
in 1870 and a rebellion on the Saskatchewan in 1885. The political
life of Manitoba and eventually of Canada was convulsed in 1889
and 1896 by similar problems arising out of the transfer of 1870,
and still others await a solution. The process of actual settlement,
however, was peaceful and rapid. The causes and personnel of
the migrations from Eastern Canada, the effect of the route through
the United States in deflecting on the way the bulk of this migration from a destination in the Canadian West, and the net result
of the boom of 1880–1881 are problems of this period. To this
period also belong the beginnings of group settlements—the Ice-
landic and Mennonite migrations, which have remained among the
most distinctive in Western Canada. The records of Dominion
policy over a wide range of problems now supply data of exceptional value. A series of Indian treaties and the Northwest Mounted
Police inaugurated a tradition of law and order seldom equaled
in pioneer settlement.

Problems of Land Settlement To Be Solved

In one respect a pioneer belt survey for Western Canada is
singularly appropriate. An historic cycle in the administration
of public lands is now drawing to a close, and a policy that owed
its beginning to national emergencies in 1870 is now, after fifty

years of controversy, about to be abrogated. Between the federal control of public lands in Western Canada and that still to be found in the public land states of the American Union there have been many technical similarities of actual administration. Their origins and constitutional basis, however, have been vastly different, a fact that goes far to account for the recent success of the Prairie Provinces in regaining control of the natural resources within their boundaries. Under the Hudson's Bay Company the tenure of land was primitive and as a rule unrecorded. In accepting the transfer in 1870 Canada not only validated all Hudson's Bay grants in the registers but made special grants to placate the métis after the Riel Insurrection. But the land policy of the Dominion was dominated by larger national issues. What were the historic reasons for withholding from Manitoba in 1870 and from Saskatchewan and Alberta in 1905 the control of their public lands? What was the relation between the expansion of Canada to the Pacific and the building of the Canadian Pacific Railway, between the "land grant" system for the Canadian Pacific Railway and the free homestead system, between the free homestead system and indiscriminate immigration, between indiscriminate immigration, again, and the railways? What has been the net result of the land grant system for the railways and of the free homestead system for the country as a whole? Would the provinces be well advised to continue either with the unalienated resources which yet remain? What deductions are to be drawn from the administration hitherto of Hudson's Bay lands, of Canadian Pacific Railway lands, of school lands and university lands, of the preëmption features of the free homestead system? Are there any feasible methods of registering unimproved or idle lands for sale under government auspices? These and other problems of land settlement are now, for the first time perhaps, approachable from data sufficiently ample and convincing to warrant general conclusions.

IMMIGRATION AND COLONIZATION IN CANADA, 1900-1930

D. A. McArthur

THE last decade of the nineteenth century, which opened in Canada on a scene of gloom and depression, departed amidst feelings of buoyant hope and expectancy. Attention was being directed from many quarters to the prairies of Western Canada as an attractive field for settlement. The era of cheap land in the western United States had come to an end, and those who sought new land were obliged to turn northward to Canada. In the closing years of the century many thousands had crossed the northern frontier, carrying with them a moderate amount of capital and, what was more significant, a fund of experience and skill in the use of land similar to that of the Canadian prairies. They proved to be excellent colonists, and their success became an effective advertisement for Canada in Europe as well as in the United States.

The opening years of the new century likewise marked the emerging of Canada to a new position of prominence in the thought of the people of Britain and of Europe. The diamond jubilee of the accession of Queen Victoria had been celebrated with magnificent pageantry; the reality and the extent of the Empire had been impressively demonstrated, and with it there came a realization of the rapid growth—even approaching maturity—of the senior members of the British family and of their ability to bear a portion of the burden of imperial partnership. Canada's participation, along with the other dominions, in the military campaign in South Africa directed to her the attention of the peoples of western Europe as well as of Britain. A new star had emerged on the transatlantic horizon. The name of Canada was on the lips of thousands of persons to whom it was entirely unknown a decade earlier. It was known to be a country of vigorous people, sparsely inhabited, and having vast stretches of excellent agricultural lands awaiting the productive energy of the settler.

THE STAGE OF DEVELOPMENT OF THE PRAIRIE PROVINCES IN 1901

The total population of Manitoba and the Northwest Territories had increased from 220,000 in 1891 to 415,000 in 1901 while the area under crop increased in the same period from 1,420,000 acres to 3,600,000 acres. This settlement naturally was distributed chiefly along the lines of railway. In addition to the main line of the Canadian Pacific Railway there were branch lines extending from Calgary northward to Edmonton and south to Macleod, from Dunmore Junction to Lethbridge, and from Regina to Saskatoon and Prince Albert, besides the Manitoba and Northwestern, the Manitoba and Southwestern, and the Northern Pacific, with a line running from Emerson on the United States boundary to Winnipeg, and with branches to Brandon and Portage la Prairie. Mackenzie and Mann had already begun the construction of certain of the roads later to be incorporated in the Canadian Northern system and had a line running from Port Arthur westward across Manitoba with a branch extending northward from Gladstone to Dauphin. The construction of these railways had been made possible through the grant of financial assistance by the government of Manitoba, in certain cases, and in others by extensive concessions of land from the federal government. In all, the railways had received nearly 32,000,000 acres of public lands in Western Canada and became deeply interested in the problem of settlement not only as a means of providing profitable traffic but to give value to the lands which had been used as security for the bonds sold to provide funds for railway construction.

Western Canada had already attracted special groups of settlers from continental Europe. By the end of the century more than 25,000 Ruthenians were settled in western Manitoba, northern Saskatchewan, and northern Alberta. The Dukhobors had but recently been given lands along the Canadian Northern Railway in northern Saskatchewan. These, in addition to the Ukrainians and an infiltration of Danes, Poles, and Austrians, constituted the chief European continental elements in the population of Western Canada. The Canadian population that had migrated from the eastern provinces was reinforced by nearly 50,000 Americans, not all of American origin but almost wholly English-speaking and committed to the maintenance of ideals similar to those of the Canadian people.

STIMULATION OF IMMIGRATION AND ITS EFFECT, 1901–1911

The stage was now set for the operation of an aggressive and extensive campaign for immigrants under the able direction of the Hon. Clifford Sifton, who was familiar with the western country and knew its possibilities. Numerous immigration agencies were opened in the United States, in Britain, and on the Continent; literature advertising the attractions of the Canadian West was scattered broadcast; free land for the farmer and the opportunity of profitable employment for the laborer became the inducement to attract people to Canada. The elaborate organization created for the discovery of prospective immigrants was able to capitalize the publicity acquired by Canada during the Boer War. The interest of the government did not end, however, when the settlers arrived in Canada. Agencies were created for the reception of the immigrants and for the supervision of their ultimate distribution in Western Canada.

In the first decade of the new century Canada undertook a program of railway construction unparalleled in its history. Two new transcontinental lines, the Grand Trunk Pacific and the Canadian Northern, were projected and placed under construction, while many new branch lines were built where the advance of settlement seemed likely to provide traffic. This extensive railway construction required the labor of many thousands of workmen who could not be supplied by the Canadian market and were imported from abroad as immigrants. The results of an aggressive immigration policy in meeting an abnormal demand for labor and in peopling the western prairies were reflected in the census returns of 1911. The total immigration into Canada during the last decade of the nineteenth century was about 370,000, of whom nearly one-half came from the British Isles. The immigration during the first decade of the new century was nearly 1,500,000. The population of Manitoba had increased from 255,000 in 1901 to 461,000 in 1911. The population of the district that became the Province of Saskatchewan increased from 91,000 to 492,000 and that of Alberta from 73,000 to 374,000.

An analysis of the census returns of 1911 indicates the extent to which this increase is attributable to immigration. The following table (Table I) shows the origin of the population of the three Prairie Provinces.

During the decade the British-born population of Manitoba had increased from 33,000 to 90,000, of Saskatchewan from 9000 to 76,000, and of Alberta from 7000 to 65,000. The population of European birth had increased in Manitoba from 32,000 to 78,000, in Saskatchewan from 22,000 to 91,000, in Alberta from 12,000 to 58,000, whereas the population born in the United States increased

TABLE I—ORIGIN OF THE POPULATION OF THE PRAIRIE PROVINCES, 1911
(IN PER CENT)

	NATIVES OF THE PROVINCE	NATIVES OF OTHER CANADIAN PROVINCES	BRITISH BORN	FOREIGN BORN
Manitoba . . .	37	21	21	21
Saskatchewan . .	21	30	16	33
Alberta	20	23	19	38

in Manitoba from 7000 to 16,000, in Saskatchewan from 3000 to 70,000, and in Alberta from 11,000 to 81,000. The population of European birth was drawn largely from Germany, Austria, and the Scandinavian countries.

RESULTING PROBLEMS

The influx of such a large immigrant population created a series of problems that come within the scope of the survey undertaken by the Canadian Pioneer Problems Committee. Not the least important of these was the problem of land granting. The crown lands in the possession of the federal government were appropriated, largely on a basis of free grants, as a means of attracting settlement. As an incident of this policy a system of preëmption was introduced by which persons already possessing homesteads could secure additional land in the vicinity of the homestead on the payment of a small sum and the performance of certain work of clearing and breaking the land. At the same time, the railway corporations were selling lands near the railway lines as a means of securing a revenue for the companies. The operation of these various methods of disposing of land is receiving the attention of the Committee.

Arising out of this same situation are kindred problems of economic and social adjustment—problems of transportation, of marketing, of credit, and a large group of problems associated with the transplanting to the Canadian West of the social institutions and culture of many of the older European peoples.

The Creation of Provincial Administrations in the Area

When the great rush of migration had set in to the Canadian prairies the region extending westward from the Manitoba boundary to British Columbia constituted the Northwest Territories, which were governed by a lieutenant governor and a council responsible to an elected legislature. This government, however, did not possess the powers of a provincial administration; it could not levy taxes or borrow money and did not enjoy the right of creating companies. The new problems of legislation and administration emerging out of the rapid advance of settlement could not be solved by the existing system of government. In 1905 the portion of this territory south of the 60th parallel of latitude was erected into the provinces of Saskatchewan and Alberta, with powers of administration similar to those possessed by the older provinces. The organization of provincial administrations paved the way for the introduction of a system of local government suitable to the needs of the new communities. A consideration of these institutions of government necessarily comes within the scope of the present survey.

The Course of Immigration, 1911–1921

The movement of migration to Canada continued into the second decade of the century and reached its peak in 1913, when the total immigration amounted to 402,432. Of this number 150,000 had come from the British Isles and 140,000 from the United States. The maximum of migration from non-English-speaking peoples occurred in 1914, when the number reached 134,000. The total immigration into Canada during the first fourteen years of the century reached nearly 3,000,000, an average annual immigration of slightly less than 210,000. The tracing of the course of this migration and the mode of its adjustment to Canadian conditions comes within the scope of the Committee's survey.

The World War naturally interrupted the course of migration from all European countries to America. During the four years from 1915 to 1918 the total migration to Canada was less than 350,000 and fell below the total for each of the single years 1912, 1913, and 1914. Apart from the war, however, it is most probable that the wave of migration Canada-ward would have subsided after 1913. The western provinces had passed through the trying experience of a land boom that brought highly inflated prices and in its train the inevitable reaction and decline. The peak of employment in railway construction had been passed, and many of the immigrants who came during the previous decade left Canada, going in large numbers to the United States, where the demand for labor was greater. Much of the immigration of the pre-war years of the present century constituted, as it has been described, a short-term loan of European labor for purposes of railway construction. The period of deflation following the war involved serious readjustments in the industrial life of Canada and extensive unemployment. It is not surprising, therefore, that there should have been a substantial emigration from Canada to Europe and particularly to the United States, whose large industrial centers seemed to offer better opportunities for regular employment. During several years the emigration from Canada to the United States exceeded the total new immigration. An examination of recent census reports indicates that by 1921 about 75 per cent of the immigrant population had departed from the country. This phenomenon raises questions regarding the conditions determining the extent to which an immigrant population can be absorbed. The survey may indicate that Canada was "stuffed" with immigration much beyond her powers of assimilation. It may be possible to discover some of the characteristics of the settler who is likely to remain permanently in the country as distinguished from the transient and of the conditions of settlement most likely to contribute to his success.

Effect of the World War on Immigration

The World War, directly and incidentally, completely changed the character of the problem of immigration in Canada. The enormous loss of life in Britain consisted largely of men between the ages of 20 and 40, the group from which under normal conditions immigration to Canada would have been drawn. The readjustments in the economic organization of the country left little unemployment in agriculture but created a large number of unemployed in industry by reason of the decline of certain staple industries and of the difficulties met by workmen of a certain type in fitting themselves into the new industrial organization. In general these changes operated to the disadvantage of Canada in that the class best fitted by training and experience to become adjusted readily to her economic requirements was not inclined to emigrate, while those who wished to migrate were not the best suited to her system. The belligerent nations of continental Europe were not inclined to encourage emigration of their nationals during the years of reconstruction, when man power became an asset of great value. For some few years after the war the attitude towards former enemy states was not such as to permit any extensive migration of their peoples to Canada.

Effect of United States Immigration Restriction on Canada

The change in the immigration policy of the United States involved in the introduction of the quota system likewise materially affected migration to Canada. By reason of the conditions of post-war Europe and of the imposition of the quota, emigration from southern and eastern Europe to the United States fell rapidly— from 872,000 in 1913 to 23,000 in 1925. The Atlantic passenger fleet had been constructed to meet the demands of a much larger movement of people. Because of this decline in passenger traffic, and because of other conditions, the fares on transatlantic vessels were greatly increased and the high cost of transport erected an effective barrier to much of the immigration which under other conditions would have moved across the Atlantic. To encourage emigration to Canada it became necessary, therefore, for governments in Britain and in Canada to embark on a policy of subsidies. The imposition of restrictions on the legal admission of Southern and Eastern Europeans to the United States tended to encourage attempts to gain entrance through the back door by way of Canada. The extent to which this occurred is indicated by the fact that of the total immigration entering the three Prairie Provinces in the period 1921–1925 only one half remained in those provinces in 1926. Inquiry will probably indicate that much of the Canadian immigration since the World War was of a transient nature and regarded the United States as its ultimate destination. The survey is undertaking an examination of the ultimate disposition of this later migration.

Soldiers' Settlement and Other Supervised Forms of Colonization

The demobilization of the armed forces of the nation at the end of the war involved the adjustment to civilian life of thousands of men whose training had been interrupted by the war or who were unable to return to their former vocations. The government sought to meet this problem by offering special inducements to returned soldiers to undertake settlement in the western provinces. An elaborate scheme of soldiers' settlement was evolved whereby aid was granted in the purchase of farms and of agricultural equipment under the supervision of government. The operation of this most interesting experiment in controlled settlement comes within the scope of this survey. As incidents of the post-war adjustments in Britain, agreements were made between the governments of Great Britain and of Canada by which part of the passage money was paid for children, the wards of voluntary emigrating societies, and families and single men going to settle on the land, and more extensive aid was provided in special cases where families settled on improved farms. The operation of these special forms of supervised settlement is receiving the attention of the Committee.

Recent Canadian Attitude Towards Immigration

In recent years certain fairly clearly defined, though not wholly consistent, views have emerged with respect to the problem of immigration and settlement. The agrarian movement, which has assumed most substantial proportions in the Western Provinces, is based both in its economic and political phases on a very definite group consciousness. It has served to clarify and consolidate western rural opinion with respect to conditions affecting agriculture. The coöperative efforts of the western farmers have been successful because the rural population has been capable of appreciating the benefits of such coöperation and of fitting into the coöperative enterprise. The western farmer, therefore, has a direct interest in the character of the new immigration to the Prairie Provinces. Experience of a quarter of a century has indicated fairly clearly certain conditions necessary to success alike in the type and outlook of the settler and in the character and location of his land. In these circumstances western opinion has favored carefully controlled and selected immigration and has been inclined to regard with suspicion the subsidizing of immigration from the public treasury.

Another section of public opinion has been apprehensive lest immigration from continental Europe should increase to such an extent as to threaten the dominance of British ideals and institutions in the Western Provinces. The two large corporations, one publicly owned, that control the transportation situation likewise have an interest in immigration because of its relation to the problem of both passenger and freight traffic. Each company maintains an effective organization for the recruitment of immigration in Britain and on the European continent and for the placement of settlers on suitable lands in Canada. The aggressiveness of these railway organizations has occasionally aroused the concern of those interested in the effective control of immigration, and their activities on the European continent have been quite definitely limited by an agreement with the federal government. In general, the latest tendencies in policy have operated to encourage agricultural immigration from the British Isles and to place fairly definite restraints on immigration from southern and central Europe.

The recent transfer of the natural resources, including ungranted lands of the three Prairie Provinces, from the federal government to the several provinces will give those provinces a much more direct interest in the problems of immigration and colonization and may conceivably effect changes in the machinery for the control and direction of immigration. The prediction may be made with safety that the problem of immigration will receive much attention in the Western Provinces during the next few years. For that reason special value may be attached to the results of the experience of several decades in immigration and colonization as they may be discovered by an investigation such as that being undertaken by the Canadian Pioneer Problems Committee.

ECONOMIC FACTORS AFFECTING THE SETTLEMENT OF THE PRAIRIE PROVINCES

D. A. MacGibbon

IF we apply the tests of pioneer living[1] to the Canadian provinces of Alberta, Saskatchewan, and Manitoba, from their southern boundary to a line drawn through Edmonton, North Battleford, Prince Albert, and Dauphin, they must be regarded as having, except in one particular, passed beyond the primitive pioneer stage. In the region thus defined there is a rural population of about 1,200,000 people and an urban population of about 700,000. The provinces are organized politically as constituent parts of the Canadian Commonwealth. Each has established its own municipal institutions. Each has its own state university and a system of secondary and primary schools. A wide network of railway communications leaves very few districts farther than 12 miles from a railway. Surveyed roads, comprising 240,372 miles, are in use. There are more than 100,000 miles of improved earth roads, and graveled arterial motor roads either connect the principal cities or are under advisement. The number of automobiles currently registered totals 311,821. The despatch of grain, the outstanding farm product, is facilitated by more than 5000 country elevators located at 1800 shipping points. Banking facilities are provided by the chartered banks of Canada, which have established 951 branches. Each province has its own system of rural telephones, and the number in use is placed at 110,734. In certain districts there are rural mail delivery routes. The gross revenue from agricultural products produced in 1929 is estimated at $642,019,000, and manufactures are placed at $352,967,078.

In respect to land settlement and land utilization, however, even the most densely settled portions of the rural parts remain in what might be termed an advanced stage of pioneer development. South of the line suggested there are still considerable areas of virgin soil open for settlement, due to land grants made to encourage railway construction, to certain grants made to the Hudson's Bay Company, and to the policy of setting aside sections of land for school purposes. Since in many districts unimproved sections of

[1] Isaiah Bowman: The Pioneer Fringe, *Amer. Geogr. Soc. Special Publ. No. 13*, New York, 1931.

land lie contiguous to land that has been taken up, as this land is
sold to immigrants, certain of the conditions more particularly
associated with pioneering life persist. The writer has observed
on the same day, in central Manitoba, settlers of European birth
coming to town in automobiles, in wagons drawn by horses, in
wagons drawn by oxen, and walking, barefoot, with loads upon
their shoulders. In a rough way the mode of transportation
indicated the number of years of settlement.

The Northward Drive of Settlement

Beyond the Edmonton-Battleford-Prince Albert-Dauphin line
lies the true pioneer fringe of the Western Provinces. It is an
immense area. More than half of each of the three provinces lies
north of this line. The expansionist movement into this area, un-
critical and optimistic, is in full tide. This drive to the north owes
its vigor to at least three factors: (1) After many years of agitation
by Saskatchewan and Manitoba, the federal government has been
induced to complete the Hudson Bay Railway. The first shipments from Churchill, the northern terminus, took place in the
autumn of 1931. Popular expectations forecast a rapid development of this port and of the territory contiguous to the line of
railway. (2) Discoveries of important ore bodies in northern
Manitoba have kindled the imagination of the public, which expects
a mining development in the Northwest comparable to that achieved
in northern Ontario. (3) In the last five years there has been a
flow of population into the Peace River country which transcends
any previous movement of population into that region. Settlers
are now located 75 miles from the end of steel, and all of the conditions indicative of pioneer methods of living are to be found in
the Peace River country. This movement of settlement northward
is not confined to Alberta but is also characteristic of northern
Saskatchewan.

Economic Factors Affecting Settlement

The chief economic factors that must be investigated in this
vast region are (1) the natural resources within the territory;
(2) the transportation facilities and other public works necessary
to give access to the region; and (3) the method of financing governmental expenditures necessarily incurred in throwing open the
country to settlement. Incidental to such an investigation there

should also be studies of the problems involved in making credit available to the settlers, organizing market facilities, and adjusting taxation to the scanty resources of the newcomer.

Natural Resources: Land

The natural resources of the country furnish the subject matter for four studies upon farming, mining, fishing, and lumbering. The importance of land utilization surveys has been dwelt upon in a preceding article. These surveys should indicate the areas that should *not* be thrown open to land settlement, the areas that should first be made available to settlement, and the economic size of the farm unit. This may vary from one part of the territory to another, depending upon the nature of the soil and the type of agriculture recommended. Finally, it should be possible to place a valuation upon the land that would correspond to its value for farming purposes. In many parts of the country settlers who were unfamiliar with the variations in the crop results from year to year have been induced, in a period when there have been substantial harvests, to purchase land at a price much beyond its permanent value for farming operations.

Minerals and Timber

The location, extent, and richness of mineral deposits demand the most careful consideration. It is believed that the northern area is highly mineralized, and important mining developments are now in progress in northern Manitoba. Railways have been constructed to the chief ore bodies proved up, and mining companies recently have been making expenditures at the rate of $6,000,000 a year in this province. The other northern areas are being searched with extraordinary intensity for ore deposits. Exploration is being carried on in a large way by trained geologists equipped with hydroplanes, with supply depots at convenient points. Mining development may cause the appearance, adjacent to the mining fields, of a type of agriculture really subsidiary to and subsisting upon the local market provided by the mining population. An investigation of this situation should consider the probable life of the mines with a view to shaping agriculture in their vicinity on the basis of permanency. Otherwise, when the mining population moves on to other fields, drastic reorganization will be necessary.

In Alberta coal deposits extend from the southern boundary at least well into the Peace River area. Production of coal in Alberta in 1930 amounted to 5,754,752 tons. Coal mining has an interesting bearing upon pioneer settlements. Since the chief demand for labor at the mines exists during the winter, when many types of agricultural employment are at a standstill, a certain interchange between farm employment in the summer and mining in the winter occurs each year. The production of crude petroleum in 1929 in Alberta amounted to 988,675 barrels. Reconnaissance work is being carried on at many points in search for new wells. In the northern part of the province, beyond the limits of the present settlement, occurs an immense deposit of tar sands. Here also research has been in progress with a view to exploitation. It seems likely that it will be only a matter of time before economic methods of use will be devised. The utilization of this deposit would have a most important influence in opening up northern Alberta for settlement. Perhaps in no part of Canada does the problem of mining development in relation to land settlement need more careful study than in Alberta.

The total stand of merchantable timber in the Prairie Provinces is placed at 56,826,000,000 cubic feet. The lumbering industries play a similar rôle, in pioneer development, to mining. Timber resources also present the additional problem of determining whether certain wooded areas should be cleared for land settlement or should be conserved permanently for lumbering purposes.

FISHERIES

Along with mining and lumbering, consideration must be given to the fishing industry. Recent official reports point out: "Lake Winnipeg, Lake Winnipegosis, Lake Manitoba and the smaller lakes to the north and west furnish most of the fish products of Manitoba. . . . " "In Saskatchewan and Alberta, commercial fishing is confined to the regions north of the Saskatchewan River, where whitefish in large quantities are taken. The problem of transportation is keenly felt; some of the greatest lakes of the continent—Reindeer, Athabaska, Great Slave, Great Bear—and hundreds of smaller bodies of water are still beyond reach from a marketing point of view. The lakes of the west, however, repeating the part which the St. Lawrence played in the days of the French *régime* and the cod banks in the history of New England, have assisted greatly in the settlement of the country by providing a much needed food supply for the pioneers."[2]

[2] Canada Year Book, 1929, Dominion Bureau of Statistics, Ottawa, 1929, p. 322.

The utilization of land for agricultural purposes is thus very closely related to the exploitation of these natural resources. No fair view of the possibilities of agricultural settlement within the northland can be obtained without considering the development of mining, fishing, and lumbering. In one part of the region mining may be the dominant factor; in another, fishing; in the third, lumbering.

TRANSPORTATION

Transportation has always been one of the chief economic pre-occupations of the people of the Prairie Provinces. Until connections by rail were established with Eastern Canada, farm settlement was virtually at a standstill. The rapid development of the southern part of what is now the three provinces was made possible by an equally rapid expansion in railway mileage. The railways have always been powerful agents for colonization, settlements being encouraged by them directly through subsidiary agencies.

The first aspect of the railway problem to develop was that of outlets to enable the settlers to ship their goods to market and to import their needed supplies. The first railway connections were southward through the United States to Minneapolis and Duluth. This was followed by the completion of the Canadian Pacific Railway, which gave access to Eastern Canada and to the Pacific coast. Subsequently the construction of railway lines that later became the Canadian National Railways gave additional outlets in both directions.

A second phase of the transportation problem was that created by the need for branch lines. These branch lines sometimes precede but often follow the colonization of areas suitable for agriculture. The economic problem to be resolved in connection with branch lines is at what distance from a railway does it cease to be economic to carry on farming operations. The Board of Railway Commissioners take the view that haulage beyond 12 miles is uneconomic, but the problem has scarcely been studied in all its aspects. Finally, along with the necessity of actually securing the physical facilities of traffic, there has always existed that of determining fair rates to charge upon the traffic carried. It was really in connection with this problem that the Dominion government created the Board of Railway Commissioners. Transportation problems of the nature set forth are still in the foreground in Western Canada and are more particularly acute with regard to the pioneer fringe.

After a long agitation carried on by the people of the West, the Dominion government has completed the railway to Churchill on Hudson Bay. This line will give Western Canada a northern outlet direct to tidewater. In the Peace River district in Alberta there is a strong demand both for a direct outlet to the Pacific and for additional branch lines. Indeed, all along the northern fringe of settlement there are demands for additional lines of railway, striking more deeply into the northland. While there have been numerous appeals to the Board of Railway Commissioners to settle the rail structure of Western Canada, it has not been wholly stabilized. At the present time litigation is pending for the reduction of rates between Alberta and British Columbia. A study of the railway situation in Western Canada should indicate where railway outlets and branch lines are needed, and whether the present level of freight rates constitutes an undue burden on the agricultural or other economic activities of the west.

TAXATION

The problem of providing public works necessary to open up new country to settlement raises a serious problem in government finance. This problem is aggravated in difficulty by reason of the federal organization of Canada. Under the British North America Act most of the advantages of settlement seem to accrue to the Dominion government, while, on the other hand, the chief burdens of providing roads, bridges, schools, hospitalization, and other facilities necessary to make settlement reasonably attractive fall upon the provincial governments. This problem in itself is a constitutional one between the provinces and the Dominion, but, indirectly, it affects the taxation burden that now falls upon the farm settlements of Western Canada.

THE SOCIAL STRUCTURE OF A PIONEER AREA AS ILLUSTRATED BY THE PEACE RIVER DISTRICT

C. A. DAWSON

THE social structure of any region rests upon a geographical substratum. This includes the topography, the natural fertility of the soil, the climatic features, and the lines of transportation both within the region and with the outside world. These features determine, in the main, the typical occupations, the divisions of labor, and population selection. At strategic points centers spring up, within which are concentrated the institutional services of a people. The geographical features and the location of institutions can be mapped. So also can be mapped population units showing varying degrees of concentration.

These are the more visible and tangible geographic and social characteristics of an area. Such characteristics determine the direction and extent of communication by means of which is developed the less tangible social structure of the region—the more intimate phases of its culture. The attitudes, notions, and opinions constitute the more subjective side of this culture, and the traditional and more formally organized institutional practices form its more objective side. These comprise the network of communal ties that make concerted action possible. It may be conceived as some sort of organic whole which in new areas has its thin spots and patches where communication is almost if not quite discontinuous. This communicational aspect of social structure may be seen only by means of the scientific imagination. Nevertheless, it is a structure quite as real as the physical structure and quite as worthy of scientific study. Those who ignore it find themselves confronted by its subtle pervasiveness at every turn.

THE SELECTION OF REGIONS FOR INTENSIVE RESEARCH

The three Prairie Provinces (Manitoba, Saskatchewan, and Alberta) may be viewed as a regional whole. Indeed, an analysis of this area is the chief objective in the research plans of the Canadian Pioneer Problems Committee; and, when this study is completed, its geographic, economic, and social structural data will be presented systematically. A region so large may be divided into

37

smaller natural areas or subsidiary regions, as for instance, the
Carrot River valley in Saskatchewan, the Medicine Hat area in
southeastern Alberta, which is characterized by very light rainfall,
and the relatively isolated Peace River valley in northwestern
Alberta. Each of these lesser regions may be studied as geographical units, with their own peculiar topographical features
and soil types and their own means of transportation and communication. In each, nature presents its peculiar problems. While
wheat culture, as a cash crop, dominates most sections of the
Canadian prairies in their earlier stages of development, it cannot
remain the main source of livelihood in sections that all too soon
prove unsuited to its cultivation. Wheat-growing has a social
as well as an economic status; hence its wide prevalence as a culture pattern. It is hardly necessary to remind the reader that
the type of production of a given area and its social organization
do not rest on a narrow geographic determinism. The elements
of population drawn to a region tend to impose upon it their traditional material and social culture. Far more mixed farming than
elsewhere is found in those grain-growing districts of the Peace
River that have been settled by Germans and Southern Europeans.
The most successful creamery of the north is maintained by a
homogeneous Norwegian settlement. But in time wheat culture
has threatened the very existence of this dairy venture. In due
course there will be an adjustment between natural conditions and
an imported culture—a compromise between nature and nurture.

The very extent of the prairie region has made it necessary to
select sample areas for intensive field study. These areas represent
in each case either a particular soil type or rainfall régime, mode
of agricultural exploitation, marked isolation, age of settlement,
religious and racial backgrounds, the presence of irrigation, or close
association with industrial enterprises. The elements of social
structure have emerged under a great variety of determining conditions which the writer has endeavored to keep in mind in the
selection of subsidiary areas.

THE PEACE RIVER DISTRICT: ITS GEOGRAPHICAL SETTING

Geography conspires to give each region topographic features
that mark it off in some degree from all other regions. From this
point forward I shall draw upon the Peace River region[1] for descrip-

[1] This region was visited in the summer of 1930 as part of the Canadian Pioneer Problem Committee's program of research. The area studied was restricted to the communities north and west
of the Peace and between the Peace and its southern branch, the Smoky River.

tive data (Fig. 1). The valley of the Peace is separated from other
settled areas by long stretches of poor soil, muskegs, and timber.
The early settlers had to proceed 150–200 miles through such
territory from the end of steel. For a good many years this fertile
northern area was without a railroad or a permanent highway.
The railway reached there about fifteen years ago. The high- *1917*

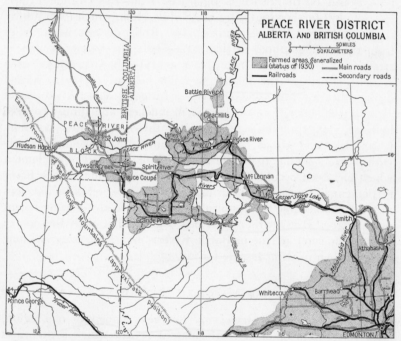

Fig. 1—Settled areas in the Peace River district of Alberta and British Columbia (approximately
status of 1930). Scale, 1 : 6,000,000. (Based on manuscript map prepared by the Canadian
Pioneer Problems Committee.)

way is much more recent and during a wet period is impassable
for motor cars. Until the year 1930, when this study was made,
there were two passenger trains a week from the outside and it
was a twenty-four hour journey from its "capital," Grande Prairie,
to the nearest city, Edmonton. The area now enjoys three trains
a week. Its potential acreage for agricultural production is estimated at 18,000,000 acres. It has a population of 40,000 and is
the most important far-northern populated district in Canada.
It has developed under a measure of isolation that has fostered
a marked degree of regional self-consciousness. Within this area

physical features play their rôle in dividing the area into minor divisions. The Peace River, with its banks rising 800 to 1000 feet above its level and a wide margin of "breaks" on either side, acts as a barrier that cuts off from each other the settlements north and south of the Peace. The employment of a ferry rather than a bridge accentuates this divisiveness. The Spirit River settlement lying south of the Peace is separated from the Grande Prairie district, still farther south, by the Saddle Hills, which form a hilly timbered barrier 8 miles across. The Rolla district is 50 miles from the main southern settlement. There the barrier is wide—stretches of timber covering a poorer soil type that has not yet been settled. North of the Peace, 50 miles beyond the main settled district, lies the Battle River area—a fringe area in the process of rapid settlement. Here the barrier of muskegs and timber-covered light soil plays an important part in this settlement's isolation. Clear Hills and Hines Creek settlements are fringe settlements with barriers similar to Battle River. Rolla is a fringe settlement which has been occupied nearly as long as the older Peace River settlements (20 years) and during most of the period of its development it has been 50 to 80 miles from the railroad. During recent years a good dry-weather road has connected it with the end of steel. The same is true of Battle River, but its highway has long periods when it is impassable for automobiles.

Its Central and Marginal Settlement Centers

The Peace River country exemplifies one's conception of a region, with its centers of older settlement and with fringe settlements at the circumference. It is dotted with larger and smaller towns and villages from the center to the fringe. The one large town, Grande Prairie, with 2000 inhabitants, occupies the key position for the whole region, while the town of Peace River plays a secondary rôle. The latter has been kept in the running only by its proximity to the northern settlements. Grande Prairie is the focal point of transportation and communication within the region and with the outside. Its business turnover stands at the top. Its stores and professional services show quite extensive specialization. It is a minor wholesale center subsidiary to Edmonton and other large centers outside. For certain goods and skills all the inhabitants of the region must come to Grande Prairie. It has the only talking picture theater in the northland. It is the headquarters of numerous clubs and other social organizations. Out from it range the lesser villages on the railroad, and out from these the crossroad centers of the fringe territory. Here, too, the mail order houses find the largest number of their customers. Medical, religious, educational, and recreational services become more rudimentary and meager as one moves toward the fringe. There one finds with few exceptions the itinerant minister holding occasional services in the homes or in the log schoolhouse when it is built. The doctors live in the larger towns and penetrate the surrounding country at a mileage rate of fifty cents for each mile traveled. (A settler living 30 miles out has to pay $30 to bring the doctor to his home unless the doctor adjusts the customary charge to the financial condition of the patient.) The six months' one-room school under an inexperienced teacher is frequent in outlying districts. Here factional fights about school matters flare up perennially. It gives democracy a chance to express itself in a very elementary form. Here there is practically no formally organized social or recreational life. The population depends upon a frontier sports day with all its trimmings and an all-night dance to conclude it. Whole families attend, and the very young children are put to sleep and placed together in a space set aside for the purpose just beyond the blare of festivity. An orchestra from the town provides the music, and the town baseball team competes with a pick-up team from the local community. The residents of the older communities attend in large numbers and experience an emotional revival of earlier memories. Informality and kindliness still prevail on the fringe of this modern settlement, but these have been somewhat disciplined by the diffusion of urban culture. Fifty miles rather than 150 miles from the railroad make a tremendous difference in this respect.

The Process of Settlement

The whole process of settlement in this region may be presented briefly. The two older settlements of Fairview in the north (about 12 miles southeast of Hines Creek, Fig. 1) and Grande Prairie in the south (see Fig. 1) began about the same time and in the same way about twenty years ago. The land in the vicinity of Fairview and Grande Prairie is of the best soil type in the region. Formerly covered with timber and light brush, fires swept over the territory before active settlement began, leaving a relatively open and fairly easily broken area near the two towns just mentioned. These open patches formed the geographical nuclei of settlement. The constituent fringe was covered with more brush and timber on a poorer soil type, and it was more difficult to settle. Here transportation was attempted on rough roads, often impassable. Settlement was scattered, and the population turnover was high. Little land was broken, and this very fact often made these farms "frost wells" in the wilderness. The first settlers in Fairview and Grande Prairie walked or drove a distance of 150 to 200 miles with a grub stake and a few agricultural tools. The religious, educational, and medical facilities lingered in the rear of population entry; but most tardy of all was the railroad. It was warmly welcomed, but its coming disturbed the locating of practically every village in the region and also many of the school districts. Many evidences of the wastage of unplanned settlement were here seen. The insecurity of foothold on the land was observed and the drifting away of most of the early settlers in the whole constituent fringe of settlement. Almost simultaneously the section of more open land at Griffin Creek just south and west of the present village of Berwyn was settled. The soil is similar to that of Fairview. One does not go far north before striking the lighter soil, under brush and timber, harder to clear and less fertile. The old homesteaders on the more favored land have remained in quite large proportions; but the constituent fringe has marked time, and the agricultural death rate among the original settlers has been excessively high. Even those who have remained on these outlying areas have maintained a bare existence supplemented in a small way from wages earned away from the farm. Frontier schools, churches, and other inadequate facilities are still prevalent after many years of attempted settlement.

Battle River is a typical newly settled fringe sub-area. This little prairie nucleus with its fertile soil lies 50 miles north of Berwyn. The highway connecting it with the railroad crosses muskegs, gravelly soil, and stretches of bush. During wet weather this road is impassable for trucks. Surrounding the good land is light soil under brush and timber, which has been settled very rapidly in the recent rush. The settlers are living on relatively poor land, far from the railroad and hard to clear, and many of them have little capital. Their possibilities of maintaining a stake in this land are not great, although they have settled on free homesteads of 160 acres. This has been the prevailing mode of initial settlement throughout the whole Peace River region. Very many of these fringe settlers except on the fertile soil nucleus hang on for a brief space and pass on. Their holdings are consolidated, and after this land has changed hands several times a more permanent settler family has found itself on the land. Their predecessors were unproductive, had few of the amenities of life, and have added little to the process of settlement. They were too far ahead of adequate transportation, were often unsuited to agriculture, and had insufficient capital. Their excessive mobility has kept back satisfactory settlement and the founding of efficient local social institutions. It has been said that the settlers in the older settlements started with little or no capital. In many instances this was true, but they started on the best land in the north country, and they supplemented their early agricultural products by freighting, railroad building, and laboring for the settlers in other districts. The mechanization of agriculture has done away with most of this latter form of opportunity. The era of extensive railroad building is past. In the main, the new settler must rely on the products of his own land or be eliminated, as have been many of these modern settlers. As soon as our field men left the main road in these fringe sub-areas of Battle River, Clear Hills, and Hines Creek, transportational difficulties became obvious. They had to vacate their cars and use saddle horses in gathering schedules from the various farmsteads. Many of these initial settlers were asking for direct relief long before the world financial depression emerged. For a great many families the existence level was precariously low.

HANDICAPS OF THE FRINGE SETTLEMENTS

The description of fringe settlement just given by no means tells the whole story of the cost of the settlement of new areas. Every social institution is heavily subsidized from the outside older areas. The schools receive grants in aid, and even then they are not a very effective means of education, despite many heroic efforts that have been put forth in their behalf. The churches are built on outside capital, and for years receive most of their operating expenses from their denominational headquarters. In the new Battle River district the United Church gave the community a new modern church and manse free from debt and is paying most of the minister's salary. This case is somewhat extreme, but it will illustrate the trend of denominational practice. Battle River has a doctor whose salary is paid by the Province of Alberta.

The local community provides her with a very humble frontier frame shack and a saddle horse. In some of the newer areas state-supported nurses are provided in the absence of other medical services. The Battle River people are 75 miles from a hospital, with the means of transportation none too certain. Freight rates from the Peace River region had to undergo a special adjustment in 1925 to keep the farmers in the world wheat market. The money spent on highways is raised in outside areas with very little returns from the new district for this initial expenditure.

The Rolla sub-area, when this study was made, lay 50 miles from the railway and on the main trunk road from Peace River town to Fort St. John. This road has been modernized during the past few years. For many years this area was developed far distant from the end of steel and without any means of motor transportation. Yet the district seemed to achieve an agricultural success somewhat comparable to the older districts of Grande Prairie and Fairview despite the distance handicap through the barrier mentioned above. It was our aim to discover why a stable community could emerge with such a transportational handicap. It is a very beautiful district in the eyes of the traveler by the main highway and shows many signs of prosperity. As our research proceeded it soon became apparent that the British Columbia government had made an earnest effort to bring success to its far northern agricultural settlement. Taxes were reduced to the minimum. In recent years ready money has been made current in this area by means of extensive road building and the construction of telegraph lines. Its hospital costs have been very heavily subsidized by the outside health organizations. Its schools have received a larger subsidy than in any other area that has come under our observation. The district has been too far from the railway for banks and machinery companies to take as heavy a toll as in older districts. They are slow to risk too much in these fringe districts. The subsidy for religious and other institutions is in keeping with the other fringe districts studied. Despite all this aid from the older communities and from the state, it was discovered in the survey of individual farmsteads that their agricultural achievements were much more apparent than real. A very small percentage of the land long settled had been broken, and the shipments of its agricultural products had been small when compared with older districts settled close to the railroad. This has led to the conclusion that no important agricultural production has taken place at any very great distance from the railroad. Fifteen to 20 miles under certain conditions seems to be the limit beyond which agricultural communities mark time as far as grain growing is concerned; and wheat production is the dominant aim of practically all settlers in the Peace River country.

SOCIAL CENSUS OF SETTLERS BY INDIVIDUAL FAMILIES

Whatever the costs of settlement in terms of subsidy from the resources of well-established regions, the final measure of success or failure can be understood only in terms of the modes of production and the standard of living of the individual family. The social problems of settlement rest most heavily on the life of each member of the pioneering family. Our field men used a lengthy schedule in gathering details of the settler's holdings, his progress, his standard of living, and the participation of the members of each family in the activities of the accessible forms of social organization. In this way we were able to ascertain the specific utilization of educational, medical, religious, governmental, and other institutional resources in the family's struggle for a satisfying existence. The ultimate efficiency of these institutions lies in their measurable use by the members of the settler's family. In many cases rather complete life histories of typical settlers were obtained, which disclosed the successive emergence of formal social institutions at the different stages of frontier development. The intensive schedules of farm families totaled 332. They are representative of all types of soil and all the typical sub-areas of the Peace River region from the center to the circumference. We have been able to make numerous comparisons between the older settlements and the raw crude experiments in settlement now taking place in the outlying districts.

FAMILY COMPOSITION

Our sample for the whole area revealed that 39 per cent of all households have no children and that 11 out of every 12 of these no-child households are carried on by an operator without a homemaker—in most instances bachelors. In this element the fringe shows a proportionately greater number. In the more recent settlement by means of the railroad the tendency is for family rather than bachelor households to predominate in comparison with the long trek settlement of the early days in the Peace River country, when the bachelors greatly outnumbered the family men. Approximately 60 per cent of all children under 17 are between the ages of 1 and 8. Grande Prairie is the only district in which the number of children between the ages of 1 and 8 is less 'than the number between 9 and 16. Fairview, Berwyn, and the fringe show the highest percentage in the younger group. The fringe shows a somewhat larger percentage of children under 17 away from home. The average number of children for families with one child or more is 3.5 for this area; for all households it is 2.1. The ages of settlers vary from 18 to 60, but they are mainly in the 20's, 30's, and 40's, the last group being the largest. Range of average age for these operators is from 42.1 on the fringe to 51.7 in Fairview. It is 45.6 for the sample reduced to 313. As with the operators, the home-makers have the lowest average on the fringe, 37.3. The average age of the home-makers for the whole area is 40.4. In newly settled regions one may expect many households without home-makers and a swelling of the ranks of those between 20 and 50. One would also expect the sample to show the presence of a larger number of young children in the families who have children in comparison with like families in regions long settled. Pioneer regions are areas where the adults are in their productive prime and in which the numbers of young and aged are disproportionately small.

TERRITORIAL ORIGIN

The pioneer nature of the area is also indicated by the fact that operators and home-makers were born outside the region. The proportion of the operators born in the west of Canada is strikingly small—about 6 per cent. There came from Ontario, Quebec, and the Maritime Provinces 29 per cent; while the United States and Great Britain produced 20 per cent each. The remaining 25 per cent are from Continental Europe and are mainly Scandinavians, Germans, and Russians. It is significant to note that 22 per cent of the operators were not born on the farm but are urban-born, from the British Isles for the most part. Only in experimental regions like the Peace River with their frontier glamor would one expect to find the population trend from the city to the country so large. Not only do the operators and home-makers show a heterogeneity in respect to birthplace, but they exhibit a marked residential mobility. A few moved directly from their boyhood homes to the region, but the great majority made two, three, four, or five moves before they made their home in this far north agricultural area. We found many operators who had "tried it out" for a time on practically every new agricultural frontier in the great West, north and south of the international boundary line. We found in out-of-the-way corners the human "sweepings" of the prairies. New regions are not only the stamping ground of the young and efficient, for they also attract in the initial stages of their development a goodly number of the shiftless and incompetent from the agricultural and urban classes.

OCCUPATIONAL AND EDUCATIONAL BACKGROUND

The occupational backgrounds of the operators in this region show a great variety of non-agricultural pursuits. Of the 332 operators 94 had no other occupation than farming, 127 had had one other occupation, 74 two other occupations, 7 four other occupations, 1 five other occupations. The 332 operators indicated that they had previously given full time for an extended period in a variety of non-agricultural occupations which totaled 396 for the whole group. About 30 per cent of the occupations are of the unskilled variety followed by a mobile population. About 30 per cent of the group are clerks, office workers, and the like. Eleven per cent of the occupations are of the unskilled roustabout type. About 5 per cent of the total are from the professional occupations (8 teachers, 2 clergymen, 6 engineers, 1 lawyer, 3 surveyors, 1 army officer). The sifting process will go on as the region goes through the life cycle of its development. Non-agricultural occupational backgrounds will be reduced to a small proportion, and a typical homogeneous agricultural population composed of farmers born and bred will emerge. As would be expected, the educational backgrounds are also varied. Thirty-nine per cent of the operators and 29 per cent of the home-makers did not reach Grade VIII. Thirty-seven per cent of the operators and 40 per cent of the home-makers completed Grade VIII. Ten per cent of the operators and 8 per cent of the home-makers had some high school work. Nearly 4 per cent of the operators and nearly 5 per cent of the home-makers are high school graduates. Two per cent of the operators and 1 per cent of the home-makers are college graduates. About 5 per cent of the operators and 15 per cent of the home-makers have received normal, nursing, teaching, business, musical, or other education. Eight per cent of the operators stated that they had had no schooling.

Standard of Living

Among those living in this region are a large number who have known something of urban standards of living, comforts, and conveniences. General cultural diffusion, furthermore, has given an urban slant to the needs of most of these settlers. Consequently, accessibility to a good town with up-to-date stores, clubs, theaters, hotels, athletic teams, and all that is meant by a modern centralization of services is their persistent demand. Such a town is Grande Prairie; and all the lesser towns and villages go as far as they can in this direction. No village on the railroad (and they are practically all so situated) is too small to have its local board of trade agitating for better roads into its constituent territory. No village is too small to have its athletic associations, bridge, and other social clubs. In these days of rapid transportation, the social life of the region centers in the town and village. Otherwise it is practically non-existent except for a few informal gatherings and visits. For the people a decent standard of living demands the roads, the car, and the clothes that will make a visit to the town feasible and satisfying. If one cannot farm efficiently enough to accomplish this, he has little social status among his occupational peers. He suffers isolation and loneliness. Modern settlers refuse to return to the manner of life of their old stone age prototypes of a generation ago. The exceptions to this statement are the low-standard Southeastern Europeans who have entered the region in considerable numbers on the difficult uncleared and infertile land on the fringes of the outlying sub-areas. But even these had asked for governmental assistance for the year 1929–1930 before our study was made.

While it cannot be presented here in detail, we have been able to show statistically the depression of the standard of living as one moves out from the center to the constituent fringe of the older areas. It is most meager, and life is most unstable of all, in the fringe sub-areas like Battle River. Here one finds a preponderance of one and two-room log houses with little furniture or equipment, as compared with the more commodious frame houses closer in. The region as a whole has few really modern dwellings as yet. At this point it must be remembered that in the Peace River country the wells are deep and far apart. Only 13 per cent of the families have telephones. Forty-three per cent of the 332 families had cars. The fringe sub-areas had no telephones, and only 5 per cent had cars. Radios were found in one house out of every 6 for the whole area, but in the fringe districts where they are most

needed only 5 per cent of our sample had them. Thirty-six per cent
had a piano or gramophone for the whole sample, while the fringe
sub-areas had a little more than 20 per cent of the same. For the
whole sample 36 per cent take a daily paper, 68 per cent a weekly
paper, 70 per cent an agricultural paper; 8 per cent take a religious
paper, 40 per cent read popular magazines, and about 5 per cent
read foreign papers. As one moves out to the fringe the dailies
(from outside the area) dwindle to a small percentage. The same
is true of the current magazines. There is also a reduction in the
reading of the weeklies and the agricultural papers, but it is not so
great. The attendance of fringe people at theaters, concerts,
athletic games, lodges, and organization meetings is excessively
low—quite in keeping with their income and their remoteness from
the towns and villages in which these forms of associated life find
expression. Under such conditions it is not strange that the fringe
population mobility is high and its productive efficiency low.

Wastefulness of Too Rapid Colonization

It has taught some of our Western Provincial governments that
the drift policy in pushing out too rapidly and precariously the
settlement of new areas is economically and socially wasteful.
The settlement of these fringe areas might better wait the solid
extension of settlement, transportational conveniences, and social
organization. Then such land becomes economically valuable;
it attracts those who have the capital to utilize it properly (which is
the eventuality in any mode of settlement), and the settlers have
near at hand the resources for living the social life that the more
or less sophisticated present-day settler feels that he must have.

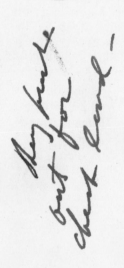

THE POSSIBILITIES OF AGRICULTURAL
SETTLEMENT IN ALASKA

C. C. GEORGESON

The future of Alaska cannot be evaluated solely by a comparison of her resources with those of the more favored and more accessible parts of our country.
It is frequently asked "Why go to Alaska when we have much closer at hand
the climate of California, the great wheat fields of the Northwest, the timber
of Oregon, the iron and copper of Michigan, and the coal of Pennsylvania?"
Such a question ignores the industrial changes which will be forced on the nation
by increased population. Older parts of the world have long since been driven
to use natural resources far inferior to those which our nation has so long
enjoyed.

A journey to Finland would be an excellent prelude to an understanding of
the future of Alaska. The Finlanders are a sturdy, progressive, cultured people,
who have developed their high civilization under the most adverse climatic
conditions and in a land but scantily endowed with natural wealth. Much of
their crops are grown on land which in Alaska would not now be classed as having
agricultural value. By industry, thrift, and application of science, the Finlanders have overcome their adverse physical conditions and have made themselves a prosperous nation. . . .

Alaska has every advantage over Finland and Sweden both in food resources,
measured by areas of arable and pasture lands and fisheries, and in potential
energy, measured by water power and mineral fuel. Her metallic resources,
with the exception of iron, which has not been sought for, are known to be far
greater than those of the other two countries. Three quarters of Alaska has
a climate entirely favorable to occupation by the white race and better than
that of Finland and much of Sweden. On the basis of comparison with Finland
we may look forward to the time when Alaska will eventually support a population of ten million people.

Thus concisely did that leading authority on Alaska, the late
Dr. Alfred H. Brooks of the U. S. Geological Survey, sum up the
future prospects of this northern territory.[1] No more fitting introduction than this could be supplied to a discussion of Alaska as
a region of pioneer settlement.

The value of Alaska's resources in minerals, furs, fisheries, and
timber is well known. Its agricultural resources and potentialities
are less known, and as it is on these that real settlement depends,
they will form the main theme of the present brief article.

[1] A. H. Brooks: The Value of Alaska, *Geogr. Rev.*, Vol. 15, 1925, pp. 25–50, with three maps in
1 : 10,000,000 of land classification, transportation, and mineral resources. The quotation above
is from pp. 48–49.

The Agricultural Areas[2]

The area of lands capable of agricultural development in Alaska has been variously estimated. Perhaps about 47,000 square miles, or 30,000,000 acres, may be considered as potential crop land, and a like area as grazing land. The possibilities that these figures imply are thrown in bold relief when it is stated that according to the Fifteenth Census the total acreage of crops harvested in Alaska in 1929 was 3875 acres. According to the same source improved land in 1930 amounted to 8825 acres, having increased from 5736 acres in 1920. Of the total population of the territory of 55,000 (in 1920; nearly 60,000 in 1930) Brooks estimated[3] 1000 as being engaged in agriculture.

The principal areas (Fig. 1) in which farming is carried out at present are the Susitna and Matanuska Valleys in south-central Alaska, which extend inland from Cook Inlet, and the Tanana Valley in the interior. Other areas where farming can be carried on successfully are the Yukon Valley, both above and below the confluence of the Tanana, the west side of Kenai Peninsula, and parts of the valleys of the Copper River and its tributaries. Part of southwestern Alaska is suited for grazing during at least a portion of the year. The Kuskokwim Valley probably represents another belt of agricultural land, but owing to its remoteness and inaccessibility its development is likely to be postponed beyond that of the other areas mentioned. In the "Panhandle" of southeastern Alaska truck farming is practiced in limited areas at the heads of fiords or on the tidal flats. This mountainous region in itself is not suited to agriculture, but owing to the local outlet provided by the relatively concentrated population in this area market gardening has developed there.

[2] General Information Regarding the Territory of Alaska, edit. of June, 1931, U. S. Dept. of the Interior, Washington, pp. 32–36.

Information for Prospective Settlers in Alaska, *Alaska Agric. Exper. Stas. Circular No. 1* (current edit., revised Oct. 15, 1930, by H. W. Alberts, based on three earlier editions by the writer: (1) Suggestions to Pioneer Farmers in Alaska, *Alaska Agric. Exper. Stas. Bull. No. 1*, 1902; and (2) and (3) with same title as *Circular No. 1*, editions of May 11, 1916 and Oct. 15, 1923).

L. A. Wolfanger: Economic Regions of Alaska, *Econ. Geogr.*, Vol. 2, 1926, pp. 508–536.

H. H. Bennett and T. D. Rice: Soil Reconnaissance in Alaska, with an Estimate of the Agricultural Possibilities, *U. S. Dept. of Agric., Field Operations of the Bur. of Soils, 1914*, Washington, 1919, pp. 43–236, with reconnaissance soil maps of the Cook Inlet-Susitna region, 1 : 625,000, and the Yukon-Tanana region, 1 : 1,000,000.

H. H. Bennett: Report on a Reconnaissance of the Soils, Agriculture, and Other Resources of the Kenai Peninsula Region of Alaska, *ibid., 1916*, Washington, 1921, pp. 39–174, with soil maps of Kenai Peninsula, 1 : 250,000, east side of Knik Arm, 1 : 125,000, and east side of Cook Inlet north of and including Kachemak Bay, 1 : 125,000.

[3] *Op. cit.*, Table I, on p. 49.

Except for the natural grasslands, which occur in relatively small areas on the east side of the Alaska Peninsula, on Kodiak Island, and some of the near-by Aleutian Islands, all the areas suitable for agriculture are timbered. Although in south-central and interior Alaska this timber, mainly spruce, birch, and alder, is of relatively light growth, it remains that practically every square

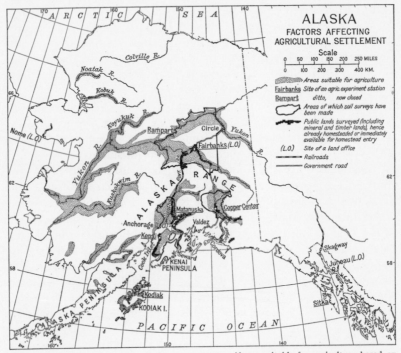

Fig. 1—Agricultural Alaska. Scale, 1 : 20,000,000. (Areas suitable for agriculture based on map in "Information for Prospective Settlers in Alaska" mentioned in footnote 2.)

foot of soil has to be cleared before it can be put under cultivation. In interior Alaska the ground is often covered with moss, underlain by frozen subsoil, a survival from the colder climate of Pleistocene time which owes its preservation to the non-conducting properties of the moss cover. As Russian experience in Eastern Siberia shows, removal of the surface mat of moss and grass and cultivation cause permanent ground ice to disappear or to sink to a level permitting the growth of crops. Indeed the presence of a frozen subsoil is an advantage in supplying moisture during exceptionally dry seasons.[4]

[4] Brooks, op. cit., p. 36; Bennett and Rice, pp. 143–144.

CLIMATE[5]

Climatically Alaska falls into four major provinces: the Pacific coast region, which, besides including the immediate coastal belt, extends in south-central Alaska to the arc of the Alaska Range; the interior region; the Bering Sea region; and the Arctic Sea

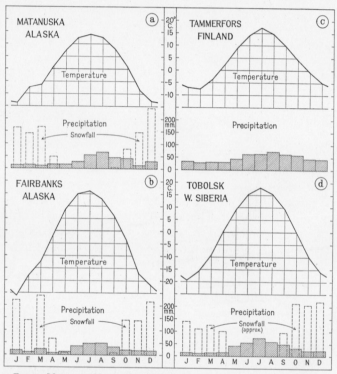

FIG. 2—Mean monthly temperature and precipitation at Matanuska and Fairbanks, two stations in the agricultural area of Alaska, compared with stations of similar climate in Finland and Western Siberia, where farming has long been carried on. For the position of Tobolsk in relation to the crop land of Siberia see, below, Figure 3 on page 249.

region. From the standpoint of agriculture the south-central Alaskan portion of the Pacific coast region and the interior region mainly come into consideration.

South-central Alaska as exemplified by the west side of Kenai Peninsula and the Susitna-Matanuska Valleys (Fig. 2a) has tem-

[5] Summaries of Climatological Data by Sections, *U. S. Weather Bur. Bull. W*, 2nd edit., Washington, 1926, Vol. 3, Sections on Alaska.

E. M. Fitton: The Climates of Alaska, *Monthly Weather Rev.*, Vol. 58, 1930, pp. 85–103.

perate summers, moderately cold winters, and a moderate rainfall. The interior region (Fig. 2b) has light precipitation, cold winters, and comparatively warm but short summers. In the Matanuska region, the frost-free period, or growing season, averages some 115 days, from about May 20 to September 15. In the Tanana Valley, at Fairbanks, the growing season averages some 90 days, about from May 25 to August 25. This shortness, however, is compensated in both areas by the length of daylight and its influence on plant growth. During the growing season the days are long. At Fairbanks the approximate hours of sunrise and sunset are as follows: May 1, 4 a. m. and 9.30 p. m.; June 1, 2.30 a. m. and 10 p. m.; July 1, 1.30 a. m. and 10.30 p. m.; August 1, 2 a. m. and 10 p. m. During June and July and parts of May and August twilight is continuous throughout the short night.

CROPS

The most important cereal crops grown in the Matanuska Valley are spring wheat, oats, and barley. The yields per acre in a continuous period of six years were 22 bushels for wheat, 51 bushels for oats, and 24 bushels for barley. Potatoes form the most important money crop and yield from 200 to 300 bushels an acre. In the Tanana Valley grain and potatoes are likewise the most important crops.

In the interior only early maturing grains will mature in the short summer. The seeding begins usually the first week in May, and the crop must be ready to harvest by the end of August or early September, according to the season. Only spring-seeded grain can be depended on. Fall-sown or winter wheat is a failure. Hardy varieties of winter rye can be sown in the fall. Field corn cannot be grown. The staple crops are barley, oats, and spring wheat, and only early maturing sorts of these. Field peas and flax can be grown. Potatoes and root crops are successful. But even these must be chosen for their earliness. Forage plants and grasses, which have done well, are a hardy alfalfa (*Medicago falcata*), field peas, Alsike clover, white clover, smooth brome grass (*Bromus inermis*), slender wheat grass (*Triticum spicatum*), and, of course, all native grasses and plants. Red clover and common alfalfa cannot be grown. They winter-kill.

A tenet in successful management is to plow the fields in the fall so that they may be ready to sow as soon as the snow leaves and get the full benefit of the short summer.

Work of the Agricultural Experiment Stations[6]

The development of agriculture in Alaska has been closely associated with the work done at the agricultural experiment stations of the Federal Government.

In 1898 Congress authorized the investigation of the agricultural possibilities of the Territory and the establishment of experiment stations. The writer was placed in charge of this work with authority to select suitable sites for the stations.

The first station was located at Sitka, which was then the capital of the Territory. A station was also established at Kodiak Island that year. In 1899 a tract was selected at Kenai on the Kenai Peninsula, and the work of clearing was begun immediately. In 1900 a station was established at Rampart in the Yukon Valley in latitude 65° 30', and in 1902 another at Copper Center in the Copper River Valley. In 1905 a tract near Fairbanks in the Tanana Valley was selected on which development work was begun as funds became available; and finally in 1917, when the Alaska Railroad from Seward was built to that point, an experiment station was established in the Matanuska Valley. It will be noticed that these stations are widely scattered, hundreds of miles apart. This was for the purpose of testing the adaptability of the different sections of country for farming purposes. It was soon discovered that these regions differed in their adaptability to certain crops. It was found that hardy vegetables can be grown with eminent success, but this was not the case with grain. Sitka station in southeastern Alaska is in the rainy belt, and, while grain could be grown there, it could seldom be saved in the fall after maturity on account of the rainy weather. Kenai and Kodiak stations were found to be better adapted to cattle raising and a general livestock industry than to grain growing. At Rampart, within one degree of the Arctic Circle, early varieties of grain matured every year, and in some respects the most important work in grain growing was carried on at this station. Here nearly all of the many hybrids among the grains were produced. It has been demonstrated that at Fairbanks and Matanuska stations grain growing and general farming can be made a great success. Only four of these stations are in active operation at this time. The other three have been closed for various reasons, chiefly for lack of adequate funds to operate them. The work at all these stations has proved that

[6] On this work see the Bulletins, Circulars, and Annual Reports of the Alaska Agricultural Experiment Stations (list in General Information Regarding the Territory of Alaska, p. 123).

Alaska has great agricultural possibilities and that the land is ready to produce foodstuffs for some millions of people as soon as it is settled and intelligently cultivated.

At the Sitka station it was soon discovered that the wet climate of southeastern Alaska was not adapted to general farming. The station was therefore devoted to horticultural work. It was found that strawberries imported from the States were unsuited to the climate. There are two wild species of strawberries indigenous to Alaska, *Fragaria chiloensis* in the coast region and *F. platypetala* in the interior. In 1904 hybridization was begun by the use of the pollen of these hardy wild species on cultivated varieties. It proved a success and eventually more than 12,000 hybrid seedlings were raised and tested at this station. About ten per cent were superior varieties which, in competition with each other, were later reduced to about two per cent. These hybrids proved to be hardy enough to thrive in the interior region, where all varieties brought from the States were winter-killed.

Potatoes were in like manner raised from seed balls, and some 1500 seedling varieties were tested. Many of these proved to be specially adapted to Alaska. All kinds of fruit bushes and hardy ornamental shrubbery were propagated at this station and distributed free of charge to settlers in the territory in order to test them under various conditions and to encourage settlers to grow them. Seeds of hardy vegetables were distributed likewise. The result has been gratifying.

The work of the stations at Rampart, Fairbanks, and Matanuska has demonstrated the agricultural capacity of this central section of Alaska. Every variety of grain, forage crop, and vegetable that was likely to succeed was tried at these stations; and, in addition, efforts were made to create new varieties that should be better suited to the climate than varieties grown in the States. The hybridization of grains was done at Rampart station. My theory was that anything that succeeded in latitude 65° 30' would succeed in any section of Alaska suited to agriculture.

A small-grained, early maturing, hard spring wheat obtained by the writer from an experiment station at Tulun, Siberia (54° 33' N., 100° 22' E.), has been the earliest variety of the hundreds tested. It has matured repeatedly at 65° N. in 82–90 days (110-115 days are required for spring wheat to mature on the fringe of the wheat area of the Canadian Northwest). Occasionally when less favorable seasons occur it will require 100 days in which to mature, from the date of seeding until harvest. Pollen of this variety has been used to cross-fertilize later and more vigorous varieties of spring wheats, with the result that some of these hybrid new creations approach the Siberian wheat in earliness, while they are more vigorous growers and better yielders. Several varieties have thus been established that were born and bred under the climatic conditions of Alaska and will eventually become the standards for wheat growers in those latitudes.

Many varieties of barley in common culture will mature in latitude 65°, where they have a growing season of 90–100 days. In like manner, new varieties of this grain have been established by cross-fertilization which are earlier and better adapted to the climatic conditions than most of the barleys in common culture. Through the Department of Agriculture the writer was supplied many years ago with a very early but dwarf barley which was grown on a plateau of the Pamir Mountains of Central Asia at an elevation of 11,000 feet. By crosses with this early variety new creations have been established which are large, vigorous growers and still early enough to mature every year in latitude 65°. The original barley from India grew only two feet high, had very short heads and very long beards. In the hybrids the beards have been eliminated. The beards are a handicap to the crop. The rain and wind, aided by the beards, break down the straw and the grain lodges and does not mature. Some stiff-strawed, beardless varieties have been developed by the experiment stations and are now introduced to Alaska farmers.

HOMESTEADING LAND

Land for farming purposes is acquired in Alaska mainly by homesteading. The government does not sell land, and there are but few and small tracts in private ownership that can be acquired by purchase. The homestead law has undergone some changes. In 1903, when the first homestead law was passed by Congress, it permitted a qualified person to take up 320 acres. It was argued, and justly so, that nearly every half section has more or less waste land on it, which is unfit for actual culture and which could be used for stock raising to better advantage by the homesteader; but, as the towns of Anchorage and Fairbanks grew in population and all settlers wanted to get as close to the town as possible, it was found that this liberal homestead law excluded many settlers from the town. More could be accommodated if the homesteads were smaller. Therefore in 1916 the size of the homestead was reduced by law to 160 acres, and that is the law today. Smaller homesteads may be taken if a settler desires it, but the maximum he may take is 160 acres.

The conditions on which homesteads may be acquired are liberal and easy to comply with. The applicant, man or woman, must be a citizen of the United States. He must follow the instructions issued by the General Land Office for administration of the law. Among these regulations are: he must clear within five years, and put into cultivation, one-eighth of the land he has applied for; he must establish a home and live there, but he can get leave of absence for five months each year and can then seek work elsewhere. When the regulations are complied with he must pay $1.25 an acre. The Land Office will then give him title to his homestead, which, once issued, is irrevocable. During the period of probation he is allowed to sell a relinquishment to some other person, who will assume the obligations of the original homesteader and carry on in compliance with the law. A person who has used a homestead right in the States can take up another homestead in Alaska.

Only some four hundred actual homesteads have been taken up and are now occupied by farmers throughout this immense territory. Certain areas of the most available homestead lands have been surveyed by the government, and where these surveys are made a homesteader can pick out his quarter section wherever it may suit him. A homestead can even be taken up on unsurveyed land, and when the regulations in such cases are complied with the government will send a surveyor to survey the settler's land free. The law is liberal. The requirements are reasonable and just, and when title is acquired no man has a more secure right to property in land anywhere on earth than the homesteader.

Farms are also obtainable through purchase from homesteaders. A number of good farms which were homesteaded by men as early as 1915 are now being offered for sale at reasonable prices. Farms with some buildings and 160 acres of land—a part of which has been cleared—may be obtained at $1000 to $2000 each. These farms are now owned by homesteaders who are too old and feeble to work the land.[8]

Land or property outside of incorporated towns is at present

[8] Information for Prospective Settlers in Alaska, edit. of Oct. 15, 1930, p. 22.

not subject to taxation in Alaska. All male settlers between the ages of 21 and 50 years are required to pay a school tax of $5.00 per annum. The funds of the Territory are raised by licensing certain industries, including fisheries, cold-storage plants, and mining.[9]

DATA ON PRESENT HOMESTEADS

There are at present three land offices in Alaska, one each at Anchorage, Fairbanks, and Nome. The Nome district has no farm lands, and homesteads taken for trading purposes need not be considered here. The Register of the Land Office at Anchorage writes[10] that there are a total of 798 locations on record, 286 of which are in the Matanuska Valley. The rest are scattered in the Copper Valley, the Kenai Peninsula, and elsewhere; but this includes mining claims and trading posts, and he does not mention how many homesteads have been abandoned.

The Register at the Fairbanks office writes[10]: "There are about fifty settlers now living on land in this district more or less dependent upon agriculture. Approximately 2000 acres are held under various squatter claims not of record. About 1500 acres are held in patented or pending entries. About 2000 acres are abandoned or relinquished." Neither office gives exact information as to farms. The land offices do not distinguish between trading sites and farms.

Trading sites are usually only from one to five acres. This fact is to be noted. There are but few real farmers in the Territory. The homesteaders are mostly disappointed gold seekers. They are generally bachelors. Many fail to comply with the requirements of the law and move to other sections. Some relinquish their rights for a small sum to a successor, and a small percentage remain and undertake to farm in earnest. Again, many of these first-generation settlers do not know how to farm in the north, and their lack of instant and conspicuous success discourages them. The most successful are immigrants from Finland, Norway, and Sweden, who are familiar with a cold climate and with the crops that can be grown.

Farmers raised in the corn or wheat belt of the United States are likely to be discouraged by the long severe winters that go hand in hand with the agreeable summers. The best solution, if it were

[9] *Ibid.*, p. 23.
[10] Personal communications to the writer, spring, 1929.

possible, would be to have settlers come direct from these northern countries—settlers who have never known anything better. Alaska would be a paradise to them.

It is perhaps the corn and wheat belt farmer that the Government handbook on Alaska has in mind when it says:[11]

"No one should think of engaging in agriculture in Alaska without first giving careful consideration to the topography, climate, soils, crops, population, markets, transportation, and mining development. It would be unwise for the prospective agriculturist to rush into this country without some preliminary knowledge of the true conditions. The same is true of all new regions.

"It must be remembered that in many parts of Alaska strictly pioneer conditions still obtain and that home markets are at present restricted to a small population, as compared with many sections of the States. . . .

"The indications are that agricultural development will be gradual, growing with the construction of highways and railways, with the development of mining industries, and accompanying increase of population."

[11] General Information, etc., p. 33, based on Bennett and Rice, *op. cit.*, pp. 43–44.

GOVERNMENT RESEARCH IN AID OF SETTLERS AND FARMERS IN THE NORTHERN GREAT PLAINS OF THE UNITED STATES

O. E. Baker

IN the United States, as in most other countries of the world where pioneer lands[1] are being occupied, the advance of agricultural settlement during the past quarter century has been in general onto lands less and less favorable for crop production or lands that required more and more capital for their utilization. Before the World War this advance in the United States was principally along four fronts (Fig. 1): (1) in the upper Great Lakes region, where the best of the cut-over or forest land was being cleared for crops, mostly by recent immigrants from Europe willing to accept a sub-American standard of living; (2) in the South, where the use of mineral fertilizers and cheap negro labor was making it profitable to clear the rather infertile forest and cut-over land and in some cases to provide drainage also, particularly in the lower Coastal Plain; (3) in parts of the Far West, where the production of alfalfa, fruit, sugar beets, and other crops yielding a high value of products per acre made it possible to irrigate arid land, mostly along the rivers, particularly after the Reclamation Act of 1902 provided a government subsidy; (4) in the semi-arid Great Plains region lying east of the Rocky Mountains, where the introduction or development of drought-resistant cereal crops and the application of large amounts of power per man in crop production, by means of tractors or horses in multiple hitch, facilitated by the level character of the land, excellent railroad connections, and much free government land made it possible to push forward the frontiers of crop production from 50 to 200 miles, and even 300 miles in places, during the quarter century before the World War.

Of these four pioneer belts the last is the most important, and it is the only one in which an advance is occurring at present (Fig. 2). It is the last agricultural frontier in the United States, although in other parts of the world there is much land of similar character yet unused for crop production. For these reasons, and because

[1] The word pioneer is used here with reference to a region where crop cultivation is advancing into forest land, grassland, or absolute desert and where living conditions are more or less primitive.

of the limitations of space, the methods of study of the agricultural and social conditions in this semi-arid belt alone will be discussed; and, in order to simplify the situation still more, only research in aid of farmers in the northern portion of the Great Plains will be noted.[2]

The description that follows is limited to research by government agencies, both state and federal, but this fact should not lessen its suggestiveness as to studies that might be carried on in other pioneer belts. These studies in the Northern Plains states are modest in cost and might well be duplicated, with appropriate modification, by other countries faced with a similar situation.[3]

THE PROBLEMS CREATED BY THE EMERGENCY OF 1916–1923

The agricultural problems in the Northern Great Plains region arise largely out of its semi-arid climate[4] and its location in the center of the continent remote from markets. These problems may be classified primarily into six groups: (a) land utilization—Which land should be used for crops and which for grazing? (b) agronomy and animal husbandry—How should the crops be grown, the pastures improved, and the animals fed and cared for? (c) farm management—What sizes of farms and systems of farm organization are most profitable? (d) credit—How can capital be obtained at the lowest rate (always a problem in a pioneer region), and under what conditions should loans be made? (e) taxation and social organization—How can roads, schools, churches, and other social institutions be best maintained by a sparse population? (f) marketing—How can the cost of the long haul to the seaboard or to the eastern centers of population, and of the many services connected therewith, be reduced?

[2] For a study of pioneer conditions in a selected area of this region (Garfield County, northeastern Montana) the reader is referred to Isaiah Bowman: Jordan County, *Geogr. Rev.*, Vol. 21, 1931, pp. 22–55 and *idem:* The Pioneer Fringe, *Amer. Geogr. Soc. Special Publ. No. 13*, New York, 1931, pp. 122–142. The agricultural geography of the Northern Great Plains is discussed in the writer's Agricultural Regions of North America: Part VI, The Spring Wheat Region, *Econ. Geogr.*, Vol. 4, 1928, pp. 399–433.

[3] It will be observed that the studies hereafter described are mostly economic in character. This is owing primarily to the writer's acquaintance with this aspect of the work and not to any lesser degree of activity by the agronomic and animal-industry research agencies.

[4] The physical conditions and their influences upon the development of agriculture are described in four papers published in Vol. 13, 1923, of the *Annals of the Association of American Geographers:* "The Climate of the Great Plains As a Factor in Their Utilization," by J. B. Kincer, of the U. S. Weather Bureau (pp. 67–80); "The Soils of the Great Plains" by C. F. Marbut, Chief of the Bureau of Soils (pp. 41–66); "The Natural Vegetation of the Great Plains Region," by H. L. Shantz, formerly of the Bureau of Plant Industry (pp. 81–107); and "The Agriculture of the Great Plains Region" by O. E. Baker, of the Bureau of Agricultural Economics (pp. 109–167).

These problems became increasingly acute during the years 1916 to 1923, when the partial destruction of the 1916 crop by black rust was followed by four years of unprecedented drought and these, in turn, by three years of low prices for grain. A series of "wet" seasons culminating in 1916 had encouraged a wave of settlement by grain growers, who homesteaded the public range

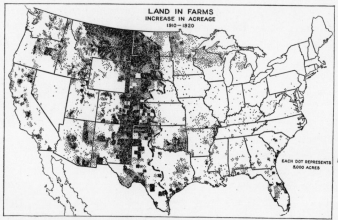

FIG. 1—The great increase in acreage of land in farms in the Great Plains region before the World War was due principally to the enactment of homestead acts in 1909 and 1916 which authorized entry on 320 and 640 acres respectively. The dashed line is drawn along the eastern margin of the Great Plains region. (Bureau of Agricultural Economics, U. S. Department of Agriculture.)

in 320 or 640 acre units or bought from homesteaders, built houses and barns (often shacks only), purchased livestock and machinery, and began to break the short-grass sod and sow the land to flax and wheat. Roads and branch railroads were built, villages were started and grew rapidly, local politicians persuaded the people to vote many of these villages into county seats of new counties, and land rose in value from $2 or $3 an acre to $20 and even $30 an acre. The open range of the cattle-and-sheep man was being transformed into farming country.

Then came the drought of unprecedented duration, each year drier than the preceding until 1919 and with the 1920 season almost as dry in some localities. Many of the settler-farmers had enough capital to survive these five years of adversity, but upon the return of heavier rainfall in 1921, 1922, and 1923 the price of wheat dropped below cost of production for most farmers. It was these later years that broke the backs of so many settlers. A few banks had failed during the dry years, but now they failed by the score, as the farms could not be sold for nearly as much as the banks had loaned on them as security. Many farms were deserted, thousands of people left the region, store buildings and village houses became vacant, taxes could not be collected, and some of the new counties defaulted their bonds.

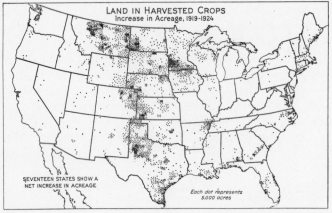

FIG. 2—Most of the increase in acreage of harvested crops from 1919 to 1924 took place in the Great Plains region. The development of drought-resistant grains, the use of dry-farming methods, and the increase in the area one man can cultivate owing to the mechanization of agriculture have made crop production possible in this area of relatively level topography and subhumid to semi-arid climate. (Bureau of Agricultural Economics, U. S. Department of Agriculture.)

Many farmers could not grow nor purchase even enough seed to plant their fields. Hence in 1918 and 1919 the President of the United States allotted $5,000,000 in all from the War Emergency Fund for seed loans, and in 1921 and 1922 Congress appropriated $2,000,000 and $1,500,000 respectively for this purpose.

The Spring Wheat Regional Council and Its Work

The disbursement and later the collection of these loans devolved upon the United States Department of Agriculture, thus bringing it into intimate contact with conditions in the region; while the agricultural colleges, experiment stations, and extension services in the Northern Plains states likewise became deeply concerned about the situation. This resulted in the formation, late in 1922, of the Spring Wheat Regional Council, composed of representatives of the United States Department of Agriculture and of the state agricultural institutions, which met in St. Paul in January, 1923.

The Department of Agriculture members of the council, before the meeting, were formed into two committees, one on the marketing of agricultural products of the region and the other on agricultural production ("Types of Farming Committee"). Each committee prepared a preliminary report, that on marketing being devoted to assuring a fair grading of the grain and payment of a reasonable price, to freight rates, to coöperative elevators, and to other problems in merchandising the crops. The report of the committee on production dealt with more permanent factors affecting the situation; and, as it represented the judgment of many competent men as to a research program to help this pioneer belt solve its agricultural problems, it seems worth while to quote it in full.

REPORT OF TYPES OF FARMING COMMITTEE OF THE SPRING WHEAT REGIONAL COUNCIL

The Types of Farming Committee suggests the following subjects for the consideration of the Spring Wheat Regional Council:

PHYSICAL CONDITIONS

That data on the physical conditions of the region be assembled and made available:

(a) Climate—To show the climatic conditions in the various parts of the region that influence the production of crops and livestock.

(b) Water Supply—To show the availability of water for household use, livestock production, and irrigation, especially in the drier parts of the region.

(c) Topography—To show the distribution of tillable and untillable lands.

(d) Soils—To show the distribution of soils differentiated on the basis of those characteristics that are known to be important in agricultural production.

(e) Natural Vegetation—To show the distribution of the various types of natural vegetation, with particular reference to their value in livestock production and as indicators of agricultural possibilities.

AGRICULTURAL DEVELOPMENT

That data on the agricultural development of the region be assembled and made available:

(a) The experience of the farmers as well as the general history of crop and livestock production, to assist in determining the proper utilization of the land and the best selection of crop and livestock enterprises.

(b) The stage of economic development of the different parts of the region, especially in relation to other regions, as indicating readjustments in the system of farming.

(c) Changes in transportation facilities and rates, as an aid in the selection of crop and livestock enterprises.

(d) Changes in world production and market conditions, as they affect the relative profitableness of crops and livestock enterprises in the region.

PRESENT UTILIZATION OF LAND

That available data on the utilization of land in the region be studied with special reference to determining the extent to which present utilization corresponds to the adaptation indicated by the physical conditions for (a) crop production, (b) pasture and grazing, and (c) timber production.

CROP PRODUCTION

(a) That available data on the adaptation of crops and varieties, and of crop rotations and tillage methods, to the conditions existing in the different parts of the region be assembled and summarized.

(b) That farmers be urged to sow only seed of adapted varieties and that in the choice of varieties of cash crops, such as wheat and potatoes, they give particular attention to market demands.

(c) That the standardization of varieties of cash crops on individual farms and in communities be recommended as a means of lessening mixtures and thus assuring better returns.

(d) That farmers be urged to use clean seed, as free as possible from mixture of other crops and varieties, weed seed, and diseases.

(e) That the adoption of rotation practices and tillage methods best suited to a profitable and permanent agriculture be recommended.

(f) That farmers be urged to adopt approved methods of controlling the grasshopper and cut-worm pests and form coöperative organizations for this purpose.

LIVESTOCK AND DAIRYING

(a) That attention be given to the selection of types and breeds adapted to the conditions that prevail and suited to market demands, particularly with reference to the use of superior sires and to the maintenance of proper ratios between sires and dams.

(b) That attention be directed to grazing and feeding practices which will result in (1) the best utilization of pastures, especially the prevention of overgrazing by limiting the number of livestock to the carrying capacity of a normal season and by deferred grazing, seeding, and other means of promoting revegetation, (2) the practicable utilization of roughages produced on the farm, and (3) the keeping of young and breeding animals in a thrifty condition.

(c) That due consideration be given to the importance in livestock management of providing an adequate water supply, reducing losses by saving the newborn and protecting from starvation, severe weather, predatory animals, diseases, and poisonous plants.

(d) That consideration be given to the classes of livestock adapted to the several areas in the region, especially the place of dairying in the agriculture of each area, taking into consideration its effect upon the seasonal distribution of labor and the stabilizing of the farmer's income.

(e) That attention be directed to the necessity of increasing the average production of dairy cows in the region and of providing a constant supply of roughages, by means of storage in silos or otherwise of the excess of moist years for use in dry years.

(f) That a study be made to determine the most practical methods of livestock production to provide the farm family with meat, milk, butter, and eggs at all seasons of the year.

Home-Grown Supplies

That farmers be urged to give increased attention to the farm garden and the home production of livestock products, as a means of conserving the cash income, reducing the cost of living, and at the same time safeguarding the health of the family. The importance of producing on the farm most of the food consumed by the family is made more urgent by the increase in freight rates and the high cost of processing and of retail distribution.

Costs of Production

That data on the costs of producing different crops and kinds of livestock and livestock products be assembled and made available and that farmers be urged to adopt methods and practices which reduce production costs. This is especially important in view of the low prices of most of the products of the region and is probably the most immediately effective method by which farmers can improve their financial condition.

Farm Organization

That data on the organization of farms in the region be assembled and made available, with special reference to the combination of farm enterprises which make the best use of land, labor, and capital, reduce the risk of losses in unfavorable years, and give the most profitable returns.

Agricultural Areas

That consideration be given to the feasibility of delimiting the agricultural areas in the region on the basis of physical and statistical data now available.

Systems of Farming

That consideration be given to the feasibility of formulating statements with regard to the systems of farming best adapted to the several agricultural areas, taking into consideration the physical conditions, the differences in the characteristics of the individual farmers and their farms, the costs of production, and the trend of prices of the commodities that can be produced in each area.

January 15, 1923

Report of Committee on Farm Organization

At the meeting of the Regional Council in St. Paul several committees were appointed, but space permits including only the report of the committee on farm organization:

Gentlemen of the Council:

Your Committee on Farm Organization has had two meetings and has laid out a plan of operation essentially as follows:

The work contemplates two general phases, one pertaining largely to the temporary emergency situation of agriculture and the other pertaining to the long-time program of farm organization for the region. Some recommendations regarding immediate action are appended hereto.

It is recognized that the types of farming and farm practices in operation at present are the outgrowth of years of experience and the accumulation of practical first-hand knowledge on the part of the farmers who occupy the land. In a large majority of cases the combined judgment of farmers of a community is correct as to the most economic organization of the farm business. When there is a well-defined type of agriculture in a region it should be disturbed only when there is reasonable probability of improvement, and then but slowly.

It is recognized that the difficulty in which agriculture finds itself today is due far more to the disparity in prices between farm products than to errors in farm organization or practice.

THE LONG-TIME PROGRAM

This contemplates the assembling of all available information from the various states and from the United States Department of Agriculture, or from any other available source, with the object of first locating the various areas of similar agricultural conditions and, second, presenting rather definite and specific recommendations as to systems or types of farming for the respective areas.

For the purpose of furthering this plan of work it is recommended that the council take the following action.

First. Urge upon the United States Department of Agriculture the importance of locating as quickly and as accurately as possible, in coöperation with the various states, by means of maps and otherwise, and of presenting in published form the main agricultural areas of the region as a basis for developing a program of agricultural production, particularly with reference to types of farming.

Second. Request the United States Department of Agriculture to make available at once to the Committee on Farm Organization, by photostats or otherwise, the maps and other data showing climate, topography, soil types, natural vegetation, and water supply and correlate with those physical data the maps and material relating to the agricultural development of the region, utilization and ownership of land, the geographic distribution of crops and livestock, crop practices and rotation, livestock production, size of farms, and systems of farming.

Third. Request the several states in the conference likewise to make available such data, maps, and material as they possess, these to be combined with the material from the United States Department of Agriculture and prepared for publication by that department (see First, above) and by the several states or otherwise.

Fourth. Assist in providing for the publication of this material as the basis for making detailed plans for types of farming and for farm organization suited to each of the various agricultural areas. Publication of the material already available is fundamental to the proper development of plans for a profitable agriculture and for advising as to types of farming and schemes of farm organization that will be suitable to each area.

Fifth. We recommend that each state agricultural college organize a permanent state agricultural program committee, which shall include definite assignments from interested divisions of the college, experiment station, and extension service, for the purpose of unifying and clarifying the program for agriculture for which those institutions shall stand. This committee may coöperate with other state agencies in the determination and development of this plan.

January 22, 1927
University Farm,
St. Paul, Minnesota

COROLLARY RESEARCH, PRINCIPALLY ECONOMIC, BY DIFFERENT GOVERNMENT BUREAUS

Before the meeting of the Spring Wheat Regional Council, the Bureau of Agricultural Economics of the United States Department of Agriculture had undertaken a series of farm organization and settlers' progress surveys in coöperation with the agricultural colleges and experiment stations of Montana, North Dakota, and South Dakota and also had begun the preparation of an Atlas of Physical Conditions and Land Utilization in the Northern Great Plains Region. The Bureau of Plant Industry, which had established, ten to fifteen years previously, a number of experimental farms in the region, conducted in coöperation with the state agricultural experiment stations, intensified the plant breeding, pasture, and tillage work and extended its barbary eradication (wheat rust) campaign; while the Bureau of Animal Industry, soon after the Council meeting but not as a result of it, established a large livestock and range management station at Miles City, Montana. The Weather Bureau also increased the number of "coöperative" observers' stations in the region, while a soil survey of the area east of the Rocky Mountains in Montana was undertaken by the Bureau of Soils in coöperation with the Montana experiment station. The state experiment stations likewise expanded their work, especially in the field of agricultural economics.

FARM ORGANIZATION AND SETTLERS' PROGRESS SURVEYS

The local farm organization and settlers' progress surveys revealed that a few farmers, even in the less favored districts, had accumulated a competence ($5000 to $15,000) in the course of the ten to fifteen years since agricultural settlement began and that, where the physical conditions were more favorable, a surprising number of farmers were what one might call successful. Some of the causes of success and failure were revealed by the survey records, and the first report on each survey consisted largely of a description of the systems of farming in the district, especially with reference to success or failure.[5] The second report showed the financial progress made by the farmers during one good and one fair year.[6] A third report suggested the size of farms and a system of farm organization that would give the largest returns in the next few years, based on what was considered the best system of farming methods and practice in livestock management used by the farmers interviewed.[7] A fourth report suggested minor modifications for the year following to conform with recommendations in the "Agricultural Outlook" report of the Department of Agriculture with reference to prospective production of crops and prices, both in the United States and abroad. This fourth kind of report, of course, should be issued annually.[8]

The agricultural experiment stations of the states in the region carried on other economic studies, some simultaneously. Notable among these was a farm survey in the very dry "triangle" of Montana, the corners of which are Great Falls, Havre, and Shelby;[9] studies of developing farms in western South Dakota and of

[5] L. A. Reynoldson: Farming in Northeastern Montana: A Preliminary Report on the Farm Business and Financial Condition of 151 Farmers in Sheridan and Daniels Counties, Bur. of Agric. Economics, Washington, D. C., Jan., 1923. Mimeographed.

Idem: The Progress of Farmers in Southeastern Montana from the Time of Their Settlement in the Area, Bur. of Agric. Economics, Washington, D. C., Feb., 1924. Mimeographed.

L. A. Reynoldson and R. E. Willard: An Economic Study of Farming in Southwestern North Dakota, *North Dakota Agric. Exper. Sta. Bull. No. 180*, July, 1924.

[6] L. A. Reynoldson: The Progress of Farmers in Northeastern Montana for Two Years: The Farm Business and Financial Condition of Farmers in Sheridan and Daniels Counties for Two Successive Years, Bur. of Agric. Economics, Washington, D. C., Dec., 1923. Mimeographed.

[7] L. A. Reynoldson: An Organization System for Farms in Northeastern Montana, Preliminary Report. Bur. of Agric. Economics, Washington, D. C., Feb., 1925. Mimeographed.

Idem: An Organization System for Farms in Southeastern Montana. Bur. of Agric. Economics, Washington, D. C., March, 1925. Mimeographed.

E. R. Johnson and C. G. Worsham: The Organization of Farms in Western South Dakota and Progress of Farmers Who Have Settled in the Area, Bur. of Agric. Economics, Washington D. C., Aug., 1924. Mimeographed.

[8] L. A. Reynoldson: The Effect of the Agricultural Outlook for 1925 on the Organization System for Farms in Northeastern Montana, Bur. of Agric. Economics, Washington, D. C., Feb., 1925. Mimeographed.

[9] M. L. Wilson: Dry Farming in the North Central Montana Triangle. *Montana Agric. Extension Service Bull. No. 66*, Bozeman, Mont., June, 1923.

M. L. Wilson and H. E. Murdock: Reducing the Cost of Montana's Dry Land Wheat Harvest, *ibid., Bull. No. 71*, June, 1924.

An Agricultural Program for Montana, by several authors, *ibid., Bull. No. 84*, May, 1927.

farming systems in the eastern part of the state,[10] and studies of type-of-farming areas in North Dakota.[11]

The homesteading of the public land in this region and the erection of fences were a calamity to the cattle and sheep raisers, who had previously had free use of the range. In addition, the price of cattle after the World War fell to a point far below the cost of production for many cattlemen. Not only the grain growers but also the livestock ranchers needed help in the reorganization of their business. This need prompted the Bureau of Agricultural Economics, in coöperation with the agricultural experiment stations in Montana, Wyoming, and the Dakotas, to undertake the study of ranch organization. One report has been published[12] and another is in press. In these studies also the survey method was largely used.

THE ATLAS OF PHYSICAL CONDITIONS AND LAND CLASSIFICATION

The Atlas of Physical Conditions and Land Utilization under preparation by the United States Departments of Agriculture and the Interior consists of (1) a series of climatic maps and graphs based largely on an analysis of rainfall and temperature as these affect crop production and use of pastures; (2) generalized maps of the soils of the region, of the natural vegetation, and of the carrying capacity of the range; (3) a series of land classification maps, on a scale of eight miles to the inch, showing three grades of crop land, irrigated and irrigable land, land suitable only for grazing, national forests, etc., and (4) a series of maps, showing, by the dot system, acreage of harvested crops, of crop failure, of crop land lying idle or fallow, of plowable pasture and non-plowable pasture in farms, and of woodland in farms pastured and also not pastured, the num-

[10] C. G. Worsham: Studies in Developing Farms on Western South Dakota Ranges, *South Dakota Dept. of Agric. Circular 5*, June, 1923. Preliminary Report.

M. R. Benedict: The Business of Farming in the South Dakota Wheat Belt, *ibid., Circular 6*, 1923. Preliminary Report.

C. A. Bonnen and R. H. Rogers: Profitable Farming Systems for the Intensive Spring Wheat Area in South Dakota, *South Dakota Agric. Exper. Sta. Bull. No. 235*, 1928.

C. A. Bonnen and J. B. Hutson: Profitable Farming Systems for East Central South Dakota, *ibid., Bull. No. 226*, 1927.

[11] R. E. Willard and O. M. Fuller: Type-of-Farming Area in North Dakota, *North Dakota Agric. Exper. Sta. Bull. No. 212*, July, 1927.

F. F. Elliott, J. W. Tapp, and R. E. Willard: Types of Farming in North Dakota, *U. S. Dept. of Agric. Technical Bull. 102*, Washington, D. C., 1928.

R. E. Willard: Cost of Producing Crops in North Dakota, *North Dakota Agric. Exper. Sta. Bull. No. 199*, 1926.

[12] M. L. Wilson, R. H. Wilcox, G. S. Klemmendson, and V. V. Parr: A Study of Ranch Organization and Methods of Range Cattle Production in the Northern Great Plains Region, *Bur. of Agric. Economics Technical Bull. No. 45*, Washington, D. C., March, 1928.

ber of farms, the value of farm land and buildings per acre, and the number of people engaged in agriculture according to the census, which data were tabulated by enumeration districts (townships usually). The land classification maps and the accompanying text have been prepared by the Conservation Branch of the Geological Survey of the Department of the Interior, under a coöperative arrangement with the Department of Agriculture, and were based on the reports of the inspectors on application for entry of land under the Grazing Homestead Act and other acts.[13]

The original plan of the atlas included a series of graphs showing the relation of crop yields to climatic conditions, according to the records of the ten agricultural experiment stations in the region operated by the Bureau of Plant Industry in coöperation with the state experiment stations. These have been issued separately.[14]

CREDIT STUDIES

Little work has been done in the Northern Plains states in studying farmers' credit. This is, perhaps, owing to the fairly adequate private banking facilities in the region, also to the enactment of the Federal Farm Loan Act, which makes long-time loans available to farmers of the region on the same terms and rates as in other parts of the United States, and to the Intermediate Credit Act, which provides for short-term credit, particularly useful to cattlemen and sheepmen. In addition there has been the emergency legislation of the seed loan acts previously referred to.

The only study of the credit needs of farmers in the region has not been published,[15] but similar studies in the Southern Great Plains region are suggestive.[16] In the Oklahoma studies, which were made by a modified survey method, the needs of short-time

[13] Most of the maps for the atlas, including the land classification maps, were completed by 1925, but publication has been delayed, awaiting the completion of the natural vegetation and soil maps. The land classification maps have been published beforehand separately by both departments concerned under the title "Land Classification of the Northern Great Plains," 8 sheets on the scale of 1 : 500,000, accompanied by mimeographed text, A. E. Aldous and J. F. Deeds, assisted by others: Land Classification of the Northern Great Plains, Montana, North Dakota, South Dakota, and Wyoming, U. S. Geol. Survey, Washington, D. C., 1929.

[14] E. C. Chilcott: The Relations Between Crop Yields and Precipitation in the Great Plains, U. S. Dept. of Agric. Misc. Circular No. 8, Washington, D. C., 1927.

[15] This study, entitled "Financing Farmers and Stockmen in Southeastern Montana," was made by Elmer A. Starch of the Montana Agricultural Experiment Station, in collaboration with W. G. Murray of the U. S. Bureau of Agricultural Economics.

[16] J. T. Sanders and A. N. Moore: Credit Problems of Oklahoma Cotton Growers; idem: Credit Problem of Oklahoma Wheat Growers—two bulletins in preparation by Oklahoma Agric. Exper. Sta. and U. S. Bur. of Agric. Economics coöperating.

V. P. Lee: Farm Mortgage Financing in Texas, Texas Agric. Exper. Sta. Bull. No. 330, April 1925.

Idem: Short-term Farm Credit in Texas, ibid., Bull. No. 351, March, 1927.

credit were considered primarily. The schedule used secured data on the purposes for which money was borrowed, the sources and costs from each source, the kinds of credit needed by seasons, merchant credit, cash credit, etc., and cost of each kind, the security offered by the farmers, separately for owner, tenant, and laborer, and the losses, etc. In the Northern Great Plains it would be desirable to include the credit requirements in different years and the effect of credit on bank deposits, on the movement of wheat and cattle to market, and on other aspects of marketing.

In this connection a very interesting experiment in Montana should be noted. This is the establishment on new farms, largely by means of credit, of men who were familiar with local conditions but who had lost out because of adverse seasons. The experiment is known as the Fairway Farms and consists in the careful selection of the land and of the men and the guidance of their labors, first as tenants under a contract to buy the land, later as owners under a mortgage. The project is supervised by M. L. Wilson of the Montana Agricultural College.[17]

SOCIAL STUDIES: TAXATION

It is evident that most of the economic studies that have been made in this pioneer belt, especially since the meeting of the Spring Wheat Regional Council, have related either to the cost of producing crops or to the size and organization of farms. This is fitting; for, until the agriculture of a region is established on a sound and enduring basis, all social institutions are in a precarious position and efforts to provide the amenities of modern life may prove futile. At present the farmers in the region are accumulating capital, which will help greatly to tide over the dry seasons that are certain to occur again, and it would appear that the time has come to consider the improvement of social conditions in the region.

The improvement of social conditions will involve serious problems of taxation; for better schools and roads, libraries, and other institutions and services must be paid for. In a semi-arid region like the Northern Great Plains the farms must of necessity be large in area and the population correspondingly sparse. The cost of roads and schools per capita will be greater normally than

[17] Since this was written, Professor Wilson has advised the writer that, although most of the men are getting along well and are repaying the loans, a serious error was made in deciding on the size of farms. These farms ranged from one (640 acres) to two sections in size but should have been three or four sections in size. Larger-sized farms have been made more economical by the development of larger tractors and the great success of the "combine" in harvesting grain.

in more populous districts, while the capacity of the people to pay taxes, for several years at least until wealth accumulates, will be less. In Montana the tax burden was unnecessarily increased by the unwise division of old counties into several new counties, each with a staff of salaried officials. In many cases it appears inevitable that the state will need to bear part of the expense of maintaining facilities for education and communication in the newer or poorer districts, and doubtless the richer communities sooner or later will raise the question how far such a policy is justifiable.

Meanwhile some of the drier or poorer lands may be taxed out of use, i.e. become delinquent and revert to the county or state, as is now happening on a large scale in the northern portions of the Great Lakes states.[18] Such a process, like a snowball rolling down hill, becomes cumulative; for, as a part of the land fails to pay taxes, all other lands in a county usually have to pay more, and this causes still more land to become delinquent. On the other hand, taxes on good farm land tend to force it into use for crops, or, if already in use, to be cultivated more intensively. In this Northern Great Plains region it appears likely that the emphasis on farm management surveys will soon be shifted to taxation and land utilization studies.[19] Among the phases of the subject that should be studied

[18] A quarter of the land in some counties in northern Wisconsin has become tax-delinquent and is reverting to the county (see B. H. Hibbard and others: Tax Delinquency in Northern Wisconsin, *Wisconsin Agric. Exper. Sta. Bull. No. 339*, June, 1928).

"Taxes levied on all enterprises in any industry tend to eliminate the marginal producer and thereby to affect supply and price of the product" (Eric Englund: Research in Farm Taxation [a paper read at the 18th annual meeting of the Amer. Farm Economics Assn. at Washington, D. C., Dec. 28, 1927], U. S. Dept. of Agric., Washington, D. C. Mimeographed).

[19] Two taxation studies have been made in the Northern Great Plains region, viz.:

R. W. Newton and A. H. Benton: Some Tax Problems of North Dakota Farmers, *North Dakota Agric. Exper. Sta. Bull. No. 203*, Oct., 1926.

E. P. Crossen: Taxation and Public Finance in South Dakota, *South Dakota Agric. Exper. Sta. Bull. No. 232*, June, 1928.

Several other excellent studies have been completed in the Central Plains, as follows:

Eric Englund: Assessment and Equalization of Farm and City Real Estate in Kansas, *Kansas Agric. Exper. Sta. Bull. No. 232*, July, 1924.

Idem: Tax Revision in Kansas, *ibid., Bull. No. 234*, Dec., 1924.

Idem: The Trend of Real Estate Taxation in Kansas from 1910 to 1923, *ibid., Bull. No. 235*, Sept., 1925.

Idem: Federal Aid As a Part of a Long-time Agricultural Policy, *ibid., Bull. No. 237*, Oct., 1926.

Whitney Coombs, L. A. Moorhouse, B. D. Seeley: Some Colorado Tax Problems, *Colorado Exper. Station Bull. No. 346*, Sept., 1928.

Worthy of note also, although dealing with states outside the Great Plains, are the following bulletins:

J. E. Brindley and Grace S. M. Zorbaugh: The Tax System of Iowa, *Iowa Agric. Exper. Sta. Extension Bull. No. 150*, Jan., 1929.

R. W. Newton: Taxes on Michigan Rented Farms, 1919–1925, *Michigan Agric. Exper. Sta. Technical Bull. No. 91*, Jan., 1928.

In the northern counties of Michigan surveyed (a partly pioneer area) taxes were taking nearly all the net rent of farm land, and, in the southern Michigan counties, about one-half of the rent. These southern counties have good soil and have been settled nearly a century.

are the sources of funds, the distribution of expenditures, the ratio of assessed value to real value of farm land compared with urban property, changes in the relation of taxation to market value of farm real estate and likewise to the net income from farm property, including tax delinquency,[20] and especially the relation of the township to the county, the county to the state, and the state to the nation in reference to the amount of taxes paid and the benefits received.

SOCIAL ORGANIZATION

It is inevitable in a pioneer region that more attention will be given to making a living than to advancing culture and acquiring the comforts and amenities of life. Nevertheless, the social side of life has not been neglected by the people of the Northern Great Plains, and in particular they have provided courageously for the education of their children. This has been achieved despite the sparse population and the consequent difficulty in gathering children in schools[21] and the even greater difficulties of taxation. There is a smaller percentage of rural illiteracy in the Dakotas and Montana than in any of the other 45 states except Idaho and Nebraska.

The agricultural experiment stations in the region have realized the pressing economic needs of the farmers and have devoted most of their attention in the field of the social sciences to problems of farm management and marketing of farm products. However, an excellent description of social organization agencies, with suggestions for improvement, has been made in North Dakota,[22] and a notable study of the factors involved, both economic and social,

[20] The percentage increase in delinquent taxes in certain counties in the major agricultural sections of Kansas between 1917 and 1922 was as follows, according to the *Kansas Agric. Exper. Sta. Bull. No. 234,* p. 19:

Year	Corn Belt	General Farming	Flint Hills	Wheat Belt	Grazing
1917	100	100	100	100	100
1918	122	113	120	152	133
1919	141	68	121	161	215
1920	222	99	126	219	275
1921	343	232	433	409	417
1922	264	271	742	570	468

The five grazing counties, which are also marginal wheat counties, reported nearly half the aggregate amount of delinquent taxes in the 27 counties for which figures were obtained; but the value of taxable property in these counties was only about 3 per cent of the total in the 27 counties.

[21] J. E. Richardson and J. W. Barger: Public School Dormitories for Rural Children in Montana, *Montana Agric. Exper. Sta. Bull. No. 201,* Feb., 1927.

[22] E. A. Wilson: Social Organizations and Agencies in North Dakota, *North Dakota Agric. Exper. Sta. Bull. No. 221,* Aug., 1928.

in the movement of settlers from farms,[23] also a study of standards of living in farm homes;[24] but, with these exceptions, little has been published by experiment stations in the region. A series of studies that have been made in Wisconsin have developed methods of research which, with some modification, would appear well adapted to research and the planning of a program for rural improvement in the Northern Great Plains region.[25]

MARKETING

The marketing of the farm products, especially wheat, has involved serious problems ever since the settlement of the region. Proper payment for the high protein of wheat, especially in dry years, freight rates, elevator charges, dockage for weed seeds, and other items that enter into the "spread" in the price of wheat between the terminal market at Minneapolis and at the country elevator, have provided the issues for many political campaigns; nevertheless, not until recent years have the experiment stations conducted any large amount of research in the subject. There are now one or two men in each of the three agricultural colleges and experiment stations in the region working on marketing problems, and a number of valuable studies have been issued.[26]

[23] E. A. Wilson, H. C. Hoffsomer, and A. H. Benton: Rural Changes in Western North Dakota, *North Dakota Agric. Exper. Sta. Bull. No. 214*, 1928.

[24] E. L. Kirkpatrick: Annual Family Living in Selected Farm Homes of North Dakota: A Preliminary Report. (In coöperation with North Dakota Agricultural College.) Bur. of Agric. Economics, Washington, D. C., Aug., 1928. Mimeographed.

See also J. D. Black and C. C. Zimmerman: Family Living on Successful Minnesota Farms, *Minnesota Agric. Exper. Sta. Bull. No. 240*, Nov., 1927.

[25] C. J. Galpin: The Social Anatomy of an Agricultural Community, *Wisconsin Agric. Exper. Sta. Research Bull. No. 34*, May, 1915.

J. H. Kolb: Rural Primary Groups: A Study of Agricultural Neighborhoods, *ibid., Bull. No. 50*, Dec., 1921.

Idem: Service Relations of Town and County, *ibid., Bull. No. 58*, Dec., 1923.

J. H. Kolb and C. J. Bornman: Rural Religious Organization: A Study of the Origin and Development of Religious Groups, *ibid., Bull. No. 60*, June, 1924.

J. H. Kolb: Service Institution for Town and County, *ibid., Bull. No. 66*, Dec., 1925.

J. H. Kolb and A. F. Wileden: Special Interest Groups in Rural Society, *ibid., Bull. No. 84*, Dec., 1927.

[26] E. J. Bell: Larger Markets for Montana Wheat, *Montana Agric. Exper. Sta. Circular No. 135*, 1927.

Idem: Markets for Farm Products of the Billings Trade Area, *Montana Agric. Exper. Sta. Bull. No. 212*, 1928.

Idem: Marketing High Protein Wheat, *ibid., Bull. No. 213*, 1928.

A. H. Benton: Dockage in Wheat in North Dakota, *North Dakota Agric. Exper. Sta. Bull. No. 172*, 1924.

Idem: Advertising Farm Products by Farmers and Farm Organizations, *ibid., Bull. No. 185*, Jan., 1925.

A. H. Benton and M. F. Peightal: Farmers' Elevators in North Dakota, *ibid., Bull. No. 206*, Feb., 1927.

A. H. Benton: Poultry and Egg Marketing in North Dakota, *ibid., Bull. No. 215*, 1928.

A. H. Benton and H. E. Seielstad: Coöperative Live Stock Marketing in North Dakota, *ibid., Bull. 223*, 1928.

Pioneer Belt Agriculture Largely Commercial

Farmers in most, if not all, pioneer belts in the modern world make their living largely by producing commodities for export or at least for shipment outside the region. Argentina and Australia ship abroad wheat and beef and wool, Manchuria sends soy beans and wheat, the Great Plains of North America export or ship to the Eastern States wheat, beef, and dairy products. Pioneer belts are, therefore, more dependent on the world's market than longer settled regions; their economic welfare depends more directly on weather conditions and the progress of agricultural technique in other parts of the world, also on changes in the purchasing power and the diet of foreign peoples, than does the economic welfare of agriculture in more densely populated areas.

Furthermore, it must be recalled that the pioneer belts of today possess less favorable physical conditions, either of climate or soil or of land surface (topography), or else require a larger investment of capital to make the land suitable for agriculture (by irrigation, draining, clearing, etc.) than do most longer settled regions. Quite commonly, too, they have a further handicap of longer hauls and higher freight rates. The investments which have been made in pioneer belts, therefore, will be more promptly and sharply effected by improvements in agricultural practice (whether these lower costs or increase production at the same cost) than will investments in more fortunately endowed or more favorably located agricultural regions.

For these reasons it is especially important to the farmers of pioneer belts that the agricultural land resources of the world be estimated and the advantage of different regions in the production of a commodity compared. There has been much waste of human life and labor in the settlement of hilly lands, poor lands, and other lands ill adapted to agriculture, which could have been avoided if the settlers had known of better lands available elsewhere. The need of such a survey of resources and classification of land is further indicated by the fact that the principal importing regions of the world—northwestern Europe and eastern North America— are rapidly approaching a stationary population.

It is also especially important to farmers in pioneer regions to keep abreast of improvements in agricultural technique, particularly in the use of power and machinery. Since farmers in pioneer belts commonly labor under the handicap of natural conditions below average, the artificial conditions created by them must be above the average if a normal return of their labor is to be secured. This may be one of the reasons why farmers in many pioneer belts are among the most progressive in the nation—the unprogressive cannot survive.

RAPID MECHANIZATION OF AGRICULTURE AND ITS EFFECTS

Just at present the farmers in the Great Plains belt in North America are enjoying the benefits of a very rapid advance in the technique of the production of cereal crops. The tractor has been greatly increased in reliability and usefulness in recent years, and the new "combines" have reduced the number of hours required to harvest the small grains to one-third or even one-fourth that required five years ago. In Montana, for instance, the number of farmers and farm laborers has not increased since the World War, but the acreage and production of wheat have doubled.[27]

With the three-plow tractor outfits wheat is being grown and harvested at a labor cost of only 2½ man-hours an acre, including the cultivation of a second acre of summer fallow; and the six-plow outfits are reducing this figure to 2 man-hours an acre. The six-plow outfit, operated by one man, except in harvesting, for which two men are required, will plow 15 to 20 acres, or duckfoot-cultivate 75 to 100 acres, or seed about 100 acres, or harvest 50 acres, in a ten-hour day.[28]

This Great Plains belt is now the most dynamic agricultural region in North America. Land that was sub-marginal for crops a few years ago has now become clearly super-marginal. The sale of tractors in Montana was nearly fourfold greater in 1928 than in 1925, and the sale of combines was sixteen times greater. A survey by the Montana experiment station of one hundred successful wheat farmers in that state revealed that the average size of their farms had increased as follows: from 1045 acres in 1924 to 1130 acres in 1925, to 1250 acres in 1926, to 1625 acres in 1927, to 1900 acres in 1928, remaining at about the same figure in 1929. A similar increase in size of farms is occurring in western Kansas. Family farms of such size raise many problems of social organization, but it seems probable that the automobile will greatly aid the solution of most of them.

[27] As sometimes happens, inventors and the manufacturers of farm machinery have done more to solve the production problems of agriculture in the region than the government agencies, either federal or state. But increased production has made the marketing problems even more difficult. In this field the work of government agencies has been and must continue to be of supreme importance. There are also many serious production problems awaiting solution.

[28] With a large tractor hauling several drills, another man may be necessary to keep the boxes supplied with seed, and in harvesting with several outfits an extra man is usually employed to haul oil and gas and water, in addition to the man or men hauling the grain from the combine.

In the semi-arid steppes of Soviet Russia, likewise, the tractor and combine are being introduced, and the number in Manchuria is increasing rapidly. Most of the pioneer belts of the world are pioneer because of deficient rainfall and because of lack of progress in the development of machinery that increases the acreage of crops per man engaged in agriculture. In such of these belts as can produce 10 to 12 bushels of wheat per acre with summer fallow, or 6 to 8 bushels or more without summer fallow, the tractor and the combine seem likely to transform much of the grassland into grainland, double the density of population, and rouse in the people of the region new aspirations and interests.

However, it should be recalled that the area of these semi-arid lands in the world that have thus suddenly, by the development of large units of power, been made available for profitable cereal production, is very great. It is possible there may develop such a rapid increase of production, particularly of wheat, and perhaps of cotton, as to depress the price seriously and thus, especially in times of local drought, bring distress upon these pioneer regions. For several years the price of wheat in the United States has been lower than that of most other major agricultural commodities when compared with the pre-war prices. But the greatly lowered cost of production by these modern methods makes the cultivation of wheat still profitable in the Great Plains region. Some of the farmers operating a very large acreage cleared as much as $50,000 on their operations during the season of 1928, and most of the smaller farmers did well.

However, in general, those farmers did best who grew sweet clover and corn as well as wheat and who kept a large acreage in pasture. In the long run what the farmer sells is his labor and managerial ability. Without sacrificing the acreage in wheat he can produce other crops at those times of year when wheat does not need attention, and during the long winters he will find it profitable to sell his labor, even at a low price, by feeding and caring for livestock.

Although invention seems to have solved the most serious problem at present of this pioneer region—how to produce crops at a profit—and in doing so has made possible the agricultural exploitation of a vast area of land in various parts of the world, the need for scientific research will always remain urgent. In particular, let us hope that science will solve the next great problem of these semi-arid lands, which will develop probably in a few decades— the maintenance of soil fertility.

OPPORTUNITIES FOR AGRICULTURAL COLO-
NIZATION IN THE EASTERN BORDER
VALLEYS OF THE ANDES*

Raye R. Platt

ASK a citizen of any of the west coast republics of South America north of Chile where in his country there are opportunities for agricultural settlement, and he will, almost without exception, point to the eastern border valleys of the Andes and the adjacent lowlands. Pressed for information on the region he may paint a broadly impressionistic picture of fertile soils, equable climate, abundant rainfall, cheap land. Rarely will even the best informed be able to give any of the details that the immigrant or native farmer looking for new land wants to know. Questioned as to why, when his country must still import large quantities of farm products from abroad, there has been no large-scale movement of native farmers and farm laborers into the region in recent years and no successful colonization from abroad, he can only shrug his shoulders and lay the blame on the failure of his government to provide the transportation facilities that to his mind are all the region needs to bring its potentialities to full fruition. The better informed may have vague ideas of the need for systematic efforts at disease prevention in order to make the region safe for white colonists, for careful consideration of suitable crops based on the demands of the market, for experimental work and instruction in cultivation methods; but the transportation problem looms so large that all other problems that must be solved before the region can be successfully colonized are almost completely obscured by it.

*Venezuela has not been included in this discussion of possibilities for agricultural settlement in the eastern border valleys of the Andes and the adjacent lowlands for two reasons. First, the zone of eastern border valleys is so narrow (Fig. 1) as to offer little room for settlement. Second, whereas the lowlands immediately adjacent to the eastern border of the Andes in Colombia, Ecuador, Peru, and Bolivia are suggested as suitable for white colonization on account of their greater elevation and consequently more temperate climate than the semi-tropical lowlands farther east, the lowlands adjoining the eastern border of the Andes of Venezuela do not properly constitute a separate zone but are a part of the great llanos region that stretches all the way from the foot of the Andes to the mouth of the Orinoco.

Opportunities for settlement in the eastern border region in Argentina south of latitude 38° S. are discussed in the article on Patagonia in the present volume.

The general question of colonization in South America is dealt with in Otto Nordenskjöld: Südamerika, Ein Zukunftsland der Menschheit, Stuttgart, 1927, especially in Chapter 12, in which the author takes up the regions offering future opportunities for white settlement (see also his map, p. 187). The eastern border valleys of the Andes are discussed on pp. 195–199.

Causes of Neglect of Eastern Border Valleys As Colonization Region

It is true that, in spite of a long-professed desire on the part of the governments of Colombia, Ecuador, Peru, and Bolivia to attract agricultural immigrants to this belt of eastward-facing valleys and bordering plains and to provide there opportunities for their own agricultural population, no definite, practical steps have ever been taken in that direction. But the indifference of governments is not the real reason. The real reason lies in the fact that none of these countries has yet arrived at a stage of agricultural development that makes the demand for more land sufficiently urgent either to force their governments to take the steps necessary for opening the eastern region to large-scale colonization or to bring about broad colonization projects financed by private capital.

This does not mean that these countries are so completely self-supporting agriculturally that they have no need at present for either more extensive or intensive utilization of their cultivable land. Quite the opposite is the case. Their governments as well as their private capital have been so largely concerned, however, with the production of certain export products of high value—minerals in Bolivia; minerals, sugar, and cotton in Peru; cacao in Ecuador; coffee in Colombia—that little attention has been paid to the production of food for local consumption. Comparable statistics on the production and importation of farm products in these countries are difficult to obtain. The following list of food products imported into Peru in 1925, selected from official statistics,[1] is significant, however, in that it indicates how far even this country, which has made more progress than any of the others in attempts at agricultural development along modern lines, is from being self-supporting:

Wheat	77,404,631 kilograms
Rice	32,330,837 "
Flour	7,019,325 "
Lard	5,828,001 "
Potatoes	3,198,181 "
Fruits (fresh and dried)	3,007,896 "
Butter	749,652 "
Prepared and conserved meats	490,513 "
Rough cocoa	308,823 "

Comparable statistics on local production are available only for

[1] Statistical Abstract of Peru, 1928, prepared by the Bureau of Statistics, Department of Treasury and Commerce, Lima, 1929, pp. 93–97, 125, and 128.

wheat and rice. They show that nearly half the amount of these two basic foods consumed in Peru is imported.

More Accessible Regions Given Preference

If the time ever comes in these countries when serious consideration is given to the development of their agricultural potentialities and intelligent efforts made in that direction, it seems certain that such efforts will be directed, in the first instance, not towards the colonization of the eastern region but toward the development to their maximum productivity of lands which, by comparison with the eastern region, may be described as easy of access to railways and roads or to river and ocean transportation. In support of this may be cited the efforts made in Peru in the past few years under President Leguia's administration toward the improvement and extension of the irrigation systems of the coastal valleys.

The Example of Peru: Irrigated Coastal Valleys

The Leguia government recognized, as has perhaps no other government in the history of South America, the desirability of creating a class of small landowners. It might have been expected that its efforts toward that end would be devoted to opening up the eastern region by providing the roads and railways needed, establishing experimental farms there, setting up the machinery necessary for the combating of disease and insect pests, and undertaking the shifts in population required to give the region an adequate labor supply. But, instead, the eastern region was all but forgotten in costly measures for the improvement and extension of the irrigation systems of the coastal valleys in order to provide a full perennial supply of water for the lands already occupied and to add new land to them for sale in small lots. A few experimental farms were established for various purposes in the plateau regions, a few trails into the eastern valley region were improved or extended; but the real work of the government toward the development of the country's agricultural resources was done in the coastal valleys. The reason was that, because of the proximity of these valleys to ocean ports, they could pay a return on money invested in improvements that the eastern region could not pay because of the heavy cost of the long haul to market, however efficient transportation facilities might be provided.

The result is sufficient evidence of the administration's farsightedness. In a few years the production of sugar and cotton in the coastal valleys was brought to a point where the annual exports of these two products equaled in value the total annual exports of silver, copper, and petroleum. With the returns the country could buy in the foreign market the agricultural products that it needed more cheaply than they could be produced in and shipped from the eastern region.

In Bolivia Intensification of Agriculture on the Plateau

Bolivia also, under President Siles' administration toward the end of the last decade,[2] laid plans for agricultural development that quite definitely postponed to the far distant future all efforts on the part of the government at actual colonization measures east of the Andes. There the government came to the wise decision that its efforts toward making the country agriculturally self-supporting should be devoted first to bringing to their maximum productivity the lands already occupied on the *altiplano* and in the nearer valleys of the Eastern Cordillera. It was believed, with good reason, that, by the introduction of modern methods of cultivation, production could be so increased that, in addition to largely supplanting with domestic products the foodstuffs now imported from abroad, land would be freed for sale to native small farmers and even to foreign colonists.

The Siles government has fallen, and its successors may repudiate its plans or shelve them for the time being. But, with a policy of such evident practicability once promulgated, it would seem that until the hopes held out to them by the Siles government have been in part, at least, fulfilled, no large-scale expenditure of government funds for colonization purposes where colonization has so frequently failed would be countenanced by the people of the *altiplano*, on whom, in Bolivia, all governments must depend for support.

No Immediate Need for Colonization of Eastern Border Valleys

The time may come when the products of the eastern valleys and lowlands are so much needed in the markets of the world that private capital may be moved to undertake their development— cultivating them on a large scale, either as private enterprises

[2] Eduardo Romecin: Agricultural Adaptation in Bolivia, *Geogr. Rev.*, Vol. 19, 1929, pp. 248–255.

or by allotting them to colonists and financing the construction and operation of roads, railways, and river-steamer lines. One can conceive, for example, of the possibility of the establishment of packing-house enterprises in the llanos of Colombia and the low-lands of Bolivia, if the grazing lands of the world now occupied become too valuable to be used for that purpose. Until such a time comes, successful colonization in the eastern region must depend upon government coöperation at least in the building of roads and railways and the development of river transportation. It would seem reasonable to prophesy, from the evidence afforded by the attitude recently taken in Peru and Bolivia by the Leguia and Siles administrations, that such coöperation on any large scale must wait until the demand for the development of the eastern region becomes a really pertinent need. The need may be hastened by the failure of the market for the present basic exports from these countries, by the exhaustion of mineral resources, or by the pressure of agricultural population increased to a point where neither the present industries nor the land at present occupied can support it. Meanwhile it would seem wise for the local governments to under-take or foster scientific studies of the region to the end that, when the need does become pertinent, plans may be made and executed with full knowledge of the problems to be met.

Conditions in the Eastern Border Valleys in General

At present the belt of potentially colonizable country in the eastern border valleys of Colombia, Ecuador, Peru, and Bolivia, and the adjacent lowlands (Fig. 1) is probably less known than any other region in the world of comparable potentialities. Its climate has been sketched only in broad outlines except for a very few small sections. Its soils are known only from a few studies in widely scattered areas and from deductions made on the basis of vegetation, rainfall, slope of the land, etc. The greater part of it has never been mapped in anything like the detail required for the intelligent location of colonies or the planning of transportation routes. Little is known of the measures that must be taken to protect men and animals from local diseases. No reliable figures are available on its present population or its annual production of vegetable crops and livestock. Its inhabitants have in general been so long out of touch with the people of the plateau and coastal regions that there has not even grown up that body of information carried from

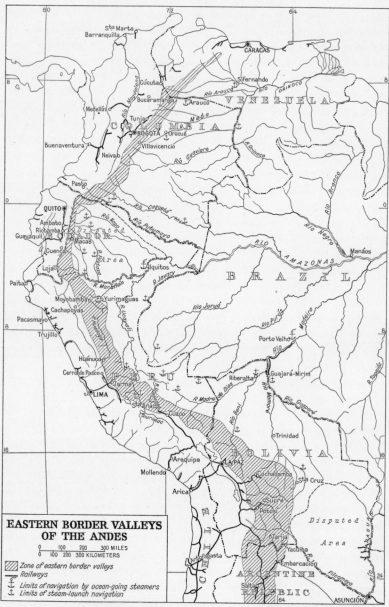

Fig. 1—General map of the belt of eastern border valleys of the Andes from Venezuela to northern Argentina.   Scale, 1 : 28,000,000.

mouth to mouth that played so important a part in the westward movement of farmers in the United States. Little is known of the distribution of land still in the public domain and, for that reason, presumably open to colonists free of charge or at low cost, of the extent of privately owned land, or of the possibilities of purchasing land from private owners.

Movement into the region began early in the seventeenth century. At a time when all transportation in the Andean region was by mule or on the backs of Indian bearers the steep descents from the plateau summit into the eastern valleys were only a part of the difficulties that movement and transportation everywhere encountered. As long as mules or Indian bearers were the only carriers throughout the west coast countries these eastern settlements could transport their products to the plateau markets with some hope of competing there with products from other sections; but with the construction of roads and railways elsewhere their markets were gradually lost in favor of sections to which these facilities brought cheaper transportation. Every new railway or road that has been built on the plateau or between the plateau and ocean ports has made the isolation of the majority of these eastern settlements all the greater, until in many sections their inhabitants have settled down to a self-contained existence without trade of any sort at all worthy of mention.

As a result, although many of the people of the region, perhaps the majority of them, live on farms or village plots that have been occupied by their families for generations and even centuries, yet they live today, as they have always lived, under essentially pioneer conditions. In places, as in the Urubamba and Chanchamayo valleys, they are pioneers in fact with a pioneer's ambitions and hopes; but for the most part they are pioneers in outward appearance only, long since settled into a state of apathetic contentment quite foreign to the true pioneer.

In each of the four republics whose territory extends into the region under discussion the problems involved in the agricultural development of the eastern border valleys of the Andes and the adjacent lowlands are to some extent problems peculiar to the country. The barrier offered to transportation and communication by the steep descents from the plateau to the eastern valleys is, however, common to all. There are few passes from the plateau that are feasible for railway and road construction if freights or tolls are to be sufficient to meet even maintenance and operation costs and still permit the farmer to realize a reasonable profit on the produce that he ships to the plateau. Perhaps the ultimate solution will be the construction of trunk lines over the few feasible passes and a feeder network made up of railways, roads, and navigable rivers. Steam-launch lines on the larger rivers have been suggested, with a network of connecting roads across the interstream areas and canoe connections with the sections that are remote from heads of steam navigation but still accessible to rivers navigable for canoes. But the question of where to get men capable of handling the large fleets of canoes that would be required is one that will arise at once in the mind of anyone who knows from experience how difficult it is even now to get good canoemen in the region.

Indeed, whatever direction suggestions for the improvement of opportunities for agricultural development in this eastern region may take, the problem of where to secure the additional labor that will be required is a serious one; not only the more or less specialized labor required for the operation of transportation systems, whatever the type that may be developed, but farm labor as well. The indigenous population is not large in most sections, and such as exists is little adapted to any but the most primitive sort of agriculture, while the transference into the lowlands of farm laborers from the highlands has never been a success.

COLOMBIA

THE CATTLE-RAISING LLANOS

Settlement in Colombia in the eastern border region (Fig. 2) has been chiefly confined to the llanos—the grass-covered plains drained by the Colombian tributaries of the Orinoco River—and the adjacent valleys of the Andes. Cattle raising was introduced into the llanos shortly after the Conquest and developed steadily up to the outbreak of the War of Independence (1810–1819). The chief cattle-growing section of the llanos now, as in colonial times, is the triangular area bounded by the Eastern Cordillera and the Arauca and Meta Rivers, known as the Casanare region. There are no official figures as to the number of cattle in the region, but what is considered to be a reliable estimate made in 1907[3] gave 150 ranches of various sizes with about 250,000 cattle and 50,000 horses in an area of about 15,000 square miles.

South of the Meta River cattle raising has never been extended

[3] P. J. Eder: Colombia, London, 1913, p. 230.

eastward beyond what are called the Llanos de San Martín and the Llanos de San Juan—relatively small areas along the mountain border. Villavicencio, the chief town of this section of the llanos, with an estimated population of 6000 to 8000, is the largest settlement in Colombia east of the towns of the Eastern Cordillera.

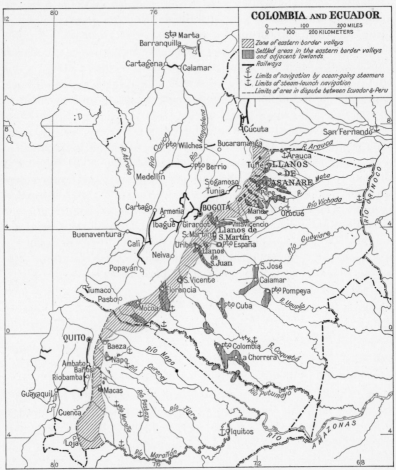

FIG. 2—The settled areas in the eastern border valleys of the Andes in Colombia and Ecuador. Scale, 1 : 16,000,000.

But its size is due to its nearness both to Orocué, the head of wet-season steam-launch navigation on the Meta, and to the best and shortest trail between Bogotá and the llanos, and not to the prosperity of the district of which it is the administrative capital.

The region between the San Martín and San Juan llanos and the upper Orinoco is much less known than the Casanare region, the cattle industry having never been introduced into it because of its distance from navigable tributaries of the Orinoco and from trails up to the Eastern Cordillera. It is described,[4] however, as much better suited to cattle raising than the Casanare region, with a generally cooler climate, more luxuriant grasses, and less protracted periods of drought.

This southern section of the llanos experienced its era of greatest prosperity during the period in which the collecting of quinine bark was at its height (1872 to 1887) and also during the rubber-collecting period (1887 to 1912), when ranches were established in the San Martín and San Juan llanos to raise cattle for food for the collectors and mules for transport.[5] Considerable areas in the adjacent valleys of the Cordillera were also planted to coffee and cacao at that time. With the failure of the rubber market in 1912 large numbers of the inhabitants left the region. Those remaining in the valleys have continued their cultivation of small patches of cacao and coffee, while those remaining in the llanos section still carry on a little cattle raising and the cultivation of a few crops for food. A few of the larger cattle ranches still ship a considerable number of hides to the plateau; but, for the smaller farmers, trade with the plateau returns so little profit because of the cost of transportation over exceptionally poor trails that most of them have settled down to the self-contained existence characteristic of the people of most of the settlements of the eastern mountain border region.

Decline of the Cattle Industry

The northern llanos still hold a place of considerable importance among the sections of the country where cattle are raised for hides, but the course of the industry there under the republic has been progressively down grade, and the herds today number but hundreds where there were thousands at the outbreak of the War of Independence. Many factors have contributed to this decline. The War of Independence made the first great inroads in the industry. Owners and herdsmen joined the revolutionary army, and such of the herds as were not slaughtered for food soon scattered

[4] F. O. Martin: Exploration in Colombia, *Geogr. Rev.*, Vol. 19, 1929, pp. 621–637; reference on pp. 623–626.

[5] *Ibid.*, pp. 630–631.

or completely disappeared for want of care. Civil wars (the last of which was finally put down only in 1904) further reduced the herds that were reassembled, although by no means on their former scale, after the establishment of the republic. During the periods when the collecting of quinine bark and rubber in the Amazonian forests of the southern part of the lowland region was at its height, many were called away from the ranches to what appeared, at least, to be more lucrative labor. But more important still was the development in other parts of the country of new export products—chiefly coffee—turning men away from the llanos to better opportunities. Moreover the Cauca valley, the high savanas of both the Eastern and Central Cordilleras of the Andes, and the Caribbean plain gradually assumed the place once held by the llanos as cattle-grazing lands, not only because of their easier accessibility to local markets and to river and ocean ports but also because of their more luxuriant grasses and their greater freedom from drought and from diseases and insect pests.

Lack of Transportation .

Lack of transportation has been, however, the most serious factor in the decline of the cattle industry in the llanos. It is a factor that must be removed by government action or by heavy investments by organizations prepared to wait for far-distant returns, before successful colonization can be expected. In the early days of the industry large numbers of cattle were driven up to the settlements of the Eastern Cordillera savanas, particularly to the Bogotá region, and sold for meat. But the trip over difficult trails frequently took weeks. Every drive left its toll of exhausted, starving cattle by the way, and those that completed the journey arrived at the market reduced to skin and bones. The result was that, as cattle raising was gradually developed in the Cordillera savanas themselves, fewer and fewer head were driven up from the llanos, and hides rather than cattle for food came to be the chief export. In the northern section of the llanos—that is the section accessible to transportation on the Arauca and Meta Rivers—a large proportion of the hides soon began to find its way to market by way of the Orinoco River, and today most of them are shipped that way. In the section south of the Meta, where grazing lands have never been occupied so far eastward as to be accessible to navigable rivers, the hides were, and still are, exported by way of the Villavicencio-Bogotá trail.

The construction of a rail route from the Eastern Cordillera to the northern llanos is so little feasible that, as far as can be discovered, no definite proposal for one has ever been made. This is significant in a country noted for the number and impracticability of railway plans officially or privately proposed. The only feasible route would be a line over the Paso de Las Cruces (6146 feet), about 100 miles south of Bogotá, to connect the southern section of the llanos with the Huila-Caquetá Railway now building southward by way of Neiva from a connecting point on the Bogotá-Girardot-Ibagué line; but a branch line of impracticable length would be necessary to connect this railway with the northern llanos. It would seem, therefore, that if the llanos are ever to be afforded effective transportation it must come through the improvement of the river routes to the Orinoco. At present the Arauca and Meta Rivers are called navigable for steam launches as far as the towns of Arauca and Orocué, respectively, and even beyond in seasons of particularly high water. The navigable season, however, is very short and comes at a time when much of the interstream areas is flooded and movement over them practically impossible. Navigability, as applied to these rivers, is, furthermore, a purely relative term. At best they are, when in flood, full of floating trees and shifting sand bars which, if not an actual menace to steam-launch navigation, suffice to make it slow and difficult.

In addition to the lack of transportation the Casanare section, at least, is by no means the cattle-raising country par excellence that enthusiastic prophets of the future of the llanos would have one believe. During the height of the wet season—and the wet season lasts for eight or nine months—the large rivers overflow their banks, flooding large sections of the interstream areas and even menacing the settlements. On the other hand, the drought at the height of the dry season is so severe that, except for a strip close to the mountain border and a few places along the river channels, the grasses are burned out, while water is to be had only in the larger streams.[6] It is possible that the larger rivers of the region could be leveed against floods and irrigation works provided to tide over the annual periods of drought, but the work would involve expenditures that could be undertaken only by a prosperous government and will be practicable only when and if the day comes that the relinquishing of the present grazing lands of the world to more intensive types of agriculture makes the development of the grazing potentialities of the llanos an imperative need.

[6] Eder, *op. cit.*, pp. 231–233.

COFFEE AND CACAO OF THE BORDER VALLEYS

In the border valleys of the Andes adjacent to the llanos the cultivation of coffee and cacao was introduced by the Spaniards at an early date. Neither has, however, ever attained to any real importance among the exports from the region; not because of lack of suitable soil and growing conditions but because they have never been able to pay transportation costs and compete with the products of areas more easily accessible to domestic markets and to river and ocean ports. Along the border of the Cordillera, as at Arauquita on the upper Arauca River, whose shipments of cacao by the Orinoco route are of some importance, there are areas still largely undeveloped where good soils and freedom from drought favor the growing of a variety of crops—rice, cacao, sugar, and maize.

FOOTHILLS AT HEAD OF CAQUETÁ AND PUTUMAYO RIVERS

Another section of the eastern region of Colombia that has had considerable agricultural development, particularly during the rubber-collecting period, is the foothills of the Eastern Cordillera at the headwaters of the Caquetá and Putumayo tributaries of the Amazon. Diversified farming with some cattle raising, undertaken originally to provide food for the rubber gatherers, is still carried on there, and the region is reported as being highly favorable to white settlement.[7] In fact this is the only section of the eastern region in whose colonization possibilities the Colombian government has at all interested itself in recent years. Access to the Pasto region, where there is a large and industrious white and Indian population, is relatively easy, and the government has done considerable work in opening trails to the Caquetá-Putumayo region from across the Eastern Cordillera. If the Huila-Caquetá Railway is ever completed, it is probable that this Caquetá-Putumayo region will come to be one of the important agricultural districts of the country.

ECUADOR

Of all the countries under discussion Ecuador (Fig. 2) offers certainly the least opportunities for successful colonization east of the Andes. The descent from the plateau to the lowlands is

[7] Demetrio Salamanca T.: La Amazonia Colombiana: Estudio geográfico, histórico y jurídico en defensa del derecho territorial de Colombia, Bogotá, 1916, pp. 90–125.

See also "República de Colombia, Memorias del Ministro de Gobierno al Congreso en sus sesiones ordinarios de 1925," Bogotá, 1925, pp. 113–133.

exceedingly abrupt. The streams that flow eastward descend to the lowlands more precipitously than anywhere else along the eastern front of the Andes. The few trails, following these streams as the only possible way of making the descent, are, once they have left the plateau, at all seasons of the year mere mud wallows passable only on foot.

EARLY GOLD MINING DISTRICT ON THE UPPER PASTAZA

Because of the abrupt descent of the eastern border of the Andes and its lack of cultivable valleys near the populous districts of the plateau summit, there has been no opportunity for the gradual filtering of plateau dwellers down toward the lowlands. Gold, washed from the river sands, did attract considerable numbers of white men to the region at an early date; and, during the 1550's and 1560's a number of fairly large settlements, chief among them the famous and now somewhat mythical Sevilla de Oro, were established in the most important gold-bearing region on the upper Pastaza and Upano Rivers (the latter a headwater tributary of the Moroña), as well as several smaller settlements farther north along the upper Napo and its upper tributary, the Quijos. In 1599 a revolt of the lowland savages practically wiped out the settlements of the Pastaza-Upano region. Those of the settlers who remained in the region after the massacre ultimately built the village of Macas near the old site of Sevilla de Oro.[8] This village is now the only settlement of any size in the whole of the Oriente region, as it is locally called.

ISOLATION OF ITS MODERN SUCCESSOR, THE MACAS-NAPO REGION

Macas stands in the midst of a highly fertile district and is really a group of small farms supporting about five hundred people.[9] Its fine cattle are known, by hearsay at least, throughout Ecuador, but it is rarely that any are driven up to the markets of the plateau. The long trail to Riobamba, the only route from the village to the plateau, is at all seasons of the year so deep in mud that cattle cannot stand the journey over it. One wonders, indeed, how and why such a settlement as Macas exists. But it must be borne

[8] Alfred Simson: Travels in the Wilds of Ecuador and the Exploration of the Putumayo River, London, 1886, pp. 49–60.

[9] J. H. Sinclair and Theron Wasson: Explorations in Eastern Ecuador, *Geogr. Rev.*, Vol. 13, 1923, pp. 190–210.

in mind that the inhabitants, as in certain sections of eastern
Bolivia, Colombia, and Peru as well, are of a type of which white
men elsewhere can scarcely conceive. They are with few exceptions
a people long since reduced, because of their inability to engage in
trade of any importance, to a state in which they have no desires
that cannot be satisfied by the land on which they live. Shelter
and food are their chief wants. The few articles of their monotonous
diet are easily grown. Their huts of bamboo slats and mud plaster
are easily constructed from material immediately at hand. On their
infrequent trips to the plateau they may carry with them a bit of
gold washed from a near-by stream, a little crude alcohol distilled
from cane grown on a river playa, a few home-made cigars, a little
coffee or cacao, wherewith to purchase the few yards of cheap cloth
needed for clothing. Their life is easy, tranquil, and even plentiful
within their conception of plenty. The region could undoubtedly
support many more people in such a state of plenty and tranquillity,
but such a life could scarcely satisfy the desirable type of colonist,
either local or foreign, who breaks old ties and traditions to set
out to find a better life in new lands.

The five hundred people at Macas and perhaps a hundred more,
scattered—a few families in a place—at such points as Archidona,
Napo, Mera, and Baeza, make up the whole of the so-called white
population of the region. There are no continuous grassy plains
in the Ecuadorean Oriente comparable to the llanos of Colombia,
but in the Napo region are tracts of grassland of considerable
extent where several fairly large cattle ranches have been established. There is, however, no possibility of driving cattle to the
plateau, and the shipping even of hides is not feasible because all
transportation out of the region is by Indian bearers except for
small amounts that are reported as occasionally shipped by canoe
down the Napo River to Iquitos. Some coffee, of fair quality, is
grown in the Napo district, but little of it ever reaches the markets
of the plateau. Sinclair, who made important explorations in the
region in 1921 and in 1927, reports that the few exports from the
Napo region that reach the plateau are carried on the backs of
Indians over the Papallacta trail to Quito—a journey of ten days
at the least and an utterly impossible journey when the rivers
are in flood. If the so-called Curaray Railway, a 180-mile line
proposed from Ambato to the Curaray River, first surveyed in
1905 and now in operation for about 16 miles from Ambato to
Pelileo, is ever completed, or the work now under way by an Ameri-

can petroleum company on a road from Baños to Mera over the same route as that proposed for the Curaray Railway, as part of its concession agreement, is carried out, the Napo district should come into considerable prosperity; but even with the transportation problem satisfactorily solved there will remain the problem of securing sufficient labor for more extensive agricultural operations. The Indian population on which the present white settlers depend for labor is not large, and such as is available is already attached to the various settlers under a patron system that is little better than slavery.

No Immediate Prospect for the Development of the Ecuadorean Oriente

Even the most patriotic of Ecuadoreans have little hope of agricultural colonization on any large scale in the Oriente. As far as the Ecuadoreans themselves are concerned there will be no actual need of colonization there for many years to come. The regions of the country that are, at least by comparison with the Oriente, easy of access to roads and railroads and to river and ocean ports are greatly underpopulated. The need of more farmers and farm laborers is generally recognized in Ecuador, but it is for the development of land on the plateau and on the broad Pacific plain, already occupied but sparsely peopled and inefficiently worked, that they are needed.

PERU

Early settlement in the eastward-facing valleys of the Peruvian Andes took place in four separate sections—in what may be called the Moyobamba section, the Huánuco-Cerro de Pasco section, the Tarma-Chanchamayo section, and the Urubamba valley (Fig. 3). These remain today the only sections of the region at all important from the standpoint of population or the exportation of agricultural products. In the Huánuco-Cerro de Pasco, Chanchamayo, and Urubamba sections there has been a slow but fairly steady increase in utilization of the land and the production of export crops. The Moyobamba section, once considered the most promising of them all and still second only to the Huánuco-Cerro de Pasco region from the standpoint of population, has been reduced by various vicissitudes to a point where it has no trade of any importance.

The Moyobamba Region: Its Early Prosperity and Subsequent Decline

Existing settlements in the Moyobamba region date for the most part from early colonial times. The movement of settlers into the region was purely a natural movement of men looking for land

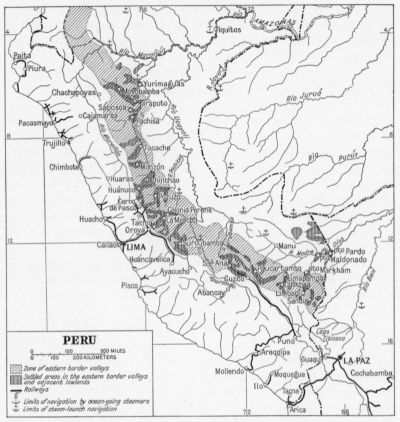

Fig. 3—The settled areas in the eastern border valleys of the Andes in Peru. Scale, 1 : 16,000,000.

into an area of good soils and favorable climate with no added incentive of supplying provisions to near-by mining centers such as has been the case with other important settlements in the eastern valleys of Peru.

Not only in early colonial times before the Spaniards had begun the restoration of the irrigation systems of the coastal valleys which had been largely abandoned by them in their first feverish efforts at exploiting the mineral resources of the Andes, but even well up toward the end of the nineteenth century there was, however, a sufficient demand for the diversified products of the Moyobamba region in the mining centers of the plateau and in the coastal towns to make it profitable to export them in spite of the long distances that they had to be transported on mule back. Because of the altitudinal climatic zones which within short distances extend from tropical valley bottoms to temperate valley heads, a great variety of crops thrive in the region—wheat and corn at the valley heads and on those upper slopes that are sufficiently level to be worked; cacao, coffee, and tobacco in the moist, warm, middle valleys; rice and sugar in the valley bottoms.

The region prospered for generations. In the 1850's and 1860's the weaving of Panama hats came to be its most important industry, although coffee, cacao, tobacco, and sugar were still exported in considerable quantities.[10] But the beginning of the rubber boom in 1887 called the men away by hundreds to what they believed to be the speedy amassing of fortunes in rubber collecting. Many of them never returned, and the atmosphere of gloom and sadness that settled upon the villages of the region came to be proverbial.

With the end of the rubber boom in 1912 some of the rubber collectors found their way back. But the days of prosperity in the Moyobamba region were over. In addition to lack of sufficient labor to work the land during the rubber boom, the coffee market had failed because of the establishment of plantations elsewhere in sections more accessible to markets, and, whereas the region had for many years had what amounted to a monopoly of the hat-weaving industry, other sections of the country now took it up. The result was that those among the rubber gatherers who returned came back to a district practically without trade of any sort. That the majority of them remained in the region was due to the ease with which a plentiful living could be had from the soil provided that only shelter and food were demanded. It is reported that during the rubber boom the town of Moyobamba alone fell in a short time from 12,000 to 5000 inhabitants and that today at least 40 per cent of its houses are deserted.[11]

[10] Hildebrando Fuertes: Loreto: Apuntes geográficos, históricos, estadísticos, políticos y sociales, 2 vols., Lima, 1908; reference in Vol. 1, pp. 59–82.

[11] G. M. Dyott: Silent Highways of the Jungle, New York, 1922, p. 74.

Present Conditions and Transportation Outlook

The region now produces little more than enough to feed its own people, and Panama hats are the only product that it sends to the plateau or the coastal region. A few products are brought down by trail on the backs of Indian bearers to the Huallaga River for shipment to Iquitos by steam launch—a little tobacco, coffee, cacao, and alcohol. From plantations near the river a few bales of poor, ungraded cotton are shipped. Whatever the grower receives after the transportation charges have been paid he rates as profit; but it is a profit only because it is realized on surplus products that would otherwise be left on the ground and not by any means a profit based on land values and labor costs. No value can be placed on either land or labor in the region, for there is no market for either.

Lack of transportation is the chief drawback to the development of the region. A railway has long been proposed through it from the Pacific port of Pacasmayo or from a new port to be established near Pacasmayo to the port of Yurimaguas on the Huallaga River and during the past few years has frequently appeared to be at the point of construction. If it is built it will provide an opportunity for colonization not to be had anywhere else in Peru. A recent concessionaire for the construction of this railway included in his plans the establishment of a large European colony beyond the mountain border on lands close to Yurimaguas on the left bank of the Huallaga. His plans for the colony included a careful study of soils and climatic conditions, sanitation and control of disease, and an experimental farm and school for training the colonists in the selection of crops and methods of cultivation—all necessary to the success of such a colony. It must be borne in mind, however, that, no matter how successful the sanitation methods adopted may be in keeping such a colony in good health, it will still be a colony in tropical country to which desirable European colonists must adjust themselves by a process long and painful if successful at all. Its products, moreover, will be tropical products for which there is little demand in the country itself and will, therefore, have to make the long and expensive trip by rail to the Pacific coast or down the Amazon to the Atlantic and still compete in a market already oversupplied from more conveniently located areas. It would seem that efforts at colonization in the more temperate mountain valleys of the region, where crops demanded by the local markets could be raised, and for which the haul to markets could be shorter and cheaper, would be more certain of success than any scheme for the colonization of areas in the tropical lowlands.

The Prosperous Huánuco-Cerro de Pasco Region

The Huánuco-Cerro de Pasco region—that is the district centering in these two towns—is the largest settled area in the eastern border valleys of the Peruvian Andes. It has prospered chiefly because of its neighborhood to the markets furnished by the mines at Cerro de Pasco and to the Central Railway of Peru, which by connecting with a good motor road between Cerro de Pasco and Huánuco brings the latter town within less than twenty hours of Lima. There is, however, little room for colonization within the sections nearest the good transportation routes. The deep valleys such as those of the Yanahuanca and upper Huallaga Rivers are intensively cultivated and well populated.[12] In the section immediately north of Huánuco and west of the northward-flowing section of the Huallaga River there are coca and coffee plantations that market their products by way of Huánuco. No information is available as to the amount of land open for settlement in this section, but it is evidently underdeveloped, since its exports by way of Huánuco are relatively small. It suggests itself, therefore, as worthy of study as a possible field for colonization.

Bordering on the Huallaga River on the east and extending northward well toward the lower river are what are called the Pampas de Sacramento. Very little is known of them, but they have been described by the few explorers who have crossed them as luxuriant grasslands broken only by thin stands of timber and have been pictured as the great future grazing lands of the country. They, too, need exploration and study before any suggestions can be made as to their suitability for colonization.

The Backward Pozuzo Colony in That Region and Other Colonies Along the Pachitea River

In the foothills of the Andes, which in the latitude of the big bend of the Huallaga River below Huánuco extend eastward well over toward the Pichis River, is the Pozuzo colony,[13] the only settlement of colonists direct from Europe that has endured in all the region under discussion. It was founded with high hopes by some

[12] O. M. Miller: The 1927–1928 Peruvian Expedition of the American Geographical Society, *Geogr. Rev.*, Vol. 19, 1929, pp. 1–37; reference on pp. 21–25.
[13] *Ibid.*, pp. 25–29.

hundred and fifty families that migrated there from Bavaria in the 1860's. At the present time it has about 600 inhabitants not concentrated in villages but scattered on separate farms among the hills.

The Pozuzo colony cannot be in any sense described as a success. At first sight the neat appearance of its houses and its well-cultivated fields suggest prosperity of a high order. It is, however, in fact, not unlike the settlements of the Moyobamba region, with this difference that, in addition to growing food in plenty for their own use, the people of the community exercise considerable energy in keeping their houses in repair, constructing furniture, and the like. The colony lacks only transportation to make it truly prosperous, but under present conditions its products have to be shipped by the long steam-launch route to Iquitos or transported over bad trails to Huánuco or Cerro de Pasco and there compete with products grown close at hand. The colonists might in part combat the heavy cost of transportation by using cheap Indian labor for the cultivation of their crops, but they have failed to do this either because they do not care to mix with the Indians or because they have not learned how to handle them. At any rate the colony's exports are small, and it cannot be said that it is doing better than merely holding its own.

The Peruvian government has long been concerned with the establishment of colonies along the Pachitea River north of the Pozuzo colony, but its efforts there have all failed. Several years ago a colony from California, said to have numbered about one hundred families, was established on the river at a point a short distance above the head of steam-launch navigation at Puerto Victoria, but the project was abandoned in a few months. Now a new port some distance farther downstream—Puerto Leguia—has been established on the river, and considerable work has been done on the constructing of a trail to it from Huánuco, but it is difficult to see how any colony in the region can ship products by trail, however good, and compete in the Cerro de Pasco and Huánuco markets with products grown close at hand. As to the futility of expecting successful colonization based on transportation over the thousand-mile river route to Iquitos under present market conditions, the stagnation of the many settlements long ago located under similar physical and climatic conditions along the Ucayali River is sufficient evidence.

The Tarma and Chanchamayo Valleys

In the establishing of their early settlements in the Tarma and Chanchamayo valleys (actually two sections of a more or less continuous valley, the former with its center at Tarma and the latter at La Merced) the Spanish were following the example of their Inca predecessors, the remains of whose stone-walled terraces for the cultivation of coca are still to be seen in many places throughout the region. The early plantations, with coffee on the warm moist valley slopes, cotton on the valley floors, and sugar on the river playas, prospered until 1742, when they were almost completely wiped out by a revolt of the lowland savages. For more than a century thereafter, until in 1847 a garrison was established at San Ramón, settlers slowly returning to the valley were constantly menaced.

Even then the reëstablishment of the plantations of the valley proceeded slowly because of the difficulty of transporting products up to the plateau; but the completion of the Central Railway from Lima to Oroya and the improvement of the trail into the valley as a part of the overland route from Lima to Iquitos gave the valley a transportation system that permitted it once more to realize a profit on its products in the plateau and coastal markets. The recent construction of a motor road from Oroya down into the valley as far as La Merced has given it transportation facilities not possessed by any other section of the eastern border of the Andes. At that, the cultivated areas are still widely scattered and limited as yet to the most easily worked land—coffee plantations here and there on flat-topped spurs, plantations of sugar cane, tropical fruits, and some cotton and rice on valley flats. Coffee, of which practically the entire supply for central Peru now comes from the Chanchamayo valley, and alcohol are the chief exports because even with the improved means of transportation shipping costs are still high.

The Perené Colony in That Region

A few hours by trail eastward from La Merced is the famous Perené colony of the Peruvian Corporation where an experimental settlement established in 1890 has made noteworthy progress in the growing of coffee, cotton, rice, and tropical fruits and now has a total of about 4000 hectares under cultivation in a concession of 50,000 hectares. The colony is greatly in need of a motor-road connection with La Merced, but its success in growing a large variety of tropical products is evidence of the future in store for great sections of the eastern border valleys of the Peruvian Andes when the demands of the market force the construction of transportation routes.

The Urubamba Valley

The Urubamba valley is, as the result of Bowman's studies in 1911,[14] the best known of all the eastern valleys of Peru from the standpoint of scientific examination of its potentialities and its needs. Physically as well as in its economic organization the valley is typical of many of the eastern valleys of Peru. In the upper valley in the vicinity of the village of Urubamba a combination of winter rains and light frosts produces conditions favorable to the growing of good wheat, and wheat and bread are exported in considerable quantities; but the demand is far greater than the supply, and Cuzco, only a few hours away by rail, must still import flour from abroad. The lower valley begins at 8000 feet and extends down to 1000 feet at the Pongo de Mainique in the Urubamba River. The two sections of the valley, separated by the Torontoy Canyon, are only about twenty miles apart, but their difference in altitude is 3000 feet. As a result there are frosts at Torontoy, at the lower end of the upper valley, and none at Huadquiña, at the head of the lower valley. Torontoy produces corn, and Huadquiña cane. In the lower valley irrigation is required during part of the year. Little or none is required from December to March, inclusive; but from June to September frequent irrigation is necessary.

Handicap of Insufficient Labor and Inadequate Transportation

In the Urubamba valley, as elsewhere in the eastern border valleys, poor and inadequate transportation facilities are the chief obstacle to progress. Labor, too, is scarce and inefficient. It is the chief problem of the planter to adapt his crops so as to get the best possible results from both. About 50 miles of the 112-mile railway from Cuzco to Santa Ana in the lower Urubamba valley— long awaited as the salvation of the region—are now in operation. Although the railway has not yet reached the lower valley, its

[14] Isaiah Bowman: The Andes of Southern Peru, [Amer. Geogr. Soc. Special Publ. No. 2], New York, 1916, Chapters 2 and 6.

ultimate effect may be judged from the fact that in 1924 the 48 miles completed in 1923 carried 34,568 tons of freight and 36,385 passengers.[15] Yet even before the road was built thus far the valley was famous for its prosperity. So greatly needed were its products that those of high value in relation to their bulk and weight such as coca, cacao, and alcohol could stand the heavy transportation costs and still return some profit. The combined freight charges and taxes, however, took a large part of the returns on the crop. How much the construction of the railway into the upper valley has reduced the cost of transportation is not known; but in 1911, when the price of coca paid the producer was 20 cents per pound the average return per acre after labor and transportation costs were paid was estimated at $140, from which must be deducted the value of the planter's time, interest on his investment, etc.

TROPICAL PRODUCTION IN LOWER URUBAMBA VALLEY

In spite of the cost of transportation, if labor were plentiful and cheap, this and other eastern valleys could still find considerable prosperity in the intensive cultivation of products such as coca, cacao, and coffee. But labor is scarce, and planters must use it to the best possible advantage. The solution in the lower Urubamba valley has been the production of alcohol from sugar cane. Not only does the whole process from the cultivation of the cane to the distilling of the alcohol require less work than coca or cacao, but it can be so handled as to provide employment for the available labor throughout a great part of the year. Unfortunately the planter, because of high production costs, feels that he must sell his alcohol where he can, with the result that large quantities are consumed by his laborers and their efficiency greatly reduced thereby. The vicious circle thus created can be broken only by cheaper transportation rates to the plateau and by the laying of such taxes on alcohol as to make it less profitable than sugar.

Since so little information is to be had on the availability of land for colonization throughout the belt of eastern border valleys and lowlands it is worth while to cite some details from Bowman's report[16] on the Hacienda Sahuayaco in the lower Urubamba valley. The property—an estate of 400 square miles, yet rated as one of the smaller estates of the valley—was purchased a few years pre-

[15] W. Rodney Long: Railways of South America, Part II, *Bur. of Foreign and Domestic Commerce, Trade Promotion Ser. No. 39*, Washington, 1927, p. 248.

[16] Bowman, *op. cit.*, pp. 78 and 83.

vious to Bowman's visit there in 1911 for $6000. The estate is ten miles wide and extends across the valley from side to side for a total distance of 40 miles. About ten square miles are on the valley floor where coca, cacao, cane, coffee, rice, pepper, and cotton are

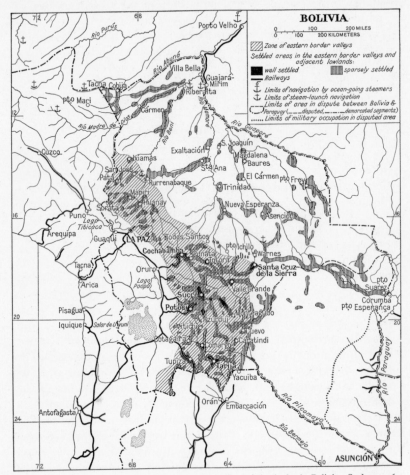

FIG. 4—The settled areas in the eastern border valleys of the Andes in Bolivia. Scale, 1 : 16,-000,000.

grown. The remaining 390 square miles include some mountain country with possible minerals and a great deal of fells country suitable for pasture and containing here and there patches of arable land. But it is hill country suitable only for the small farmer who supplements his vegetable food supply by keeping cattle, mules, pigs, and poultry and raising coca and fruit. On all of the estates of the valley there is, of course, much arable land that is still uncultivated. There is no information available, however, as to whether there is still public land open for colonization or as to the possibility of purchasing or leasing land from the present owners.

BOLIVIA

Of the whole belt of country under discussion no section would seem destined to a brighter future than the Bolivian section (Fig. 4). All things considered—possibilities for transportation development, relative size and distribution of areas requiring a minimum of clearing and other reclamation work, climatic conditions attractive to a great variety of tastes and suitable for a great variety of crops, water power potentialities, timber resources, grazing lands—it would seem reasonable to place Bolivia first among the countries offering opportunities for colonization in the eastern border valleys of the Andes and the adjacent lowlands. Its zone of border valleys is broader than that of any of the other Andean countries; its plains tracts suitable for grazing lands are larger than the llanos of Colombia even though the section of the Chaco region disputed with Paraguay be excluded.

Railroads under Construction or Projected: Down Into the Eastern Valleys

Here, as elsewhere in the eastern border region, lack of transportation is the chief obstacle to successful colonization. The problem of constructing a system of transportation lines is, however, by no means as difficult of solution as in most sections of the eastern regions of Colombia, Ecuador, and Peru. Two railways have already penetrated for short distances down into the eastern valleys from the altiplano—the Oruro-Cochabamba railway and the railway now in process of extension from Potosí to Sucre. The fact that these lines, short though they are, traverse country as difficult as any that may be encountered in railway construction anywhere in the eastern valley region has been generally accepted as proof of the feasibility of ultimately extending them eastward to the border of the Cordillera. But it seems evident that the way out for the products of the greater part of the eastern region will not be by means of trunk and feeder systems built to connect with these lines. The cost of constructing them has been enormous, and the Oruro-Cochabamba line is obliged to charge such exorbitant shipping rates that it has actually contributed very little to the agricultural prosperity of the Cochabamba region.[17]

FROM SANTA CRUZ ALONG THE ANDEAN FRONT AND ACROSS THE CHACO

When railways are built to serve the eastern region (unless the Bolivian government for strategic reasons decides that the outlet for the region must be by way of the altiplano and undertakes to construct, and perhaps in large part to maintain, extensions to the Potosí and Cochabamba lines) they will be the long-hoped-for 400-mile line across the northern Chaco from Santa Cruz de la Sierra to a port on the upper Paraguay River and the extension north to Santa Cruz along the western margin of the Chaco of the railway now building northward from Embarcación toward the Argentine-Bolivian border. Easily constructed roads and branch railways connecting with these two trunk lines would afford an outlet for all the best grazing and farm lands of the northern and western Chaco region and foothill valleys of the Cordillera. For the great lowland section of northeastern Bolivia the natural outlet would seem to be by way of roads and canoe routes connecting with the heads of steam-launch navigation on the Madre de Dios, Beni, Mamoré, and Guaporé Rivers. The Madeira-Mamoré Railway built by the Brazilian government in accordance with the terms of the boundary settlement of 1904 provides a portage around the worst of the rapids that obstruct the navigation at the mouth of these rivers, and only short extensions of the line are needed to carry it above the rest.[18]

The construction of the railway from Santa Cruz to the Paraguay and the extension northward of the line from Embarcación are both projects within the scope of private capital, and there are reasonably good prospects that one or both of them may be undertaken at an early date. The development of a transportation system of roads and navigable rivers on the now little-inhabited northeastern lowlands must in all probability await the day when large land companies heavily capitalized may undertake the development of the grazing possibilities of the region.

Prospects are that the section of eastern Bolivia that will be first opened to successful colonization is the foothill region between

[17] Romecin, *op. cit.*, pp. 250–251.

[18] See Isaiah Bowman: Trade Routes in the Economic Geography of Bolivia, *Bull. Amer. Geogr. Soc.*, Vol. 42, 1910, pp. 180–192.

Santa Cruz and the Bolivia-Argentine boundary. This is the only section that has any prospects of railway penetration in the near future. The region in part falls within the areas reserved by decree of the federal government in 1905[19] for colonization, and although no information is available on the areas there now privately owned, there is presumably still much land in the public domain. Mather[20] describes this foothill section as "preëminently a cattle country," but he also describes the streams of the section for irrigation purposes and mentions the excellence of the kitchen gardens and vineyards cultivated at the Franciscan missions as indicative of the adaptability of the region to diversified farming.

CONCLUSION

It seems evident that we have in this zone of eastern border valleys and adjacent lowlands the curious anomaly of a tremendous total acreage of land climatically suitable for white colonization and capable of producing a wide range of temperate and subtropical crops and livestock for human consumption yet so shut off from the rest of the world by mountain barriers on the one side and by distance from ocean ports on the other that, for the most part, it scarcely merits classification with the pioneer lands of the earth at all. Every step that is taken to increase the productivity of lands already under cultivation and to shorten the time and cheapen the cost of transporting their products to the consumer further postpones the far distant day, now difficult to visualize, when the demand for its land and its potential products is such that governments will be forced to establish the needed transportation routes or private capital find it profitable to do so.

[19] Paul Walle: Bolivia, Its People and Its Resources, Its Railways, Mines, and Rubber-Forests, London, 1914, pp. 388–389.
[20] K. F. Mather: Along the Andean Front in Southeastern Bolivia, *Geogr. Rev.*, Vol. 12, 1922, pp. 358–374.

CONDITIONS AFFECTING SETTLEMENT ON THE MATTO GROSSO HIGHLAND AND IN THE GRAN CHACO

W. L. SCHURZ

NATURAL CONDITIONS

THE area under consideration in this study as a possible reserve of lands for future settlement lies in the heart of South America. It extends in the form of an inverted U from the upper Paraná and its head, the Paranahyba, on the southeast, first as the Matto Grosso Highland, then as a region of intermediate elevation opposite the great salient of the Andes at Santa Cruz de la Sierra, and last as the Gran Chaco lowland, to its southwestern termination in the Pilcomayo River (Fig. 1). Although physically the three regions merge into each other, politically they belong to three different nations, Brazil, Bolivia, and Paraguay. (The Argentine portion of the Gran Chaco, between the Pilcomayo and the Salado, is not considered in the present article.) Physically the three regions have in common that they are all more or less open grassland, the conditioning factors being similar, as, among others, latitudinal position and elevation compensate each other. Most important of the three regions and most promising as a field for human settlement is the Matto Grosso Highland (with an area of more than 300,000 square miles and a population of 600,000) which is comprised by the southern part of the Brazilian states of Matto Grosso and Goyaz. The intermediate region lies in the Bolivian department of Santa Cruz, and that portion of the Gran Chaco here considered is situated in Bolivia and Paraguay.

THE MATTO GROSSO HIGHLAND

The Matto Grosso Highland, except where it is drained by the headwaters of the north-flowing Araguaya, which forms the boundary between Matto Grosso and Goyaz, lies almost entirely within the basin of the Paraguay River and so to the south of the Amazon jungle. The Amazon-Paraguay divide therefore lies close to the northern edge of the highland and, although not constituting a hard-and-fast line of demarcation between two regions respectively suitable and unsuitable for colonization, may be accepted as roughly the northern limit of the area practicable for human settlement under the material conditions demanded today by settlers of the white race. Though climatic conditions in the forested plateau country about the headwaters of the Amazon tributaries from the Madeira east to the Tocantins do not constitute an

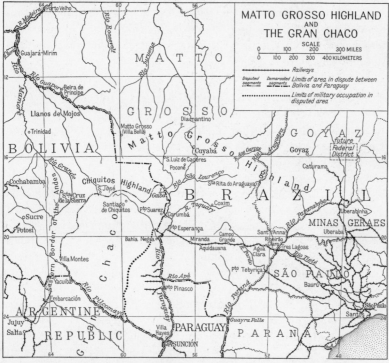

FIG. 1—Map of the Matto Grosso Highland in Brazil and the Gran Chaco in Bolivia and Paraguay showing the features mentioned in the text. Scale, 1 : 21,000,000.

insuperable obstacle to settlement, difficulties incident to the exploitation of jungle lands for agricultural purposes exclude these regions from consideration, except for their possible occupation by immigrants of inferior cultural levels, to whom the heavy physical effort required in clearing the land is easily compensated by whatever promise of subsistence is offered.

The name Matto Grosso, or "great forest," is a misnomer as applied to this region. Natural conditions over much of the plateau are unsuited to the development of a true forest growth, and most of the tableland, known as *chapada* or *chapadão*, is covered only with herbaceous plants, scattered bushes, sparse grass, and clumps of palms.

The rainfall within this area is markedly seasonal, the bulk of the precipitation occurring between October and April. At Cuyabá there is very little rain during the three months of June, July, and August. Rainfall in the Cuyabá-Corumbá belt varies from 39 to 59 inches a year and, for the rest of the area under consideration, between 59 and 79 inches. Records of rainfall and temperature taken at five representative points over a number of years give the following data:

TABLE I—TEMPERATURE AND RAINFALL IN THE MATTO GROSSO HIGHLAND

PLACE	ANNUAL RAINFALL (mm.)	NUMBER OF RAINY DAYS	MONTHS OF GREATEST AND LEAST RAINFALL (mm.)	AVERAGE ANNUAL TEMPERATURE (C.)	EXTREMES OF TEMPERATURE (C.)
Cuyabá . .	1,460	130	241 (Jan.) 3 (June)	26.5°	37.2° (Sept.) 9.9° (July)
São Luiz de Caceres .	1,289	120	20 (Feb.) 6 (July)	25.6°	40.6° (Nov.) 3.8° (May)
Corumbá .	1,258	80	208 (Dec.) 6 (July)	26.7°	40.6° (Oct.) 0.8° (May)
Tres Lagoas	1,141	76	141 (Jan.) 26 (July)	24.4°	41.0° (Sept.) 1.5° (July)
Goyaz . .	1,689	89	308 (Jan.) 0.2 (July)	24.4°	40.0° (Sept.) 5.0° (July)

The Matto Grosso Highland is bounded on the west and south by well-defined lines of escarpments, below which lies a secondary zone known as the *pé da serra*, or piedmont belt. The valleys of the rivers incised in the plateau contain belts of true forest, which give way to lines of *burity* palms in their upper reaches. The *chapada* or *chapadão* is largely covered with a sparse scrub vegetation that gives evidence of the poor quality of the soil. These steppe lands are known locally as *campo cerrado*, or "closed country," to distinguish them from the *campo limpo*, or "clean country," i.e. treeless lands, which lie to the south of the plateau or cover the slopes of the valleys of the west-flowing tributaries of the

Paraguay. The wide expanse of the *campos de vaccaria*, or cattle country, lying largely to the south of the Northwestern Railway between the Paraná and the Paraguay (roughly along the 20th parallel), forms the largest single area of this open prairie country. As its local name signifies, it is well suited to the raising of cattle. The piedmont zone of the west-facing edge of the plateau has likewise long been the center of an important cattle industry. Thus a series of famous old *fazendas*, or ranches, follows the line of this intermediate zone from São Luiz de Caceres in the north (lat. 16° S.) around by Poconé, Coxim, Aquidauana, and Miranda in the south (lat. 20° S.). Between this westward-sloping piedmont and the Paraguay River lies the vast low region of the *pantanal*. Though furnishing excellent pasturage during much of the year, this zone is subject to inundations that cover most of its extent with a shallow layer of water, forcing herds to be driven to higher ground until the flood has receded. On the right, or Bolivian, side of the main river there are a number of so-called *lagunas* (*lagoas* in Portuguese) which serve as vast storage reservoirs for the flood waters of the Paraguay and so retard somewhat the fall of the river after the annual rise.

THE INTERMEDIATE REGION

In the intermediate region between the Matto Grosso Highland and the Gran Chaco the open plains about the city of Santa Cruz de la Sierra, in spite of occasional excessively prolonged periods without rain, possess most of the natural conditions required for successful agriculture and stock raising. Summer temperatures are generally high, but in the winter the winds blowing from the south give them a bracing climate.

The western limits of these plains are marked by the eastern foothills of the Andes. To the north lies a belt of low jungle country that separates the prairies of Santa Cruz from the vast open *llanuras*, or plains, of Mojos in the Bolivian department of El Beni. Though this district between the Beni and the Mamoré has long been the seat of a primitive cattle industry, its almost level surface makes it liable to widespread annual inundations that would render any general settlement of this area impracticable.

To the south and southeast of Santa Cruz and beyond the great bend of the Rio Grande, as the uppermost course of the Mamoré is called, lies a large region whose scanty rainfall and lack of surface

water make it an unfavorable field for settlement. On the southeast
this region merges into the general area of the Gran Chaco, but on
the south it meets a belt along the upper Pilcomayo where cattle
raising is practicable.

To the east of Santa Cruz and beyond the Rio Grande a belt
of wilderness known as the Monte Grande separates the plains
from the higher land of the Chiquitos area. This latter is a region
of low ranges, among which lie considerable tracts of land suitable
for agriculture or raising of cattle. Though much of these lands is
wooded, the problem of clearing it is much less serious than in the
heavier tropical jungle to the north. The southern limit of this
region is roughly the line of the old trail between Santa Cruz and
Puerto Suarez on the Paraguay, which passes through the upland
villages of San José and Santiago de Chiquitos. Beyond the eastern
limits of the Chiquitos hill country there is a low belt of sandy
lands reaching to the Paraguay. This zone is covered with a scrub
forest growth in which palms are prominent. During the dry
season it is waterless and during the rainy season inundated. These
lands are unfit for any kind of development.

THE GRAN CHACO

The portion of the Gran Chaco here considered comprises the
territory lying between the Paraguay and the Pilcomayo. The
long north-and-south trail between Santa Cruz and Yacuiba in
Argentina, which crosses the Pilcomayo at Villa Montes, may be
roughly taken as the western limit of the Chaco. The Santa Cruz-
Puerto Suarez trail may be accepted as its northern boundary. The
Gran Chaco was long shrouded in mystery, and much of it is still
unexplored. The disputed boundary between Bolivia and Paraguay
runs across it.

The Gran Chaco consists of a low plain that falls gently and
almost imperceptibly towards the east and southeast. Its almost
horizontal surface, combined with the impermeability of its subsoil
and the heavy rains of the summer season, accounts for the defective
drainage that keeps much of its area covered with water for long
periods during each year. The so-called rivers that cross it are
sluggish streams with such suggestive names as Rio Confuso
(confused), Rio Pérdido (lost), and Rio Salado (salty). They have
little or no erosive force, and their water is generally brackish. In
fact the scarcity of potable water is one of the problems involved in

the development of this region. These natural circumstances, combined with the troublesome insects that infest it and the hostility of the Indians, have been the decisive factors in retarding the opening up of the Chaco.

The main feature of the vegetation of the Chaco is the large stretches of open savana interspersed with frequent islands of forest. These wooded tracts usually consist of more or less dense tropical jungle, but large clumps of palm trees are common. The open lands are covered with a growth of tall grasses, but the layer of surface water during the rainy season prevents its full utilization for grazing purposes, while the long dry season tends to reduce its value as pasturage during the winter months.

In spite of all these disadvantages the Chaco, especially the belt along the Paraguay River, is the center of a growing cattle industry, whose herds appear to flourish reasonably well. There is adequate pasturage during most of the year, and the industry is capable of considerable expansion; though the disadvantages of the region as a field for human settlement will militate to a certain extent against its development. In any effort to utilize the limited agricultural possibilities of the Chaco something might be learned from the experience of Argentina in its territory of El Chaco lying to the south of the Pilcomayo.

HISTORY OF SETTLEMENT AND DEVELOPMENT

The Early "Bandeirantes" and the Jesuit Missionaries

The first efforts to penetrate Matto Grosso were made by Portuguese slave hunters from São Paulo before the end of the sixteenth century. These raids, or *entradas*, were later followed by the long treks of the Bandeirantes, bands of Paulistas, who reached the valley of the Paraguay and, crossing the low imperceptible divide between that river and the Guaporé, entered the basin of the Madeira. The use of river valleys as lines of penetration and the open character of most of the country facilitated the advance into the far interior. Thus, the Paulistas followed the Tieté and the Paraná to the Pardo, ascended that river and crossed by the Campoá portage to the Taquary, and then went up the Paraguay and the São Lourenço. Gold was the primary objective of this movement into the vast wilderness of western Brazil, and, though the washings never yielded such rich returns as in Minas Geraes, enough gold was found in the rivers to sustain the original object of the expeditions.

The Bandeirantes found gold in the vicinity of Cuyabá in 1719. After 1734 they pushed on to the Guaporé. In 1746 diamonds were first discovered. At the end of the eighteenth century one Brazilian authority, Ricardo Franco, gave the population of the captaincy of Matto Grosso as 24,000. The Bandeirantes drove herds of cattle with them and carried seeds for planting, but stock raising and agriculture long remained subordinate to the search for gold and diamonds. Before the end of the eighteenth century Cuyabá and other places had been founded, and the Portuguese crown had made good its dominion to the present frontier at the Guaporé.

In the seventeenth century the Jesuits established a series of missions in the Chiquitos country to the west of the Paraguay and attempted to create Indian communities similar to those of the "Reductions" in Paraguay and the Argentine missions. They introduced the cultivation of cotton and other plants and dis-covered sources of gold whose existence still lures prospectors to that region. Meanwhile farther to the west Spaniards from the plateau had begun the raising of cattle on the grassy plains of Santa Cruz, bringing with them sugar cane and other plants, which they cultivated in a rudimentary fashion.

To the south of the Chiquitos highlands the waste of the Gran Chaco still lay untouched. An expedition of Spaniards crossed it on their way from Asunción to the Peruvian Andes before the middle of the sixteenth century. They found no reason for dis-puting its possession with the Indians, and it remained in the mystery which still envelops much of its surface.

DEVELOPMENTS OF THE NINETEENTH CENTURY

Matto Grosso vegetated through most of the nineteenth century. The old gold washings no longer repaid their working, and no new fields of importance were discovered. Most of the dredging enter-prises begun in the latter decades of the century were failures; Cuyabá and the other towns declined in population and activity. Villa Bella on the Guaporé is long since a ruin, and Diamantino is a sleepy hamlet. Only Corumbá has shown any vitality or signs of progress. In the meantime the fast-multiplying herds of cattle, that today form the chief wealth of the state, roamed the ranges without a market, except for an occasional *boiada* that was driven across the Paranahyba into São Paulo. The new interest in rubber, dating from about 1896, sent some of the more adventurous into the forests to the north and northwest of Cuyabá in search of the *Hevea*. Some rubber came into Corumbá for shipment from north-eastern Bolivia, but the total of all this was small compared with what went out by the Amazon. However, the export tax collected at Manáos on rubber from Matto Grosso was welcome to the treasury of a state whose revenues were hopelessly inadequate to the task of providing for even the most perfunctory public administration. It was from this circumstance that there developed the present antagonistic dualism within Matto Grosso, whereby the open cattle-raising southern part of the state, lying within the drainage basin of the Paraná-Paraguay system, holds the balance of political control over the jungle-covered, rubber-producing section lying within Amazonia.

RECENT IMMIGRATION INTO THE REGION

Considerable impulse was given to the development of Matto Grosso, but particularly to the western part of the state, as a result of the Paraguayan War (1865–1870). Not only were the designs of the Paraguayan dictator Lopez on that region definitely dispelled by his defeat and death, but the Paraguay River was opened to international traffic as a result. Moreover, realizing the necessity of further strengthening its hold on the upper Paraguay country, the Brazilian government pushed the Northwestern Railway to completion in 1914, thereby linking the Paraguay River with São Paulo and Rio de Janeiro. With the railway there has come a new current of immigration and added impetus to the opening up of the southern zone of the state.

Considerable numbers of immigrants from the states of São Paulo and Rio Grande do Sul have moved into the districts of Campo Grande and Tres Lagoas. Many Japanese have also settled in this part of the state. Furthermore, the founding of large *frigorificos*, or packing plants, in the state of São Paulo has provided a better market for the cattlemen of Matto Grosso and is forcing them gradually to improve their stock. Great ranches like the "Descalvados" of the foreign-owned Brazilian Land, Cattle, and Packing Company have grown up on the upper Paraguay and wherever there are large areas of good pasture lands. Some of these cattle find their way in increasing numbers to the *frigorificos* of São Paulo; the rest supply the local *saladeros*, or jerked-beef plants, whose product is shipped to the River Plate or eventually to the Cuban market.

THE PRESENT STATUS OF ECONOMIC DEVELOPMENT

THE MATTO GROSSO HIGHLAND

In this country land is still held in large holdings, the average size of a ranch being over 5000 acres. It is estimated that there are now over 6,000,000 head of cattle in Matto Grosso and Goyaz.

There is little agriculture, except in the neighborhood of such towns as Cuyabá. Manioc, corn, beans, rice, tobacco, and crude sugar are the principal crops raised. Some of the black tobacco of Goyaz finds its way to São Paulo and Rio de Janeiro, where it is made up into cigarettes. One of the export products of Matto Grosso is ipecacuanha, which is found in the region tributary to the towns of Cuyabá and Diamantino.

The diamond rush of the past few years to the Rio das Garças (a left tributary of the upper Araguaya in 16° S.) is only a sporadic phase of the economic development of the state. Local business has profited to a small degree from supplying the needs of the several thousand *garumpeiros* engaged in the washings; but strikes of this kind are, after all, inimical to the sounder growth that is desirable for the state. Under normal market conditions it is unprofitable to work the rich deposits of manganese ore in the Urucúm hills near Corumbá, owing to the long distance from seaboard.

The extent of the foreign trade of the state of Matto Grosso for the years 1922–1924 is shown by the following figures:

	Exports	Imports
1922	£143,073	95,947
1923	204,275	67,364
1924	226,554	106,169

However, these figures evidently do not include indirect importations made through São Paulo but would appear to show only the commercial movement through the customs port of Corumbá. Exports consist largely of jerked beef, hides, rubber, yerba mate (Paraguay tea), and ipecacuanha.

THE INTERMEDIATE REGION

The development of the Santa Cruz district of Bolivia has been retarded by the lack of satisfactory connections with the outside world. Neither of its four outlets furnishes economical transport for its products to the market where they might find acceptance. The long trail over the mountains to Cochabamba is too exhausting to its cattle, but a few are driven south into Argentina. Some are killed for their hides, which are cured and sent to the plateau to be sold as sole leather. The sugar cane of the region is ground to make alcohol, the trade in which, owing to the lessened cost of transport, is more profitable than would be a business in sugar with the plateau country. The government *estanco*, or monopoly, has been an impediment rather than an incentive to the cultivation of tobacco. In an effort to solve the transportation problem and to bind the eastern lowlands to the plateau, the Bolivian government has decided on the construction of a railway between Cochabamba and Santa Cruz. Though an automobile road would probably be preferable to such a costly undertaking, some convenient connection is necessary to keep the Santa Cruz region from being drawn into the commercial sphere of attraction of Argentina and so eventually being lost to Bolivia. Once the railway is completed, it should give an impulse to the production of cotton and sugar for supplying the needs of the plateau population. On the other hand, a more practicable outlet for the petroleum deposits of the country to the southwest of Santa Cruz would probably be to the Paraguay-Paraná.

Several attempts have been made to develop the Chiquitos country lying to the north of the Santa Cruz-Puerto Suarez trail. The ambitious project of a Belgian colonization company with a river port on the Laguna Gaiba ended in failure. An English land company is now making efforts to attract settlers to the same general region. All of these enterprises suffer from the fundamental problem raised by the long and expensive haul necessary for their products to reach a market. Meanwhile the interior of that region has long been stagnant, only a few cattle being driven out to the river at Corumbá and the transit trade in rubber having declined to only a fraction of its former volume. Of the long extinct Jesuit régime nothing remains but the peaceful character of the inhabitants and isolated patches of crops introduced by the missionaries.

THE GRAN CHACO

Two factors have been responsible for a certain development of the zone of the Gran Chaco that lies within easy reach of the Paraguay River. One of these is cattle raising, the other is the

production of tanning extract from the quebracho tree. Although
all this region is in dispute between Paraguay and Bolivia and the
interior is little explored, the Paraguayan government has given
away most of the Chaco in large grants to individuals and private
companies. Several of these grantees were of Argentine nationality, and one was an American. A number of quebracho extract
plants have been installed at different points on the Chaco side
of the Paraguay by American or Argentine capital. Railway lines
have been built into the interior for bringing out logs, and numerous
feeder trails have been opened up for the ox trains. Large stretches
of the open country within the river zone are now given up to cattle
raising. As most of the cattle are inferior stock, their meat is suitable only for canning, and hence, with the decreased demand for
canned beef in Europe, the local industry has declined in importance
during the past few years. There has been practically no development of agriculture, except in a small area about Colonia Hayes near
Asunción. The new Mennonite colonization on the upper river
should serve as a test of the agricultural possibilities of that region.
However, nothing at all comparable in importance to the cotton-
growing industry of the Argentine Chaco has been developed so
far.

Communications with the Outer World

Six main routes connect Matto Grosso and the Chaco with the
settled rim of South America and with the sea. To the north the
various links in the Amazon system supply an outlet to the Atlantic.
The western part of Matto Grosso has a connection with the
Madeira by way of the Guaporé, the Mamoré, and the Madeira-
Mamoré Railway. There is a regular transportation service to
the head of navigation on the Guaporé, whence a trail leads over-
land to the upper Paraguay country about São Luiz de Caceres.
This road is a link in the old route of the Portuguese from São
Paulo to the Madeira basin, for the protection of which they con-
structed in the eighteenth century the pretentious fort of Beira de
Principe on the Guaporé. Farther to the west the Mamoré and
its confluents offer a means of access to the plains of eastern Bolivia.
Beyond the reach of the little stern-wheelers which ply up the
Mamoré from Guajará-Mirim across the low Mojos country, ox-
carts and mule trains continue the route into Santa Cruz de la
Sierra.

EXISTING AND PROJECTED RAILROADS

From the south Brazilian coast two railway lines penetrate this area. The most easterly of these is the line from São Paulo, which is slowly advancing north towards the heart of the state of Goyaz. From its present terminus beyond the Paranahyba there is an automobile road to the small city of Goyaz, the capital of the state, whence an old trail, opened in 1736, leads west across the Araguaya into Matto Grosso. The city of Goyaz is about 600 miles distant from the coast at Rio de Janeiro, and the length of the projected railway connection with São Paulo is about 750 miles. The Goyaz Railway crosses the important cattle country of the "triangle" of Minas Geraes by way of Uberaba and will pass near the reservation set off as the future Federal District of the republic. The federal government also plans to extend the Central Railway from Rio de Janeiro into Goyaz from its present terminus beyond the São Francisco at Pirapora. The usefulness of the Goyaz Railway is lessened by the difference in gauge with the Mogyana Railway, over which it enters the state of São Paulo.

Longer and more important than the Goyaz route is the line of the Northwestern Railway, which continues the rail connection of the São Paulo system from Bauru 1272 kilometers across the breadth of Matto Grosso to the Paraguay River, the great north-and-south route between the River Plate and Cuyabá.

Its western terminus is at Porto Esperança, about 55 miles below Corumbá, to which point it is planned to extend the railway. This line is federal property and is operated by the national government. Its service is extremely inefficient, and operating costs are high in relation to revenues, resulting in heavy annual deficits. In 1924 it carried 785,560 passengers (total passenger kilometers, 52,186,663) and 196,160 tons of freight (total ton kilometers, 47,258,318). This railway has been the principal avenue for the settlement of southern Matto Grosso, and a number of growing towns have sprung up along its line.

Roughly paralleling the Northwestern Railway to the north, the old trail has survived over which cattle are still driven to railhead in the state of São Paulo, fording the Paranahyba at Sant' Anna. Another road, used by automobiles, leads from the line of the Northwestern Railway at Ribeirão Claro north to the diamond fields of the Rio das Garças. From Ribeirão Claro to Santa Rita do Araguaya the distance is about 324 miles and thence to

Engenheiro Morbeck or Lageado another 144 miles. The diamond fields are in the vicinity of Lageado and Cassanunga. Santa Rita can also be reached by automobile from Uberabinha, some 572 miles to the east. West from Santa Rita a mule trail leads about 400 miles across the great *chapada* to Cuyabá.

There exists a project, fostered by the well-known General Rondon, for a branch of the Northwestern to terminate at Cuyabá. This branch would leave the main line at Agua Clara. An older railway project provides for a line that would continue the Araraquara Railway from the state of São Paulo northwest across the Paraná at Sant' Anna to the same destination. Surveys have been made for a railway from the line of the Northwestern south to the Paraguayan border. A project for which a concession is held to link Cuyabá with Santarem at the confluence of the Tapajóz and the Amazon would appear to be financially impracticable for some time to come.

River Arteries

The Paraguay River furnishes through water communications at all times of the year between Corumbá in Matto Grosso and the River Plate, though there is only six feet of water on certain passes in the dry season. Corumbá lies about 1422 miles above Buenos Aires. The Paraguay River still constitutes the main artery of traffic for the western part of Matto Grosso. The exigencies of the radical crews of the river steamers are a more serious obstacle to the future development of this route than are the natural limitations to the navigability of the river. The Paraná is open to through navigation only from where it touches the corner of Paraguay at the great cataracts of the Guayrá. The small steamers that run on the open stretch of river above these falls and connect at Porto Tebyriçá with the terminus of the Sorocabana Railway from São Paulo are of merely local importance. The upper Paraná is so broken by rapids and falls, like those of Itapura, as to render it of negligible value to the economic life of the tributary region.

Of other rivers, the great Rio São Francisco is impracticable as a gateway to the Atlantic. The upper navigable section of the river is separated from the Matto Grosso Highland to the west by parallel ranges on the borders of Goyaz, and in its lower reaches all navigation is interrupted by the Paulo Affonso Falls on the frontier between the states of Bahia and Sergipe.

The dual Tocantins-Araguaya system, which drains eastern Matto Grosso and most of Goyaz and flows north across some fifteen degrees of latitude to debouch near Pará, would appear to offer an excellent outlet for this region. However, its course is so broken by rapids and shallows that it is useless as a through route of communication. Though there is steamer or launch navigation on certain isolated stretches, it can be ascended to its upper reaches only by canoes, many weeks of painful effort being required to make the journey.

Outlet Routes of the Santa Cruz Region

Another through north-and-south route is that between Santa Cruz de la Sierra and Buenos Aires. This connection between the Bolivian plains and the River Plate is by way of the long road to the terminus of the Argentine rail system at Embarcación and thence by Tucumán and Córdoba into Buenos Aires. Automobiles now reach Santa Cruz by this overland route, which was until recently restricted to oxcarts and mule trains, but through traffic over it is still small.

Of the four outlets of eastern Bolivia the most important is the connection with the Pacific via Cochabamba. From Santa Cruz a trail leads westward some 350 miles across a series of mountain ranges up to railhead at that city. Mule trains cover the distance in about two weeks, and a recently inaugurated air service in a few hours. Work is now on the point of being initiated on a long-projected railway line to bind the eastern lowlands of Bolivia with the plateau.

From the terminus of the main river steamers at Corumbá smaller light-draft boats ascend the Paraguay and its confluents to Cuyabá and São Luiz de Caceres. The old trail from Santa Cruz leading east nearly 500 miles across the Chiquitos country to Puerto Suarez, the small Bolivian frontier post opposite Corumbá on the Lagoa de Caceres, has already been mentioned. This route, much of whose length suffers from either a scarcity or an excess of water, has declined considerably in importance during the past two decades. There has never been much through traffic over it, but it has preserved a certain interest as a link in a possible trans-continental railway project between Arica and Santos.

Problems of Public Administration and International Relations

The maintenance of law and order naturally presents serious problems in a region so large and thinly settled as is Matto Grosso. It is impossible for the state, with the limited means at its disposal, to make its authority felt everywhere. The small force of state militia has proved incompetent to put down local opposition to the government at Cuyabá such as occurred when the famous Morbeck refused to allow the state to collect the export tax on diamonds in the Rio das Garças country. Cattle thieving has also been common and flagrant at times along both the Bolivian and Paraguayan borders, the presence of Paraguayan renegades aggravating the disorder. Moreover, the state government of Matto Grosso has at times shown little consideration for formal agreements made with private interests, as in the notorious case of the concession of the General Rubber Company in the upper basin of the Tapajóz. The Indian tribes in Matto Grosso do not present any serious problems for future settlers. Beyond the limits of the Amazon jungle they are entirely pacific, and their tribal rights are well guarded by the federal government of Brazil, which aims to protect them from exploitation by the whites. In 1924–1925 large parts of Matto Grosso were seriously disturbed by the depredations of *revoltosos*, or bands of rebels, who took refuge there after the failure of the São Paulo uprising of 1924.

Beyond occasional depredations along the Brazilian border disorders are few in the Chiquitos region of Bolivia, and in the department of Santa Cruz serious violations of law and order are infrequent. However, wild Indians in the wilderness of the Monte Grande have sometimes attacked travelers along the Santa Cruz-Puerto Suarez trail.

In the Gran Chaco the only menace to the public peace has been from the occasional demands of the *peonada*, or labor force, of the quebracho establishments along the river. On at least one or two occasions these demands have resulted in serious strikes, as at the Puerto Pinasco plant of the International Products Company. Also, wherever there have been revolutions on the left bank of the river in Paraguay proper, the activities of the revolutionists have sometimes extended over into the Chaco side. In the interior some of the Indian tribes oppose the entrance of the whites into their land, and their hostility still constitutes an obstacle to the exploration and opening up of much of the country. Probably a more serious impediment has been the unsettled title to the Chaco. In an effort to assert their claims the Bolivians have slowly advanced down the Pilcomayo, establishing small military posts at each step. On the other hand, the Paraguayans have pushed into the Bahia Negra region, where they have a strong post on the site coveted by the Bolivians as the river terminus of an outlet for the whole eastern part of their country. An armed clash between forces of the two nations in this neighborhood in December, 1928, almost led to open war. Formal hostilities were averted by an agreement to submit the long-standing dispute to arbitration.

PRESENT STATUS AND FUTURE POSSIBILITIES OF AGRICULTURAL LAND UTILIZATION IN PATAGONIA[1]

WELLINGTON D. JONES

AN observer traversing the length and breadth of Patagonia would see a landscape displaying few conspicuous traces of human occupation. The face of nature, in its larger lineaments and in detail, is today essentially as it was before this frontier land began to be settled some fifty years ago. Present settlement is sparse, and the earlier nomadic hunting Indian population, which lived largely on guanacos and wild ostriches, was even more thinly scattered.

TABLE I—AREA AND POPULATION OF THE SOUTHERN TERRITORIES OF ARGENTINA AND CHILE, 1920*

TERRITORY	AREA IN SQUARE MILES	POPULATION	AVERAGE POPULATION DENSITY PER SQUARE MILE
Neuquén	40,500	30,677	0.76
Río Negro	79,800	42,652	0.53
Chubut	93,500	31,021	0.33
Santa Cruz	109,100	18,462	0.17
Tierra del Fuego . .	8,300	2,608	0.31
Magallanes (Chile) .	64,800	28,960	0.45
Total	396,000	154,380	0.39

*The figures in the tables are either taken directly from the official statistical publications listed in the Bibliography under "República Argentina" and "República de Chile" or are calculations based on figures from these sources.

The government censuses taken in 1920 showed a total population of 154,380 in the 396,000 square miles of the southern territories of Argentina and Chile that approximately comprise Patagonia (Fig. 1 and Table I). Although not dense anywhere, this population

[1] This study is based primarily on field investigations made in 1911 and 1912 by the Comisión de Estudios Hidrológicos of the Bureau of Railways of the Ministry of Public Works of the Argentine Government. Professor Bailey Willis was chief of the commission, and the author of this paper was a member. Surveys of various sorts, including an appraisal of land utilization possibilities, were made in a zone along the railroad then under construction west from San Antonio to Lake Nahuel Huapí and in a zone in and just east of the Andes north from Lake Nahuel Huapí to latitude 39° 40′ S. and south to latitude 43° 40′ S. The available literature on the parts of Patagonia not covered by these surveys has been consulted in the preparation of this paper, at the end of which the more valuable of these sources are listed.

is rather unevenly distributed (Fig. 5), and the evidences of human occupation and use of the land vary correspondingly in intensity.

THE AGRICULTURAL REGIONS OF PATAGONIA

On the basis of differences in agricultural utilization, which differences are based fundamentally on differences in natural conditions, four major divisions of the area embraced in the six political territories listed in Table I can be distinguished (Fig. 1):

1. The sheep ranching region of the dry plains and low plateaus.
2. The oases of irrigation cropping, along the rivers of the northern half of the dry region.
3. The cattle ranching zone of the East Andean border.
4. The non-agricultural zone of the rainy, forested Andes.

Patagonia is defined in the present paper as including the southern parts of Argentina and Chile, extending from the Atlantic to the Pacific and from the southern extremity of the continent to the northern boundaries of the divisions listed above.

THE SHEEP-RANCHING REGION

The eastern two-thirds of that portion of South America that extends from somewhat north of the Río Colorado all the way south to Tierra del Fuego is very sparsely settled, semi-arid to arid plains and low plateau country that is devoted to sheep ranching (Figs. 1–3) except in the restricted areas described below. The rainfall is too low (less than 400 millimeters) for growing crops without irrigation, and, except in the valleys of a few major streams traversing the area, the possibilities of irrigation are slight. Large tracts of land in this dry plains and low plateau region are owned by companies that have fenced their properties and carry on sheep rearing by much the same methods as those practiced in the western United States and Australia. Land not in possession of the large ranching companies, however, still constitutes the bulk of the area of the region. Much of this land is unused and government-owned; some is owned and used by small landowners with relatively small flocks of sheep, and some is occupied temporarily by squatters. Both the quality of the scattered bush and bunch-grass vegetation and the possibilities for watering livestock, as well as the strong and persistent west winds, are much less favorable for cattle than for sheep, and consequently the latter everywhere predominate (Figs. 4 and 7).

TABLE II—ELEMENTS OF THE LIVESTOCK ASSOCIATIONS IN TYPE AREAS OF THE AGRICULTURAL REGIONS OF PATAGONIA AND ITS BORDERLANDS, 1920

TYPE AREA	PER CENT OF TOTAL LIVESTOCK UNITS*				
	Sheep	Cattle	Goats	Hogs	Horses and Mules†
Sheep Ranching Region of the Dry Plains and Plateaus					
Northern part (Department of 25 de Mayo, Río Negro Territory)	65	8	5	0	22
Central part (Department of Deseado, Santa Cruz Territory) .	77	13	0	0	10
Southern part (Department of San Sebastian, Tierra del Fuego Territory)	93	2	0	0	5
Cattle Ranching Region of the East Andean Border (Department of Los Lagos, Neuquén Territory)	7	52	16	0	25
Cattle Ranching Region of the Monte (Department of Añelo, Neuquén Territory)	4	43	15	0	38
Grain Farming Region of the Outer Pampas (Department of Bahía Blanca, Buenos Aires Province)	31	40	0	2	27
Livestock and Grain Farming Region of South Chile (Department of Osorno, Llanquihue Province) .	7	79	3	3	8

*1 livestock unit = 1 horse = 1 head of cattle = 7 sheep = 7 goats = 5 hogs. These conversion figures are based on feed requirements.

†In all cases mules are much less numerous than horses.

Ranching has altered only in slight degree the natural conditions as they were when the first settlers came into the region. Widely separated ranch houses, with their associated corrals, dipping vats, sheds, windmills, and irrigated garden patches, long stretches of wire fence far apart, an occasional gaucho on horseback, scattered flocks of grazing sheep, and the isolated huts of the poor squatters do not bulk large in a monotonously uniform landscape of plains, mesas, and canyons, with dull gray-green or gray-buff semi-desert vegetation hundreds of miles in extent.

Livestock density per square mile in this extensive region inevitably is low (Fig. 6), since the stock is grazed on the sparse natural vegetation and in most cases is given little or no supple-

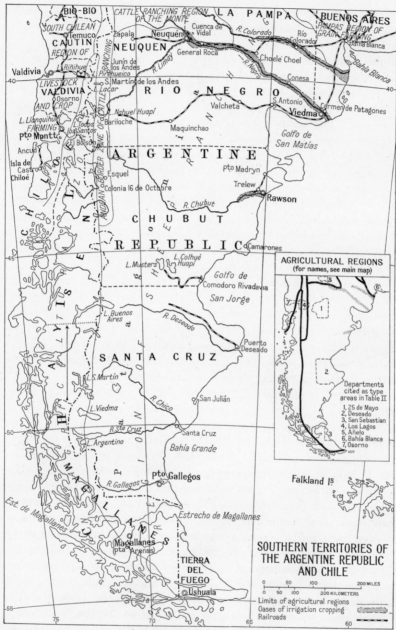

FIG. 1—Geographical features of Patagonia referred to in the text. Scale, 1 : 12,000,000. Boundaries of territorial subdivisions of Chile are shown as defined by the decree of Dec. 30, 1927 (*Geogr.
Rev.*, Vol. 19, 1929, pp. 61–77). In addition, the boundary between the Province of Llanquihue
and the Territory of Magallanes, for which 1920 statistics have been employed both in text and
maps, is shown at latitude 47° S.

mentary feed from crops (Fig. 8). The average livestock density per square mile, however, varies greatly from one part of the region to another, as the map shows. In part this variation in density reflects differences in carrying capacity of the ranges, due primarily to differences in vegetation that grow out of differences in climate. In part, however, this variation in livestock density probably is due to the fact that in places the available grazing land is not fully utilized. The better ranges in southern Patagonia carry as many as 200 sheep to the square mile, but throughout much of the ranching region the density is less than one third this figure. As a consequence, even the smaller ranches, with 8000 to 10,000 head of sheep, occupy several square miles, and the leasings or holdings of the companies with large herds are immense. The Compañía Explotadora de Tierra del Fuego with 3,600,000 acres and 1,125,000 sheep, the Sociedad Industrial y Ganadera de Magallanes with 1,240,000 acres, and the Argentine Southern Land Company with 730,000 acres are among the larger companies.

The canyons that in many places are cut into the plateau surfaces play a significant rôle in sheep ranching, especially in the winter and particularly in the southern latitudes, in that they offer places of shelter for the flocks from the cold winds. Furthermore, on the floors of these canyons greater soil moisture than on the plateaus results in better winter pasture, and, although permanent streams are rare, springs are not uncommon in the canyons.

The ranch centers are for the most part located at springs issuing from the base of mesas or canyon walls, at which sites water is available for watering stock and for ranch-house uses and in not a few cases is employed to irrigate a small garden and a few acres of supplementary forage. Such sites also give protection against the blustering winds that so frequently blow.

Towns within the region of sheep ranching are restricted to the Atlantic coast (Figs. 1 and 5), at places so located as to serve as exporters of wool and, in recent years, of some frozen mutton. Eleven such ports, most of which have a population of between 1000 and 3000, take care of the bulk of the trade of Patagonia. At all of these ports, except Magallanes and Puerto Madryn, ships must anchor offshore and load from and to lighters. Goods unloaded at these ports are not subject to the import duties (Magallanes recently was taken off the free list by Chile) imposed at ports serving the more highly developed parts of Argentina and Chile.

TABLE III—CHIEF PATAGONIAN EXPORTS TO FOREIGN COUNTRIES BY PORTS

PORT	METRIC TONS OF WOOL*	METRIC TONS OF FROZEN MUTTON†
Ushuaia	38	2,914
Magallanes	11,417	17,975
Puerto Gallegos	863	3,266
Santa Cruz	49	. . . . . .
San Julián	749	1,758
Armour	. . . . . .	2,636
Puerto Deseado	2	674
Comodoro Rivadavia	1,122	. . . . . .
Camarones	162	. . . . . .
Puerto Madryn	1,337	. . . . . .
San Antonio	3,853	. . . . . .
Total	19,592	29,223

*1925 for Magallanes (formerly Punta Arenas), 1923 for other ports.

†1925 for Magallanes, 1927 for other ports. The figure for Ushuaia is for Cia. Frigorífica Argentina, the location of which in Tierra del Fuego is unknown to the author of this paper.

To these ports each year after the shearing season long lines of carts loaded with wool make the slow (in many cases several weeks long) journey necessary to get the chief export of the region to a point where ocean carriers can take it to the markets of Europe and North America. From these ports the carts return to the ranches, laden with the variety of products, largely manufactures and foodstuffs, needed but not produced on the ranches.

The several railway lines reaching various distances inland from the Atlantic (Fig. 1) have in recent years greatly shortened the cart hauls from ranches in their respective zones of influence. A few years after construction was begun on these railroads the automobile was introduced into Patagonia. It seems not to be much used yet for trucking, probably because of the absence of sufficiently good roads. For transporting people and mails and light goods, however, it has proved of great value, for much of the dry plains and plateau country can be traversed even where little or no road construction has been done.

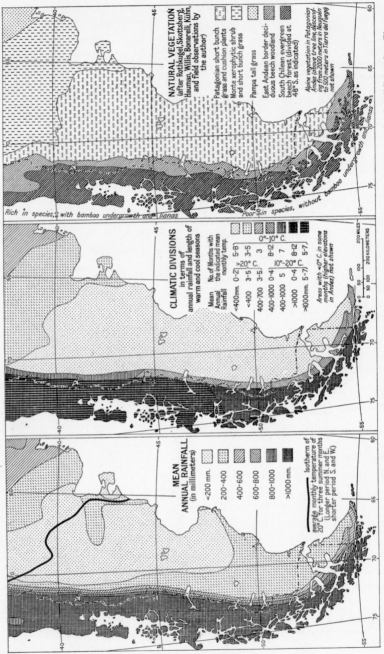

FIGS. 2–4.—Rainfall, climatic divisions, and vegetation of Patagonia. Scale, 1 : 20,000,000. (Based on publications cited in the bibliography: Figures 2 and 3 on G. G. Davis, Figure 4 on the authors enumerated under the title.) Since the meteorological stations are far apart in most of Patagonia, the lines drawn on Figures 2 and 3 involve a series of plausible assumptions based on the relief and natural vegetation.

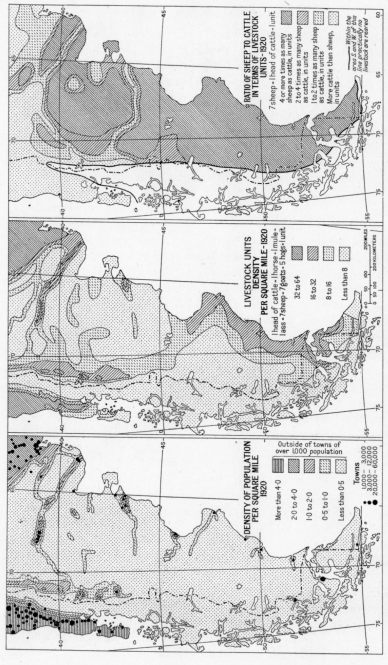

Figs. 5–7—Population density, livestock density, and ratio of sheep to cattle in Patagonia. Scale, 1 : 20,000,000. (Based on the map and the publications cited under República Argentina and República de Chile in the bibliography.) The densities were calculated from the areas of the departments, measured by planimeter on that map, and the statistics in the government publications. The isopleths were then drawn with reference not only to these densities but also to facts observed by the author in the field and obtained in the literature.

The Oases of Irrigation Cropping

In the valleys of the Río Negro and the Río Chubut, which cross Patagonia from the Andes to the Atlantic, irrigation cropping has been developed and supports a population considerably denser than that in the sheep ranching country traversed by these streams (Figs. 1, 5, and 8). Of these irrigated oases, the flat-floored, bluff-bordered valley of the Río Negro, cut 100 to 300 feet below the general level of the plateau, is the most important. The irrigated zone in this valley extends, with some interruptions, from near the junction of the Río Neuquén and the Río Limay to the Atlantic Ocean. A variety of crops is raised, but alfalfa dominates areally in the crop association (Table VII, p. 140); the vine for wine yields greatest cash returns. The availability of alfalfa forage presumably is what makes possible the considerably denser livestock population in and near the valley (Fig. 6) than is the rule elsewhere in the dry region and likewise the dominance of cattle over sheep (Fig. 7), although definite statements to this effect have not been found. Traversed by the railroad from Bahía Blanca to Zapala (Fig. 1), this ribbon of cultivation, with green fields, fruit trees, vineyards, irrigation ditches, and farm villages, offers a delightful and economically significant contrast to the sheep ranges stretching away on either side for many miles. Six towns in the Río Negro oasis, each with a population of between 1000 and 3000, bear testimony to the much higher productivity of the irrigated crop lands as compared with the dry ranching lands.

Along the lower course of the Río Chubut another stretch of irrigated land, less extensive than that along the Río Negro, supports a second group of distinctly denser population than is characteristic of the sheep ranching country (Figs. 1, 5, and 8). Alfalfa again is here the dominant crop, in this case shipped in significant amounts to the ports farther south along the Atlantic. Four towns of between 1000 and 3000 population are located in this irrigated area.

A third area of irrigation cropping, as yet but little developed, lies along the Río Colorado, extending downstream in a tenuous line from a point some 80 miles above the town of Río Colorado.

Other than these three major irrigation areas in Patagonia, there are only small patches of irrigated land a few acres in extent near ranch centers, supplied with water from small streams which head in most cases in springs at the base of plateau scarps and flow only a few miles before disappearing.

THE CATTLE RANCHING ZONE OF THE
EAST ANDEAN BORDER

Along the western border of the dry sheep country, close to the eastern edge of the Andes, between latitudes 37° and 44° S., is a long and narrow zone of hill and valley country with between 400 and 1000 millimeters of annual rainfall and originally with a patchy

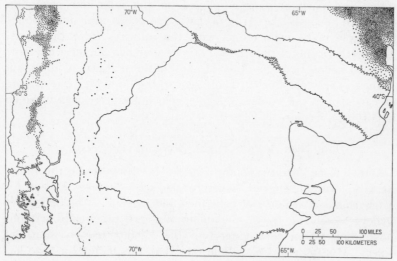

FIG. 8—Land in crops in northern Patagonia, 1920. Scale, 1 : 10,000,000. One dot represents 250 hectares, approximately one square mile. The part of Patagonia south of the map has almost no land in crops except a little along the lower course of the Río Gallegos.

vegetation cover of grassland and deciduous forest (Figs. 3 and 4). In this zone cattle rather than sheep ranching has been developed (Figs. 6 and 7), in connection with which much of the forest has been burned off to add pasture area. The pasturage is luxuriant, favoring cattle rather than sheep rearing and supporting a denser total livestock population than does the vegetation of the dry region to the east. Some crops, chiefly wheat, also are raised (Fig. 8) without irrigation; these in part are used to feed the local population and in part furnish supplementary fodder to livestock. The density of population of this Andean border zone in places approaches that of the irrigated oases, although in general it is intermediate between that of the latter areas and of the sheep country (Fig. 5).

Strongly isolated at the present time, this Andean border zone of ranching and some farming supports only one town having a population of as much as 1000. Connections with the outside world are westward across the Andes to Chile or eastward to the Atlantic ports (Fig. 1). On the two main routes across the Andes launches or small steamers traverse Lakes Nahuel Huapí, Todos los Santos, and Llanquihue on the route to Puerto Montt and Lakes Lacar, Pirehueico, and Riñihue on that to Valdivia, with carts or riding and pack animals employed on the inter-lake stretches. Eastward towards the Atlantic carts for goods and automobiles for people make connections with the railways from the ports. The northern end of the Andean border zone has the most effective external connections, by way of the Southern Railroad to Bahía Blanca, over which line cattle are sent to the Pampas. The driving of cattle over the Andes to Chile, which formerly was of some importance, has largely ceased.

The Non-Agricultural Zone of the Andes

West of the cattle ranching Andean border zone lie the rainy, heavily forested, rugged, severely glaciated Andes. Except for a few small settlements of fishermen and loggers at the mouths of valleys along the coast, the mountains are practically without population where they extend to the Pacific, namely south of Puerto Montt ($41\frac{1}{2}°$ S.). The fact that this mountain zone has but little flat land, and that its rainfall is excessive, has precluded and probably will continue to prevent crop raising, and livestock rearing will be carried on only in the summer on alpine meadows.

Agricultural Regions Bordering Patagonia

The type of agricultural land utilization in each of the three regions that border Patagonia may be briefly characterized as follows (see Figs. 1–8 and Table II):

1. Adjoining the sheep ranching region on the northeast is the grain farming region of the outer pampas. In this plains region of fertile, dark-colored grassland soils and light to medium rainfall the growing of wheat on large farms for export is the major agricultural interest. No small part of the area, however, still remains in the hands of ranchers, who graze cattle and sheep on the natural grass.

2. North of the sheep ranching region and west of the grain farming region of the outer pampas is the cattle ranching region

of the *monte*, a dry, bush-covered country unsuited to cropping except in districts where water is available for irrigation and poorly suited to sheep rearing because of the thorny bush cover.

3. West of the Andes in Chile, and extending northward from the island of Chiloé (about 43½° S.), is the livestock and grain farming region of southern Chile, where pioneer farming is gradually expanding as the forests are cleared.

History of the Settlement of Patagonia

The history of white settlement in Patagonia, and of the accompanying economic development, is a short one. Although explorers touched at various points along the coast subsequent to Magellan's discoveries in 1520 and Jesuits from Chile established short-lived mission stations near Lake Nahuel Huapí in the late seventeenth and the early eighteenth centuries, practically nothing was known about the interior of Patagonia until Captain Musters in 1869–1870 traversed the land east of the Andes from the Strait of Magellan to Lake Nahuel Huapí and thence went east to the mouth of the Río Negro. Following Musters a number of explorers sketched in the outlines of a fair knowledge of the interior before settlement began in the early eighties of the nineteenth century. It is not strange that, except for a tiny colony on the lower Río Negro at Carmen, a small group of Welsh settlers on the lower Río Chubut, a few Chileans in the vicinity of Punta Arenas, and a few more Chileans near the Andes, settlement of Patagonia was delayed until so late. The Pampas region of Argentina and the Great Valley of Chile sufficed until about this time to take care of immigration and the natural increase of population. The Atlantic coast of Patagonia, with its barren semi-desert landscape and its few and poor harbors, offered no attractions; the rainy, densely forested, mountainous Pacific coast south of Puerto Montt was equally uninviting. Furthermore, the native Indian population of Patagonia was hostile to settlement by the whites.

The Indians, however, were subdued in a series of campaigns between 1879 and 1883, and soon thereafter three streams of population began to move into Patagonia and to occupy the land, one southward from the Pampas along the Atlantic coast and thence into the interior, a second northward from Punta Arenas, and a third eastward across the Andes from the Great Valley of Chile. Independent of these movements, settlers from the Welsh

Table IV—Number of Livestock in the Southern Territories of Argentina and Chile, 1888–1920*

Territory	1888			1895			1908			1914			1920		
	Total Livestock	Sheep	Cattle	Total Livestock	Sheep	Cattle	Total Livestock	Sheep	Cattle	Total Livestock	Sheep	Cattle	Total Livestock	Sheep	Cattle
Neuquén	?	?	?	297.5	51.1	173.7	427.2	96.1	193.7	412.2	113.2	152.3	376.3	103.0	139.5
Río Negro . . .	135.4	41.1	77.4	267.6	144.2	82.1	1154.4	674.9	279.5	672.1†	400.3	91.0	641.7†	379.3	104.1
Chubut	?	?	?	50.0	6.8	29.9	809.4	303.4	335.0	542.7†	292.4	135.8	453.5†	260.1	87.6
Santa Cruz . . .	?	?	?	71.2	52.7	10.6	403.4	341.1	25.3	657.1	562.9	43.5	742.9	627.6	60.3
Tierra del Fuego	0.1	0.0	0.1	2.1	1.0	0.8	214.1	191.8	11.9	123.4†	112.0	6.3	108.8	96.7	6.5
Magallanes (Chile)	?	?	?	?	?	?	307.7	257.2	32.0	328.5	284.0	28.7	288.3	260.0	14.9
Total							3316.2	1864.5	877.4	2736.0†	1764.8	457.6	2611.5†	1735.7†	412.9

*In terms of 1000 livestock units (rating 1 livestock unit as 1 horse, 1 head of cattle, 1 mule, 1 ass, 7 sheep, 7 goats, or 5 hogs).
†The reason for this marked decrease from 1908 to 1914 is not known to the writer. The lack of a notable increase from 1914 to 1920 may be the result of disturbed markets during and following the World War.

colony on the lower Chubut, established in 1865, went west to the eastern Andean border in 1888 and founded the colony of Diez y seis de Octubre (16th of October).

DEVELOPMENT OF RANCHING

Sheep were introduced into southern Patagonia about 1880 from the Falkland Islands and subsequently into northern Patagonia from the Pampas. Presently large blocks of land were obtained from the Argentine and Chilean governments by sheep ranching companies, and by 1895 livestock rearing had become well established. The major development of ranching, however, came after about 1900, with the establishment of regular steamship services along the Atlantic coast and the consequent assurance of a means of export of wool. Still another

factor in stimulating the development of sheep ranching seems to
have been the increase in alfalfa growing in many places in the
Pampas region, with a resulting tendency to feed cattle on this
crop rather than sheep on the natural pasture. In the humid
East Andean border cattle were introduced from Chile and furnished the basis of a livestock industry markedly different from
that which developed in the dry country to the east. Table IV
shows quantitatively the development of ranching in Patagonia.

IRRIGATION

Irrigation works were constructed in the upper Río Negro
valley in 1885, and subsequently additional works were built farther
down stream. Irregular variations in the flow of the Neuquén,
which is a tributary of the Río Negro, resulted in occasional disastrous floods in the irrigated lands along the latter stream. Studies
were made, therefore, and construction was completed in 1916,
of storage works whereby the flood waters of the Río Neuquén
are impounded a few miles above the mouth of the river in a great
natural depression, the Cuenca de Vidal, and later released for
irrigating additional acres. The Río Limay, which also is a tributary
of the Río Negro, possesses in its headwaters in the Andes a series
of lakes that help regulate the flow of the river.

RAILROADS

The Southern Railroad completed its line west from Bahía
Blanca to Neuquén in 1899 and subsequently extended it to Zapala
(Fig. 1). This line from Bahía Blanca has proved a boon to irrigation farmers in the valley of the Río Negro, to sheep ranchers in
the sections of the dry region within reach of the rails, and to cattle
raisers in the northern part of the East Andean border zone. About
1910 the Argentine government began the construction of railroads
westward from several of the Atlantic ports of Patagonia. These
railroads were planned to open to more effective development
both the ranch lands and the potential crop lands of considerable
areas. The line west from San Antonio has been constructed to
within a few miles of Bariloche and facilitates wool export from
the zone traversed. The short line from Puerto Madryn serves
the irrigated district of the lower Chubut valley. The lines from
Comodoro Rivadavia and Puerto Deseado serve sheep country.
It is planned to extend the lines from San Antonio and Puerto
Madryn west to the productive East Andean border zone, and if

this is done no doubt development of this now isolated part of Patagonia will be stimulated, with consequent increase in railway traffic. Surveys also have been made for extending one or both of the lines from Bahía Blanca and from San Antonio across the Andes to Chile.

GROWTH OF POPULATION

Although population density is low in Patagonia, there has been a steady increase since settlement began in the eighties of the nineteenth century, as is shown by Table V.

TABLE V—POPULATION GROWTH IN THE SOUTHERN TERRITORIES OF ARGENTINA AND CHILE, 1865–1920

TERRITORY	1865	1875	1885	1895	1912	1920
Neuquén	?	?	?	14,517	27,474	30,677
Río Negro	?	?	?	9,241	34,229	42,652
Chubut	?	?	?	3,748	23,316	31,021
Santa Cruz	?	?	?	1,058	8,192	18,462
Tierra del Fuego . .	?	?	?	477	2,275	2,608
Magallanes (Chile) .	195	1,144	2,085	5170	17,330*	28,960
Total	?	?	?	34,211	112,816	154,380

*Population in 1907.

THE FUTURE OF AGRICULTURE IN PATAGONIA

The agricultural possibilities of Patagonia, both for rearing livestock and for raising crops, are, in certain sections at least, far from being fully utilized. A good deal is known as to these as yet unutilized possibilities, but various studies should be made, including the correlation of data now in the hands of several Argentine government bureaus, in order that so far as possible mistakes may be avoided in the future and past mistakes be rectified.

IN THE SHEEP RANCHING REGION

In the dry sheep ranching region further development undoubtedly will be along lines similar to those so far pursued. Data should be gathered, however, as to the carrying capacity of the ranges in different parts of the region at different seasons of the year and as to desirable consequent seasonal movements of flocks. The scarcity of water for stock in summer now keeps the number of animals grazed below the carrying capacity of the vegetation on certain ranges. Artesian and other water possibilities should be investigated. Wherever possible, land still available for allotment should be sold or leased in blocks so laid out with reference to water holes as to make possible the maximum utilization of the ranges. Methods to prevent overgrazing and consequent decline in the carrying capacity of the ranges should be developed. The possibilities of growing alfalfa or other forage crops on small irrigated patches throughout the region should be canvassed, as well as the possibilities of obtaining such forage crops from the larger irrigated areas within the region and from the East Andean border, since supplementary winter feed probably would considerably increase the number of livestock that could be reared.

In southern Patagonia, where the climate of the sheep ranching region is less arid and the carrying capacity of the pasture consequently higher, the rearing of sheep for frozen mutton as well as for wool has led to some replacement of merinos by Lincolns, and the export of frozen meat from refrigerators at coast ports is increasing. The extent to which this change in type of sheep reared may well be encouraged is worthy of careful investigation.

In the Irrigated Areas

The irrigation cropping possibilities in the valleys of the Río Negro, the Río Chubut, and the Río Colorado have been studied primarily from the engineering viewpoint. Further studies in these areas as to lands suitable for development should be carried out, studies involving availability of water, cost of supplying water, character of soils, kinds of crops that might be raised, and the probable soundness of such development. It would appear that the chief function of these larger irrigated areas, as of the small ones, may well be the supplying of supplementary feed to the sheep ranches, and the finishing of stock brought from the ranches, rather than the raising of crops to be exported from Patagonia. Certain types of crops, such as vegetables, may be raised to supply food to the local population, but wheat probably can better be imported from the Pampas farming region. At present there is only a very small acreage of any kind of crop grown south of the lower Chubut valley on the Atlantic coast or of latitude 44° S. along the margin of the Andes (Table VI). Judging from the kinds of crops grown on the few acres now in cultivation and the climatic data available, summer temperatures in these southerly

TABLE VI—AREA UNDER CROPS IN THE SOUTHERN TERRITORIES OF ARGENTINA AND CHILE (IN HECTARES), 1895–1920

TERRITORY	1895	1914	1920
Neuquén	3,512	10,784*	9,459
Río Negro	1,458	37,166	42,606
Chubut	5,556	13,742	9,784
Santa Cruz	.....	1,945	4,515
Tierra del Fuego	.....	87	109
Magallanes (Chile)	.....	....	619
Total	.....	....	67,092

*Area in 1912.

TABLE VII—AREAS IN SPECIFIC CROPS, SOUTHERN TERRITORIES OF ARGENTINA AND CHILE (IN HECTARES), 1920

TERRITORY	ALFALFA	WHEAT	OATS	MAIZE	BARLEY	VINEYARDS	POTATOES	ETC.	TOTAL
Neuquén	2,705	4,487	816	391	507	77	117	359	9,459
Río Negro	26,983	4,827	2,320	3,096	2,005	1,581	497	1,297	42,606
Chubut	4,559	3,517	886	22	388	39	209	164	9,784
Santa Cruz	4,183	4	103	1	22	.....	84	118	4,515
Tierra del Fuego	......	......	84	.....	10	.....	...	15	109
Magallanes (Chile)	......	......	598	.....	.....	.....	21	.....	619
Total	38,430	12,835	4,807	3,510	2,932	1,697	928	1,953	67,092

latitudes of Patagonia are not sufficiently high to afford a period long enough to ripen wheat or maize (Table VII). Forage crops of several varieties, however, can be grown in the dry region with irrigation wherever water is available and in the Andean border without irrigation.

In the East Andean Border Zone

The somewhat greater density of population and of livestock and the presence of some crop growing in the Andean border zone as compared with the sheep ranching region (Figs. 5, 6, and 8) suggest that in this mountain borderland the possibilities of development may be considerable. As a matter of fact, the potentialities of this zone constituted a major reason for beginning the construction of railroads westward up the valley of the Río Negro and from San Antonio and Puerto Madryn. In the Andean border the rainfall is sufficient to produce natural pasture with a much higher carrying capacity than exists in the drier region to the east, and crops can be grown, except on the more porous soils of glacial outwash flats, without irrigation (Figs. 9A and 9B). More studies must be carried out, however, before precise estimates can be made as to how much land can be put into crops and as to how much more livestock can be reared in the area. Three types of commercial agriculture seem to have promise in addition to cattle ranching, namely dairying, apple growing (summer frosts may make this impracticable), and the production of forage crops to be sold to the sheep ranches to the east.

Economic Possibilities in the Patagonian Andes

A not unimportant phase of the economic development of the Andean border is closely related to the non-agricultural forested mountains to the west. This latter zone is one of great natural beauty. Its heavily glaciated mountains and valleys with many arrestingly beautiful lakes and streams are a resource that has been recognized by the Argentine government in its establishment of the Parque Nacional del Sur and in the proposal of the Chilean government to establish a similar recreation reserve. If this mountain zone develops into tourist country, as it well may, the agricultural border zone is the area where hotels will be established and various other means of caring for visitors set up. An important local market for the products of farms and ranches will thus develop, and the prosperity of the area be increased. From the tourist standpoint further study of both the Andean border and of the mountain zone is desirable.

In addition to the value of the Andean forests in Patagonia as regulators of stream flow and as elements in the scenic beauty of the landscape, they constitute a readily available source of fuel and

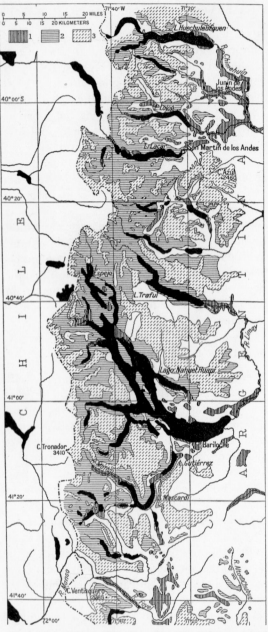

FIG. 9A (continuous with Fig. 9B) — Classification of land in Argentine part of Andes and in East Andean border, between 39° 40′ and 43° 40′ S. Scale, 1 : 1,400,000. Key to symbols: 1, land suitable for crops, in part requiring irrigation; 2, virgin forests suitable for timber supply; 3, alpine zone, above about 1500 meters, with grassy meadows suitable for summer grazing.

building material for near-by agricultural settlements. On the Chilean side certain species, particularly the alerce (*Fitzroya patagonica*) and the roble (*Nothofagus obliqua*), are cut and sold for timber outside the region. The forests as a whole are not composed of valuable timber species, but the character of the climate is such that it has been suggested that the native species of trees be replaced by several desirable varieties of conifers from the Puget Sound region of North America. Such replacement will only be practicable on a large scale, if at all, in the somewhat distant future.

Bailey Willis has stressed the significance of the hydroelectric possibilities of the Patagonian Andes. Heavy rainfall in the mountains gives rise to streams of large volume. The gradient of these streams is high, and consequently the power resource is great. At present, however, no important use is made of this resource. With the building of railroads to and across this section of the Andes, hydro-electric power might be used to run the trains, for coal imported from overseas would be costly. The demands of the local population for current for light and for small amounts of power in the towns and on ranches could also be met. Whether or not any considerable manufacturing industries will develop to use much of the possible electric power is highly conjectural.

Ranching Probably the Dominant Industry of Patagonia in the Future

No mineral wealth of significance except the petroleum field at

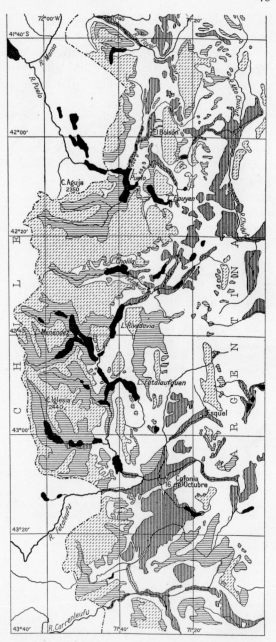

Fig. 9B (title concluded)—Lakes are in black. The white areas in Argentine territory represent grazing lands, composed of recently burned forest areas, brushy mountain slopes, and drier grassland areas east of the Andes. The map is reduced and generalized from the land classification maps on a scale of 1 : 200,000 in Bailey Willis: Northern Patagonia, New York, 1914.

Comodoro Rivadavia has been discovered in Patagonia. It appears likely, therefore, that, except for a possible future tourist business in and near the Andes, continued development of the southern territories of Argentina and Chile will rest on agriculture—sheep or cattle ranching for the most part, with subsidiary crop raising in places.

The pioneer character of agricultural development in most parts of Patagonia is strongly pronounced. The relatively new and unstabilized sheep ranching industry dominates the economic life; changed though it may become in numerous respects, ranching undoubtedly is the best use of most of the area and will continue economically supreme. Close settlement can never be expected except in the larger irrigated valleys and in the East Andean border. In the latter areas lies most of the land now under crops, and only in these areas can there ever be much increase in crop acreage.

BIBLIOGRAPHY

Anderson, Hans. Die natürlichen Grundlagen und die gegenwärtigen Ver-hältnisse der landwirtschaftlichen Produktion in Chile, *Tropenpflanzer*, Beiheft No. 2 of Vol. 28, 1925.

Bonarelli, Guido. Tierra del Fuego y sus turberas, *Anal. Minist. de Agric.: Sección Geol., Mineral. y Minería*, Vol. 12, No 3, Dirección General de Minas, Geología e Hidrología, Buenos Aires, 1917.

Davis, Gualterio G. Servicio Meteorológico Argentino: Historia y organización, con un résumen de los resultados. Ministerio de Agricultura, Buenos Aires, 1914.

Denis, Pierre. The Argentine Republic: Its Development and Progress. London, 1922.

Eickhoff, Fritz. Patagonien (Südargentinien). Leipzig, no date [1925?].

Franze, Bruno. Die Niederschlagsverhältnisse in Südamerika. *Petermanns Mitt. Ergänzungsheft No. 193*. 1927.

Hauman, Lucien. Étude phytogéographique de la Patagonie, *Bull. Soc. Royale de Botanique de Belgique*, Vol. 58, 1926, pp. 105–179.

Hosseus, C. Curt. El proyectado Parque Nacional del Sud, *Bol. Minist. de Agric. (República Argentina)*, Vol. 20, 1916, pp. 647–700.

Jefferson, Mark. The Rainfall of Chile. *Amer. Geogr. Soc. Research Ser. No. 7*, New York, 1921.

Jones, Clarence F. Agricultural Regions of South America, *Econ. Geogr.*, Vol. 4, 1928, pp. 1–30, 159–186, 267–294.

Krüger, Paul. Die Patagonischen Anden zwischen dem 42. und 44. Grade südlicher Breite. *Petermanns Mitt. Ergänzungsheft No. 164*. 1909.

Kühn, Franz. Die patagonischen Häfen Argentiniens, *Zeitschr. Deutsch. Wissenschaftl. Vereins zur Kultur- und Landeskunde Argentiniens*, Vol. 1, 1915, pp. 65–80.

Kühn, Franz. Die atlantische Küstenschiffahrt Patagoniens, *Mitt. Deutsch-Südamer. Inst.*, Vol. 8, 1920, pp. 39–48.

Kühn, Franz. Physiognomie argentinischer Wirtschaftslandschaften, *Petermanns Mitt.*, Vol 70, 1924, pp. 224–229 and 271–276.

Kühn, Franz. Argentinien: Handbuch zur physischen Landeskunde. 2 vols. Breslau, 1927.

McBride, G. M. The Agrarian Problem in Chile, *Geogr. Rev.*, Vol. 20, 1930, pp· 574–586.

Nordenskjöld, Otto. Südamerika: Ein Zukunftsland der Menschheit. Stuttgart, 1927.

Nordenskjöld, Otto. Wissenschaftliche Ergebnisse der Schwedischen Expedition nach den Magellansländern 1895–1897 unter Leitung von Dr. Otto Nordenskjöld. 3 vols. Stockholm, 1905–1907.

Provincia de Buenos Aires. Anuario estadístico para el año 1924. I, Territorio y población. Dirección General de Estadística de la Provincia de Buenos Aires, Buenos Aires, 1926.

República Argentina. Anuario del comercio exterior . . . años 1921, 1922 y 1923, y noticia sumaria del período 1910–1923. 2 vols. Dirección General de Estadística de la Nación, Buenos Aires, 1924.

República Argentina. *Boletín Mensual de Estadística Agropecuaria.* Buenos Aires, monthly.

República Argentina. Censo general de los Territorios Nacional, 1920. 2 vols. Ministerio del Interior, Asesoría Letrada de Territorios Nacionales, Buenos Aires, 1923.

República Argentina. Mapa de los ferrocarriles de la República Argentina. 1 : 1,500,000. Dirección de Tierras, Colonización y Fomento de los Ferro-Carriles del Estado, Buenos Aires, 1922.

República Argentina. Tercer censo nacional (1914), Vol. 6: Censo ganadero. Buenos Aires, 1917.

República de Chile. *Anuario Estadístico.* Oficina Central de Estadística, Santiago, annually.

República de Chile. Censo de población (1920). Dirección General de Estadística, Santiago, 1925.

Richelet, J. A. La ganadería en los Territorios del Sud, *Bol. Minist. de Agric.* (*República Argentina*), Vol. 19, 1915, pp. 655–675.

Rothkugel, Max. Los bosques patagónicos. Oficina de Bosques y Yerbales, Dirección General de Agricultura y Defensa Agrícola, Ministerio de Agricultura (Argentina), Buenos Aires, 1916.

Schmieder, Oscar. Länderkunde Südamerikas. (Series: Enzyklopädie der Erdkunde). Leipzig and Vienna, 1932.

Skottsberg, Carl. Übersicht über die wichtigsten Pflanzenformationen Südamerikas S. von 41°, ihre geographische Verbreitung und Beziehungen zum Klima, *Kungl. Svenska Vetenskapsakademiens Handlingar*, Vol. 46, 1910, No. 1.

Soldano, F. A. Le barrage du Neuquen et les irrigations dans la vallée du Río Negro. Buenos Aires, 1919.

Steffen, Hans. Westpatagonien. 2 vols. Berlin, 1919.

Willis, Bailey. Northern Patagonia. One vol. of text and one case of maps. Comisión de Estudios Hidrológicos, Bureau of Railways, Ministry of Public Works, Argentine Republic, New York, 1914.

PIONEER SETTLEMENT IN THE UNION OF SOUTH AFRICA

John H. Wellington

Amount of New Land Still Available

IN the Union of South Africa the age of the pioneer settler is fast drawing to a close. Since the Act of Union in 1909 successive governments have realized the importance to the country of liberal schemes of land settlement, and, since the World War of 1914–1918, the disposal of crown lands to settlers has proceeded so rapidly that at the present time but little remains for white settlement. It is expected that within a few years all the available crown land worth purchasing will have been sold to settlers, who, according to the terms of their agreements, must occupy and develop their holdings. On the face of things, therefore, it would appear that the "waste spaces" have almost been filled up and that there is little opportunity in South Africa for the pioneer settler. But, in actual fact, the opportunity is not quite so far gone. Several millions of acres of undeveloped land are at present held by land companies that are disposing of ground for settlement in various parts of the Transvaal and Natal. Indeed, this appears to form the bulk of land in the Union available and suitable for pioneer farming, since it is generally admitted that the crown lands still to be disposed of are of comparatively small value.

No Land Available from Subdivision of Older Farms

It may be inquired if land will be available for settlers as the result of a possible division of farms in the more developed parts of the country, where intensive methods of farming have greatly increased production. In a few instances this is probably so, but in general there seems to be a tendency for farms to become larger instead of smaller, for, with the occupation of land inferior in quality to the picked farms of the early settlers, it is found that a greater area for general farming is necessary. In times past the practice of dividing farms into separate holdings for the sons of the family has led to disastrous results: it has been largely responsible for the development of the "poor white" now forced to earn his livelihood in competition with the native. The process of farm subdivision is not likely to be adopted to any great extent, and land

146

for settlement on a considerable scale is not to be expected from this source. The immigrant with capital will, of course, always be able to acquire land in the more settled and prosperous parts of the country, and, in so far as he introduces improved methods and new ideas, he will be in a sense a pioneer. For the present,

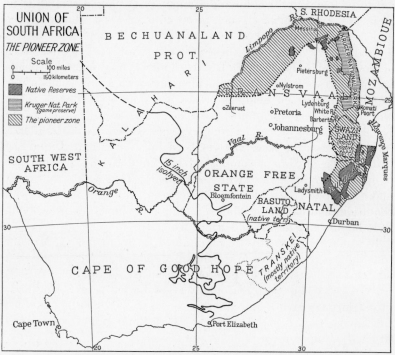

FIG. 1—The location and extent of the pioneer zone in the Union of South Africa. Scale, 1 : 16,-000,000. The Native Reserves, including rather more than half of Swaziland, are not open to white settlement. The Kruger National Park is also not available for settlement. The area to the west of the 15-inch isohyet is too dry for extensive settlement, and in the south and southwest of the Cape Province, where the rainfall is sufficient, there is little suitable land unoccupied.

however, it will be convenient to limit this inquiry to the case of the settler who is confronted with the task of occupying and developing virgin land on the confines of civilization.

LIMITATIONS DUE TO WATER SUPPLY[1]

In estimating the area still available for pioneer settlement in the Union of South Africa (Fig. 1) consideration must be given to

[1] On this general topic see H. D. Leppan: The Agricultural Development of Arid and Semi-Arid Regions, With Special Reference to South Africa, Johannesburg, 1928. Chapters 1–7 and 13 deal with South Africa.

two different sets of factors: water supply and the reservation of land for various purposes by the Government. The former factor is of the utmost significance, and the isohyet of 20 inches (Fig. 6) will be taken as a convenient boundary of the area suitable for settlement on a considerable scale. It is true that many excellent farms are to be found in areas having a much lower annual rainfall than 20 inches, but, in general, such farms enjoy the special advantages of perennial streams or of exceptionally good supplies of underground water. Moreover, there are still vacant considerable areas of crown land in the southern Kalahari, but occupation here depends on the success of the boring machine, and with a precarious water supply, ranching on holdings of not less than 10,000 acres is the only type of settlement unit possible in this area. Although the Kalahari is bush or savana country and excellent as pasture land, its water resources have not yet been fully investigated, and the little boring already accomplished has emphasized the difficulty of opening up this area to white settlement. It is a tract that must make its appeal to those who have been born and bred in such conditions and who know almost instinctively how to wrest a living from land nearly devoid of surface water.

It would undoubtedly be maintained by many South Africans that the 20-inch isohyet in the summer rainfall region is too low a limit for settlement in a region of such uncertain rainfall. Admittedly it is low, but with reasonably favorable subsidiary conditions mixed farming is not infrequently successful in such areas when the human factor is right. Most of the land recently settled is situated within the 20–30 inch rainfall zone.

LIMITATIONS DUE TO NATIVE AND GAME RESERVES

The second limiting factor is the establishment of Native Reserves, and, in the eastern Transvaal, of the Kruger National Park as a game sanctuary. The native areas as they exist at present within the pioneer zone are shown on the accompanying map (Fig. 1). It should be recognized that Basutoland and Swaziland are administered and controlled by the Imperial Government, Basutoland being occupied entirely by natives and about one-half of Swaziland being native territory; the remainder is held by white settlers under concession. The Transkeian territories of the eastern Cape Province are almost entirely occupied by native tribes, so that these large areas are ruled out of account as possible land for white settlement. The whole question of segregation of natives in reserves is at present under consideration by the Union Government, and the Prime Minister's proposals trend in the direction of the enlargement of these areas by allowing natives to purchase land on the margins of them. Considerable areas of crown land in the vicinity of the Native Reserves are, therefore, being held for the possible extension of the native areas when the policy of segregation comes up for consideration during the lifetime of the present parliament.

There is no likelihood, either, of the area occupied by the Kruger National Park being reduced to make room for white settlers. The recent enlargement of this game reserve by the linking of the Shingwedzi portion in the north to the Sabie Reserve in the south has necessitated the provision of land outside of the reserve for settlers who have thus been displaced. So long as the game flourishes the South African Government will undoubtedly maintain this reserve, of which the country is justly proud. With the arid and semi-arid areas and the reserves eliminated, the land still unsettled or only recently settled is reduced to the areas indicated in Figure 1. It will be recognized, however, that there are little "islands" of sparsely settled land still comparatively undeveloped that are not included in this zone. They are due in the main to local conditions specially unfavorable for settlement and can scarcely be considered in a general survey of this kind.

PHYSICAL CONDITIONS IN THE PIONEER ZONE

Physical Regions: The Limpopo Valley

The topographic features of the pioneer belt may best be considered by reference to the physical regions shown in Figure 2.[2] It will be seen that a considerable part of the zone lies within the Limpopo Valley, a wide, shallow, pre-Karroo (Paleozoic) feature of which only the southern part falls within the boundary of the Union. The topographic character of this region is comparatively simple: the river has cut a wide plain in the old granite which forms the base of the continent. Most of the surface is covered

[2] For a more detailed description of the physical character of the pioneer belt see J. H. Wellington: The Natural Regions of the Transvaal, *South African Geogr. Journ.*, Vol. 10, 1927, No. 10, pp. 5–24.

with a light sandy soil,[3] weathered from the granite and apparently of low fertility. Little soil investigation has as yet been made in this region, but it seems probable that only the narrow alluvial strips along the stream courses can be considered as areas of good soil. At present most of the region is covered with dense bush increasing in density to almost corridor-forest character along stream courses. Few mountains break the even surface of the region, and only here and there do kopjes, formed by fragments of the Karroo system (Permo-Triassic), interrupt the level character of the plain. The area lies for the most part below the altitude of 3000 feet and may therefore be considered as Low Veld.

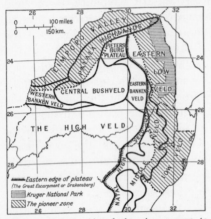

FIG. 2—Relationship of the pioneer zone to the physical regions of the northeastern part of the Union of South Africa. Scale (as also of Figs. 3, 5, 6, 7), 1 : 20,000,000. High Veld is land over 4000 feet in altitude, Middle Veld is from 3000 to 4000 feet, Low Veld is below 3000 feet.

THE PALALA HIGHLANDS

To the south of this region the pioneer belt merges into the Palala Highlands, which comprise the Waterberg in the south and the Zoutpansberg in the north. This region, in contrast to the Limpopo Valley lowland, is extremely uneven and rugged owing mainly to the occurrence of bold escarpments of Waterberg sandstone facing the center of the Transvaal. A great deal of the area is thus excessively rocky, and between the ranges the valley plains are often covered with deep sandy deposits weathered from the ridges. Most of the fertile soil is located along the stream courses, and these alluvial strips have an enhanced value because of the perennial character of the streams which derive their water from the sandstone beds. It should be noted, however, that these same streams, such as the Sand, Palala, and Magalakwin Rivers, become intermittent in flow when they pass into the preceding region owing to evaporation and the loss of water by percolation in the sand. Some idea of the topographic control of settlement in this region may be derived from the fact that one land company has

[3] On the soils of South Africa see the Official Soil Map in 1:3,000,000 accompanying Official Soil Map of the Union of South Africa, *Science Bull. No. 79 (Div. of Chemistry Series No. 94)*, Union of South Africa Dept. of Agriculture, Pretoria, 1929.

farms for sale in this area varying in price from about 5 shillings to more than £ 4 a morgen (a morgen = 2.17 acres). Farms at the former price consist mainly of stony outcrops with little or no arable land and water difficult of access, whilst the higher prices are determined mainly by the location of the farms in river valleys with a higher percentage of arable land, in consequence, and facilities for a certain amount of irrigation. In a region of such topographical diversity the situation of a farm becomes of primary significance in estimating its value. The valleys in this region lie approximately between the altitudes of 3000 and 4000 feet and may, therefore, be considered as Middle Veld, but the ridges and higher slopes exceed 4000 feet above sea level and these may be grouped as High Veld areas. In the extreme northeast of this region, i.e. in the eastern valleys of the Zoutpansberg, the land is more distinctly of the pioneer type than anywhere else in the Union. It is unsettled and unsurveyed crown land which is not being alienated by the government so as to allow for the possible extension of the adjoining Bavenda Native Reserve.

The Central Bush Veld

It will be noticed from Figure 2 that a small part of the Central Bush Veld of the Transvaal has been included in the pioneer zone. Most of this central basin has been settled within the last ten or fifteen years, and through the Springbok Flats, which form some of the best arable land of the region, a railway now runs from Naboomspruit to Zebedelia (see Fig. 10). A few farms held by the land companies, however, are still unoccupied, but most of the region has already passed out of the pioneer state of development.

The Eastern Low Veld

The remainder of the zone includes those extra-plateau areas that lie to the east of the Great Escarpment, or Drakensberg (Fig. 2), known as the Eastern Low Veld, extending southwards into Zululand. In this region the Kruger National Park occupies a great strip of country along the boundary of the Transvaal. The land still unsettled or only recently occupied lies near the western margin of this reserve. The surface of the area is formed of the denuded older granite like that of the Limpopo Valley, and the rolling surface is broken occasionally by granite tors, or monadnocks, such as Legotte's Peak near the White River settlement, or by fragments of the pre-Paleozoic Swaziland system which forms ranges such as the Murchison and Sutherland Ranges and the Barberton mountain land. The general character, however, is that of a plain descending from rather over 3000 feet at the foot of the Drakensberg to about 1000 feet at the western boundary of the park. As in the Limpopo Valley, the soils of the area are sandy and porous, the richest ground lying in the stream valleys. Rainfall and water supply, which will be considered later, constitute the main difficulties in the development of this area, but in the vicinity of perennial streams the intensive cultivation of tropical and sub-tropical fruits can be carried on with great success, as the well-established settlement at Tzaneen has proved. In this area crown land has recently been sold at £ 10 a morgen, but it must be admitted that the conditions here are not quite typical of the greater part of the region farther removed from the edge of the plateau. Over most of the region, however, the bush-covered country is eminently suitable for stock farming, and the occurrence of East Coast fever can be held in check by systematic dipping. The presence of the game reserve necessarily entails a certain loss of stock, for *Felis leo* has not yet learned to respect the rather unconvincing reserve boundary. On one ranch of 100,000 morgen the loss due to vermin does not exceed about fifty head of stock annually, and, since the size of farms in this area is generally less than 4000 morgen, marauders from the reserve tend to add spice to life rather than to constitute a serious menace to settlement.

In Zululand the pioneer area is comparatively small on account of the great extent of the Native Reserves. The land still unsettled or in the pioneer stage of development is situated mainly in the coastal plain, here formed chiefly by alluvial deposition, and lies mostly below 3000 feet. This Low Veld area, however, merges into a Middle Veld region westwards (see Fig. 2), and the even character of the plain gives place to rolling upland country with deep-cut wide valleys whose grass slopes form admirable pasture land. The flooded plains of the larger rivers, such as the Umkuzi and Umfolozi, are arable areas of as rich soil as any to be found in the Union. Immediately after the World War, when the cotton boom was at its height, the government, in response to popular demand, disposed of considerable areas of crown land mainly to ex-service men with capital, who were eager to develop this virgin country. The prospects for cotton and sugar cane appeared to be incomparably good; but the results, despite adequate capital and unstinted hard work, have been little short of disastrous. The causes of this failure are mainly climatic and will be considered later.

TOPOGRAPHY AND HEALTH

The exceedingly healthy character of the South African climate is well known, and, if the somewhat high daytime summer temperatures of the lower areas be excepted, the climate is almost ideal for white settlement.[4] But topography has a special significance in its relationship to the incidence of malaria in South Africa. In Figure 3 are shown the three generally recognized malarial areas. The zone where the disease is "serious" is confined mainly to the Low Veld areas, comprising the pioneer belt, and extends towards the center of the Transvaal along the river valleys. The unfortunate fact must be stated that the best agricultural lands in this zone are often most adversely affected by the disease, which in years of good rainfall constitutes a serious

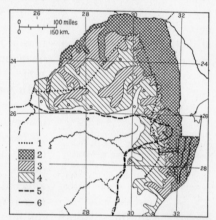

FIG. 3—Conditions affecting health. 1, limit of pioneer zone; 2, malaria serious—invariably a summer epidemic, in parts of Zululand continuous; 3, malaria moderate; 4, malaria slight, occasionally epidemic; 5, southern (in the Transvaal) and western limit of *Bilharzia* after A. Porter (see the text); 6, outline of area (in Zululand) where nagana, a disease transmitted to livestock by the tsetse fly, is prevalent; o, location of certain towns (for names see Fig. 10).

menace to white occupation in these areas. There is no doubt, of course, that with proper precautions the anopheles may be kept out of dwelling houses and reduced in number by the draining of pools and marshes, but the pools are valuable for watering stock in the dry season when many of the rivers cease to flow, so that the control of the pest by this means has this disadvantage. Many settlers in the "serious" malarial zone send their families to High Veld areas for the summer months, and others leave their farms in summer entirely to the supervision of natives. The necessity for some such procedure is recognized by the government in the conditions of

[4] J. H. Wellington: Some Physical Influences in the Human Geography of South Africa, *South African Journ. of Sci.*, Vol. 26, 1929 (Being the Report of the South African Assn. for the Advancement of Sci.), pp. 80–94.

tenure for crown lands, for, whilst in other areas personal occupation of the farm is required for eleven months of the year, in this zone only six months' occupation by a white owner is insisted on.

In response to widespread demands the present Union government has announced its intention of taking immediate steps to eradicate malaria. Presumably these efforts to exterminate the anopheles will be made in conjunction with the governments of adjoining low-lying territories, and there is every reason to believe that there will soon be a great improvement in the situation.

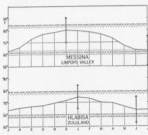

FIG. 4—Mean monthly temperature (curve), mean annual range (shaded belt), and mean monthly range of coldest and warmest month (double-headed arrows) at two representative stations in the pioneer zone.

In the health map (Fig. 3) the limits of the incidence of bilharziosis, a disease communicated by a parasitic worm (*Bilharzia*) found in watercourses, are also shown. Most of the streams in the pioneer zone are inhabited by affected snails, and, although the disease is no barrier to settlement, it does lower the vitality of both adults and children in this area. Steps are being taken to disseminate information as to methods by which the affected snails may be removed from the rivers and pools.

In a small area in Zululand shown on the map the tsetse fly is present, and nagana, the disease transmitted to livestock by that fly, has up to now prevented stock farming on a large scale in the excellent pastoral country in this part of the pioneer zone. Parts of the northern Transvaal were formerly "fly areas" but are now quite free of the pest. Investigations at present in progress promise well for the extermination of the tsetse in Zululand, when pastoral farming will be possible in the bush and grass country of the Low and Middle Veld.

CLIMATIC FACTORS: TEMPERATURE

So far as crop production is concerned, the temperature conditions of the pioneer zone call for little comment. They are everywhere sufficiently high for the cultivation of tropical crops. Two representative stations may be taken to show the mean monthly temperatures and the mean temperature ranges. Messina (22° 20′ S. and 30° 3′ E.; altitude 1950 feet) is typical of most of the Limpopo

Valley, and Hlabisa (28° 8′ S. and 31° 52′ E.; altitude 800 feet) in Zululand is fairly representative of the eastern area. The mean monthly temperatures and the temperature ranges at these two stations are shown in Figure 4.

The mean maximum temperatures suggest a high evaporation factor, but unfortunately there are no evaporation tanks in any part of the zone, and hence no records are available. The average annual evaporation from a free-water surface at Johannesburg, Cape Town, and at five conservation dams in the southern Cape Province is about 75 inches. It is probable that in the Limpopo Valley of the Eastern Low Veld the annual evaporation exceeds this amount; over the Zululand region estimation is more hazardous and might be definitely misleading.

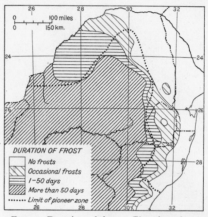

FIG. 5—Duration of frost. The pioneer zone is mostly Low Veld (below 3000 ft.) or Middle Veld (3000–4000 ft.). In consequence frosts are nowhere sufficiently severe to handicap seriously the cultivation of tropical and sub-tropical crops. (Figs. 5, 6, 7 based on maps by Union Meteorological Office.)

The duration of the period in which frosts may occur in the pioneer zone is shown in Figure 5, based on the frost map prepared by the Union Meteorological Office. The whole of the eastern area is shown as being frost free, but, in fact, light ground frosts do occasionally occur in the valleys in northern Natal and Zululand, but they are not of sufficient severity to preclude the successful cultivation of sugar cane. In the Palala Highlands region, where the frost period is in most parts of less than fifty days' duration, cotton and tobacco are grown successfully. There is thus little direct control of agricultural production by temperature conditions.

RAINFALL

It is, however, otherwise with rainfall, which is by far the most important factor controlling agricultural development in the zone.[5] From Figure 6, based on the map published by the Union Meteorological Office, it will be observed that the Limpopo Valley and

[5] F. E. Plummer and H. D. Leppan: Rainfall and Farming in the Transvaal, *Transvaal Univ. College Bull. No. 12*, Pretoria, 1927.

the Eastern Low Veld are areas of low rainfall when compared with the rest of the Transvaal. The Limpopo Valley is, in fact, the worst watered area of considerable size in the province, but the parts of the Eastern Low Veld removed from the edge of the plateau appear from the scanty records to be rather more favored. Messina (Grenfell Camp), with an annual total of 15.51 inches,

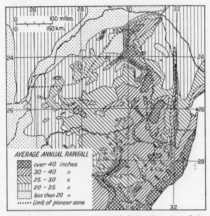

FIG. 6—Average annual rainfall. In spite of the predominantly summer type of rainfall orographic influences are discernible in the heavy rains of the edge of the plateau (Drakensberg) and in the Palala Highlands region (see Fig. 2). The best-watered part of the pioneer zone is Zululand.

may be taken as a fairly typical station in the Limpopo Valley, although its annual total is probably rather below that of the valley as a whole. It will be realized that the paucity of the recording stations in the pioneer zone, and the short records of most of those that do exist, make it impossible to give more than approximations for the regions as a whole. From the monthly averages shown in Figure 8 it will be observed that very little winter rainfall occurs (April–September), 93 per cent of the total annual precipitation occurring in the six summer months. In Figure 7 the seasonal distribution of the rainfall is shown based on the map published by the Meteorological Office.

RAINFALL RELIABILITY, ESPECIALLY IN SPRING

In agricultural matters by far the most critical feature of the rainfall over most of South Africa is its degree of reliability. This may perhaps best be expressed by the average deviation of the annual totals from the mean for the available period.

In the case of Messina the deviation is 25 per cent from the mean of the period 1907 (when the records began) to 1925, reckoned by hyetal years (July to June). Of more particular significance is the reliability for the first three summer months, when rain is needed for the starting of the crops. The mean of the quarter October to December for the period 1907–1925 is 6.41 inches, and the percentage deviation 37. In the Waterberg, to the south of the Limpopo Valley, the average annual rainfall is considerably higher, and the area is altogether better watered. For the Eastern Low Veld the recording stations in the heart of the pioneer zone have records that are too short to give a fair indication of the rainfall conditions. The selected representative station, Free State Camp

(23° 51′ S. and 30° 40′ E.), at the foot of the northern slopes of the Murchison Range, over a period of eight complete years has a mean annual rainfall of 23.6 inches and an average deviation from the mean of 25 per cent. The average for the October to December quarter is 8.9 inches, and the average deviation 26 per cent.

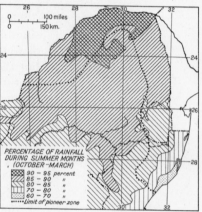

FIG. 7—Seasonal distribution of rainfall. Except along the coastal plain of Zululand the rainfall in the pioneer zone is everywhere mainly associated with the high temperatures and low pressure of the summer. In Zululand a considerable rainfall derives from the atmospheric depressions which sweep northwards along the coast in winter.

In Zululand, although this part of the zone is of small area, two hyetal regions must be recognized. The Lebombo Range, which trends north and south along the eastern boundary of the Transvaal and Swaziland, extends southwards into Zululand, where it is known as the Ubombo Range. To the east of this feature the rainfall varies from about 28 inches to over 48 inches along the coastal strip. To the west of the range, however, a rain shadow appears to be formed; and the average annual totals are in many places less than 25 inches. From the point of view of health conditions the western drier area is higher and more suitable for white settlement than the wetter coastal region. Rain gauges in the unsettled parts of Zululand are very scattered and have only recently been set up. The selected station, Nongoma (27° 53′ S. and 31° 36′ E.), lies to the west of the Ubombo Range at an altitude of 2500 feet, and its average annual total of 37.1 inches would appear to be rather higher than the totals for some of the unsettled or recently settled areas. The average deviation from the mean during the period is 30 per cent. For the October to December quarter the mean is 14.2

inches, and the average deviation from the mean for this quarter is 26 per cent.

The actual annual rainfall at these three stations and the October to December totals are shown in Figure 9.

TYPES AND INCIDENCE OF PRECIPITATION

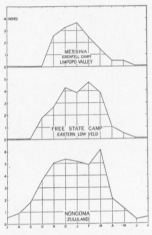

FIG. 8—Mean monthly rainfall at three selected stations in the pioneer zone.

These figures are eloquent as to the suitability of the seasonal distribution of rainfall for agricultural development, but the types and incidence of the precipitation call for some comment. Unfortunately there is little reliable information available regarding these matters in the pioneer zone, and it is not even certain to what extent it shares with the central Transvaal and Free State the high intensity usually associated with the showers of the thunderstorm type. On the Witwatersrand the average intensity for 24 hours during the period 1897 to 1906 has been calculated by H. E. Wood and found to be as follows:

TABLE I—INTENSITY OF SHOWERS

Amount of Rainfall Within 24 Hours	Mean Amount Expressed As Percentage of Average Total Annual Rainfall
0.01–0.10 inch	7
0.11–0.25 "	13
0.26–0.50 "	24
0.51–1.00 "	33
1.01 inches and over	23

It seems probable, however, that intensities in the Eastern Low Veld and Zululand would be rather lower than at Johannesburg.

In many parts of the summer rainfall region of South Africa the occurrence of hail associated with thunderstorms causes a certain amount of loss of stock and of crops. In the pioneer zone, however, hailstorms do not appear to be frequent or severe and apparently do not often cause serious damage.

SURFACE WATER SUPPLY

The critical feature about the rainfall of the pioneer zone is that, except in parts of Zululand, the average annual means are barely sufficient for successful agriculture, as distinct from stock farming; and the liability of droughts, as shown in the percentage deviations from the normal, makes cropping a hazardous undertaking without some subsidiary source of water supply. At present no large conservation dams have been constructed in the pioneer zone, and it is doubtful if large schemes will be considered in this part of the country for some time to come. The settlers would have to be prepared to construct small dams on their own farms to eke out the uncertain supplies of water from rainfall.

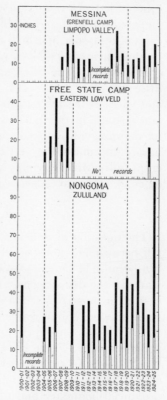

The character of the river régime has naturally a bearing on this matter. In the Palala Highlands or Waterberg region the streams are perennial, as has been previously noted, and in the Eastern Low Veld most of the streams deriving from the plateau are perennial for some distance from the Great Escarpment. Elsewhere in these regions the streams are definitely intermittent and consist in the dry winter season of a series of pools which are of the greatest value for watering stock and indeed often for human consumption as well. In Zululand the large rivers coming down from the High Veld and the interior are perennial, but the smaller

FIG. 9—Actual annual rainfall at the same three stations of the pioneer zone (the rainfall year is July to June). The full height of each bar is the total annual rainfall. The lower blank portion is the rainfall for the quarter October-December.

tributary streams in the Low Veld area are intermittent. Moreover, the flat character of the Low Veld here and the spasmodic heavy rainfall constitute another drawback, for the arable lands are subject to heavy flooding. In the Mkuzi and Hluhluwe settlements in northern Zululand the experience of settlers since 1923 has been sufficiently remarkable to warrant citing the following

details.[6] Since 1924 there has been an alternation of low and excessive rainfall, so that in 1925 the first crops after the land had been
cleared were almost entirely swept away by floods. The following
year was one of drought, with the consequent failure of the cotton
crop, and the occurrence of a further season of intense heat and
drought led to a reduction of the original price of the farms by the
Department of Lands. In spite of continued energy, sufficient
capital, and good methods, many of the settlers have had to give
up their farms and seek employment of any kind to make a living.

It should not be inferred from this that the pioneer zone is of
little value for settlement. On the contrary, many settlers have
met with great success, but it seems to be generally agreed that it
is a mistake in this part of the country to depend on the rainfall
for cropping and, indeed, that agriculture is likely to be extremely
hazardous unless the settler has stock to fall back on when his
crops fail. Mixed farming with, if anything, a greater dependence
on stock seems to be necessitated by the climatic régime.

UNDERGROUND WATER SUPPLY

The question of underground water supplies must be mentioned,
not because boreholes can supply sufficient water for crop growing
but because in some localities they form the sole source of drinking
water in the dry seasons. Fortunately boring has been fairly successful in most parts of the pioneer zone. In the old granite of
the Limpopo Valley water has been found at an average depth of
73 feet, and at the depth of 112 feet the average yield is over 21,000
gallons a day. There have been about 25 per cent failures in the
boreholes of this region. In the Eastern Low Veld conditions would
appear to be similar, except in the Lebombo Flats adjoining the
provincial boundary and to the south of the Komati River, where
parallel dolerite dikes are responsible for the great difficulty in
finding water. In Zululand, where the water table might be expected
to be high, the low yields from boreholes already sunk in the Karroo
beds are due apparently to the amorphous or colloidal matter
derived from the weathering of the constituent minerals of these
beds.[7] The difficulty of finding good supplies of underground
water in Zululand is another of the unexpected factors affecting
settlement prospects in this area.

[6] For an account of the vicissitudes of the Zululand settlers see: Report of the Department of
Lands for the Period 1st April, 1926, to 31st March, 1927, *Union Government Publ. 17*, Pretoria,
1928, pp. 43 ff.

[7] For an authoritative account of these conditions see A. L. Du Toit in *Journ. South African
Soc. of Civil Engineers*, Vol. 26, 1928.

HUMAN CONDITIONS IN THE PIONEER ZONE

NATIVE LABOR

The relationship of the native in South Africa to land development is the subject of a paper by Dr. C. T. Loram in this volume. It will suffice to say here that native labor is almost indispensable to the white settler in the pioneer zone on account of the high summer temperatures and the scarcity of white labor. Native workers generally can be obtained in most parts of the zone at low rates of wages, although Transvaal farmers are at present raising an outcry against the economic conditions that are causing a drift of the native population to the towns. For the present, however, there is no real scarcity of native labor in the pioneer zone, and it is impossible to predict the future trend of events in matters of this kind. Although recent disturbances in Natal show that the native population is not everywhere content, in most parts of the country there is a disposition on the part of the native to accept the white man's domination without question. The settler, sooner or later, recognizes that the native laborer is generally not very efficient, that he demands little, and that he has a highly developed sense of justice, which is sometimes evinced in his acceptance of punishment or in his resentment of ill treatment. There is no danger to be feared from the native in the pioneer zone unless unjustly repressive legislation provokes him to make a stand for the recognition of his rights.

WHITE SETTLERS MOSTLY OF SOUTH AFRICAN ORIGIN

In the Limpopo Valley and in the Eastern Low Veld an overwhelming majority of the settlers are of South African origin, the sons of farmers who have succeeded in the more settled parts of the country.

There does not appear to be a great inclination on the part of the older farmers to migrate to the new areas unless misfortune has dogged their steps. Some of the less valuable crown land has been occupied, with government assistance, by farming folk having little or no capital and accustomed to low standards of living. In very many cases such settlers have failed to succeed and have left their holdings owing to their inability to make a living. It must be admitted, however, that with the stoutest heart in the world successful farming in years of drought is impossible and that the element of luck is often the deciding factor in the settler's career.

The misfortune of having two years of drought at the beginning of his career would probably make it impossible for a settler to regain the lost ground before the next dry period overtakes him.

South African settlers in the pioneer zone carry their habits and customs with them to their new farms: there is little change in the manner of life. Oversea settlers, however, usually find it necessary to adopt new habits. The settler's house, unless he has considerable capital, is small, as is the case the world over, and his food is largely produced on the farm; in South Africa, maize enters largely into the diet. In many parts of the country it is advisable to seek shelter from the summer sun in the early afternoon, and, in many Low Veld towns, business houses are closed in summer between the hours of two and four in the afternoon. Beyond such changes, there need be little to alter the usual habits of the European settler.

METHOD OF LAND DISTRIBUTION

The land available for settlement in the pioneer zone is almost entirely held by the Government as crown land and by three or four land companies. The former had in December, 1929, about 600 farms still to be disposed of consisting mostly of land of an inferior type; the land companies have rather more than 3,500,000 morgen. The settlement of these areas is encouraged by the Union Government by every possible means. Under the Land Settlement Acts the Minister of Lands is empowered, *inter alia*, (1) to acquire private land by purchase or exchange for land-settlement purposes; (2) to make advances not exceeding £500 to lessees for developing their holdings; (3) to cause boring operations to be effected or improvements of a substantial nature to be erected or constructed and to add the cost thereof to the purchase price of holdings.

Five Land Boards assist the Minister in an advisory capacity for the disposal of crown lands. The qualifications of each applicant are considered in the allocation of a farm, and, although no reasons are given for the selection of any applicant, it is generally understood that the board's selections are based on the fitness of applicants to succeed under the local conditions. There can be no doubt that in most of this zone some experience of South African conditions is necessary for successful farming.

Crown land and also land purchased by the government for general settlement is leased to the successful applicant for five years, at the end of which period he has the option of purchasing the farm over a period of forty years, interest on the purchase price being 4 per cent. For the first year of the lease no rent is paid by the settler; for the second and third years, 2 per cent per annum is paid on the purchase price; and during the fourth and fifth years, 3½ per cent.

Under the "contributory purchase" scheme the Government buys a farm desired by the settler, the settler being required to pay not less than one-tenth of the purchase price before the farm is allotted to him. The remainder of the price is paid over the forty years period of the lease, but the lessee is not required to pay instalments for the first two years.

Certain conditions govern the granting of a lease to settlers taking up land under these schemes. There must be personal occupation of the farm for eleven months of the year, except that in the malarial areas already referred to the period insisted on is only six months. For the remainder of the year the farm must be left under competent supervision. Among other conditions the lessee is required to use the land for agricultural and pastoral purposes, and during the first five years the land must be improved, where no improvements exist on allotment, to the extent of 10 per cent of the value of the holding.

Under these schemes the Department of Lands is empowered to make advances to lessees up to the amount of £500 for the purchase of stock, implements, seeds, and "other things necessary for the development of the holding." A settler may, of course, acquire land held by the private land companies under the "contributory purchase" scheme. This, in fact, is often done, but the land companies themselves, of course, sell direct to the settlers, the terms being one-fifth down and the remainder to be paid over a period of ten years. No loans or advances are made by the land companies to settlers, but the companies are on the whole generous in their treatment of purchasers when instalments are not paid owing to drought or to other misfortunes.

Societies for Agricultural and Financial Help

Settlers' associations in South Africa, such as the well-known 1820 Association, exist for the purpose of advising settlers and assisting them in difficulties attendant on taking up domicile in the new country. They do not finance the settlers, but their work includes arranging for immigrants with capital to be apprenticed to experienced and successful farmers for a period before the decision is made to purchase a farm in any part of the country. The wisdom of this procedure is evident; in South Africa it is almost essential for successful settlement by immigrants.

For the general farmer there exist coöperative societies and companies supported by the Land and Agricultural Bank of South Africa. In 1928 there were 132 companies with limited liability and 259 societies with unlimited liability of members, covering almost every branch of agricultural and pastoral activity. The Land Bank makes advances to these associations to guarantee the fulfillment of their contracts, as well as for the purchase of machinery and equipment necessary for farm development. The Land Bank further makes advances to individual farmers for the erection of fences, the construction of dipping tanks and silos, the supply of water by boring or otherwise, and for other purposes. Loans are made for these purposes to settlers who hold land under agreement of purchase or lease from the Crown, and the repayment of such loans is guaranteed by the Minister of Lands. The Land Bank is indeed the main financial anchor of the farming community in South Africa, but there are also other sources of financial aid available to the settler. Storekeepers are usually willing to give credit on the basis of a first mortgage or the advance sale of the coming harvest. Whilst this provides temporary financial accommodation for the farmer, it is regarded as an evil rather than as a boon to the struggling settler. Unfortunately it is often the only course open to him if he has had the misfortune to start under adverse climatic conditions, and the hold on the land by the store-keepers is frequently a bitter theme for the invective of the farmer who happens to be a victim of circumstances. The coöperative system backed by the Land Bank is steadily improving the position of farmers, although it is still regarded by many as a halter round the neck of private enterprise.

COMMUNICATIONS

River transport in South Africa scarcely exists: almost all transport is by road and rail. The more important roads and railway lines and their connection with the main centers of population are shown in Figure 10. In the whole of the pioneer zone good roads are the exception; for the most part they are made by the farmer himself until the locality attains sufficient importance to warrant an official program of road construction by the Provincial Council.

A new and interesting development, however, is taking place in this connection. The railway system of South Africa is supplemented by the service of motor buses and lorries from railheads. Such motor services necessitate the construction of roads, and, although the heavy vehicles rapidly cut up the road surface, a

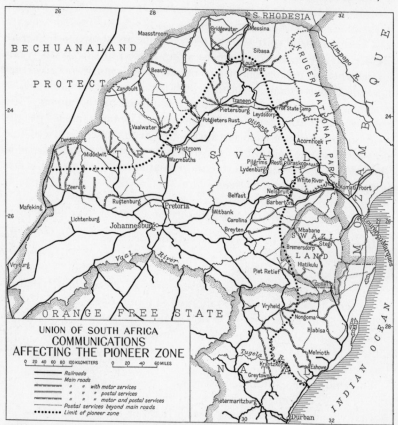

FIG. 10—Main transportation lines and postal services affecting the pioneer zone. Scale, 1 : 8,-000,000. The road motor services by coach and lorry are run in conjunction with the government railways. These services are being rapidly developed, and changes are made from month to month. The termini of the postal routes in the pioneer zone are generally branch post offices where telegrams are accepted for transmission by telephone to the nearest trunk line office.

great advantage to the locality results from the necessary road building as well as from the regular services maintained by the government railway administration.

Proximity to a railway line or a bus route naturally enhances the value of a farm, but generally this factor is far outweighed by others, such as topographical character and water supply. There are crown land farms in the Zoutpansberg district within five miles of the railway line that are valued, nevertheless, at little more than a shilling an acre, whilst other farms in the same district, fifteen miles from the railway, have recently been sold for £5 an acre. In South Africa the principle is amply demonstrated that a railway is important in land development only in so far as the land is capable of development.

The main postal routes in the pioneer zone are shown in Figure 10. Telegrams are received at offices along these routes. With regard to telephones, expansion of the net depends on the progress and success of settlement. Farm telephone lines are constructed in response to demand by farmers and are limited by the money voted each year by Parliament for this purpose. The farm line is intended to link up not more than ten farms to a trunk telephone and telegraph office; the rental of £3 10s. a mile is shared equally by all the farmers on the line. In the more sparsely settled areas the cost is prohibitive to most settlers.

Size of Farm Unit and Amount of Capital Necessary

It is impossible to generalize satisfactorily with regard to the size of the farm unit. In the areas where there is no water for irrigation and where, for the time at least, the rainfall is the only source of water supply, the average area of crown land farms is at present about 2000 to 3000 morgen (4300 to 6500 acres). In the light of recent experience it is now generally thought that in such areas the unit should be not less than 4000 to 5000 morgen. The more arable land a farm contains, the smaller, naturally, will be the unit of size.

The amount of capital necessary for stocking farms in the pioneer zone varies, of course, according to the type of farming adopted. Actually, some settlers succeed with little or no capital and repay in time the advances made by the Land Bank. For most settlers, however, some capital is essential, and £1000 is considered little enough to purchase stock, build a house, and provide sustenance for the inevitable years of drought which may unluckily occur at the beginning of the venture.

Relation of Settlers of English and Dutch Origin

With the density of population of one family to about seven square miles, it will be apparent that the population is scattered, and that, in the absence of towns or dorps at frequent intervals, the social life of the pioneer is largely restricted to the circle of his immediate neighbors. To some extent the racial origin of the settlers has a bearing on this question. The white population is composed predominantly of settlers of both English and Dutch origin, with a small percentage of other nationalities. It would be out of place to discuss here the relationship between the English and Dutch sections, nor is it possible to generalize in this matter. In spite of considerable difference of outlook between the settler from overseas and the South-African-born settler of Dutch extraction, there is often the friendliest coöperation between them, but it must be admitted that in other instances the differences in political sympathy and outlook are sufficiently emphasized to make social intercourse difficult. Amongst many Dutch South Africans there is still a feeling of hostility to the "uitlander," and too often the settler from overseas develops a complete intolerance for what he considers the intense parochialism and narrowmindedness of his Dutch neighbors. But the best influences at work in South Africa are gradually improving this position; progress, however, is slow in some parts of the country, and unfortunately there are other influences seeking to increase and exacerbate ill feeling between the white races. The language question, too, sometimes adds to the difficulty of the settler's social relationships, and the disinclination of the Dutch churches to accept religious interpretations adopted by most English churches has made progress towards coöperation in religious matters slow and difficult. These facts will suffice to point out a certain general lack of harmony in the social structure as between the white races, but it must never be lost sight of that the utmost good feeling often obtains between the two types of settlers in spite of considerable differences in outlook.

LOCAL URBAN CENTERS

The comparative loneliness of the pioneer settler's life can occasionally be relieved by visits to centers of population such as Pietersburg in the north; and, in the south, Johannesburg and Pretoria are accessible by motor car in two days from most parts of the zone. For Zululand the large center is Durban. In addition to the larger centers there are smaller villages or dorps where stores supply the necessaries of life and where the moving picture theater with its weekly show provides entertainment and some form of contact with the outside world. In the pioneer zone, however, entertainment of this kind is rarely accessible to the majority of the settlers.

Educational Facilities

The education of the settlers' children presents difficulties not yet entirely overcome. Government farm schools are the general rule where sufficient children can attend; but, in a mixed population of English and Dutch, the language medium is sometimes difficult to settle. In most of the larger towns secondary schools are available, and at Johannesburg, Pretoria, and Pietermaritzburg university education is provided. The University of Pretoria provides special courses in agriculture and farming practice.

Standard of Living

The standard of life of the settlers varies greatly according to circumstances. In some settlements, such as that of White River, where citrus cultivation has necessitated considerable capital, the standard of living is in general high, and many of the settlers have constructed dwellings that compare favorably with country houses in any part of the world. Usually, however, the settler's house is of the simplest type: a wood-and-iron structure or a thatched rondavel built by native labor at little cost. As might be expected, there are all gradations from this unassuming beginning to the elaborate bungalow sometimes built by the settler with plentiful resources. Usually, however, dwellings and habits of life are of necessity marked by extreme simplicity.

CONCLUSIONS

The pioneer zone in South Africa, although small in extent, is attractive to the settler who is prepared above all to grapple with the climate, in which the outstanding feature is a fickle rainfall. Years of drought in all parts of the zone are certain to occur, and one good year in four or five is the most that the settler can depend on. This condition overshadows all others and, in fact, necessitates a period of apprenticeship on the part of the settler from overseas who has had no experience of such conditions. Many farmers with long experience in South Africa would certainly advise a newcomer to put his money into less land in the more settled parts of the country, where intensive agriculture can be practiced, where irrigational facilities may be available, and where possibilities have been fairly tested. Success in the pioneer zone goes not necessarily to the man with much capital or even with energy and resourcefulness, but to the farmer who by experience or by instinct is equipped to play nature at her own game, by using the prodigality of the full years to counter the dry, lean years that are sure to come.

NATIVE LABOR IN SOUTHERN AFRICA*

C. T. Loram

A SUPPLY of native labor is indispensable to the pioneer in Central and South Africa. In other parts of the world, such as the United States, Canada, Australia, and New Zealand, it has been possible for the white man to build his home, till his land, and look after his stock without the help of aboriginals. The position, however, is different in Africa. The debilitating influence of a tropical and subtropical climate, the prevalence of insect-transmitted bacterial diseases, and the depredations of stock-consuming wild beasts make farming impossible in the pioneer belts without the aid of the native. Besides, he is there. Why not use him?

It may safely be said that the native is found in practically all the pioneering belts in Africa. The possible exception would be the high veld plateaus such as are found in Kenya, the Transvaal, Orange Free State, and elsewhere. These plateaus were too cold and too windswept for the warmth-loving African, besides which it was not always safe to live in the flat country and so be exposed to attacks from enemies.

MODE OF OCCUPATION OF LAND BY NATIVES

Hence, when the white pioneer comes along he finds the land already in the occupation of natives. This occupation for the most part is not close, nor are the natives engaged in any systematic cultivation of the soil or in the deliberate breeding of good stock. On the contrary the occupation is of a scattered nature, the natives

*The question of native labor represents a special problem of pioneering in tropical and sub-tropical countries with an available labor supply and hence is of particular interest. In temperate countries the pioneer either becomes a jack-of-all-trades and does all the rough work himself or he uses machines and avoids it. In Central and South Africa he can get his crop hoed by hand with native labor and for that matter have all the work of the field done for him on a low wage scale. An African pioneer thus becomes a manager of men from the start. This makes it necessary that he be also a small capitalist. For this reason the government agencies directing oversea settlement to these parts of Africa emphasize the need of men with capital. It is cheap labor and land that the African pioneer seeks, not, like his Canadian or American counterpart, just cheap land.

In view of this special interest of the problem, two papers are devoted to it in the present volume, this one by Dr. Loram and the next one by Mrs. Jollie, each the outgrowth of the author's experience and intimate contact with the African native, the one as an investigator and director of native education, the other as a practical pioneer and legislator.—EDIT. NOTE.

congregating along the river banks or round the water holes and practicing in the valleys just sufficient agriculture to provide themselves with food. Such occupation on land is generally designated "squatting."

A native squatter is always a member of some tribe and owes allegiance and certain dues of a feudal nature to his chief. Unless, however, the land on which he is living has been expressly set aside by the white man's government as a Native Reserve, the native squatter is not regarded as the owner of the soil he tills or the veld on which he pastures his herds. Such land is either expressly or by implication regarded as belonging to the Crown or European government administering the territory, and the native squatter usually pays a rental on a hut basis for the land he occupies, in addition to the poll or other form of general tax which he pays to the government.

Natives as Tenants of White Farmers

A "squatter tenancy" is a tenancy at will, except that native custom, which gives the occupant the right to reap his crops before leaving his land, is generally observed by the European government. It frequently happens that, when undeveloped or crown land is sold to a white pioneer or settler, it is sold without reference to the squatter occupation. When the new owner of the land enters into possession he generally summons a meeting of the squatters, informs them that he is the new owner of the land, announces how many native families he proposes to retain on his property, selects those he desires, and gives the remainder notice to quit at a certain date after they have reaped their crops. The dispossessed natives have the alternative of seeking a new landlord who will receive them as "labor tenants" or of attempting to find a place in a near-by Native Reserve or of gravitating towards an urban area.

In the Union of South Africa it was made illegal by the Land Act of 1913 for a white man in a so-called European area to sell or let land to a non-European without the consent of the government or to enter into any agreement with a native on a crop-sharing basis. Before 1913 it was possible for a white landowner to allow a black man to live as a tenant on his land either for a cash rental or more commonly on a crop-sharing basis, whereby the native plowed and tended the field and at harvest time gave his landlord a portion of the yield. This practice was held to be conducive to bad farming and also to prevent the sale or lease of lands to Europeans, hence it was abolished in 1913 in the Union of South Africa. It still obtains, however, in other parts of Africa.

While the white farmer in the Union of South Africa is not allowed now to charge rent to those natives who remain on his farm, he almost invariably enters into an agreement with them whereby in return for the right to live on his farm they give him three months' labor free of wages. Labor above the three months' limit is paid for sometimes in cash but often by stock. For the most part the total amount of labor given is six months. At the time when European landowners were allowed to charge rent, "Kafir farming," as it was contemptuously called, was a very profitable occupation; and owners of large farms—generally land companies—were unwilling to improve or sell their land, the easily collected rents from the tenant providing a sufficient return on the money invested.

Natives who live on the farms of Europeans, whether as rent payers under the old system or as labor tenants under the new system, are generally given a loosely defined area of land to cultivate and to build their huts on. In addition, they are usually allowed to graze a limited number of stock. Inasmuch as this stock is usually of very inferior quality—the "scrub" bull is a universal danger—and is difficult to limit, the present-day tendency in the Union of South Africa is for the farmer to refuse to allow his native labor tenants to have stock and, if the tenant objects, to eject him in favor of another or to rely entirely on native "servants," i.e. whole-time employees who receive payment all the year round but no privileges other than housing and food. The tendency of recent legislation in the Union of South Africa is to encourage servants rather than labor tenants; but this does not always work out to the benefit of the white employer, who now finds that he has to compete with the employer of native servants in the urban areas.

DRIFT OF NATIVE LABOR TO TOWNS

In South Africa as everywhere else in the world there is a drift from the rural areas to the towns. This applies to natives as well as to the whites, and the urbanized native has become a problem both to the white man in whose cities he has gone to dwell and to the white farmer who has lost his services in the country.

Apart from the natural glamour of urban life, many natives

prefer to get to the town because of the superior conditions of employment, chief of which are a regular cash salary, municipally provided housing, and good and regular food. When the increased cost of living in urban areas is taken into account, probably the real wages of a native in the town are not better than those paid in the country; but the native thinks they are, and that settles the matter for him. The native's chief objection to living in the town is the difficulty of finding suitable accommodation for his wife and family. As the government is deliberately making it more difficult for married natives to live in towns, this may effect a slightly improved labor position in the rural areas. This position, however, will not be entirely satisfactory until the relations of master and servant have been put upon a better footing.

TERMS OF EMPLOYMENT

What are these relations at present? After the pioneer farmer has decided how many natives he requires and will allow to live on his farm, he enters into a verbal contract with them stating (a) the number of days of free labor he requires in return for the right to remain on his farm, (b) the amount of land and the number of stock the native is permitted to use and own, (c) the rate of wage for such period, and (d) what services, if any, are required of the tenant's women and children. The conditions vary in different parts, but possibly the following represent the average: (a) 90; (b) as much as he needs and, say, twenty head of stock but no bulls; (c) 20 to 30 shillings a month for as many months as the native cares to work; and (d) domestic service in the homestead paid for at the rate of 10 shillings a month and the services of the women, girls, and boys at harvest time at the rate of from six pence to one shilling a day.

In the past these conditions have seemed reasonable to the natives, but now they are beginning to be dissatisfied. The chief causes of this dissatisfaction are the increased wants of the native due to education and his imitation of the European's standard of living, the increased limitation of his stock, and the arbitrary actions of the farmer in opposing the education of his children. So great was this dissatisfaction that recently in South Africa a native labor union made a serious attempt to organize native servants and labor tenants for the purpose of improving their position. This attempt failed as the result of vigorous action on the part of the landlords and employers, who promptly ejected those natives who joined the organization. This, however, will not be the end of the natives' attempts to better their condition.

SUGGESTIONS FOR THE IMPROVEMENT OF NATIVE LABOR CONDITIONS

Inasmuch as the amount of land in the Native Reserves is insufficient, so that a total segregation of natives is impossible even if it were desirable, and inasmuch as the white farmer needs native labor and inasmuch as the native is more than willing to remain on the white man's farm provided he can have security of tenure, the proposal has been made to the government to establish tenant holdings for the natives on lines akin to the crofter system in Scotland. Under this system, in certain parts of the country, natives would be allowed to lease portions of land on condition that they use the land beneficially. Under such a scheme the native would have security of tenure and would therefore work his land better, while the farmer, in addition to getting a small rental, would have available a source of supply of native labor. Unfortunately these proposals have not received the attention they deserve in the face of the present fear complex regarding the native which obtains generally throughout South Africa.

Another suggestion that has been made for the improvement of a supply of native labor in the Union of South Africa is the application to industrial employers of rural native labor of some of the regulations of the Native Labour Act, which at present only applies to industrial occupations such as gold mining and the coal industry. Under this act a definite contract is entered into between employer and employee by which the employer on the one hand agrees to pay a certain wage in cash, to provide housing, food, and medical attention on a certain scale, and to submit his books, premises, etc., to the inspection of a government official. On the other hand the native undertakes to give certain specified service and becomes subject to the penalty of imprisonment if he breaks his contract by running away or absenting himself without leave.

This law has worked satisfactorily in the industrial occupations to which it is applied and will probably be applied before long to large-scale farming operations such as sugar-cane growing and the wattle-bark industry. It could not in its present form be applied to individual farmers, but it points a way by demonstrating the need for obligation on the part of the employer as well as of the employee if labor conditions are to be satisfactory. At present the Master and Servants Laws stress unduly the obligations on the servant.

NATIVE LABOR RECRUITING AGENCIES

Another means of securing labor, and the one that is followed by the industries to which the Labour Act applies, is through native labor-recruiting agencies. These have become a very important feature of the labor problem in southern Africa. The government issues licenses to approved organizations to recruit for labor. These organizations either have their own servants or employ traders and storekeepers in native areas to enlist men for service. Any native in these areas who finds it necessary to obtain money applies to a labor agent and offers himself for service. If he is passed by a medical officer as fit he "joins," as the phrase goes, and is sent off to some industrial area on a six or nine months' contract. As very few natives offer themselves for recruitment until they are in desperate need of money for some special purpose, such as the payment of the government tax or the settlement of a pressing debt, an advance of a few pounds is almost always made.

This system of recruiting labor has extended to other occupations nowadays, and many farmers rely on recruited labor. Although the method is expensive, inasmuch as the recruiters' fees must be paid, and somewhat risky, inasmuch as the employer never knows what kind of "boy" he is going to get, it is the only means at the disposal of those farmers who are situated in areas where natives do not live. Now that the whole system of recruiting is covered by government regulations, most of the obvious abuses of the system have disappeared.

THE NATIVE AS A LABORER

Judged by white standards the African native is inefficient as a laborer. He has nothing of the perseverance of the Asiatic nor is he so quick to learn. Under stimulus he can work very hard indeed, but he soon tires of work and asks permission to "go home and rest." Very often, too, this request for a vacation comes at a most unsuitable time for the employer. The reasons for his inefficiency are not hard to find. In the first place the South African native is a pastoralist. The little subsistence agriculture that was necessary was done by the women. In the second place the African's wants have hitherto been very few—a home, some cattle, enough food and drink for daily needs, a blanket or two, a few clothes. He asks for no more in the way of supplies, but he does ask for leisure, for time for gossip, for courting, for lying in the sun, for social entertainment in the way of beer drinks and visiting. Why should he work for twelve months in the year when he can get all he wants with four months' work? Finally, the native is not acquisitive. He does not need to save for a rainy day. His social organization is such that he can always borrow from a friend. Indeed, to have much more than one needs is folly, for others will only come and borrow.

Yet, in spite of his inefficiency, the native is liked as a laborer. His innate cheerfulness, his courtesy, his loyalty to employers whom he likes, his devotion to his master's interests make him extraordinarily likable. While whites oppose the granting of political privileges to natives, while they are apparently unwilling to give them more land, and while they will speak loud and long on the inefficiency of the native, there is no white man but will admit that he knows at least one exception. When these "exceptions" are added up they make a goodly number.

Perhaps the two factors that make the African native such an asset to the pioneering settler are his patience and his docility. The typical African is not in reality the haughty, war-loving warrior of the romantic and sensational novelists. He is a home-loving, peaceful, moderately industrious pastoralist with a code of social habits whose chief characteristics are hospitality and friendship. He readily accepts the overlordship of the European government, and, perhaps because the land is regarded as belonging to the tribe as a whole and not to an individual, he does not resent the coming in of the white man to lands he has been accustomed to regard as his own. Very often he accepts the white man as his chief and resents his strange new ways the less because he is accustomed to arbitrary and even capricious acts on the part of his chief. Perhaps patience and docility, carried to the extent to which the African carries them, cease to be virtues because they induce him to accept a position of subordination, escape from which at a later date causes serious dislocation of racial relations, such as we see taking place in the Union of South Africa today. Had the native resented the white occupation of Africa as other races have resented foreign entry into their territory, he might have secured for himself a position and a respect that he lacks today.

It is therefore extraordinarily easy for the white pioneer and settler to maintain friendly relationships with the South African natives. Of course, he must adapt himself in many ways to his new neighbors, but in this mutual understanding he will find that the black man will go far more than halfway to meet him.

ATTITUDE THE WHITE SETTLER SHOULD ADOPT TOWARD SOUTH AFRICAN NATIVES

From time to time the writer has been called on to advise the European settler as to the attitude he should adopt toward the South African natives. It may not be out of place to summarize some of his opinions here.

1. *Learn the native's language.* It is only through their language that one can get to know the soul of a people. A knowledge of the native's language helps in every way. It enables the employer to give his instructions adequately and the employee to offer his explanations. It gives the employer prestige among the natives and makes it less easy for him to be deceived. It enables the employer to know the other man's side, without which knowledge satisfactory master-and-servant relationships are difficult.

2. *Understand the native's customs and, if possible, respect them.* The native has a complete culture or civilization of his own built up through long years of experimentation. To this culture he clings tenaciously, and even when he adopts the white man's customs he still adheres to many of his own. In this respect he differs considerably from the American negro, whose civilization was crushed by slavery. Perhaps the native customs that present the greatest difficulty to the pioneer are those connected with women and cattle.

3. *Treat the native with absolute justice.* The sense of justice of the African native is very keen, and it is only on a basis of fair play that one can have satisfactory dealings with him. He has a great respect for law and order, a fact that makes possible a satisfactory solution of the South African race problem. He is quick to accept deserved punishment but sullen and morose if he feels he has been punished unfairly. Far from resenting firm handling, he appreciates and responds to good discipline.

4. *Avoid familiarity.* To the South African native the white man is a chief, and by tradition a chief is a man who gives orders. With so-called "raw" or heathen natives familiarity is regarded

as a sign of weakness, and native laborers are quick to take advantage of such weakness.

5. *Have consideration for the home life of the natives.* The patriarchal attitude, which expresses itself in such ways as providing land and stock for native laborers, helping parents to maintain discipline in their families, and seeing that the sick and needy are attended to, is well understood and much appreciated by natives.

6. *Make provision for the religious, educational, and recreational life of native servants.* Perhaps there is no more successful way of attracting and retaining native labor than by the provision of a native school. All over South Africa the native is thirsting for education, and the wise employer is profiting from this by providing educational facilities for his children. Experience has also shown that the educated native makes a better servant than the uneducated, though it is harder to retain him.

Perhaps a final word of advice to the settler in a pioneer area in search of native labor may be permitted. It is this. Cultivate friendly relations with the local magistrate or government official, the missionary, the native trader, and, above all, with the native chief. All of these can influence native labor considerably. If the settler can gain the reputation among these people of being a man who treats his labor well, pays fair wages while exacting efficient work, he will find that he has more labor offering than he can employ.

LAND AND THE NATIVE IN BRITISH AFRICA: THE SOUTHERN RHODESIAN EXPERIMENT

Ethel Tawse Jollie

THE opening of Africa to traffic from every side and the passing of nearly every part of the vast continent under the more or less direct rule of some civilized Power is a development of the last half century and has been achieved by so many different methods that it is not surprising to find a bewildering variety of conditions. Particularly as regards the position of the native peoples the most marked contrasts exist, even under the British flag, and these contrasts are found not merely between the self-governed and the home-governed countries but in those which are still controlled direct from the Colonial Office. Yet there are signs that the Bantu people, no longer isolated and now enabled to communicate through the written word as never before, are awakening to a sense of race, and it cannot be supposed that they are unaffected by the inequalities of their position. The theory that, as a whole, they are a "child race," incapable of rising above a certain level, is now generally discredited, while the ethics of today cannot tolerate the assumption that they were intended to be a race of perpetual helots. But this revised idea of their capacity and destiny does not incline all the white races who have rescued them from barbarism to the solution adopted by the French, which is that of absorption, social and political. The problem as presented to the British is how to secure a future that will give scope to both white and black without political or social fusion; and it is a problem in which the American conditions are reversed, since the ruling and directing race is in the minority.

Three Types of Native Land Tenure in British Africa

There is no more important question in this connection than that of land tenure, for the landless detribalized native presents peculiar difficulties, both administrative and social. The present system, or lack of system, inevitably leads to the emergence of a few Bantus far above the level of their race, where their position between two worlds, and with no security in either, is difficult

178

and unfortunate. There are three catagories into which the British countries of Africa fall as to land tenure: (1) those in which the land is recognized as being the exclusive property of the indigenes; (2) those in which certain parts have been assigned to them and in which they can buy land elsewhere on the same terms as white men; and (3) the dominion of South Africa, where for two hundred years Europeans have steadily encroached on the land formerly occupied by natives. As to the last it must be remembered that the earlier British and Dutch settlers encountered determined resistance to their occupation, and self-preservation forced them to retaliate unless they were to abandon altogether the effort to colonize this barbaric land. Nor did they always disturb a peaceful people in hereditary homes. Africa before the white man came was a shambles, the scene of perpetual raids by wave after wave of tribes that lived on warfare.

The traditional Bantu system of land tenure is communal, except that the land is vested in the chief, whose prerogatives are autocratic in the extreme. In practice he delegates his authority to chiefs and headmen who allot the land to each family or individual, and all have customary rights as to fallow land and grazing. The advantages of a system that protected the tribe against the intrusion of strangers or alienation of land by individuals are obvious in a savage state; but, whether because of the lack of incentive to improvements or for other reasons, the Bantu is a notoriously inefficient and wasteful agriculturist, while he is equally incompetent and careless as a stock breeder.

In the Union of South Africa

Certain tribes living within the colonies now united as the Union of South Africa succeeded by appealing to the Imperial Government in securing a national identity and the possession of their land by treaty or agreement. Such are the Zulu, Swazi, Basuto, Bechuana. The Swazi managed in a few years to barter away everything they possessed to concession hunters and had to be indemnified and protected from themselves. These countries have local self-government and white resident officials. No material is available to the writer to estimate the agricultural or economic progress they have made, but the impression left on travelers is that they have been handicapped by the lack of European capital, which has been used to develop other parts of South Africa, and that the material position of their people is not as good, in some respects, as that of their brothers in the Union. With the exception of the late chief of the Bechuana, Khama, none of these tribes has produced leaders or men of distinction, whereas several have come to the front in the Union.

The bad feature in the position of the Union native, however, is his increasing divorce from the land; for South Africa, as a country still predominantly engaged in primary production, cannot afford to pile up a large urban population. Out of about 4,500,000 natives only 123,000 are living on individually owned land, about 2,000,000 live in locations, and about 2,000,000 on land owned by Europeans, the government, or by municipalities, in which they can have no security of tenure. The landless native must form a serious competitor to the European industrialist, and his own position is precarious. Cecil Rhodes in the eighties was the first of South African statesmen to perceive the dangers of the position, and he strove, by the Glen Grey Act, to initiate a policy that would keep the native on the land and give him an interest in it. Within its limits this experiment has been justified, but something of wider application was needed; and between 1902 and 1905 a commission under Sir Godfrey Lagden investigated the position of the South African native, as part of the general "clean-up" after the Boer War. They reported[1] in favor of a division of land between the two races, neither being allowed to own land in the other area, and a subsequent development of social and political life within these native areas to run parallel with, but not be confused with, the European system. The difference of status between natives in the four provinces which existed at the time of union and has never been rectified would thus disappear.

The principle of this report was adopted by General Botha in 1913, but the difficulties in the way of translating it into practical politics have so far proved too much for any South African government, though General Hertzog is said to be prepared to go to some lengths to put it through. Objections come from the native side to the areas which it is proposed to set aside for them as inadequate and undesirable, but an even thornier question is that of the franchise which the Cape native possesses and which he would lose as the price of a general system of any scheme of local self-government and community representation. The results of two centuries

[1] South African Native Affairs Commission: Reports and Minutes of Evidence, 5 vols., Cape Town, 1906 (also issued as British Parliamentary Paper, Cmd. 2399).

of haphazard policy are not easily discounted, and it looks as if the present position were almost incapable of remedy, though many friends of the native believe the proposals to have the germs of a solution of the relations between black and white.[2]

IN THE WEST AFRICAN COLONIES

At the other end of the scale from the almost landless native of South Africa come the indigenes of the West African colonies, where, from the first, the Imperial Government has established the principle that the land belongs to the natives. "The whole of the lands of the protectorate, whether occupied or unoccupied . . . , are hereby declared to be native lands." So runs the Land Act of Nigeria (1910). On the other side of the continent the native state of Uganda secured through a treaty with its Baganda chief that all land beneficially occupied should be vested in the Baganda people, only waste land passing under the jurisdiction of the government, which is that of a colony under an Imperial Governor. In such countries Europeans may hold leaseholds or concessions or even monopolies but cannot own land.

IN THE EAST AND CENTRAL AFRICAN COLONIES

Between these two extremes come the East and Central African colonies of Kenya, Tanganyika (mandated), Nyasa, Northern Rhodesia, and Southern Rhodesia, the last being a self-governing colony while all the others are controlled by the Colonial Office. In these countries the flag followed trade, not vice versa; and Europeans and, in Kenya, Asiatics are firmly established on the land, from which, in some cases, they have evicted the native occupiers. The natives in practically all these regions are few, compared with the dense population of West Africa, and it is interesting to recall that the railway which "made" both Kenya and Uganda was built with imported Indian labor. There is no uniform policy in these four colonies, but in all the system of setting aside Native Reserves and confining the indigenous people to them is practiced, and it is not the principle but its practical working out that is a matter of controversy, particularly in Kenya and

[2] In 1916 when a commission reported on the subject (Union of South Africa: Report of Natives Land Commission, 2 vols., Cape Town, 1916) the South African native enjoyed the ownership of 7 acres a head in Cape Colony, 2 acres in the Transvaal, 6 in Natal, and $\frac{1}{6}$ in the Orange Free State. It was proposed to increase these ratios to $8\frac{1}{2}$, $11\frac{1}{2}$, 10, and $1\frac{1}{2}$ acres.

Tanganyika. A recent commission under Sir E. Hilton Young[3] tried to find a formula for a native policy that could be applied to all four crown colonies, but the proposals smacked too much of the West African school, which confines European influence to administrative officials and large concessionary companies and rules out the possibility of self-government—the goal of all white colonists. At the moment, while administrative changes are to bring the colonies nearer to each other, the question of a uniform native policy has been shelved. It must be understood that the question at issue between the settlers and the Imperial Government is not whether the former are justified in being in Africa nor whether their presence is essential to progress. As to both points the Hilton Young commission was emphatic, since without this settlement the economic progress of these regions could not have been effected; and it is difficult to separate the moral uplift of the natives from the material welfare made possible by white capital, brains, and energy. One of the inducements to white settlement was cheap and abundant native labor—and this applies to all the countries recently colonized—but this is proving such an uncertain factor that farmers and estate owners are revising their estimates and substituting machinery wherever possible. A government policy of state-aided small growers, like that of the West Coast, might introduce a competitive class with an infinitely lower standard of living, while in some regions the quality rather than the quantity of native produce causes apprehension to farmers who aim at a high standard. Politically and economically the situation is full of difficulty, and no solution that meets with general approval has been offered.

THE SOUTHERN RHODESIAN EXPERIMENT

At this juncture an interesting experiment is being initiated in Southern Rhodesia, at the instance of her own elected government, which is independent of Colonial Office control except as to native affairs, as to which sanction has to be obtained for any fresh legislation. In this country, which recently celebrated its fortieth birthday as a British possession, it is neither too late, as in the Union, nor too early, as in Kenya, to adopt some definitive scheme of division of land between the two races; and that, in effect, is what is to be done.

[3] Report of the Commission on Closer Union of the Dependencies in Eastern and Central Africa, British Parliamentary Paper, Cmd. 3234, London, 1929.

The charter with which Rhodes first opened this closed land gave him only the right to dig for gold, but he later bought from a German the concession granted by Lobengula to dispose of land as his agent. In the royal charter, under which Rhodes worked, stipulations were made as to respecting native land, and the British South Africa Company's directions were explicit as to not disturbing any native owners or "pegging" near their settlements. When in 1893 Lobengula provoked a war and lost his country by conquest, the Imperial Government confirmed the company in all administrative rights; and it is well known that, at a later date, the company claimed that the land itself had passed to them as owners. This was disallowed by the Privy Council, who declared the land to be the property of the Crown, since subjects cannot acquire by conquest; and, as the settlers of the territory had succeeded in making good their claim to govern themselves, the Imperial Government vested the land in the government of Southern Rhodesia on payment of a sum of £2,000,000 towards the compensation of the chartered company.

There has been so much written of the despoiling of the African native that it must be said here that Lobengula was a big lad when his father overran this country and enslaved or exterminated large numbers of its people and that they certainly made a good exchange in many ways when Queen Victoria succeeded the blood-stained line of Matabele chiefs. Even in the experience of such hunters as Selous, whole districts, once cultivated, had been depopulated; and as evidence of an even greater degree of cultivation at some forgotten period there are districts in which terraces, irrigation works, and other unexplained traces of a dense population remain.

The mystery of Zimbabwe is only one of the unsolved problems of the country and cannot be properly investigated without a far wider survey than at present exists of all the other prehistoric remains, the sum total of which points to some period or periods at which this country supported a vast number of people. When Europeans first knew it they considered it a land of plenty for its comparatively few tribes; and in the seventies and eighties hunters and traders wrote of rice, millet, pumpkins, cattle, goats, and fowls as plentiful and of the people as living an ideal existence in the fertile valleys.

In 1890 the Pioneer Column found great stretches of the country depopulated and traveled for miles without seeing a sign of inhabitants, for the survivors had often fled to some thick bit of scrub or to rocky forts or eminences for purposes of concealment; and, so far from its being a land of plenty, the first settlers nearly starved. In several years since British occupation bad seasons have been the cause of famine, and the government has imported food. Since the occupation over forty years ago the population has risen from 400,000 to over 900,000 natives.

History of Native Land Policy

Whether from motives of humanity or because they dare not risk antagonizing the Colonial Office does not matter, but so far as possible the chartered company did not evict natives from their ancestral lands, except in the case of those who were rebels in 1896 and who were not allowed to return to the Matopo Hills. Rhodes, however, gave land on his own estate to many of the dispossessed royal family. An Order in Council of 1898 provided that the natives should have the right to buy land wherever they wished and also that from time to time land should be specially assigned to them, thus giving them privileges greater than those enjoyed by the white man, who can only acquire land by purchase. In 1902 Native Reserves were definitely approved by the Legislative Assembly, but the status of these reserves was not finally settled until 1920, when, as the result of a commission appointed by the Imperial Government, at the request of the British South Africa Company, the areas were readjusted and the land vested in the High Commissioner for South Africa on behalf of the natives.

The Bantu system of communal land tenure was followed as closely as possible in the reserves. The allegation has been made that in allocating reserves the worst land was taken, but as a matter of fact very little was known then (or is known now) of the possibilities of the soils, and a glance at the map (Fig. 1) will show how widely distributed were the lands recognized as belonging to the natives. It must not be supposed that they were confined to these. Europeans had pegged farms with instructions to avoid native settlements, and the pegging of mining claims had led to the reservation of certain areas as "gold-belt land," on which the farmer had to accept considerable disadvantages in his title as the price for possible proximity to a mine market. The high veld, the principal mining centers, and the railways connecting them, all fell into a central zone along which European settlement was expected; but where natives were already within this zone they became tenants and as such they remain today. There are 179,000 of them living on alienated land or farms and 130,000 on government land, some of which may later be alienated. Their position is insecure, except that, as they form a reserve of labor for the owner, he is often pleased to have them there. Many of them occupy ancestral homes and do not wish to move into the reserves, where they are under the control of chiefs and headmen and subject to the fear of witchcraft, which, they think, is less potent on a white man's farm.

The wasteful character of native agriculture has led to the serious impoverishment of the Reserve land and of the government farms and privately owned land where they are "squatters." A more intensive method of cultivation in reserves is now being preached through a special government department, while the deficiency of water is being met by boreholes; but a real difficulty is that while some reserves are crowded others are very sparsely occupied, and yet native custom makes transfer a hardship. An even more serious problem is the unrestricted increase of native cattle, which has reached a point of real danger. During the summer of 1929–1930, which was one of drought, 30,000 cattle died of hunger, more than were sold or killed. The native hoards cattle, which are his hereditary form of capital, and no adequate steps have yet been devised to keep him within the limits prescribed by his veld or by good stock breeding. Where stock run on common land incentives to better methods are lacking.

Proposal of Individual Ownership of Land Within Segregated Areas

In these circumstances the proposal has been made (emanating first from the Chief Native Commissioner) that as an incentive to rise above the economic level of his tribe a native must be encouraged to purchase land. He is at present at liberty to do so, but very few can hope to compete with European buyers at the prices current, and there is moreover a prejudice against selling to a native. Native ownership in a district adjoining white men's farms would probably cause them to deteriorate in value. The natives themselves do not like a neighborship that brings them up against standards and regulations above their own level. This aspect of the case, however, was not the one that originally suggested a change, as the writer has special reason to know, having been one of the first who urged individual ownership of land as the only incentive to the native to stay on the land and keep him from drifting into a detribalized urban life. One of the worst results of urban life is that it deprives women of occupation and leads to demoralization of the native family life. As a result of discussions in the Legislative Council and elsewhere the government of Southern Rhodesia appointed a commission, consisting of the Chief Native Commissioner, the Director of the Department of Lands, and a chairman selected by the Colonial Office, Sir Morris Carter, Chief Justice of Tanganyika, to investigate the whole question.

Their report[4] was strongly and unanimously in favor of a measure that was recommended by another commission (the Lagden commission; see p. 180 above) to what is now the Union of South Africa but has never been possible of fulfilment there—that of territorial segregation. In exchange for the freedom enjoyed by both races at present (but of little practical use to the African) of buying land wherever they wish, it is proposed that both should make the sacrifice of setting certain land outside their reach. The Europeans had already done this as to 21,594,000 acres out of the total of 96,220,000 that have been set aside in perpetuity as Native Reserves. The commission proposed to add another 7,000,000 acres (in round figures), making nearly 29,000,000 acres, which will be regarded as permanently reserved for the natives. At present no change in the communal system of the original reserves is contemplated, but in the supplementary reserves, called the Native Purchase Areas, individual tenure will be given on terms of payment specially drawn up both to make them easy for the native and to insure that he does not abuse the privilege.

For instance, he will have to erect buildings of a sufficiently substantial nature and he will not be free to mortgage his property except with the consent of a board that will supervise all matters connected with these areas. The commission recommended freehold title, subject to the carrying out of certain improvements; but those natives already living in the selected areas and others who may desire to live there will be permitted to do so on payment of rent. All natives living on European-owned land who are not under a definite labor contract with the owner will gradually be moved to these new reserved areas, in the hope that, beginning as tenants, they will gradually acquire their lands as owners. It has been the practice on many European-owned estates to demand rent, or labor in lieu of rent, from native tenants; but the system

[4] Southern Rhodesia: Report of the Land Commission, 1925, Salisbury, 1925.

has not proved satisfactory either for the European or the native, as no contract entered into is readily enforceable and many natives go to the mines for years at a time, leaving their wives and families behind, whilst, on the other hand, they have no security of tenure. Nevertheless, the native living on European-owned farms, many of which belong to absentees, has had a very easy time in the past.

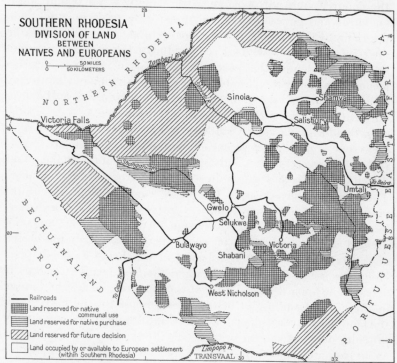

FIG. 1—Division of land between natives (ruled areas) and Europeans (blank areas) in Southern Rhodesia. Scale, 1 : 8,000,000. (Based on map in report cited in footnote 4.) Compare with the complementary map (Fig. 4, p. 202 below) showing European-owned land. The patches unaccounted for by ruling when both maps are superimposed represent crown lands not yet disposed of and, on the northern side of the railroad between Victoria Falls and Bulawayo, a forest area.

In the future he will be rounded up, probably to his own great advantage and certainly to that of the land, of which he has been wasteful because it cost him nothing.

The "Native Purchase Areas"

As will be seen from the map (Fig. 1) the Native Purchase Areas were selected chiefly for their geographical convenience as forming compact blocks adjacent to Native Reserves, and it is hoped that in these blocks native councils will spring up and develop into local government bodies in charge of matters such as roads, dipping, schools, and prevention of disease. The Southern Rhodesian native is still in a very primitive condition, and the fact that a few have shown great capacity does not do more than mark the general level. There are 919,000 indigenous natives in the country, and 587,000 live in the reserves, 300,000 (roughly) on farms and government land outside the reserves, and 22,000 in urban areas. Among the last are certainly men who are skilled mechanics and a few who are really educated; but even on the mission stations, under the most direct European influence, marriage means a reversion to old habits and ways of living, and, until some means is found of raising the women and the family as a whole to a different cultural level, this reversion is inevitable.

In dividing the land of Southern Rhodesia into white and black areas one important reservation was made. There are certain regions whose climatic and geographical position makes them difficult to settle and where, in some parts, the tsetse fly is found. These have been set aside for future consideration and form a margin of sufficient size (some 17,000,000 acres) to correct any miscalculation in the existing division. The land remaining is now divided in the proportion of about 28,000,000 acres for natives and 48,000,000 acres for Europeans, of which the natives already enjoy the use of 22,000,000 acres and the Europeans of 31,000,000 acres. The apparent inequality of these figures must be considered in the light of the use of land hitherto made by the natives and the land needed for support of an average family. The commission provided for 250,000 natives outside the reserves on the basis of about 30 acres apiece, and, as the average of cultivation is about 1½ acres apiece and has not appreciably improved during the last twelve years, this seems adequate.

ADVANTAGES AND DISADVANTAGES OF PROPOSED SEGREGATION

There is no shortage of land for Europeans at present, despite the large areas locked up by the land policy of the chartered company in the hands of companies that do not develop them, and a recent act providing for the taxation of land not beneficially occupied has already brought some of that held for speculative purposes into the market. There is not, however, a great deal of good land'in government hands within easy reach of the railway, and the patchy nature of the soil makes the ideal of small, closely settled farms very difficult of accomplishment. Cattle owning is essential in a country where fertilizer is expensive and where the soil needs building up with rather more than is taken out of it. The great drawback to farming on a small scale in Southern Rhodesia is that it does not provide sufficient margin for this, and the tendency has been to rob the soil, to cut down the timber, and generally live on capital. Quite apart from the difficulty of markets, which is a worldwide one for farmers, the agricultural problems of the colonies of East and Central Africa are of a character that seems to require either the closest and most scientific organization of individual growers or else the gradual substitution of the large, well-organized company, with the producers as its employees.

The latter is the solution that, in fact, has accomplished the economic prosperity of the West Coast colonies, the natives supplying the produce and the companies doing the marketing. The tropical type of product, such as palm oil and cacao, the geographical position and the character of the native peoples lent themselves to this form of development, but this cannot be said of the East and Central African colonies. There is not only the complication of existing white settlement, but there is the fact that the staple agricultural industries of these regions, maize, coffee, tea, tobacco, or cattle, are carried on in competition with countries possessing greater natural advantages and need scientific research, experienced handling, and a high standard of efficiency in production. All these qualities are being brought into play as the result, not of European administration or government intervention, but of the initiative and energy of the European settlers. General Smuts in his recent Rhodes lecture[5] pointed out the weakness of any country in Africa that depends upon its administration for agricultural development, and without a steady influx of European settlers it is difficult to envisage any economic future for these colonies, the bulk of whose natives are still in a primitive condition. Uganda and Nyasaland, which show steady progress in native production, owe it to missionary influence of an exceptionally practical kind; but a warning note is already being sounded as to the inevitable and rapid deterioration of the Nyasa native produce as the result of the process of living on the capital of the soil.

[5] See J. C. Smuts: Africa and Some World Problems, Including the Rhodes Memorial Lectures Delivered in Michaelmas Term, 1929, Oxford, 1930, pp. 48–52.

There is almost universal agreement by those qualified to judge that the introduction into Southern Rhodesia of the cheap plows in use by the natives means less efficient working of the land than the old hand hoe—another instance of the deceptiveness of appearances of "progress."

Need of European Stimulus for Best Interest of Native

There is a school of thought in Great Britain that is much affected by doubts as to the ethical position of Europeans in Africa and views the safeguarding of the native people and the preservation of all that is good in them as the first responsibility of administration. There is no doubt that to secure to them a reasonable share of the land is a wise policy apart from any ethical considerations; and for this, if for nothing else, the Southern Rhodesian experiment will be watched with interest. There are not wanting, however, those who say that segregation in any form means, if not stagnation, then a definite slowing down of native progress and that at the back of the whole question lies the fundamental one of psychology. Contact with the white man, and even oppression by him, applies a stimulus to native energy which is otherwise lacking; but the native achieves the higher standard of living that must be the goal of effort only at the expense of his most marked African characteristic—the utter irresponsibility of a race whose natural and sex needs are still so simple and easily gratified as to present no problem. General Smuts asserted—and most observers would agree with him—that there is no other race that has the universal characteristic of cheerful light-heartedness of the African. The secret is his irresponsibility, either for tomorrow or for his fellows, and it is incompatible with European habits or thoughts. It is also incompatible with economic development.

Where food, sex, and shelter are easily obtained there is nothing in the environment to force the "trial by error" method of development, and it is demonstrable that even white races slow down in the exceptionally easy life of Africa. If these premises are correct, the development of these young and potentially rich countries will proceed in ratio to the amount of new European brains, energy, and capital available for them; it cannot be built up on the gradual weaning of the African from his racial character, which must be a slow process and, at best, an uncertain one. As General Smuts pointed out, the most enlightened civil service cannot supply the deficiency of initiative, capital, and brains in an agricultural population. It is too soon to be sure that even the much vaunted success of the West African policy is really sound; and in any case that policy is inapplicable, so far as land is concerned, to any country with a white resident population.

The advantage of territorial segregation, as proposed in Southern Rhodesia, is that it provides a halfway house between the primitive native of the reserves and the detribalized and superficially civilized native of the towns. The growth of a middle class is by far the best chance of raising the level of a large number by slow but sure degrees, instead of pushing a few far beyond the standard of their race, which is the inevitable result of the present method of education. But the success or failure depends ultimately on the use made by the native of the land secured to him and, almost equally, on the organization of agriculture by the European farmers on sound lines both as to production and marketing. The native, whether as an industrialist or farmer, must be fitted into the economic system by the only logical means—that his work or his produce is paid for on its equality. If the white man cannot compete on these terms he will eventually disappear from the African scene. At present he seems to be not only a fixture but indispensable to the progress of Africa and the African.

PIONEER PROBLEMS IN RHODESIA AND NYASALAND

H. CLIFFORD DARBY

AFRICA south of the Tropic of Capricorn has passed beyond the initial stages of settlement. But immediately to the north there lies a region where development is not so far advanced. This is the region of the subtropical highlands of Southern Rhodesia, Northern Rhodesia, and Nyasaland. In each of these territories there are large settled areas (Figs. 4 and 5), but occupation is not continuous within any of them. Rather, the whole presents the aspect of three archipelagoes of settlement set in a sea of bush and scrub. Beyond, in Kenya, Tanganyika, and Angola, are other island clusters.

There exist among these three territories many differences, both in physical conditions and in methods of economic exploitation. Southern Rhodesia is a land where farming and mining have gone hand in hand. In Northern Rhodesia, less developed, agricultural effort has been distinct from mining enterprise. In Nyasaland the controls are yet different; here planters replace farmers and ranchers. Despite their differences, however, broad similarities of situation give to the three regions many problems in common. They agree in exhibiting to a greater or less extent the phenomena of primary settlement. There have been diversities of motive and circumstance, but there is the same community of effort and the same store of achievement in clearing the waste places of the earth.

In this process they share a common difficulty. Distinction has been made between two types of colonization, *colonisation d'exploitation* and *colonisation de peuplement*. In each case the issue is clear: in the one it is the education of the native, in the other it is the introduction of white civilization. But there is a third type: the subtropical highlands, which are intermediate in character. There the white man has gone to establish a culture of his own; yet the establishment of that culture is essentially dependent upon the exploitation of native labor, and consequently the question of settlement in these highlands cannot be approached in the same way as in other areas. The white man must always be in the position of master or foreman. In Southern Rhodesia there are eighteen natives employed in agriculture to every white man. The problem is to reconcile the interests—to say nothing of the ideals—of the immigrant and the native and to do this to the detriment of neither. To this heritage of difficulty all three areas have succeeded, and

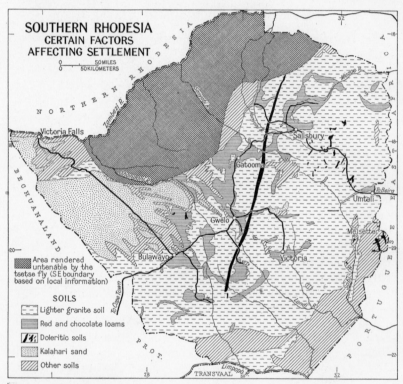

FIG. 1—Soils of Southern Rhodesia. Scale, 1 : 8,000,000. (Based on geological map by the Geological Survey of Southern Rhodesia). In the north the area in which the tsetse fly occurs is outlined from local information obtained by the author.

Figure 7 on page 207 should be consulted as a general locational map for the names of places mentioned in the text but not shown here nor on Figures 2 and 4.

the form that the compromise takes will affect the limits to which white civilization can spread.

In working out this compromise with its subsidiary difficulties, the settlers are faced with two orders of problems, economic and social. There are the material bases upon which the community rests; there is the quality of the civilization that the community evolves in its new environment.

ECONOMIC PROBLEMS

The consideration of the material bases of the community falls naturally under the headings of the three economic processes— production, transportation, and marketing.

EXPERIMENTATION TO DETERMINE SUITABLE CROPS

The advantages of improved technique are many, but modern settlers are all pioneers in the sense that they are breaking soil never before tilled. In each area man lives "a life of experiment at the edge of the plowed land." He is not yet sure what crops are best suited to his local environment. He may have to change his form of agriculture several times in an attempt to obtain some stable adjustments, and the ultimate adjustment is only attained after many failures, at the cost of many derelict homesteads.

At first in Southern Rhodesia maize was the main commercial crop. The centers of production clung to the areas of the red and chocolate loams (Fig. 1), and settlement lay along the Mazoe valley northeast of Salisbury and in the belt between Gwelo and Gatooma. On the lighter granite soils farms existed only where intrusions of dolerite increased their agricultural value. The introduction of other crops is giving a new importance to the vast area of granite veld. Some of these other crops have been tried already in the area farther north. The fluctuations revealed in the agricultural returns for Nyasaland[1] are significant.

TABLE I—CROPPED AREA IN NYASALAND

	1918	1928
Cotton	18,141 acres	1,046 acres
Fibers	1,281 "	7,863 "
Rubber	4,603 "	1,401 "
Tea	4,433 "	7,596 "
Tobacco	6,027 "	22,475 "

TOBACCO, COFFEE, TEA

When tobacco was first introduced it was found that, though many of the general principles of tobacco cultivation remained the same, details of soil and methods of curing differed greatly. Experiments were made to see which class of tobacco could be grown on each type of soil. In Nyasaland the heavy loams are

[1]Nyasaland Protectorate: Annual Report of the Department of Agriculture for 1928, Zomba, 1929, p. 5.

suited to the production of dark tobacco, which is best fire-cured; while the sandy loams produce light tobacco, which should be flue-cured. Coffee, however, took kindly neither to soil nor climatic conditions, and, on the failure of the coffee crop, tea-growing was tried upon the slopes of the Mlanje Mountains, where the rainfall, which averages 80 inches a year, is well distributed for ten months (Fig. 3). This proved a success, and it is probable that within the next few years the present tea acreage will be doubled. Coffee had also failed in the Cholo district, but this area was thought to be unsuited for tea. More recent experiment, however, has shown that tea can be grown here quite successfully, and development is going on apace. There may be other tea areas farther north, but these await transport facilities. And in Southern Rhodesia there are distinct possibilities of tea being grown in the Sabi-Tanganda valleys, but at the low level fever is prevalent. Coffee likewise is being tried in Rhodesia, to the south of Umtali; but here the activities of the stem borer and the ravage of occasional frosty nights make its success doubtful.

Cotton

The European attempt to grow cotton in Nyasaland completely broke down owing to climatic and economic conditions, and it remains a native crop grown on the unhealthful low-lying plains. When cotton was introduced into the Rhodesias this failure was repeated. Here, however, the period of trial is not yet over: experimental acreages under the auspices of the Empire Cotton Growing Corporation are being planted to discover more particularly the requirements of cotton. As far as soil requirements go, the maize land is suitable, but, if it can be proved that a good class of sand veld will produce payable yields, settlement in the area will be considerably affected.

Areas Not Suited to Agriculture

A map issued in 1906 as a guide to future settlement in Northern Rhodesia indicated the Batoka Plateau, between the Zambezi and Kafue Rivers, as "good agricultural farming land," yet today the plateau is of little farming importance. Its granitic soil has prevented it from being anything more than a cattle country. Similarly in Southern Rhodesia soil and climate, too, have made Matabeleland the main producer of cattle, but in these areas all attempts to increase the quality of the stock have been disappointing. The inability to raise high-class stock is due, it would seem, to a deficiency in the grazing grasses. The whole subject of mineral deficiencies in pastures is receiving considerable attention. Before practicable solutions can be arrived at, however, the situation in Matabeleland may have altered, owing to other prospects at present entertained for the future of the region. On the one hand the introduction of dry-farming methods is suggested, and the region has already been hailed as a potential crop-producing land. On the other hand the large area of Kalahari sand, unsuitable for cereal production, has been declared to have immense timber potentialities, and this is in a region which as yet is very thinly settled.

Government Financial and Agricultural Assistance to Settlers

This record of a few of the lines along which experiment has proceeded and is proceeding has a definite value. It shows how the conditions and soils of the area are not sufficiently known to permit any final estimate regarding its agricultural possibilities. Any statement is likely to be revalued by improvement in technique. It is safe to say only that the staples of production are problematical and that experiment has to proceed much further before any comparatively permanent constants can be evolved.

The difference in the future is that such experiment will be more definitely organized under government control and that the risk to the settler will be considerably reduced. Such government assistance is of two kinds. It may be definitely financial, or it may take the form of technical advice. The former includes the various settlement schemes and concessions in special areas, as on the occasion of the cotton and tobacco failure. Of more general importance is the existence of a Land Bank in Southern Rhodesia, started in 1924. Much lack of success results from want of capital to "carry on" after a crop failure. The purpose of the Land Bank is to provide suitable applicants with capital at a reasonable rate of interest on the security of the land, or it may assist in a projected farming enterprise. Settlers in Northern Rhodesia feel the need of such a bank greatly.

Of no less value is the assistance given by the various Departments of Agriculture, which make definite attempts to assess the physical values of different localities and to breed new varieties of seed (e. g. cotton and wheat) suited to local conditions. Experimental stations issue frequent bulletins, and their research officers visit farms to give advice. Northern Rhodesia, although less developed, has gone a stage further in advocating a more comprehensive policy and recommending[2] that an ecological survey be instituted: "An ecological survey would deal primarily with the classification of the chief types of vegetation in relation to climate, rainfall, and soil types of their habitats. Such a survey, where the country is mapped out into areas in each of which the relationship of vegetation to environment is recorded, would be of the greatest use as a preliminary guide to the possibilities of agricultural development in particular localities. The knowledge obtained would be of great assistance in delineating areas suitable for settlement."

The Question of Water Supply

Quite apart from the sphere of local experiment, there are three big problems common to the whole area: the question of water supply, the menace of soil erosion, and the economic problem of the native.

A large percentage of crop failures results from rainfall unreliability. It is indeed doubtful whether any significance can be attached to average rainfall figures. The general nature of the problem can be seen from the Northern Rhodesian statistics; and the importance of the consequent fluctuation in yields to a settler with a small capital margin cannot be overestimated.

TABLE II—RELATION OF RAINFALL TO CROP YIELD IN
NORTHERN RHODESIA

CENTERS	AVERAGES (inches)	1923–24	1924–25	1925–26	1926–27	1927–28	1928–29
Kalomo	29	15	44	43	26	27	26
Mazabuka	32	18	52	39	29	24	38
Lusaka	33	18	44	45	28	27	29
Chisamba	33	23	43	53	18	27	35
Average rainfall of season (inches)		18.5	45.8	45.0	25.3	26.3	32.0
Average maize yields for Northern Rhodesia (bags per acre)		3.08	2.67	4.87	5.50	4.90	5.50

[2] Northern Rhodesia: Department of Agriculture Report for 1927, Livingstone.

Corollary to this, there is the problem of irrigation, which assumes two aspects in different portions of the region. Ordinary crops can be grown with little difficulty where the rainfall exceeds 25 inches. The major portion of Northern and Southern Rhodesia and Nyasaland falls within this limit. But in southern and western Southern Rhodesia there is a considerable area with a rainfall deficit. The factors involved are summarized on the adjoining map (Fig. 2).[3] This is the cattle area where dry-farming methods, bore-holes, and water conservation are necessary features of ordinary farming. But within the humid region irrigation is also necessary—for even this region has long dry periods and any attempt to grow winter crops (citrus, lucerne, wheat, barley, oats, etc.) must be accompanied by irrigation facilities. The tendency towards more general mixed farming is making irrigation increasingly necessary in such areas, while, if it be found possible to extend settlement below 2000 feet, there are considerable stretches of good soil where, with irrigation, the tropical crops (rice, sugar, and cotton) could be grown.

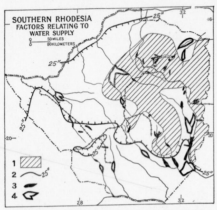

FIG. 2—Scale, 1 : 15,000,000. Key to numbers: 1, area with annual reliable rainfall of at least 25 inches—the lower limit of effective crop production; 2, isohyet of mean annual rainfall of 25 inches (toothed on inner side); 3, known and 4, probable irrigable areas.

THE MENACE OF SOIL EROSION

The problem of soil erosion is a serious factor affecting the extension of the settled area. The toll taken from uncovered soil in a few years reduces fertile land to a state where agriculture becomes impossible. It is responsible for a large decrease in the yields of many of the maize lands, where cultivation hence becomes uneconomic and where consequently the margins of the settled area retreat. In the Mazoe district it would appear that one quarter

[3] Based on the following sources: (1) C. L. Robertson: The Variability of Rhodesian Rainfall, *South African Journ. of Sci.*, Vol. 24, 1927, map on p. 103; (2) Normal Rainfall Map of Southern Rhodesia, 1898–1926, 1 : 3,000,000, Hydrogr. and Meteorol. Branch, Dept. of Agric., Salisbury; (3) A. C. Jennings: Irrigation and Water Supplies in Southern Rhodesia, *South African Journ. of Sci.*, Vol. 24, 1927, map facing p. 22.

of an inch of soil is lost annually from the cultivated land. On one farm the original yield of maize was 20 bags an acre. Green-cropping and the use of artificial fertilizers prove of little avail owing to the annual washing away of the soil and fertilizer. The problem is of course greatest in the areas of hill cultivation. Permanent extension of settlement in these areas can only be made possible

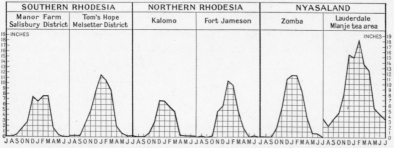

FIG. 3—Mean monthly rainfall at six stations in Rhodesia and Nyasaland. (From official figures of the respective meteorological offices.)

through remedial measures. In Nyasaland many doubted whether tea could be grown on a large scale until it was shown that anti-erosion measures could be carried out economically.

Two features combine to make soil washing particularly destructive in these parts of Africa. In the first place there is the immemorial native practice of annual grass burning, which at first was adopted by the Europeans. This reduces the humus content of the soil and makes it more liable to erosion. In the second place there is the character of the rainfall. Rain is not only restricted to a few months of the year (Fig. 3), but a large percentage falls in the form of torrential and destructive showers. Quantities of 4 inches often result from one hour's downpour. The following comparison with the régime of a humid temperate climate rainfall is instructive.

TABLE III—FREQUENCY OF TORRENTIAL SHOWERS

AMOUNT PER DAY (inches)	PERCENTAGE OF ANNUAL FALL	
	Mazabuka, N. Rhodesia	Greenwich, England
0.01–0.10	3.1	16.2
0.10–0.25	9.2	28.0
0.26–0.50	17.1	30.8
0.50–1.00	26.4	20.0
1.01 and over	44.2	5.0

Active measures are being taken to resist the menace of erosion. Government officers visit individual farms. Departmental bulletins are issued giving methods of prevention and reclamation (contouring, etc.). What is more, public opinion is gradually recognizing the value of such advice, and it is likely that ultimately there will be evolved comprehensive afforestation schemes in each of the political units of the area. Such are especially needed in the tobacco lands, where, on account of the necessity for fuel for tobacco curing, large areas of uncultivated land have been deforested and where the danger of soil erosion is at a maximum.

The Problem of Native Labor

The presence of the native offers many problems. Economically these are likely to appear in a double form. There is not only the increasing scarcity of native labor but also the danger of competition from the native himself.

The day of an abundant supply of labor is over. The demand for it has become too great, and the recent copper developments in Northern Rhodesia will intensify the situation. Here the mining companies possess an extensive recruiting organization and offer higher rates of pay and better living conditions. One factor in the failure to produce cotton in Nyasaland is the lack of labor at planting and harvesting times. And when cotton was tried in Northern Rhodesia many farmers doubted whether sufficient labor could be obtained to pick it in the event of a good crop. It is the same with tobacco and other crops. Many maize farmers are wondering how much longer they can continue producing if the native wages keep on rising. Vigorous settlement schemes for these tropical highlands are often advocated, but any sudden influx of white settlers would upset the existing balance between white and native labor and cause considerable difficulty.

The second danger, that of native competition, is also destined to become serious. Owing to his standard of living the native is able to produce maize at a price against which the European farmer is not able to compete. In 1928 from the Chiweshe Reserve alone, in the Mazoe district, 60,000 bags were sold, and it was inevitable that this secured the government contracts. If the process extends, the European farmer will be left only with the export market, with its keen world competition.

Mechanization of Agriculture As a Solution

There are two ways in which the situation is being met. In the first place there is being evolved a better technique of farming, which, among other things, implies increasing use of mechanical appliances. It is impossible to evaluate the factors involved in such mechanization because it is difficult to assess the cost of ox energy, for oxen can be sold after many years of services; their maintenance on the farm is comparatively cheap. But the efficiency of the tractor is unchallenged; and, moreover, its increased speed is important in an area where any advantage taken of favorable spells of rainfall during the sowing period is reflected in more favorable yields. The question is whether such efficiency adequately compensates for the high cost of operating. The inland situation of the area necessitates the transport of petrol and fuel paraffin over long railroad distances. Petrol at Cape Town is 1 shilling 8 pence a gallon; in Southern Rhodesia it is more than 3 shillings, and in Northern Rhodesia more than 4 shillings. It is possible that a solution may be found both in the use of new fuels and also in further technical developments in tractor manufacture. Mechanical means have to be employed within the tsetse-fly areas and are more common in Southern Rhodesia than in Northern Rhodesia.

Concentration on Crops That Do Not Require Native Labor

The other remedy lies in the nature of the commodity itself, and as time goes on development will be directed to lines that do not add to the demand for native labor, such as dairy farming and wheat and fruit cultivation. Among these, the crops that are capable of bearing the transport charges to oversea markets are particularly important. In this way a population existing on an independent basis is being created, for a white civilization based entirely on native crops would be increasingly difficult to maintain. By these means, supplemented by such economic adjustments (pools, etc.) as the circumstances of time and place demand, the possibilities of white settlement being made permanent will be increased.

Kinds of Production Suited to Company Exploitation

What conclusions can be drawn from these considerations about the unit of production in these tropical highlands? Many forms of enterprise that demand considerable outlay and provide no immediate returns are suited for a company rather than for a private individual. Ranching is one of these. As an extensive form of stock raising it can only be undertaken on the cheaper lands away from the railway. The southern part of Southern Rhodesia along the upper courses of the Sabi and Limpopo tributaries (Chiredsi, Umzingwane, etc.) contains ranches of 20,000–30,000 acres any-

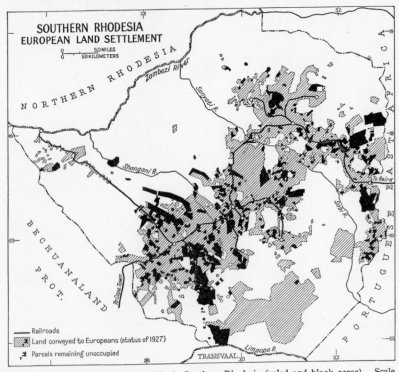

FIG. 4—Land in European ownership in Southern Rhodesia (ruled and black areas). Scale, 1 : 8,000,000. Only the black areas are not occupied. (Based on map showing status of land tenure, 1 : 1,000,000, compiled in Surveyor General's Office, Salisbury, 1927.) For native land in Southern Rhodesia, see Figure 1, page 187 above.

where up to 100 miles from the railhead, and this in a region where the altitude is not much above 2000 feet and where temperatures go above 110°. The two most outstanding establishments are those of the Rhodesia Land, Cattle, and Ranching Corporation at Nuanetsi with 100,000 head of cattle and of Messrs. Liebig's Company at Mazunga with half that number. Similarly, many crops like tea and sisal can best be exploited by a company, but in these cases the factors involved are not always simple. The case of tea is instructive. In Nyasaland tea development at Mlanje will remain a company affair; but in the Cholo district, where the rainfall, while still sufficient for the tea plant, is considerably less, it is possible for the private settler to have tobacco as an annual cash crop and use his surplus to continue the tea operations. The same considerations apply in the case of a sisal area near the railhead; there maize and beans, grown between rows of young sisal, may provide means of carrying on. These possibilities, however, are governed by the courage and initiative of the individual.

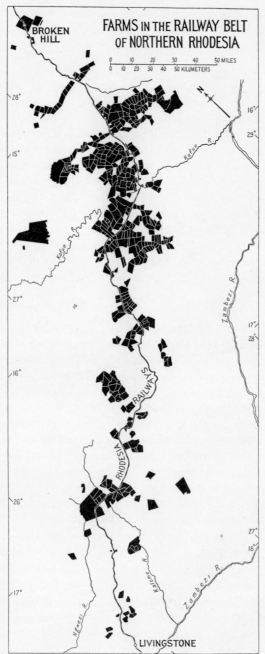

FARMS IN THE RAILWAY BELT OF NORTHERN RHODESIA

Fig. 5—Land occupied by European settlers in Northern Rhodesia in the railway belt between Livingstone and Broken Hill (for location, see Fig. 7). Scale, 1 : 2,800,000. The farms occupied up to August, 1929, are shown from information received by the author at the Government Land Office in Livingstone.

(Note that solid black in this figure represents occupied land whereas in Figure 4 it represents the unoccupied parcels within the general area of European-owned land.)

Trend to Smaller Size of Farms of Individual Settlers

Company exploitation must ever remain a valuable form of development. But the private settler is the real backbone of the community, and his estate is assuming two characteristic features. It will be smaller than hitherto, and its products will be more varied. The earlier farms were large. Land was cheap, and men came out with large conceptions of space. The idea of owning land was one of the main attractions of the area, and it is significant that until recently the question of renting or leasing land has received very little attention. Many failures in the past have been due to the fact that the settler has taken up more land than he could afford to develop, keeping but little cash in hand for bad seasons and other emergencies. The settler of the present day is content with a smaller unit, and around Gwelo original farms of 6000 acres are being subdivided into units of 1000 acres and less, while ranches of 60,000 acres are being halved.

Trend to Mixed Farming

The other characteristic of farming in the future will be its mixed character. There has been in the past too great a desire to concentrate on one crop only (e.g. tobacco). But to be successful it is necessary to spread the risk of farming and not to concentrate on a single crop; then the risks that are inevitable in all farming, and are especially great in what must long be a land of primary experiment, will be minimized. With maize, tobacco, monkey nuts (peanuts), and cotton all grown together it will take an extraordinary year to ruin the farmer. This movement in favor of mixed farming is promoted by the need of introducing crops that make but little demand on native labor. It is facilitated by the growth of towns like Umtali and Gatooma, which provide a local market for commodities such as dairy produce.

Railway Outlets to the Sea

The possibilities of production can only materialize with the aid of suitable transportation. It follows that improved transport facilities form the key to the opening up of the whole area. Such facilities are of two kinds, the construction of railway lines and the provision of subsidiary feeders.

Railway problems are concerned mainly with providing outlets for the area, that is access to the sea (Figs. 6 and 7). The main outlet at present is Beira in Portuguese East Africa, whose poor harbor is now being remedied by an extensive program of wharf construction. A very small amount of produce goes southward via Johannesburg. But alternative routes to the coast are possible. Access to the sea for Northern Rhodesia has recently been provided at Lobito by the Benguella Railway just completed through Belgian and Portuguese territory. The halfway point between Beira and Lobito is near Ndola; but geographical distance is not economic distance, and it is possible that the hinterland of Lobito may extend competitively southwards beyond Ndola into the area of agricultural settlement.

In Southern Rhodesia considerable support is given to a scheme for building a line to Walvis Bay in Southwest Africa. The great distance involved makes it doubtful whether such a line could carry economically the heavy produce of Southern Rhodesia. But it would open up to settlement considerable tracts in northern Bechuanaland, where a recent expedition not only showed the physical possibility of railway construction but also demonstrated that the region is by no means the arid waste it is often thought to be. It possesses excellent grazing land with permanent streams.

Nyasaland is also connected with Beira by railway. Continuation of the line northwards beyond Blantyre is projected; this will bring large areas to the west of Lake Nyasa within the limits of economic cultivation. But the Blantyre-Beira line is broken at the Zambezi, and produce has to be unloaded and reloaded on the other side of the river. Only commodities like tea and tobacco, which can bear the cost of such operations, can be exported from the area served by the railway. The production of cheaper crops such as maize is prohibited. There have been three proposals to eliminate this difficulty. One is the colossal undertaking of bridging the Zambezi. The other is to tap the port of Dar-es-Salaam in Tanganyika Territory around the western side of Lake Nyasa via Fife and Dodoma. A third provides for an alternative to the Beira route by an outlet at Quelimane, about 200 miles farther north. The Imperial Government favors the first proposal, and construction upon the bridge has been started. When completed the bridge will bring into the range of economical production areas that as yet lie unutilized.

SECTIONAL INTERESTS AS REFLECTED BY PROJECTED LINES AND
DIFFERENTIAL FREIGHT RATES

In any policy a certain amount of sectionalism is inevitable,
for the railway interests of one area often clash with those of another, and the sectionalism is displayed in many ways. The new
mining developments in Northern Rhodesia with the market they
provide have led to considerable agitation in Mashonaland for the
construction of a line from Kafue to Sinoia, the present railhead
of a branch leading northwest from Salisbury, thus cutting off the
detour round Bulawayo and bringing the markets of the Ndola
area much nearer Salisbury. The agitation is particularly keen in

FIG. 6—General railroad map of southern
Africa. Scale, 1 : 95,000,000.

the Logamundi district, which
would benefit most. Economic
and political motives have been
intertwined, and the situation is
complex. The proposal is generally opposed in Matabeleland,
which thinks it would lose considerably. Here, interests are intent
upon the extension of the Messina railway from the northern
boundary of the Transvaal to
connect with West Nicholson, the
railhead of a branch leading
southeast from Bulawayo. The
opening of the Limpopo bridge in 1929 makes this extension likely
within a short period. Such a line would provide an outlet through
Lourenço Marques and so enable that port to compete with Beira.

Diversity of interest may also arise from the complexities of
railway rates. A good example is furnished by the objection taken
in Northern Rhodesia to reduce the present rates on maize by 10 per
cent for the whole of Rhodesia.

Objection is taken to this proposal on the ground that it will have the
effect of further diminishing the advantage accruing to growers in the Territory by reason of their geographical position in relation to the Congo market
and markets in the northern parts of this Territory. . . .

The proposed rates will have the effect of reducing railage on maize ex
Salisbury to Congo border by 5½d per bag, ex Bulawayo by 4d and ex
Lusaka by 2d. . . . It is submitted that the protection afforded
to producers in this Territory through existing rates is fully justified by
reason of the higher cost of implements and all requirements incidental
to raising crops and should not be disturbed.

Need of Feeders to the Railroads

The railway history of the area has had in the past this peculiarity—the lines have had mineral deposits as a definite objective, such as those of Johannesburg, of Southern Rhodesia (cf. the recent

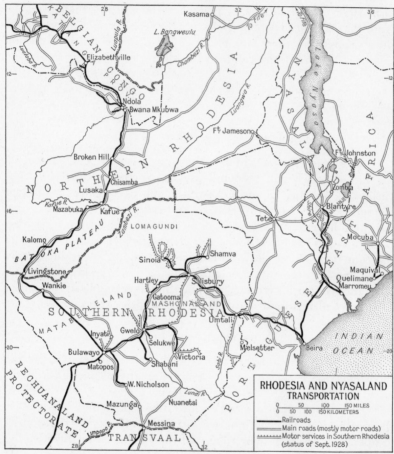

Fig. 7—Roads and railroads in Rhodesia and Nyasaland. Scale, 1 : 12,000,000. (Roads based on A. J. Clevely's maps of Northern Rhodesia and Southeast Africa and the topographic map in 1 : 1,000,000 by the Direcc. dos Serviços de Agrimensura, Colónia de Moçambique; motor services in Southern Rhodesia on map by the Rhodesia Railways.)

opening of the Shabani branch south of Gwelo), of Broken Hill, and of Bwana Mkubwa in Northern Rhodesia. This is unlike corresponding history in many other regions, where railways were run into a country to open it up agriculturally. Partly because of this peculiarity the railway track is as far as possible a "contour line," keeping to the main watershed areas and thus saving expense in the form of bridges, etc. This watershed zone has, naturally, been the area of greatest soil erosion and often is nŏt as rich as the pockets of good soil some distance away. Thus in the location of farm sites the advantage of being on the railway may often be more than balanced economically by the fertility of a more remote site. Moreover, there are many areas where conditions are not such as to warrant the capital expenditure entailed by the laying down of even a light track. In these cases feeding of the railway line is the only solution, and this involves the problematical questions of the vehicle and the road.

Formerly through Ox Transport

In early days the only mode of transport was by bullock wagon, the use of which still preponderates in Northern Rhodesia. The variability of many factors makes it difficult to estimate the limiting distance from the railway that ox transport places upon farming, but 30 miles may be accepted as an absolute maximum for maize. Lack of capital reduces the figure. If the farmer cannot buy more than one team of oxen he is economically confined to within 10 miles of the line, because only then can he bring a load a day to the railhead and so clear his crop. Only one thing can enable such a settler to go beyond this limit and that is the facilities afforded by a land bank.

Now by Motor Lorry

In Southern Rhodesia the mechanical vehicle is rapidly replacing the wagon. Here, in some areas, there is no alternative to the motor lorry. In June, 1927, the tsetse-fly menace necessitated the introduction of road-motor services into the Lomagundi district in the north (Fig. 7). Within two years the number of route-miles in operation was well over 1000. In the expansion of this idea lies a most important instrument in the opening up of new areas. At first the services were intended for perishable and dairy traffic only. But special rates in Southern Rhodesia enable them to compete with the ox wagon for bulk traffic and in some districts to extend the economic distance of maize beyond the 30-mile limit. The higher-priced crops can be grown much farther from the railhead than this. The tobacco of the Fort Jameson district of Northern Rhodesia is brought by motor lorry to the railhead at Blantyre in Nyasaland—a distance of 300 miles.

In transport as well as in production this is a land of experiment. Trials on the Rhodesian road services are being made to obtain definite information as to comparative costs of different vehicles. So far experience has shown that the two-ton six-wheeled lorry is the best type of vehicle for use in bad road and weather conditions. But it is not likely that this will be the ultimate type of vehicle, and considerable attention is being given to the matter by the British Empire Marketing Board. Emphasis is laid on the need of devising some means of movement that, owing to a big load capacity, will be cheap in cost per ton-mile and yet will not demand the building of a heavy track. The need is best expressed in this way. A train has a ton-mileage capacity per day of 150,000 and more (load 500 tons, distance 300 miles). An ox wagon has a daily capacity of less than 100 (load 5 tons, carrying distance 12 miles). The problem is to find some mean between these two extremes. The small motor lorry has a daily ton-mile capacity of about 500; this does not bridge the gap sufficiently. The considerations involved are technical in character (e.g. earth-surface pressures and fuel). Experiments are being carried now to test the practicability of a 100-ton vehicle.

Road Maintenance

Road maintenance is half the problem of transport. There are few vehicles more destructive to road surfaces than the bullock wagon, and the difficulty has been overcome by making parallel roads, one for the wagon, the other for motor traffic. Poor bridges, low-level drifts, or fords, and other deficiencies also serve to limit transport facilities. In the Mlanje district many of the most promising tea estates lie beyond the Ruo River, crossed only by a low-level drift quite impassable when the river is in flood. This is a typical complaint registered in the *Bulawayo Chronicle* (of August 17, 1929): "There was a meeting of the Inyati Farmers' Association at which strong support was given to representations to the government for making up a drift on the Ingnegiresi River on the Inyati-Insiza road. The position is impossible during the rainy season and no other outlet is available."

Local and Oversea Export Markets

The extent of the settlement of Northern and Southern Rhodesia and Nyasaland depends ultimately not on the production and transportation of crops but on their successful disposal. The market for the produce of these territories is both local and oversea. In the early days of Southern Rhodesia the market was provided by the mines. But mining operations were never on a large scale and were frequently suspended, to be renewed perhaps some years later. At such times the local farmers had to seek a more distant market. This is what happened in the area northwest of Salisbury around the extinct gold mines of Banket, Ayreshire, and El Dorado. With the growth of towns (Umtali, Gwelo, and others) and with the advent of the motor lorry, the local market for such things as dairy produce and poultry has been considerably enlarged. But relatively it has declined in importance when compared with the export market. Moreover, with the improvement of transport facilities conditions have grown more complex. The old sequence of mines followed by farms no longer holds true. A mine may derive its supplies from farms already in existence some distance away, in preference to farms near by.

In Nyasaland the absence of mines deprives farmers of a local market for maize, fruit, wheat, cattle, etc. Settlers are forced to rely entirely on the high-priced export crops—tea, tobacco, and sisal. The agricultural region of Northern Rhodesia likewise has no great local market, but it can export its produce northwards to the mineral area of Bwana Mkubwa and beyond into the Katanga district of the Belgian Congo. Within the last few years the mineral discoveries adjacent to Ndola have revolutionized settlement prospects in the territory.[4] Mining here is on a different scale from that in Southern Rhodesia; it is destined to provide a large and permanent market. A considerable amount of produce has had to be imported, and Southern Rhodesia is already attempting to compete for the market; hence the agitation in Mashonaland for the building of the Sinoia-Kafue line. This demand for foodstuffs will be trebled within the next few years. Unoccupied farms along the line in Northern Rhodesia have all been taken up, and by the end of the next decade the whole area will have been transformed.

From the foregoing survey will be seen the importance of the export market to each of the three territories on the one hand an oversea market and, on the other, a local market, namely the Ndola-Katanga region.

[4] Compare the government pamphlet "How the Mining Industry Affects the Farmer," Livingstone, 1929.

Need of Marketing Organization

From a marketing point of view the word "organization" sums up the great need of the area, organization in all branches of production. And this for two reasons. In the first place, the unit of production is small, and the demand is for large quantities. In 1928 one mining contractor was compelled to import beans because his requirements were greater than the total amount produced in Northern Rhodesia. At the same time many producers experienced difficulty in disposing of the small amounts of beans they had grown. Similarly, with better organization farmers would benefit by producing more potatoes. These considerations become important when the necessity for mixed farming is realized. In the second place, it is difficult to enter the world market in commodities that have been controlled by other countries for many years. The case of wheat is typical. The majority of flours used today are composed of blends of different wheats that have become popular. To enter into competition with these blends organization is essential.

In the old pioneering days the farmer was his own master; but today the individual cannot compete, especially in the world market, against more organized production. This was the case in the fruit industry. Up to 1921 difficulties had occurred in assembling the fruit at the ports and in arranging shipping facilities from there, mainly because the growers were unorganized. These difficulties were overcome by nearly all fruit growers coöperating to form local and district fruit growers' associations affiliated with a central body. The idea has been extended to other products, maize, milk and butter, tobacco, tea, etc.; but much more will yet be done. The tobacco failures of 1927–1929, as a result of which the settled area was considerably reduced, were due in part to the farmers' lack of knowledge of the state of the market and of the varieties of tobacco required by the buyers. The mere physical difficulty of getting farmers together in a country of great distances is an important disadvantage. When it is possible to assemble a number of farmers all living in a small area (e.g. Denmark or Ireland), the psychological factor of mutual support is very different from the state of affairs when a fraction of that number can with difficulty be drawn from an area hundreds of square miles in extent. There is some demand in Southern Rhodesia for a government policy in connection with coöperative marketing. The Union of South Africa already has a "Department of Economics and Markets."

SOCIAL PROBLEMS

The social problems presented by the lives of the settlers, men, women, and children, are best considered after a preliminary discussion of the health conditions of the area.

FACTORS AFFECTING HEALTH

The bases of the social well-being of any community are the factors affecting its health. Two disease-carrying insects present barriers to settlement, the mosquito and the tsetse fly.

TSETSE-FLY AREAS

A large part of the area north of the Zambezi is infested by the tsetse fly. By this menace the Dutch colony at Lusaka was prevented in the early days from going farther north. A belt on either side of the railway has now been freed from the parasite, and the limits of this area are extending. The position in Southern Rhodesia is different (Fig. 1). Thirty years ago, when settlement was beginning, the fly was confined to a limited area in the northwest of the territory. But in the interval it has spread considerably, and, coming into contact with the agricultural zone, has threatened a large number of farms in the Hartley and Lomagundi districts. The fly is supposed to be dependent on wild game, and operations against its spread have taken the form of bush clearing and the erection of game fences. These measures have not been as successful as was expected, and it is evident that agricultural settlement cannot protect itself against the spread of the fly, for the farmers have too little time for hunting on a large scale. Experience in the Transvaal has shown that the situation demands a different type of settlement. A chain of settlers, content with a minimum amount of agriculture and prepared to live to a large extent on the game, might be able to maintain a clear zone through which the fly could not encroach. The idea is now being applied in the Gwali area, where the advance is particularly rapid and where men are being attracted by the offer of free farms and free shooting. After the menace is over this district will be suitable for ranching.

MALARIA

Malaria retards the development of valuable areas, for the Anopheles mosquito is most prevalent in the fertile lowland valleys. Below a level of 2000 feet the risk of fever becomes too great even for the most hardy folk. But in reality malaria presents a more dangerous problem. This is the general prevalence of the disease in a milder form, not serious enough to be fatal but sufficient to wreck the constitution of the patient and make him liable to periodic attacks. In the school medical examination of Southern Rhodesia half the children gave indications of having had malaria. The gravity of the problem is increased because it is so subtle. The importance of malaria as a factor affecting the quality of the life of a country is only now beginning to be realized. The experience of classical times[5] indicates its effect upon the fiber and tone of a people. A solution is rendered all the more difficult because the remedy is a matter of individual precaution in the choice of house sites and the use of protective devices.

Nervous Strain

Apart from the definite diseases to which they are subject, there is, according to a large body of opinion both medical and general, an ailment from which white people in the highlands suffer, that for lack of a better term is called "nerve strain." This is attributed, among other things, to the effect of altitude and of the sun. On the whole these altitudes (5000–6000 feet) should have no appreciable effect upon the nervous system. But prolonged residence may alter that. It is often asserted that coastal people are much less irritable than those of the highlands. This may be due to factors other than those of altitude, but in any case the majority of settlers feel the need of a change to a coast climate at intervals. The long railway distances are as yet prohibitive, and there is some agitation for lower fares. Within the next decade or so it would seem that a coastal holiday will be a regular feature of life on these highlands. It is more likely, however, that nervous strain is due to sun effects. Here the ultra-violet or actinic rays are more concentrated than in the temperate zone and, if excessive, have a definitely harmful effect. These unexplored problems are of real importance. They will affect the quality of the life of subsequent generations and the ability of the stock to maintain its vigor. Many persons declare that children after the age of seven or eight years should spend some time out of the area. As far as the limited evidence goes it appears that the problem increases as one goes northward into Northern Rhodesia, Nyasaland, and beyond, where the altitudes are higher and the sun's rays more intense.

[5] W. H. S. Jones: Malaria, London, 1907.

South African and Oversea Origin of the Settlers

The settlers are derived from two sources, from farther south in the Union of South Africa and from overseas. Towards the end of the nineteenth century tales of the mineral wealth north of the Limpopo induced people to make their way northwards into what was practically unknown territory. Many fell before the hardships and difficulties they encountered; those who survived became hunters and prospectors, while some found areas of fertile soil and became farmers. Hastened by railway construction, hindered by the ravages of war and cattle pests, settlement proceeded and continued northward beyond the Zambezi, following the tracks of missionaries and traders in Northern Rhodesia and Nyasaland. This northward trekking, emphasized by political circumstances within the Union, has remained a permanent feature.

Among the oversea settlers there are two characteristic groups, the soldier settler and the retired colonial officials. At the close of the World War there were many who felt that they could not return again to stuffy offices and suburban garden patches. The Empire Settlement Act gave a chance to such persons, and others went with them. A certain number came out with the idea of making money and leaving the country within a few years. They soon found that money was not to be made in this way, and many began to hate the life, while some went home but normally returned again. The retired colonial officials, chiefly from India, are attracted by the climate, and farming to them is both a hobby and a supplementary source of income.

The White Settler a Manager, With a Resulting High Standard of Living

A considerable difference exists between the earlier settler and those of the last decade. When markets were distant and the ox wagon the only method of transport, the settler's produce was little more than sufficient for his own needs. But pioneering enterprise has been industrialized, and the standard of living has risen in all areas of primary settlement. It is especially high in the Rhodesias and Nyasaland. Here more than anywhere the limits to the extension of white population are set by social standards. The rôle of the white man is that of a supervisor, and settlement is therefore restricted to those with sufficient capital to guarantee this not only economically but socially. Despite the lack of social

amenities, many people are attracted to the region by the desire
to maintain a higher standard of living than is possible with the
same amount of capital in the crowded areas of the earth. A marked
contrast to these are groups of Dutch (e.g. at Lusaka and Melsetter),
who are content with a lower standard of living. While preserving
their old habit of trekking, they enter less into social contact with
the outside world and live more to themselves, comparatively
remote from the railway. The maize output of a typical hundred
farmers of the Lusaka-Chisamba district reveals the interesting
fact that 50 per cent of the farmers produced less than 1100 bags
of maize, and this does not mean a good living.

The art of living in these highlands is different from that in
the older communities. In the latter it is possible to make a livelihood without making a great success of it, but the settler in the
highlands has to make real success of his farming even to make
a livelihood at all. The word "paradox" best sums up the features
of the life; the life is one of isolation, and yet it is not.

SOCIAL LIFE OF THE SETTLER

The settlers cannot be isolated even if they would; they are
prevented economically from venturing too far from transport
facilities. Full use of these facilities is made possible because settlement in this region is of a different type from that farther south,
the cause being largely racial. In the Union of South Africa the
unit of settlement is the farm remote from its neighbor, while
here the unit is generally a group of farms remote from the next
group. Within each group the farmsteads are within four or five
miles of one another. On a small scale there are week-end tennis
parties, district football matches, and cricket leagues; and open-
hearted hospitality prevails throughout the area. On a large scale
annual agricultural shows are held in the large towns of each group.
At these and similar meetings the spirit of good fellowship has,
in the past, found its expression in an excess of drinking. But
meetings are losing much of their old social significance, for today
people are in closer touch with one another than they were ten
years ago. The motor car has altered ideas of distance, and the
possibilities of aircraft have yet to be exploited. The *Gwelo Times*
of August 16, 1928, chronicled as follows the needs of the settlers
of the Umvruna district, which have since been met: "There is a
strong demand from a number of farmers in this area for the exten-

sion of the telephone system to their holdings, and the only satis-
faction the applicants can receive is that the area is scattered.
A further effort is being made, and the services of the local legislative representative have been sought to have the matter further
ventilated."

COMPARATIVE ISOLATION THROWS SETTLER BACK ON HIS OWN RESOURCES

Yet, on the other hand, there is isolation which is largely physical
but which may be even more psychological. A farm may be isolated
for weeks and even months during the wet season, when roads
become impassable. During such a period loneliness is accentuated
by the fact that there are usually no other white folk on the farm
besides the settler's family. And at all times the settler has to do
many things he never had to do before. He may have to design
his bath and mend his own chairs, and he can never run to the
telephone to call the plumber in. In detail these are trivialities;
in the bulk they represent much of the art of living. The psychological isolation expresses itself in the absence of shops, theaters,
and all the other accompaniments of civilization. Books may be
obtained from a few rural libraries, and gramophones are abundant;
but variety, that essential feature of modern life, is lacking. Gradually one learns to do without many things, and as compensations
the local problems of farm and native come to fill up not only one's
time but one's mind.

THE WOMAN'S PART

As the unit of life more than anywhere is the home rather than
the social group, the part played by the women is greater than
in a normal community. Always in new countries the conditions
of living are much harder for the women than for the men. In
many pioneer areas they have to do the heavy work of running
a house without any outside help. Rudyard has represented the
women's point of view in British Columbia:

We have to pay for this precious state of things with our health and
our children's. . . . We have no help. A Chinaman costs fifty to
sixty dollars a month now. Our husbands can't always afford that. How
old would you take me for? I'm not thirty. Well, thank God, I stopped
my sister coming out West. O yes, it's a fine country—for men.

This may be used to measure the advantage enjoyed by women
in these tropical highlands, for here the native makes life much

easier. As with men so with women, their work consists of supervision rather than labor. They have a relatively large amount
of leisure in which to play games and take an interest in social and
political questions. A topic of great importance is the necessity
for averting the possibility of a "poor-white" problem by reducing
the dependence of the white man upon the native. The idea of
segregating the natives within their own reserves, thus preventing
their competing with the white man in the rest of the·country,
has been discussed in Southern Rhodesia. It would seem that the
men are prepared to make the financial sacrifice that this would
entail, but whether they would find the women ready to make the
social sacrifice necessitated by a return to domesticity is problematical. The introduction of cheap electric power and the increasing
use of mechanical appliances might alter the terms of the problem,
however. And the presence of the native is not without its drawback from the woman's point of view. The native servant has to
be trained and above all carefully watched; and this is no trivial
consideration in any area where inhabitants, especially the women
folks, are very liable to "nerve strain." Many women, too, live
in terror of the Black Peril; and it is never safe for a settler to leave
his family alone in the farm after dusk unless the native servants
are of long standing and trustworthy.

WOMEN'S OCCUPATIONS

One reason why life on a farm falls more heavily on the women
is that a man generally has more interests in life. But this leisure
makes a difference, from the woman's point of view. Among
other things it usually results in a garden, which is one of the
characteristic features of a Rhodesian home, and with the growth of
urban centers and with the advent of motor-lorry services a new
possibility has emerged in the keeping of poultry and the activities
of dairying. This has its economic aspect and may become an
important element in mixed farming. In the fruit areas there is
jam making, in the planting community of Nyasaland there is
clerical work, and in short over all portions of the area women
are able to participate in the task of income earning to a greater
extent than in the long-settled lands. Their status in the social
structure is correspondingly higher. Many older women in the
event of the death of their husbands carry on alone. One of the
arguments used in England in favor of women's suffrage was the fact

that a woman held the record for yield of cotton per acre in Northern Rhodesia and Nyasaland. But despite these new interests
many women are temperamentally incapable of leading such a life.
On a farm one has to make one's own entertainment, and to some
life becomes terrible. There are not a few tragedies, but that is an
individual and personal matter.

MEDICAL CARE

The common sorrow that all women have is the fear of illness,
especially with children's ailments to worry about. This is one
of the real problems of the settler in pioneer regions. There are
not only the physical difficulties of getting a doctor, but there are
economic and financial ones; for to visit an outlying farm and to
return over bad roads may occupy the greater part of the doctor's
working day. Along the railroad line between Livingstone and
Lusaka in Northern Rhodesia, a distance of over 300 miles, there
are only two doctors. That women are demanding more and more
attention is indicated in the increasing provision of better facilities,
medical and other. In 1927 in Southern Rhodesia a Women's
Institute Movement was started "to improve and develop conditions of rural life by providing centers for educational facilities
and social intercourse."

CHILDREN'S EDUCATION

In all areas of primary settlement the problem of educating
the children of settlers in remote districts is a difficult one. In this
land it is not only more difficult, it is more vital. It is more difficult
owing to transport and climatic conditions; a system of country
schools as in Australia would not meet the case. It is more vital
because the presence of a native population demands the maintenance of a high social standard if a "poor white" problem is to
be averted.

Owing to these circumstances Rhodesia has developed special
features in its educational system. The minimum number of children required to establish a government school is ten. There are,
however, many scattered farms where it was impossible to secure
a daily attendance of ten children. To meet these cases a system
of "aided farm schools" was introduced, where the government
makes a grant per scholar per annum towards the salary of a govern-
ess appointed by the parents. Two or more families near one

another may combine to establish an "aided farm school" for their children; but the standard of education thus provided cannot be high.

The other feature is the prominence attained by the boarding system for country children in the Rhodesian educational régime. Ever since 1908 the number of boarders has remained at between a quarter and a third of the total school population, a proportion not equaled elsewhere in the British Empire and probably a permanent feature in this area. But, obviously, the cost of education to the country parent is considerably greater than to the town parent. This is an outstanding problem when it is remembered that, although agriculture includes one quarter of the income earners of Southern Rhodesia, these pay only one per cent of the total income tax. In one district five of the largest farmers, with 21 children among them, have definitely decided that at the first opportunity they will get rid of their farms and clear out. The education question is an important element in the townward movement of population in southern Africa. The situation would seem to be essentially a matter for government aid, as the burden of the insufficiently educated child in this land will in the long run be greater than the cost of educating him. Northern Rhodesia has not passed beyond the state of primary schools, while in Nyasaland education still remains in the hands of missions and private teachers.

Practical Training As an Offset to Dangers of Children's Wrong Attitude Toward Labor

Continued development and closer settlement will solve many of these problems, but there are others of a different category that will not be solved so easily. These stand outside the school walls, for the community itself is the ultimate educator; they are indirectly and directly psychological. There are elements at work that sap the energies and weaken the morale of the privileged European. The report of a recent Education Commission[6] emphasizes the point: "We found among witnesses everywhere a lively and almost alarmed sense of the danger of moral degeneration which threatens the youth of a country where the services of others are so easily come by, and where the labor that serves the first needs of life is apt to be despised as menial and dishonoring."

[6] Southern Rhodesia: Report of the Education Commission, 1929, Cape Town, 1929.

It is indeed questionable whether a race freed entirely from the necessity of manual labor can retain, without some special effort, its full virility. The upper strata of every society are continually recruited from the layers beneath. This is impossible in a land where a white aristocracy rests on a foundation of black labor. And the situation is not helped by the general tropical danger of slackness. In Rhodesian schools practical training would appear to be more necessary than anywhere else as a means if not as an end of education—housecraft for girls, manual work for boys. The fact that white people are destined to become supervisors is itself a reason for training in practical operations, especially in the case of agriculture. Never before have the attractions of the city and town been so strong; the causes, economic and social, are world-wide. Educational facilities alone will do but little to keep the cityward movement in check. In Rhodesia there is evidence of a comparatively strong tendency among sons of farmers to return to the land. In one high school more than half the boys are adopting farming of some kind. It is therefore all the more important that no one be lost to agriculture for lack of suitable training. The Matopos Agricultural School is a start in the right direction.

There is, furthermore, the direct psychological effect of the native. The Rhodesian child is bereft of a large portion of the white inheritance, and the report of the Commission declares: "Children growing up in such a situation breathe as it were a psychological atmosphere which may have an effect upon their mental and emotional life that is largely unsuspected." They may come to have different standards of character, a different code of morality. Children continually and inevitably in contact with the native may adopt his habits of thought. In the tropics it is more true than anywhere else that "a man's greatest enemy is himself." The second generation of settlers always lacks many persons with the special gifts of the pioneer—with his unconscious inheritance of the standards he left behind him. To maintain these things in a tropical region will be exceedingly difficult, yet the maintenance of such standards will be the deciding factor in the ultimate fate of settlement in south central Africa.

RURAL COLONIZATION IN NORTH AFRICA
(ALGERIA, TUNIS, AND MOROCCO)

AUGUSTIN BERNARD

ALGERIA, Tunis, and Morocco, enclosed between the Mediterranean and the Sahara, are a geographic unit. From the standpoint of rural colonization and European settlement this region represents a very special case; there are few like it elsewhere in the world and in colonial history. In tropical colonies the Europeans, who are few in numbers, are administrators, heads of large undertakings, or directors of agricultural enterprises; but they stand aloof from the life of the natives and do not interfere with its course nor change its character. In colonies of the temperate zone, on the other hand, the Europeans, whether they found the country practically uninhabited or whether they decimated the native population, are in general the sole masters and can organize the administration and distribute the land at will. North Africa, in contradistinction to the great settlement colonies acquired by the white race during the nineteenth century, is not empty or nearly empty, as were the United States, Canada, Australia, and Argentina. It is inhabited by an indigenous population that does not tend to disappear but on the contrary increases rapidly. These natives are not savage hunters or fishermen, as is the case in other parts of the world. As tillers of the soil or herdsmen almost all gain their livelihood from the earth. Their civilization is very different from ours and is based on other ideas and principles, but it is nevertheless a civilization. However, they are insufficient in numbers and in degree of civilization alone to exploit the greater part of the resources of their country without the intervention of Europeans. The problem is therefore to establish a system of displacement which will not work injustice on them and to set down a numerous European population in the midst of the native population, which is and always will be the greater in numbers. As a result of the presence of natives, European settlement, which is entirely feasible in theory, i.e. so far as the environment is concerned, becomes difficult in practice. It is no longer only a question of determining which is the best area for settlement and how it can best be put to use, but rather of considering how and in what measure, owing to the native population, settlement is possible by Europeans.

THE NATURAL AND HUMAN CONDITIONS

On the map North Africa occupies a large area, especially if there be added the extensive Saharan region, which adjoins it and which is attached to it politically to a greater or lesser degree. Algeria from the administrative standpoint is divided into a northern part, Algeria proper, 207,492 square kilometers in size, and a southern part, the Térritoires du Sud, which have an area of 2,192,400 square kilometers. A similar administrative segregation of the hinterland is not made in the case of Morocco and Tunis, but if the desert is excluded the three countries have approximately the following areas: Morocco about 500,000, Algeria about 300,000, and Tunis about 125,000 square kilometers, or a combined area about equivalent to France and Spain together.

RAINFALL

Not all of this area by any means is available for agriculture or for European rural colonization. Everything depends on the amount and distribution of rainfall (Fig. 1), which is the essential factor and the one to which attention must hence be mainly directed. In general there is a decrease of rainfall from the coast toward the interior, with local increases on the higher mountain ranges and decreases in the plains and the areas screened from the influence of the sea. Certain parts of North Africa receive an abundant rainfall which, in the mountains adjacent to the sea and exposed to the damp winds, may attain and even exceed an annual average of 1000 millimeters. But, viewed as a whole, North Africa is a region of little rainfall. However, a total rainfall greater than in other countries is necessary because of the high degree of evaporation caused by sun and wind and the small amount of cloudiness. The rainfall of North Africa generally comes in the form of short and violent downpours which do not penetrate the soil. They occur only during a few months, during a few days of these months, and during a few hours of these days. Furthermore, they are extremely irregular both as to quantity and as to season.

THE THREE NATURAL REGIONS OF NORTH AFRICA

It is on the basis of the rainfall régime that North Africa may be divided into the following three regions: the Tell, with trees and agriculture; the steppe, a pastoral grassland; and the Sahara, barren, without water, without trees, without cultivation except in the oases and by irrigation. The mean annual isohyet of 300 millimeters may be considered approximately the limit between the Tell and the steppe, and the isohyet of 200 millimeters between the steppe and the Sahara. These limits can readily be plotted on a map[1] as sufficient rainfall observations are now available, but even without these observations the character of the natural vegetation would be a sure guide. Of course, these characterizations hold true only in a general way. In detail they would require a great number of modifications that cannot be elucidated except through an intensive study of the soils and the climate. It is evident, for example, that on the western coast of Morocco and on the eastern coast of Tunis, where the air is damp and there is frequent dew, cultivation, as experience shows, can thrive with much less rainfall than is necessary on the high plateaus of Algeria. It should also be stated that the Tell, the steppe, and the Sahara do not, as it is sometimes thought, represent three uninterrupted belts: there are forested and arable islands in the steppe, and even in the Sahara there are islands of steppe and in the Tell islands of desert. However, with these reservations, it remains true that the Tell, the zone of forest and agriculture, is in general not more than 100 to 150 kilometers wide along the Atlantic, the Mediterranean, and the Gulf of Gabes. As thus defined the area of the Tell may be estimated as follows: 15,000,000–18,000,000 hectares in Morocco, 10,000,000–12,000,000 hectares in Algeria, and 4,000,000–5,000,000 hectares in Tunis.

RELIEF

North Africa is a country of accentuated relief. Extensive and continuous lowland plains are met with only in western Morocco and eastern Tunis. Elsewhere merely small plains occur, separated from each other by ranges or mountain massifs. Such are the Mitidja back of Algiers, the Bougie plain, and the Bône plain. All the rest of the country is occupied by mountains or high plateaus. The mountains and forests are far from being useless in the economy of the country, but of course they withdraw large areas from cultivation. Hence, although the total area of North Africa is large, the utilizable area is very small.

[1] Augustin Bernard and R. de Flotte de Roquevaire: Atlas d'Algérie et de Tunisie, Algiers and Paris, since 1923, fasc. 3, 5, 6, and 7 (Climatologie).

A. Jury and G. Dedebant: Étude sur le régime des pluies du Maroc, *Mémoires Soc. des Sci. Nat. du Maroc*, No. 9, Rabat and Paris, 1924.

The Native Population

That is not all.   The Europeans, settlers and others, have
to divide what remains with the natives.   The natives number
about 12,000,000: 5,000,000 in Morocco (of whom 500,000 in
Spanish Morocco), 5,000,000 in Algeria, and 2,000,000 in Tunis.
The density of the native population is very uneven; three-quarters
of the natives live in the Tell and especially in its mountain areas,
for, contrary to conditions in Europe, in North Africa the moun-

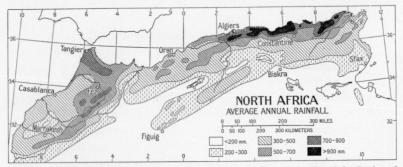

Fig. 1—Average annual rainfall of North Africa.   Scale, 1 : 19,000,000.   (Based, for Tunis and
Algeria, on annual rainfall map, 1 : 1,500,000, in "Atlas d'Algérie et de Tunisie," by Augustin
Bernard and R. de Flotte de Roquevaire, Algiers and Paris, appearing since 1923; for Morocco,
on annual rainfall map on same scale by A. Jury and G. Dedebant, *Mémoires Soc. des Sci. Nat.
du Maroc*, No. 9, Rabat and Paris, 1924.)

tainous country is more densely populated than the plains.   Certain
mountain massifs such as the Greater Kabylia region of the Djur-
djura Range (100 inhabitants to the square kilometer) are greatly
overpopulated.   Over 80 per cent of the natives derive their living
from the soil, either by agriculture or by stock raising.   They are
poor tillers of the soil and poor stock breeders.   They have only
primitive farming tools and poor cattle.   Their crops are miserably
small and just barely keep them from starving.   They practice inefficient methods of cattle raising and see their herds decimated by
drought, cold, and epizoötics.   This native population increases
rapidly.   In Morocco and Tunis the censuses are too recent to make
it possible to judge this increase properly.   But in Algeria the native
population has certainly doubled and probably tripled since 1830:
from 1886 to 1926 it increased from 3,000,000 to 5,000,000. This increase is only a source of congratulation, first, because it proves that
French rule has been beneficial to the natives by freeing them from
internecine wars, famines, and epidemics and, second, because this native population provides the necessary labor supply for the European
settlers.   But the available area is thereby reduced correspondingly.

THE COLONIZATION OF NORTH AFRICA AND ITS RESULTS

THE EUROPEAN POPULATION

Among the 12,000,000 natives there live today more than 1,000,000 Europeans (872,000 in Algeria, 175,000 in Tunis, 105,000 in French Morocco, 100,000 in Spanish Morocco). There is no longer any doubt that the European is perfectly acclimated in all of

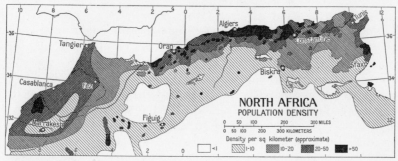

FIG. 2—Population distribution in North Africa (natives and Europeans). Scale, 1 : 19,000,000. (Generalized from population density maps of unequal value and dates: (1) of Tunis (census of 1926), in Jean Despois: La Tunisie, Paris, 1930, p. 88; (2) of Algeria (census of 1921) by Service Cartogr., Gouvt. Gén. de l'Algérie, Algiers; (3) of Morocco, in the writer's "Le Maroc," 7th edit., Paris, 1931, based on N. Larras, La Géogr., Vol. 13, 1906, p. 341.

North Africa. When Algeria was first occupied the unhealthfulness of certain plains (especially the Mitidja, where most of the settlers were concentrated), the difficult living conditions, the lack of knowledge or the misinformation with regard to the most elementary rules of hygiene produced a relatively high mortality. But since 1856 the number of births has been annually greater than the number of deaths. The death rate among Europeans in Algeria today (17 per thousand) is less than in Spain or Italy; with a birth rate of about 24 per thousand the excess of births over deaths is about 7000 to 8000 a year. As to hygienic conditions and population growth, Tunis and Morocco also are now satisfactory.

Almost all the Europeans are settled in the Tell. They do not live in a continuous belt, as do the natives, but are scattered about in larger and smaller groups. In contrast to the natives, they avoid the mountains, especially those that are inaccessible and compact. The Europeans occupy mainly the plains; from these the natives had previously withdrawn because of their openness to attack, because of malaria, and also because of the difficulty of tilling this land and its clayey soils with primitive agricultural implements. The density of the European population is generally in inverse ratio to that of the native density. Thus the department of Constantine has only 170,000 Europeans to 2,000,000 natives, whereas the department of Oran has 350,000 Europeans to 1,000,000 natives, or one European to three natives.

FRANCE'S COLONIZATION POLICY

France might have conceived her mission as limited to the carrying out of what are called the preparatory undertakings of colonization: the construction of roads and railroads, the building of harbors and of water works, the organization of credit; and she might have relied on natives alone for the cultivation of the soil. Her conception of colonization might have implied that the Europeans would live only in the cities and that they would control the higher fields of commerce and industry and direct the steamship companies, the banks, and the mining enterprises, while at the same time commanding the instruments of power, the army, the government, and the courts. But this is not the solution that prevailed nor for many reasons could prevail. For one, the natives were not sufficiently amenable or docile for the exploitation of the natural resources of the country to be left in their hands alone. Then again, North Africa was so near the relatively poor and over-populated areas of southern Europe—Spain, Italy, Malta—that their inhabitants would inevitably have poured into North Africa, both into its cities and into the rural districts. Finally, it was in keeping with the genius and tradition of France to attempt to establish new French territory beyond the Mediterranean, a New France. As a result of these circumstances the Europeans have spread out everywhere, have acquired lands, and have cultivated the soil. There is no such thing as an area reserved for the natives and another reserved for the settlers, as is the case in many parts of the world. The intention has been, as Marshal Bugeaud, who was governor of Algeria in 1840, put it, "everywhere to intermingle Europeans and natives."

STATE-INITIATED COLONIZATION

A still further step was taken, and, to the great disgust of certain economists, the system of official colonization was introduced—a system that consists of establishing in village centers French families to whom land is given free or sold at a low price with easy repayment terms, under the condition in either case of their residing upon it. This procedure was justified on various counts. In the period immediately following the conquest of the country the general security was insufficient to allow Europeans to settle on isolated farms—those who had settled in this manner were massacred during the insurrection of 1839. Furthermore, land tenure was so complicated that it was extremely difficult for individuals to buy land directly from the natives. Also, it was necessary in order to counterbalance the large emigration from the countries of southern Europe to reinforce French colonization artificially, France being and always having been a country with little emigration.

In Algeria

In Algeria this official colonization has always been successful, now more, now less. Sometimes it was carried out rather awkwardly and was open to criticism on the score that too often settlers were sent over who were not tillers of the soil at home and who were hence poorly equipped for their task, that the grants of land made were too small to provide a living, and that settlers with insufficient funds had been selected who inevitably would succumb under the initial expenses attendant on opening up new land to cultivation. The waste in undertakings of this kind is always considerable; it would have been less if better methods had been used. Nevertheless the objective of official colonization, namely to settle the rural districts of Algeria with Frenchmen, has finally been attained, as was proved by the investigation made in 1906 by H. de Peyerimhoff,[2] the report of which represents the best work on the colonization of Algeria. The degree of success of this colonization has varied with the region selected, with its accessibility, and especially with the character of the settlers. Almost no centers have arisen other than those created by official action, and on the other hand none of the centers so created has disappeared. It is official colonization that has conjured up those red-roofed villages, which are the ornament of Algeria and give a French aspect to the landscape of these old Barbary states. Official colonization established the framework that private colonization has filled out. It opened up new territory and then turned it over to private initiative. All in all the area of settlement in Algeria amounts to 2,400,000

[2] Henri de Peyerimhoff: Enquête sur les résultats de la colonisation officielle, 2 vols., Algiers, 1906 (republished by the Comité Bugeaud, Paris, 1928).

hectares, of which 700,000 have gone into European hands through private colonization and the remaining 1,700,000 hectares are due to official colonization. There are 800 European villages, 70,000 land owners, and 300,000 agriculturists.

In Tunis and Morocco

In Tunis and Morocco European rural settlement is much less developed and much more scattered than in Algeria. There are several reasons for this. In the first place French intervention in these two countries is of much later date than in Algeria. What was possible in 1830 was no longer or at least not to the same extent possible in 1881 and 1912, in view of the changed world conditions and the changed temper of the native population. Furthermore, although there is every reason to hope that colonization will finally result in an understanding and collaboration between Europeans and natives, it cannot be denied that at least at the beginning the presence of a large number of Europeans in the rural districts and their taking possession of the soil introduce a very disturbing element into native society; in Tunis and Morocco, which are protectorates established on the basis of as complete preservation as possible of native institutions, settlement could therefore not proceed as freely as in Algeria. Finally, the criticisms that had been made of the methods used in Algeria discouraged applying them to Tunis and Morocco and, indeed, led rather to a belief in the efficiency of diametrically opposite methods. Gradually, however, the two points of view approached each other; Tunis since 1900 and Morocco since 1918 have turned to official colonization, although often without much inner conviction and in any case somewhat late, in view of the fact that the best lands had already been acquired by agencies not intending to colonize them and that speculation had much raised their price. In Tunis 650,000 hectares are in the hands of Europeans, of which 275,000 hectares were acquired through official colonization. In Morocco the Europeans occupy 675,000 hectares, of which 200,000 hectares are due to official colonization. The number of European settlers actually living on their land is very slight in both countries. Nevertheless the conditions relating to settlement are practically the same as in Algeria as regards land tenure, vacant lands, and native population density, in short as regards the possibility of establishing European settlements. What has been accomplished in Algeria can and must be carried out in Morocco.

The Work of European Rural Colonization

The work of European rural colonization has consisted of extending the cultivated area, of improving the old crops, and of introducing new varieties. As Algerian agriculture suffers mainly from the scarcity and irregularity of its rainfall, the means of remedying this defect are: irrigation, which makes the farmer independent of the caprices of weather; dry farming, which stores moisture in the soil; and tree culture, which utilizes a crop element that is more drought-resistant than annuals. Numerous irrigation enterprises exist in North Africa; in northern Algeria proper the irrigated surface amounts to 200,000 hectares, and in the Térritoires du Sud the drilling of artesian wells has produced very satisfactory results. The methods of dry farming, called in North Africa preparatory tilth or cultivated fallow, applied to the growing of cereals, have made it possible to increase and to regularize the yield and to open up to cultivation the marginal belt between the Tell and the steppe, where no agriculture had been practiced by the natives. A considerable area has been planted to vineyards; these represent the most valuable element of North African agriculture. The cultivation of the olive has been made successful by the improved methods of pruning and oil-extraction. Other fruit crops occupy an important place. The cultivation of early vegetables, of tobacco, and of cotton has developed in a satisfactory manner. The European settlers have exploited a number of local products, which the natives do not know how to utilize, such as cork, esparto, and the mineral resources. The example of Europeans in the improvement of agriculture and economic conditions has been followed, although somewhat slowly and so far insufficiently, by the natives; these have been benefited by the wages paid them by the Europeans and still more by the example set them. In many places areas devoted to seasonal herding and free pasture have given way to the growing of grain; and this in turn has been replaced in the fertile plains and those near the sea by more valuable crops, such as grapes, early vegetables, and cotton. All these new resources have made it possible for a greater population to live on the territory of North Africa.

Settling the rural districts has always appeared to old African colonials as the only means of permanently establishing French superiority, because that amounts to taking possession of the soil—and in the end a country always belongs to those who till its soil. To establish and maintain as numerous a rural French population as possible is indispensable to the progress of North Africa. The presence of the European in the rural districts is the surest means of bringing the natives closer to France and of weaning them from their ancient barbarism.

THE PROBLEMS TO BE SOLVED

Is there still room in North Africa for more European settlers than those now living there? This is precisely the problem which was the subject of the Congress of Rural Colonization held in Algiers in May, 1930.[3] It is also the question which J. Célérier put to himself recently with regard to Morocco.[4] A whole volume would be necessary to answer this question. A rainfall map and a map of native population density (Figs. 1 and 2)[5] both of which it is possible to prepare with reasonable accuracy, yield important clues as to the areas where European settlement is not possible either because of insufficient rainfall or because of close occupation by the natives.

As Célérier observes quite correctly, there are no new countries other than those that are uninhabited. An old house is not so conveniently managed as is one that has been built according to one's tastes. Given the natural and human conditions of North Africa as they are, the settler there is like a delicate and valuable plant that has been transplanted at great cost and that cannot be left without constant attention lest it be choked by the natural vegetation.

In the first place, there must be preserved for the European element its legitimate rôle of landownership and its position of influence in the long-settled areas, where it is not a question of extending that influence but of maintaining it. Rural colonization in North Africa is undeniably undergoing a crisis at present, which is due to the drift of settlers to the cities, to the repurchase of land by the natives, and to the tendency to create large holdings.

THE DRIFT TO THE CITIES

The European population of Algeria is exposed to the magnetic attraction of the cities—a regrettable but, as is well known, a

[3] The proceedings of the congress were published in four volumes under the title "Congrès de la Colonisation Rurale, Alger, 26–29 mai 1930," Algiers, [1931], Vol. 1: Comptes rendus des séances du Congrès; Vol. 2: Les problèmes économiques et sociaux posés par la colonisation; Vol. 3: Monographies algériennes; Vol. 4: La colonisation rurale dans les principaux pays de peuplement. For a general account of the congress, see Albert Naud: Le congrès de la colonisation rurale (Alger, mai 1930), Renseign. Colon. (Suppl. à l'Afrique Française), 1930, pp. 513–539.

[4] J. Célérier: Le Maroc est-il un pays neuf?, Rev. de Géogr. Marocaine, Vol. 8, 1929, pp. 65–97.

[5] Figure 2, although representing total population distribution, closely reflects native population distribution inasmuch as Europeans represent only one-twelfth of the rural population (see above, p. 225).

world-wide phenomenon. Not only do colonized villages lose
population, but small cities like Blida and Tizi-Ouzou (both not
far from Algiers) experience a decline in the number of their European inhabitants other than officials. The European rural population of Algeria appears to have lost about 10,000 persons since 1911.

THE REPURCHASE OF LAND BY THE NATIVES

As regards land owned by Frenchmen, between 1880 and 1917
the natives had sold to Europeans in Algeria 1,076,000 hectares
and had repurchased from them 297,000; but during the World
War and up to 1920 they had repurchased from the Europeans
more land than they had sold them. Since 1920 the purchases and
sales of land have about balanced; and, while European holdings
continue to increase in the department of Oran, they decrease
in the department of Constantine. In Tunis the land crisis has
been even more accentuated. The repurchase of settlers' lands by
the natives has a double disadvantage: a political disadvantage
because of the check on French rural colonization, and an economic
disadvantage because, where French farms fall into the hands of
the natives, the buildings are no longer kept in shape, the cattle
are neglected, the equipment is given no care, and the soil reverts
to weeds—it is a return to barbarism.

THE TENDENCY TO CREATE LARGE HOLDINGS

Finally, the creation of what amounts to actual *latifundia*
may be observed in many places: if this development is sometimes
of economic advantage it obviously militates against a denser
European population inasmuch as a single landowner with the
help of labor almost exclusively native manages alone the territory
that before had maintained several European families.

THE SOLUTION OF THESE PROBLEMS IN ALGERIA

The situation deserves serious attention, but in our opinion
it would be exaggeration to speak of the failure of colonization.
On the whole, all Algeria withstood well the terrible shock of the
World War, and her foundations have not been shaken. However,
speed is necessary to fill the cracks and close the breaches. With
regard to the rural exodus it should be noted that the present-day
means of communication, especially the automobile, permit the

settler to live in a large city and at the same time manage a farm that is relatively far away. The repurchase of land by the natives is now rather limited and localized. Finally, it would seem possible to favor small and moderate holdings by systematic measures— by the organization of an agricultural credit system that would make it possible for the small settler to band with his fellows in order to buy large holdings and divide them up among themselves by allotment. The first attempt of this kind[6] has been carried out at Mouzaïville near Blida. An estate of 360 hectares was bought for 3,600,000 francs and divided among nine settlers' families; in the same locality another estate of 140 hectares was bought for 2,500,000 francs and was allotted to seven families. Thus, where before there were only native workers under the direction of a single European who represented the absentee landlords, there are now attached to the soil sixteen families by the powerful bond of ownership. The Bugeaud Committee advises settlers to surround themselves with families of European agricultural workers and European day laborers who, without replacing European workers, would represent an important supplementary element and would tend to become established as small landowners.

STATE AID TO ASSUME NEW FORMS

Is the work of official colonization finished, at least in Algeria? As long ago as 1906 H. de Peyerimhoff, in concluding his investigation, declared that official colonization would itself be suitable only up to a certain time, after which it should give way to free colonization, and he predicted that this moment was not far away. Of the three processes necessary for the creation of a settlement center— namely the fixing of its outer limits, the establishment of its center, and the peopling of the village—it is the last, contrary to what one might imagine, that is the easiest. In North Africa there was no lack of settlers but there was a lack of land. There is no more public domain available, and the natives in general refuse to sell their property, either because of their dislike to abandon the soil of their ancestors or because of their instinctive or systematic opposition to the establishment of new European centers. It is not the desire of the French authorities to have recourse to expropriation, although this method offers all the necessary guarantees for the protection of individual interests, and it is practically never

[6] L. Boyer-Banse: Le crédit agricole et la colonisation en Algérie, in Congrès de la Colonisation Rurale, Alger, 1930, Vol. 2, pp. 353–374.

applied. In many cases the efforts of the government are limited to opening up new areas to private initiative for the creation of access routes and to the establishment of small villages and hamlets.

This does not mean that the intervention of the state is not necessary; but this intervention in the future will take place under new forms—in the endowment and management of a colonization fund, in the organization of rural credit, in the redemption of available properties, and in their resale, with help to the settlers in financing. It is astonishing that, while great sacrifices were being made to establish French colonists in North Africa, the means were neglected to make it possible for them to succeed. If they are to take root firmly they must be maintained in their struggle with fickle nature. Of what use is it to give land to a settler who has not the wherewithal to cultivate it? Rural credit, henceforth put on an organized footing, will meet this fundamental need. It is necessary to pursue a rational colonization policy and to institute new and flexible methods intermediary between official and free colonization.

Three Objectives of Agricultural Policy

Colonization in North Africa, as has been said, may have three objectives: to increase the cultivated area, to introduce new crops, to improve the old crops. What remains to be done in each one of these three matters?

To Extend the Cultivated Area

In Algeria the southern limit of cultivation seems to have been reached, if not even exceeded. Certain settlements that had been pushed out to the border of the steppe led a hazardous existence because the grain growing that they practiced is too precarious and uncertain. The case is not exactly the same in Tunis and Morocco. In Tunis the cultivation of the olive continues to advance toward the south, and .t seems possible to extend its area, at least in the vicinity of the sea. In the Tell in Algeria there remain some arable lands that are not yet cultivated. This holds true with even greater force in Tunis and particularly in Morocco. However great one may estimate the eventual increase of native population to be, it is certainly possible for the Europeans to have a larger share in the exploitation of the soil.

To Introduce New Crops

New crops can certainly be introduced and developed. It took Algeria fifty years to realize that the cultivation of the vine would enrich her resources enormously. Morocco, in search of a valuable crop that would play the same part in her economy, hopes to find the solution in the sugar beet. Cotton growing, although the suitable areas are rather restricted, can doubtless be developed. But reliance must be placed mainly on an improvement of the old crops and methods of cultivation.

To Improve Old Methods

If North Africa is properly speaking not a "new land," it can, leaving aside mining industries and commerce, maintain by agriculture alone a much larger number of Europeans than are there at present. Seasonal pasturage as it is practiced now requires enormous areas and permits only a sparse population distribution; its methods have not been improved to their fullest extent because the Europeans so far have taken almost no interest in it; coöperation between Europeans and the natives would produce important results in this matter. The system of cultivated fallow also needs large areas, since the soil yields a crop only once in two years and hence it is necessary to have 200 hectares of land to grow 100 hectares of grain. This crop rotation is certainly the best plan at present and should not be given up; it would seem possible, however, on land sufficiently well watered and with the help of stock and fertilizer to put into effect some less burdensome combination. Fruit crops and early vegetables certainly can be much extended and will produce yields of value. Finally, in all countries irrigation can support a dense population and indeed implies its existence. Doubtless irrigation is not a panacea for North Africa; the areas suitable for irrigation will always be small and the amount of water available limited. Nevertheless the maximum possible has not been attained. In Algeria large works are being built in the Chelif valley. Morocco, although not abounding in perennial streams, is better endowed in this respect than Algeria and Tunis. On the high plateaus the number of places to water cattle can be increased in certain areas. Finally, by increasing the permeability of the soil during the rainy season, reserves of underground water will be built up with which to contend against the dry season. Simple operations and minor works undertaken by the settlers themselves, such as the reforestation of the mountains, the planting of trees, the horizontal canalization of slopes, the protection of springs, the building of revetments in gulleys, will decrease the amount of soil erosion, will retard run-off, and will increase the absorption of water by the soil while at the same time decreasing evaporation.

Conclusion: The Outlook

To summarize: We believe that further European rural colonization is entirely possible in North Africa, both in Tunis and Morocco, where it is still far from complete, and in Algeria, where it is further advanced. To be sure, for the utilization of the resources of North Africa the coöperation of the natives must in large measure be relied on; this is not only a duty to the rural population but an economic necessity. But it is indispensable that as many European families as possible be dispersed among the natives to act as their counselors and their monitors. Thus, as M. Jules Cambon said, the French will be able to apply to their work in North Africa what Burke, in his speech on conciliation with America, said of that of the Anglo-Saxon in America: "Our ancestors have turned a savage wilderness into a glorious empire, and have made the most extensive and the only honourable conquests, not by destroying but by promoting the wealth, the number, the happiness of the human race."

THE BASES OF COLONIZATION IN
NORTH EUROPEAN RUSSIA*

V. P. Voshchinin

THE North European part of the U.S.S.R.,[1] consisting of the Murmansk Area, the Autonomous Soviet Republic of Karelia, and the Northern District, including the Autonomous Area of Komi, with a total area of about 1,400,000 square kilometers, comprises several geographical belts divided into a number of regional units with different natural and economic resources, each of which has its own character and its own development prospects. The sparse population of this area (2,700,000) is mainly concentrated in the southern and southeastern parts. The density of population along the shores of the Barents, White, and Kara Seas is not more than 0.2–0.3 person to the square kilometer.

THE NATURAL BELTS OF THE REGION AND THEIR COLONIZATION VALUE

Lacking any substantial food resources the whole polar belt, owing to its severe climatic conditions, cannot be thoroughly occupied by man; all that can be done is to strengthen and rationalize the existing hunting and fishing economy. In the sub-belt of typical and southern tundra, and also the belt of forest-tundra, stock breeding (mainly reindeer) is practiced to a greater or lesser extent, and even primitive truck gardening is carried on; in this area, owing to the presence of scattered meadow and forest land, rational colonization is not out of the question, but its high cost puts it off for an uncertain time. On the other hand, the belt of *taiga* (the forested part of the Kola Peninsula, almost all of the

---

* Written with the kind collaboration of G. D. Tsinzerling, scientific secretary of the Geographical Institute of the University of Leningrad.

[1] In the present article is dealt with, as an example, one of the four regions into which the U.S.S.R., according to the author, may possibly be divided from the standpoint of colonization, the other three being (1) the Ob-Irtysh region, including northern Kazakstan; (2) the Lena-Baikal region and the Far East; and (3) Turkestan, including southern Kazakstan. North European Russia has recently been in the forefront of interest because of the rôle played by its lumber industry on the international market. The article, written early in 1930, gives an outline of the plan for its development. The region as here defined embraces the territory between the Finnish border and the Urals and between the Dc-Db climatic boundary (see Fig. 1, p. 241 below) and the Arctic Sea.—EDIT. NOTE.

Northern District, and most of Karelia) may be considered a colonization region of the near and, in some places, of the immediate future. The prospects of this colonization are determined primarily by factors of a physico-geographical order.

The Fennoscandian region of this belt (Kola Peninsula and the northern part of Karelia) is characterized by broken relief, many stones, and frequent rock outcrops, in general poor (partly podzolized and bog) soils, rapid streams, and the absence of a considerable meadow and forest area that could be utilized for farming without requiring much improvement; here farming and stock breeding are undeveloped, and the population is scattered. The other natural region of the belt—Northern Russia—has less broken relief (except the mountainous parts of the Timan Ridge and the slopes of the Urals), better soil (mainly of alluvial origin), wide river valleys and meadows, and also more valuable forests; the population in some places is quite dense (mainly along the rivers), but the forest areas are unpopulated; farming and stock breeding in the populated territory are fairly well developed. In general, the southern part of the taiga belt is richer in natural resources than the middle and northern parts: the timber there is much better in quality and in market value, and the cultivation of grain is even more reliable as to regularity and quality of crop than in the distinctly grain-growing regions of the U. S. S. R. (especially in the drought districts). This southern belt will naturally be the center of colonization activity in the near future.

But besides the main resource of the region—its timber, which covers not less than 70 per cent of the area—the North has also a multitude of useful minerals; coal (Pechora), oil (Ukhta), iron and copper ores (Vygozero, Little Pechora, Pilma), apatite (Murmansk Area), etc. With the discovery of new deposits, which is sure to result from a closer examination of the so far insufficiently studied mineral resources, new centers of attraction for labor will no doubt appear here.

Plan of Development of the Taiga Belt Centering Around the Lumber Industry

On the whole, however, the trend of present colonization will be determined by the needs of the lumber industry. The plan for the development in the North of this particular industry, which is being carried out on a considerable scale in the five years ending in 1933,[2] defines the form of all auxiliary undertakings. Of these the most important is the question of attracting to the region a permanent body of workmen and of providing the lumber industry with agricultural products.

Therefore, colonizing this northern part of European Russia involves both the hunting-industrial and the rural occupation of the land, and that determines the specific forms in which occupation must take place. Namely, in the center of forest areas in which lumbering operations are going on it is intended, first of all, to organize labor settlements, the male population of which will insure the presence of a permanent, all-year-round labor supply for lumbering in this particular district, the families of the workers concentrating their efforts in farming on good land specially designated for each such settlement. The products of the farms, in the form of different vegetables, butter, meat, and milk, will be consumed by the whole population of the lumber center. In addition to such labor settlements, it is intended to establish different wood-technical and other mills. But because the lumber industry as well as every other industry cannot be satisfied merely by permanent labor contracted for in advance, therefore, to insure an adequate supply of seasonal labor, it is intended, in addition to the labor settlements, to establish collective peasant households, mostly practicing cattle breeding, and to organize them in such a way that the occupants of these farms will have sufficient time to help in the lumber industry when the need is greatest. With periodical reinforcements for this purpose from the workmen's *artels*, these collective households will devote themselves to farming on a much larger scale than the population of the labor settlements and by their considerably larger production will guarantee that there are enough supplies for local consumption. State farms (*sovkhoz*) for the breeding of cattle and growing of forage, established when possible near the lumbering centers, will pursue the same end. To the local industry they will be tied not only by the supplying of foodstuffs and forage but also by the exchange of workmen. In the end all the newest colonization in the North will be based on the maximum rationalized balance of labor between certain regions and on their self-sufficiency in everything except food grains.

[2] The geographical aspects of the Five-Year Plan in general are well presented in the map entitled "The Five Year Plan of Economic Development of the U.S.S.R." showing European Russia in 1 : 4,500,000 and Asiatic Russia in 1 : 15,000,000 accompanied by text, "The Five-Year Plan: Introduction and Explanatory Notes to the Map," by W. P. Coates, Anglo-Russian Parliamentary Committee, London, 1930.—EDIT. NOTE.

OTHER COLONIZATION PROBLEMS OF THE REGION

Taking into account that the speed decided upon for the development of industry in the North requires the bringing together there of several thousand men in a very short period, it is apparent that the scale of the future colonization of the region will be considerable. This necessitates the development of new railroads and other means of transportation, the maximum utilization of the power resources of the region, and, above all, a comprehensive and thorough investigation of the land available for colonization. The amount of land in the North relatively fit for agriculture is estimated as 6,000,000 hectares.

The problem of today is to determine this amount more accurately and to create a plan for the combined occupation of related areas. With this is connected a long-standing problem of the North—that of distributing rationally the local population, which is quite dense in some places, as has already been mentioned. This distribution is made much easier now that the centers and the trends of colonization are already worked out in the plan of socialistic development. Undoubtedly, for the colonization of the North, special care will be exercised in the selection of the settlers.

THE CLIMATE AND SOILS OF NORTHERN EURASIA AS CONDITIONS OF COLONIZATION

L. I. PRASOLOV

OWING to their greater width in the north, Eurasia and North America do not gain the full benefit of their large size in lands valuable for their soils and climate. Millions of square kilometers are unfavorable as abodes of man and unfit for colonization.

At the north of Eurasia about 3,000,000 square kilometers are covered by the treeless Arctic tundra, and at least as large an area by the northern forest and by the mountainous districts of Siberia that lie outside of the area suited to agriculture. Even within the area bounded by the known northern limit of agriculture (Fig. 3) there is an immense belt of land that remains sparsely populated, as the conditions of existence there are severe.

Nevertheless, even these inhospitable northern areas are at present attracting more and more attention in connection with the problem of the development of natural resources and the need for colonization as a result of the increase of population in many countries.

Among the questions that investigators and directors of colonization will be obliged to solve is the question of soils.

If the severe northern climate sets a limit to the spread of agriculture and, generally speaking, makes colonization in the North difficult, then in what proportion is this limitation due specifically to the soils, whose distribution, as is known, is generally dependent on climate? What favorable or unfavorable modifications of this relationship can be expected through local topographical, geological, and other conditions?

It is the intention in the present brief sketch to answer these questions in general terms as regards Siberia and northeastern Russia within boundaries extending south approximately to latitude 50° N. in Siberia and to 60° N. west of the Ural Mountains.

The paper, therefore, within its given scope resolves itself into a discussion of the soil-geographical subdivision of this vast area on the basis of the newest climatic and soil maps and a consideration of the general characteristics of the soils and climate of the central belt that is the most important from the standpoint of colonization, namely the southern half of the forest zone.

CLIMATE

In accordance with the modern classification of climates by Köppen (1928)[1] as recently refined by Dr. A. V. Voznesenskii (1930)[2]

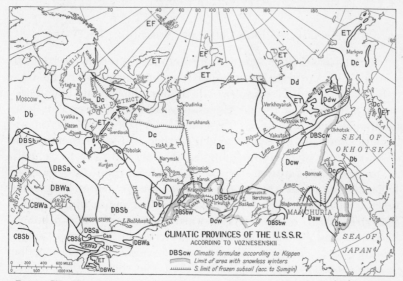

CLIMATIC PROVINCES OF THE U.S.S.R.
ACCORDING TO VOZNESENSKII

DBScw *Climatic formulae according to Köppen*
Limit of area with snowless winters
S. limit of frozen subsoil (acc. to Sumgin)

FIG. 1—Climatic provinces of the U.S.S.R., based on Köppen's classification as refined by Voznesenskii. Scale, 1 : 70,000,000. In the formulae designating the provinces the first letter represents the major climatic type (E, polar; D, boreal; C, temperate) and the following letters, both capitals and small letters, the subtypes of each. The symbols BS and SW, referring in the Köppen classification to steppe and desert climates respectively, have been modified by Voznesenskii by the addition of the letters C or D to denote the major climatic type to which the given region belongs. In so doing he has introduced the thermic element, originally lacking in Köppen's classification of 1923 (see the bibliography), and thereby defined these two types more closely. The criteria of Voznesenskii's 21 types are given in footnote 2.

[1] For references to the literature cited, see the bibliography at end of this paper.

[2] The following table is taken from page 114 of the work cited in the bibliography:

DESIGNATION AND CRITERIA OF CLIMATIC PROVINCES OF THE U.S.S.R.

DESIGNATION OF CLIMATIC TYPES	THERMAL CHARACTERISTICS		NUMBER OF MONTHS WITH TEMPERATURE ABOVE 10°C	DESIGNATION OF CLIMATIC TYPES		
	Mean monthly temperature (C°)			Precipitation deficient		
Precipitation normal	of the warmest month	of the coldest month		in winter	in steppes	in deserts
Zone I: Polar climates						
Climate of perpetual frost . . EF	< 0					
Climate of tundra . . . . . ET	< 10					
Zone II: Boreal climates						
with definite Dd	> 10	< -38	≥ 1	Ddw		
cold winters Dc	> 10	> -38	$\leq \geq 4$	Dcw	DBSc	DBWc
and annual Db	> 10 and < 22	< -3	≥ 4	Dbw	DBSb	DBWb
snow cover Da	> 22	< -3	≥ 4	Daw	DBSa	DBWa
Zone III: Moderate						
climates . . . Cb	> 10 and < 22	> -3 and < 18	> 4		CBSb	CBWa
Warm climates Ca	> 22	> -3 and < 18	> 4		CBSa	

for our territory (Fig. 1), the whole northern half of Eurasia has a boreal climate (D) or a climate transitional to that of the dry steppes (DB). Only on the extreme northern fringe is the boreal climate of the forests replaced by the polar or tundra climate (ET).

The Climatic Provinces of Northern Eurasia

On the basis of the temperature and precipitation data of 570 stations Dr. Voznesenskii compiled a climatic map of the U.S.S.R. (scale, 1:10,000,000), on which are shown the boundaries of the principal climatic provinces according to Köppen and some additional ones introduced by himself. Voznesenskii draws the climatic limit of the tundra much farther to the north than the observed limit of trees, including in the east only the Lena delta as tundra. The northeastern coast of Asia from 130° to 170° E. he assigns to the area of the coldest boreal climate (Dd) of the type of Verkhoyansk and Yakutsk, where maximum winter cold is associated with comparatively warm summers. The Chukchi Peninsula and Kamchatka are also referred to the boreal forest climate (Dc). But according to Voznesenskii an almost polar climate exists also far south within the forest zone on the summits of mountains, especially in northeastern Siberia, where the great arcs of the Cherskii, Verkhoyansk, and Kolymsk Ranges meet.

The boreal climate of the type Dc (the climate of the northern coniferous forest, or *taiga*) predominates in the greater part of Siberia and in the north of Europe. In the Far East it manifests itself in the form of the variant with a snowless winter (type Dcw), which southward goes over into the moderate-to-cold boreal climate Db (climate of the deciduous forest). Roughly south of latitude 55° N. Dc is replaced by the transitional climate of the steppes (DBS), subdivided into the colder and snowless (Transbaikal) type DBScw, the less cold West Siberian steppe type DBSb, and the comparatively warm desert steppe type DBSa. The boundaries of these climates in general outline coincide with the boundaries of the soil belts (Fig. 2), both those due to latitude and those due to altitude, the latter, even on a map of the same scale as that of Voznesenskii, appearing in considerable detail, especially in the better-known steppe zones.

In order better to characterize the above-mentioned types of climate, Voznesenskii's data for the 23 stations enumerated have been copied in the accompanying table (Table I). Ten stations of type

Dc have been included to show how much the climate of this zone varies in different latitudes and longitudes and because within this zone lies the northern limit of agriculture (Fig. 3). From the table it appears that throughout the whole great distance from the Lena River to Scandinavia in this belt 25° wide in latitude (in Siberia) the same general traits prevail: cold snowy winters with relatively little precipitation and comparatively warm and short summers with the maximum of precipitation. These are the marks of an extreme continental climate. At the same time it will be seen that annual precipitation in this zone varies from 200 (Markovo) to 567 millimeters (Cherdyn) and the mean annual temperature from −10.5° (Dudinka) to 2.3° C. (Vytegra). Farther to the east the winter temperatures are lower, and the precipitation is less. The summer temperatures vary in the same way but to a much smaller extent, so that even at the "pole of cold" at Verkhoyansk it is possible to grow some vegetables and field crops.

Proceeding along a meridian from north to south, for example through the stations Dudinka-Turukhansk-Yeniseisk, one may observe an essential difference: the mean temperatures and the amount of precipitation increase as one goes south.

The climate of the Far East in the forest zone as well as in the steppe zone is characterized by a still more uneven distribution of the precipitation: snowless winters and the maximum of precipitation at the end of the summer, as a result of which the rivers are usually subject to high floods in August.

The climate of the chernozem steppe in Western Siberia (Barnaul, Kurgan) is comparatively a little warmer than in the southern belt of the taiga (Yeniseisk) and is sensibly colder than the climate of the western forest areas (Moscow). Likewise the precipitation is less in the chernozem steppe than in the forest belt. The climate of the southern part of the Pacific Coast Province (Blagoveshchensk, Khabarovsk) is comparatively favorable as to temperature and precipitation.

CLIMATE UNFAVORABLE FOR AGRICULTURE

Throughout the whole extent of Siberia and northeastern Europe the continentality of the climate is very unfavorable for agriculture: the growing season is short, precipitation is slight, and the seasonal distribution of the precipitation makes difficult the regulation of the optimum moisture for the soil. The precipitation of summer is

TABLE I—MEAN MONTHLY TEMPERATURE AND PRECIPITATION

STATION	N. LAT.	E. LONG.	ELEVATION IN METERS	CLIMATIC PROVINCE	Length of Record in Years	Dec.	Jan.	Feb.
					TEMPERATURE IN C° (upper line			
1. Yugor Shar . .	69° 49'	60° 45'	13	ET	.. / 5	−17.2 / 6	−20.3 / 5	−20.6 / 11
2. Verkhoyansk .	67° 33'	133° 24'	100	Dd	38 / 31	−46.3 / 4	−50.1 / 4	−44.5 / 3
3. Yakutsk . . .	62° 01'	129° 43'	108	Dd	71 / 35	−40.2 / 7	−43.3 / 6	−36.2 / 5
4. Dudinka . . .	69° 24'	86° 04'	17	Dc	17 / 17	−26.9 / 6	−29.3 / 5	−26.0 / 6
5. Markovo . . .	64° 45'	170° 50'	20	Dc	21 / 21	−26.3 / 9	−28.8 / 8	−25.5 / 7
6. Turukhansk . .	65° 55'	87° 37'	40	Dc	46 / 40	−27.3 / 14	−27.7 / 12	−23.4 / 10
7. Yeniseisk . . .	58° 27'	92° 06'	80	Dc	.. / 39	−20.2 / 28	−22.5 / 21	−18.2 / 14
8. Berezov . . .	63° 56'	65° 04'	41	Dc	.. / 27	−20.3 / 14	−23.7 / 16	−18.1 / 10
9. Ust-Tsilma . .	65° 27'	52° 10'	25	Dc	.. / ..	−15.6 / 20	−18.2 / 19	−15.8 / 15
10. Cherdyn . . .	60° 24'	56° 31'	177	Dc	.. / ..	−15.4 / 42	−17.8 / 40	−13.8 / 32
11. Sverdlovsk (Ekaterinburg)	56° 50'	60° 38'	281	Dc	.. / ..	−13.5 / 27	−16.2 / 17	−13.1 / 12
12. Kholmogory .	64° 13'	41° 42'	10	Dc	.. / ..	−11.6 / 25	−13.7 / 20	−12.6 / 19
13. Vytegra . . .	61° 00'	36° 27'	40	Dc	.. / ..	−8.6 / 25	−11.0 / 24	−10.2 / 20
14. Barnaul . . .	53° 20'	83° 23'	215	Db	.. / 70	−15.0 / 24	−18.1 / 19	−16.5 / 12
15. Vyatka	58° 36'	49° 40'	164	Db	.. / ..	−12.3 / 37	−15.1 / 33	−12.3 / 32
16. Moscow . . .	55° 46'	87° 40'	160	Db	.. / ..	−7.8 / 38	−10.2 / 37	−9.4 / 34
17. Nerchinskii Zavod . . .	51° 19'	119° 37'	629	Dcw	.. / 69	−25.5 / 4	−29.2 / 2	−21.1 / 2
18. Bomnak . . .	54° 43'	128° 52'	373	Dcw	.. / 8	−30.5 / 6	−31.8 / 6	−22.1 / 5
19. Chita	52° 02'	113° 30'	674	DBScw	.. / 22	−23.6 / 5	−27.7 / 2	−22.6 / 2
20. Okhotsk . . .	59° 21'	143° 14'	6	Dcw	.. / 23	−21.9 / 3	−23.6 / 2	−21.8 / 2
21. Kurgan	55° 27'	65° 19'	88	DBSb	.. / 18	−14.5 / 13	−18.3 / 15	−16.2 / 10
22. Khabarovsk . .	48° 28'	135° 07'	75	Dbw	.. / 9	−19.2 / 8	−22.9 / 5	−17.5 / 5
23. Blagoveshchensk	50° 15'	127° 38'	150	Daw	25 / 23	−21.1 / 1	−23.5 / 3	−18.0 / 1

*All data from A. V. Voznesenskii: Karta klimatov S S S R (Map of the Climates of the

in great part useless because of losses from evaporation and drainage. Even in the northern forest zone the fields and meadows sometimes suffer from drought. But the limit of agriculture is here set principally by the low temperature of the air and soil in spring and autumn. A distinct influence on the climate is exercised by the orographical conditions. This is seen in the distribu-

AT SELECTED STATIONS IN SIBERIA AND NORTHEASTERN RUSSIA*

opposite each station) AND PRECIPITATION IN MM. (lower line)

Mar.	Apr.	May	June	July	Aug.	Sept.	Oct.	Nov.	Year	STATION
—18.4	—11.9	—3.9	2.0	5.8	6.6	2.1	—3.7	—12.2	—7.6	I
6	3	15	30	35	41	35	18	6	211	
—31.0	—12.6	2.4	13.4	15.5	10.9	2.3	—14.6	—36.7	—15.9	2
3	4	7	22	27	26	13	8	7	128	
—22.9	—8.5	5.2	15.3	19.1	14.9	5.9	—8.5	—28.9	—10.7	3
3	6	13	27	34	42	22	12	10	187	
—23.7	—15.6	—5.8	5.4	13.5	11.7	3.7	—8.8	—21.1	—10.5	4
5	7	11	30	32	43	42	18	8	213	
—23.0	—14.9	—1.0	10.5	14.5	10.4	3.2	—9.0	—19.5	—9.1	5
8	4	8	20	37	48	27	12	12	200	
—16.5	—9.6	—.05	9.1	16.3	12.8	5.1	—6.5	—20.2	—7.4	6
11	15	26	41	50	58	51	29	20	337	
—9.5	—1.2	7.4	15.8	19.6	16.1	8.5	—0.9	—12.0	—1.4	7
12	19	33	61	61	68	41	40	31	429	
—12.7	—5.3	2.5	10.2	15.8	13.1	6.2	—3.2	—14.7	—4.2	8
13	15	34	51	58	59	39	24	18	351	
—10.8	—3.0	3.1	9.7	14.4	11.6	5.9	—1.8	—10.1	—2.6	9
16	14	28	48	70	57	54	35	25	401	
—7.9	0.6	8.0	13.6	17.0	13.9	7.6	—0.7	—9.5	—0.4	10
29	23	48	51	58	76	65	49	54	567	
—7.4	1.6	9.9	14.8	17.2	14.6	8.8	0.4	—7.8	0.8	11
12	22	48	65	74	69	36	29	28	439	
—7.8	—0.4	6.0	12.2	15.7	13.0	7.3	0.4	—6.5	0.2	12
19	20	36	52	71	68	53	45	30	458	
—6.0	1.9	8.7	13.7	16.9	14.4	9.1	2.8	—3.4	2.3	13
21	21	45	50	79	72	60	49	29	495	
—9.5	0.9	11.3	17.6	20.0	17.2	11.0	2.1	—8.4	1.1	14
12	15	33	42	51	45	28	30	26	337	
—7.0	1.6	9.9	14.9	18.1	14.9	8.6	1.1	—6.8	1.3	15
26	27	49	63	62	71	58	52	45	555	
—4.9	4.2	13.4	17.4	19.7	17.5	11.4	4.6	—2.4	4.4	16
35	41	50	66	80	73	55	60	44	613	
—13.5	0.1	8.7	16.0	19.6	16.0	8.9	—1.5	—15.0	—3.3	17
5	14	29	60	112	108	46	13	7	402	
—13.9	—2.1	7.4	13.8	18.0	15.8	7.7	—3.1	—19.0	—5.1	18
6	25	47	65	76	106	56	19	14	431	
—12.2	—0.1	8.1	16.1	19.0	15.5	8.2	—1.6	—14.1	—2.9	19
3	8	28	46	90	84	33	13	5	319	
—14.2	—6.1	1.6	6.9	12.4	12.8	8.0	—3.0	—14.8	—5.3	20
4	9	20	43	59	62	51	24	4	283	
—10.3	1.2	11.2	16.2	18.3	15.8	9.6	1.0	—8.3	0.5	21
12	16	34	56	53	44	25	18	20	316	
—8.1	3.4	11.3	17.4	20.7	19.4	13.8	4.1	—8.7	1.1	22
7	24	65	98	129	125	49	34	15	564	
—9.1	2.4	10.4	18.2	22.0	19.2	12.7	1.4	—10.9	0.3	23
12	26	39	78	130	138	73	19	5	525	

U.S.S.R.), *Trudy po Selsko-khoz. Meteorologii*, No. 21, Leningrad, 1930, pp. 3–130 and map.

tion of forest and steppe in the southern part of Eastern Siberia, where steppes occupy the depressions, these generally having a warmer climate. Such are the valleys of Transbaikalia, the basins of Irkutsk and Minusinsk, and the great depression of Yakutsk (Fig. 3). These are all granaries for the neighboring forested upland regions.

Furthermore, almost all of Eastern Siberia east of the Yenisei
is located in the region of permanently frozen soil (Fig. 1), while
farther to the west this condition exists only in the extreme north.
The permanently frozen soil creates very unfavorable conditions
for the construction of buildings but does not directly put an
obstacle in the way of agriculture, as the soil thaws to a sufficient depth (except in the regions at the extreme north). Indeed
the permanently frozen soil may be favorable to agriculture, as
it holds the moisture during the period of gradual thawing.

SOILS

PODZOLS THE DOMINANT SOILS

The whole northern part of Eurasia belongs to the zone of podzol
forest soils, accompanied by bog soils (Fig. 2). The limits of this
zone, generally speaking, correspond with the zone of the boreal
climate and with the former continuous extent of the forest, mostly
coniferous. At the extreme north this zone gradually gives way
to the treeless tundra, the soils of which are closely related to the
forest soils, but are only slightly podzolized, or to the peat-bog
soils. In Eastern Siberia the zone of the taiga and of podzol soils
extends close to the southern frontier, and only comparatively
small areas in continental depressions and near the boundary of
Manchuria belong to the transitional zone of the forest steppe
and the beginning of the dry steppes of Central Asia. In these
areas the soils are: the gray soils of the deciduous forest, various
types of chernozems, and the chestnut-brown soils of the dry
steppes, accompanied by alkalines and salines. In Western Siberia
the southern limit of podzol soils approaches the 57th parallel,
projecting southward to 52° N. and beyond on the Altai Mountains
and at the southern end of the Urals. (The southern part of the
West Siberian lowland is a chernozem steppe, which farther to
the south, in about latitude 52°–53°, changes into the dry steppe
with its predominant chestnut-brown soils with different alkaline
complexes.) To the west of the Ural Mountains the southern boundary of the podzol zone passes in a general west-southwest direction
along the line Perm-Kazan-Kiev, but with marked embayments
northward and southward.

Thus, the podzol zone occupies a belt 10° to 15° of latitude in
width in the East European and West Siberian lowlands and 20°

to 25° in width on the tablelands of Eastern Siberia, comprising, with the tundra, nearly two-thirds of the territory of the U.S.S.R.

CHARACTER OF THE PODZOLS

It is understood, of course, that within this huge expanse, in which one zonal-climatic type of soil formation predominates, this type varies widely in character and presents different combinations of podzolized, bog, and meadow soils.

This variation is connected in the first place with the general change of climate with latitude, with its different degrees of continentality, and with its different local aspects; secondly, with the local geological and topographical conditions, which are independent of climate; thirdly, with the life processes of plants and animals and with the natural evolution of their associations; and, finally, with the disturbance of the natural development of the soil as a result of man's activities.

The typical northern forest soils, now called universally by the Russian common term *podzol* (meaning "ash-colored underneath"), on being cultivated become exhausted quickly and require animal and mineral fertilizers. The upper tillable layer is characterized by a comparatively small capacity for moisture absorption owing to its compactness, which also explains its tendency to erode easily. The podzol soils are poorly aërated and give an acid reaction. Their colloids are not in the form of basic compounds, and they are therefore exposed to leaching and to removal into the lower horizons. The more accentuated these properties, the more podzolized is the forest soil, i.e. the more decomposed has its mineral matter become under the action of carbonic acid and soluble humic acids, resulting in the decomposition of the forest litter.

The apparent result of this decomposition of mineral matter is the accumulation of granulated quartz silt in the soil—the ultimate decomposition product of the original rock. The mass of the soil under the humus layer becomes bleached, sometimes growing perfectly white, the clayey ingredients lose their cohesive quality and thus present a characteristic ashlike appearance. At the same time the lower horizons of the soil become more compact and impervious, sometimes preventing the deeper penetration of the roots. In the sandy podzol soils are formed hard ferruginous concretions called *ortsteins* and *ortsands*.[3]

---

[3] German terms, meaning local stones and local sands, introduced into soil science by P. E. Müller in 1887 (K. Glinka: Die Typen der Bodenbildung, ihre Klassifikation und geographische Verbreitung, Berlin, 1914, pp. 67-68).—EDIT. NOTE.

All these phenomena vary much according to the distribution of the surface moisture in relation to the relief of the ground and the character of the forest growth. In consequence of this the podzol soils usually occur in the form of intricate complexes whose members alternate within a distance of a few meters. Besides consisting of the various types of podzols, these complexes are made up of

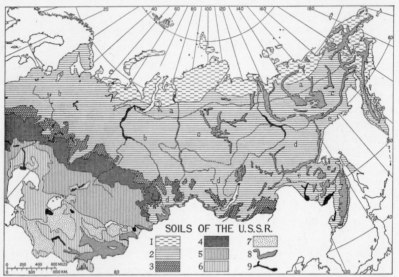

SOILS OF THE U.S.S.R.

Fig. 2—Soils of the U.S.S.R. Scale, 1 : 70,000,000. (Based on the soil maps in 1 : 10,000,000 and 1 : 16,000,000 referred to in the bibliography). Key to numerals: 1, tundra soils; 2, podzolized soils: a forest-tundra soils, b podzolized soils of the North European and West Siberian lowlands characterized by widespread development of bog (mostly peat-bog) soils, c lightly podzolized soils of the northern part of the forest belt (taiga), d lightly podzolized soils of the East Siberian plateau, e podzolized soils of the Far East and Kamchatka (Okhotsk Basin); 3, degraded and leached soils of the forest-steppe belt; 4, chernozem and chernozem-like soils; 5, chestnut-brown and brown soils; 6, gray soils (serozems); 7, sandy soils of the dry steppes and deserts; 8, mountain summit soils; 9, alluvial soils of river bottom lands.

the different transitional forms between podzols and bog soils, which are due to the gradual accumulation in the forest soil of the dead vegetational cover or by the interruption of the natural moisture régime of the soil during the cutting or burning of the forest or during the raising of the ground-water level. Of common occurrence also in the northern forest are the fresh peat bogs, developed in overgrown swamps and in abandoned river beds. In Eastern Siberia and at the extreme north of the remaining part of Eurasia the high level of the ground water and the swampiness of the forest soils may also be due to the permanently frozen ground.

Factors Defining the Agricultural Capacity of Soils

Unfortunately, the enormous inaccessible forested areas of the North have not been explored enough as yet to determine and map all their soils. Soil maps on the scale of 1:420,000 and larger exist only for the southern more populated part of the zone (former governments of Pskov, Moscow, Nizhegorod, Vyatka, etc.)

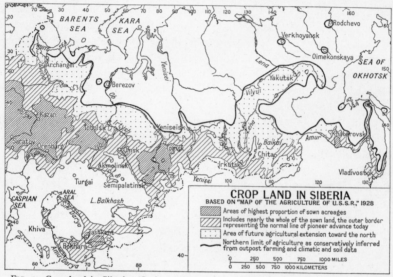

Fig. 3—Crop land in Siberia. Scale, 1 : 61,000,000. (Generalized by Bowman in his "The Pioneer Fringe," *Amer. Geogr. Soc. Special Publ. No. 13*, 1931, Fig. 188, from dot distributions on Karta zemledeliya S.S.S.R. 1927 goda (Map of the Agriculture of the U.S.S.R. in 1927), 1:6,000,000, State Institute of Experimental Agronomy, Leningrad.)

For a reasonably accurate calculation of the agricultural capacity and comparative value of the northern districts there are therefore not yet sufficient data. The principal factors necessary to take into consideration are the following three: (1) the degree of podzolization and therefore the need of lime and other fertilizers; (2) the mechanical composition of the soils, which defines the mode of tillage and in part gives an indication of their fertility; (3) the extent and character of the bogs and the bog soils.

There are some observations that show that in the northern half of the forest zone close to the tundra, as a consequence of the low temperature of the soil, the process of podzol formation is retarded and that therefore there are developed only lightly podzolized and "crypto-podzol" soils having little strength, i.e. soils

in which there is only a shallow penetration of the soil solvents.
The lightly podzolized soils also predominate for the greater part
in the mountainous tracts of Eastern Siberia, except in the belt of
land adjacent to the Okhotsk and Japan Seas.

Besides climate the petrographic structure of the parent rock
strata and orographical conditions affect the process of podzolization. The relief forms control the drainage of the excess moisture
and, according to the steepness and direction of the mountain
slopes, the conditions of insolation. On the Central Siberian
Plateau, to the east of the Yenisei, in the localities where they are
formed directly on the eluvium of the here dominant red calcareous
sandstones and diabases, the soils are usually slightly podzolized.
On the other hand, in the lowland between the Ob and Yenisei
Rivers, composed of ancient alluvium and glacial alluvium, the
typical podzols occur; in these the colorless, silica-containing
horizon attains a thickness of 25 to 45 centimeters. Besides,
a considerable part of these podzols is, as the result of the deep
degradation produced by the advancing forest, of secondary formation derived from ancient meadow or chernozem soils. But to the
north, near 62° N., beyond the Vakh River, a westward-flowing
right branch of the Ob which joins it in about 77° E., are traced
(by R. S. Ilin) slightly podzolized (primary forest) soils on the
glacial boulder deposits and *sandr* sands.

THE BOG AND PODZOLIZED SOILS OF WESTERN SIBERIA AND NORTHEASTERN RUSSIA

Here it is necessary to note that the whole lowland within the
drainage system of the Ob south to the Trans-Siberian Railway is
characterized by the widespread development of swamps. Thus,
the interfluvial spaces in the system of the Vasyugan River are
completely occupied by swamps.[4] In the Narymsk region (58° N.
and 82° E.) the swamps occupy 73 per cent of the whole surface.
Here two types are distinguished: *ryamy*, moss bogs covered with
pine trees, and *gali*, treeless meadowlike moss bogs. In the latter
the depth of the peat attains 5.5 meters, in the former 7.5 meters.
On their margin one may find semi-boggy peat soils or peaty-
podzolized soils on the so-called *suryamy*. Besides, along the rivers

---

[4] This type of terrain, photographed on the round-the-world flight of the dirigible *Graf Zeppelin*
in 1929, is shown in *Amer. Geogr. Soc. Special Publ. No. 13*, New York, 1931, Fig. 193 on p. 263.
See also photographs in *Natl. Geogr. Mag.*, Vol. 57, 1930, pp. 662–663, and in *Mitt. Geogr. Gesell.
in Hamburg*, Vol. 41, 1930, Pl. 34 and Pl. 35, Fig. 1.—EDIT. NOTE.

everywhere extend belts of *sorga*, clayey bogs full of hillocks and covered with birch. In the forested districts on the right bank of the Irtysh above Tobolsk, according to the description by Balkashin, the dry-soil forest is the least extensive. Likewise on the left side of the Ob, at the foot of the Ural Mountains, there are extensive swamps. On the other side of the Urals, in the Komi District (Zyryan Autonomous Area), according to recent fieldwork by G. N. Ognev, podzolized soils of all degrees occur in complexes with the glei-podzolized soils,[5] i.e. more or less marshy (deoxidized) podzols. Among them predominate the forest clay soils that were deposited in temporary postglacial basins and that cover the greater part of the North European Plain. These soils are by preference used in the growing of rye and barley and when fertilized yield abundant crops (from 16,000 to 80,000 kilograms per hectare). Under cultivation the soils lose their original acid reaction, while in the untilled podzols the value of rH (concentration of hydrogen ions) varies between 3.7 and 5; on old plowed lands it is usually 6. In Table II are given some of the data of Ognev's analysis of samples of the two horizons of podzol soil taken from a plowed field at the village of Nizhnyaya Voch, a little south of the Vychegda River (about $62\frac{1}{2}°$ N.):

TABLE II—MECHANICAL COMPOSITION OF TWO HORIZONS OF PODZOL SOIL

(according to Sabanin's method, in per cent)

SOIL CLASS, WITH DIAMETER OF PARTICLES	PLOWED LAYER (5–10 cm.)	LOESSLIKE LOAM (90–100 cm.)
Gravel (3–1 mm.)	0.14	——
Coarse sand (1–0.25 mm.)	0.54	0.03
Fine sand (0.25–0.05 mm.)	5.83	6.27
Silt (0.05–0.01 mm.)	50.07	46.24
Fine silt (0.01–0.001 mm.)	33.69	24.99
Clay (0.001 mm.)	9.73	22.47
Actual acidity, rH	6.3	——
Humus	2.59	——
Absorption capacity according to Gedroits, taking into account Ca	0.224	——

[5] "Glei" is a Russian term used by the common people to describe any tenacious mass like viscous mud and was introduced into soil science by Vysotski in 1900. He applied it to soil horizons that have developed mainly under the influence of ground water rising to the surface and only partially as a result of the descent of moisture into the ground (Glinka, *op. cit.*, p. 74).—EDIT. NOTE.

The most fertile soils in this region are the unpodzolized soils on the Permian marls and the alluvial clay soils, but both occur as insignificant little strips of land; and, furthermore, the seeding suffers from the spring floods of the rivers.

North of the Vychegda River, between the North Dvina and the Pechora, are situated almost uninhabited, forested, very swampy tracts. In some places the swamps cover 75 per cent of the whole area (data from the Mezen forest expedition). On the flat watersheds clayey and argillaceous podzols and peaty-podzol soils predominate. The broad old terraces of the river valleys consist mainly of sands and are covered with pine forest, in the depressions of which peat moss occurs. North of latitude 62° N. the soil is much more swampy than to the south of this latitude. The interfluvial spaces are occupied almost uninterruptedly by surficial swampy soils and by woods showing evidence of forest litter. The best forests grow along the rivers, and here also is carried on what agriculture there is, as for example along the Mezen River and its tributary the Peze. According to A. A. Krasyuk (bibliography, p. 259), even among the *taibols* of the Archangel region, where the subsandy surficial swampy soils predominate, it is possible to find not a few areas suitable for cultivation, especially in those localities where the glacial and postglacial deposits wedge out and the subsoil consists of Permian red marls.

The same conclusion was reached by Malandin and Nikitin, the explorers of the region situated at the head of the Kama River in the latitude of Cherdyn (60° 24′ N.) and northwards.

Soils of the Urals and the East Siberian Upland

Little is known about the soils of the northern Urals. In spite of their relatively low altitude (only the separate highest peaks here rise to 1600–1800 meters) these mountains are difficult of access, rocky, and almost uninhabited. Their summits rise above the tree limit and are covered with shrub, moss, and lichen tundra. The slopes are covered with pine, which predominates, cedar, and fir. At the tree limit, which in latitude 65° N. is at an elevation of only 650 meters, the larch predominates.

As on the Ural Mountains, so in Eastern Siberia the coniferous forest soils are more or less swampy in the depressions, and among them, as in the lowlands, occur moss bogs. In Eastern Siberia the so-called *erniki* are widely distributed—swamps covered with a scrub vegetation of birches and willows. From the river valleys they rise in broad, flat, undeveloped swales up to the low crests of the watersheds. Their soils are deoxidized peats and clays (semi-swamp soils). In some parts of the Central Siberian Plateau (for instance, at the headwaters of the Vilyui River) they cover as much as 60 per cent of the surface. The same type of *erniki* occurs frequently on the tablelands of Transbaikalia at the sources of rivers belonging to the Amur system (Ingoda, Onon, etc.) and on the Khamardaban.

The swampy condition of the mountain-forest soils is for the greater part limited to the surface and has its origin in the permanently frozen ground. Even in southern Transbaikalia the frozen soil appears under the forest at the end of summer, often within the upper 50 centimeters. The bogs and wooded swamps are the principal obstacles to travel in these northern forests, together with the great quantity of burnt fallen timber that covers the ground, the so-called *gari*. This fallen timber makes up the normal landscape of the region; it is difficult to find any wood untouched by fire.

The Areas of Agricultural Value in Eastern Siberia

Generally speaking, in all the forested zone and in the podzol zone there are few soils that cannot somehow be utilized for agriculture. The only ones that cannot be utilized are rocky areas and the deep peat soil. All types of podzol soils, even the characteristic podzols and also the transitional peaty bog soils and especially the silty bog soils of the lowlands, can, through melioration and fertilizing, be reclaimed for cultivation. Because these soils are not directly utilizable, however, only an insignificant part of the northern regions is at present used for agriculture. The agricultural value of the different elements of the soils of these regions cannot be considered as a unit. In what follows are discussed the various areas of fertile soils that can be conveniently and easily occupied for agricultural colonization.

It is characteristic that in Eastern Siberia and in the Far East the centers of agriculture, clearly shown on the map of I. F. Makarov,[6] are situated in the large valleys and continental depressions. Some of them lie in the forest zone, as, for example, the valley of the Amur and the Lena-Vilyui Plain near Yakutsk. Others appear

[6] Also on Figure 3, which is generalized from a similar map representing conditions in 1927 (Makarov's map is based on 1916–1917 data).

as outliers of the southern steppe zone, surrounded by mountain forests as, for instance, the Nerchinsk steppe in Transbaikalia, the deep Irkutsk basin, the Krasnoyarsk area, the deep valley of the upper Yenisei at Minusinsk, and others.

In the Amur valley from Blagoveshchensk to Khabarovsk and also near Lake Khanka the meadow soils with their dark color reminiscent of the steppe chernozems are valuable agriculturally. In these degradation has taken place only under the influence of the former forest cover and of deoxidizing processes in the lower horizon, as the result of the former excess of moisture. These soils are at present all occupied, and further colonization is possible only by clearing the forest on the podzol soils in the belt of low mountains that parallel the Amur valley on the northeast. Here, according to Koloskov, the best climatic conditions are found not in the valleys but on the uplands.

The Lena-Vilyui Plain is an immense depression of tectonic origin, filled with Mesozoic marine and continental sediments, covered by Quaternary glacial lake and river deposits. It extends east and west of Yakutsk for several hundred kilometers (from the upper course of the Vilyui River to the Aldan River) in the form of an undulating plateau 150 to 400 meters high. Near its eastern end the plateau is cut through by the Lena valley, 15 kilometers wide near Yakutsk and accompanied by clearly defined old terraces. The surface of the plateau is characterized by an abundance of long or oval-shaped formless depressions, the so-called *alasy*, with a great many small fresh-water and salt lakes.

The vegetation and soils of the Lena valley and plateau are distinguished by the intrusion of southern elements from the steppe. The upper meadow terrace in the valley of the Lena has a semi-steppe character and dark, chernozem-like soils, among which occur also alkalines and salines. In the depressions of the plateau, near the lakes, are observed the original peat-bog saline soils, which on the margins change into the dark-colored meadow *ogleënnye* (deoxidized) and also into alkaline soils. On the forest-covered slopes these alkaline soils are leached and podzolized, constituting the so-called *solodi*—the soils of the damp lower parts of the steppe. The rather low, flat watersheds between the depressions are covered uninterruptedly with the different formations of the Siberian taiga on the podzol soils. In the Lena valley and in some places on the plateau agriculture was established long ago by Russian settlers. Its expansion until now has been prevented by the economic inertia of the natives of this area.

A certain similarity to the Yakutsk anomaly is also found in the valley of the Barguzin River in the northern part of Transbaikalia, where, in the region of taiga, podzols, and bogs, dry steppe enters with soils similar, not to the chernozems, but to the more southern types of chestnut-brown soils.

In the southern part of Transbaikalia, starting in the Nerchinsk steppe, the presence of southern steppe elements in valleys in the midst of mountains covered with coniferous forest right down to the frontier of Mongolia, and in Mongolia itself, increases in frequency and continuity, so that along the frontier of Manchuria the steppe covers completely not only the valleys but also the uplands, although these latter are comparatively low (up to 1000 meters). In the soils and vegetation here are found the different transitions from the podzols and taiga of the northern zone to the chestnut soils of the dry steppes, including the different kinds of steppe chernozems. For agriculture the chernozems are used by preference. But the extension of cultivation is prevented partly by the limited amount of land fit for plowing and the numerous stony places and partly by the short growing season. To the west of Lake Baikal agriculture is practiced in a belt along the Trans-Siberian Railway but is concentrated mainly on the chernozems in the steppe and forest-steppe areas near Irkutsk, Kansk, and Krasnoyarsk; while to the north of this belt extends the sparsely populated mountainous region, for the most part forest-clad.

The limit to the southward extension of the steppe zone is set by mountains. Along the whole southern boundary of Siberia, starting from the Baikal region, extends the system of the Sayan Mountains, which sends high branch ranges to the north and is connected to the west and south with the Altai system. Their summits stand above the tree limit and during the greater part of the year are covered with snow, wherefore they are called the white mountains. In many places signs of recent glaciation in the form of cirques and moraines are observed. But living glaciers exist only in the mountain knot of Munku-Sardyk on the frontier of Mongolia.

The western Sayan Mountains and their extension, the Taskyl Range, form the southern boundary of the Minusinsk depression, the upper peripheral slopes of which have the character of a forest steppe with chernozem soils, while in the low valleys along the Abakan River and around the salt lake Shira there extend dry steppes with chestnut-brown and alkali soils. To the north the

Minusinsk steppe continues westward from the Yenisei River into the basin of the Chulym River (Ob system), where typical chernozems occur, reaching the Trans-Siberian Railway near Achinsk.

The Minusinsk depression was always the granary of the enormous Yenisei region, even though a part of it, including chernozem areas, was in the possession of semi-nomadic, little-civilized tribes, who were not much concerned with agriculture.

Near Achinsk and farther to the west the railway runs through the transitional zone, where, instead of the fir taiga and podzols, there occur the so-called *belniki*—mixed forest and dark-gray soils, related to the soils of the Central European deciduous forest and partly due to degradation of the chernozems. But this transitional, thickly populated strip of land comes to an end a little to the north of the latitude of Achinsk (approximately 56° N.). Farther to the north lies the uninterrupted zone of the taiga, with numerous bogs, where the agricultural population is settled only along the rivers and barely reaches latitude 60° N.

Thus, in general, the whole of Eastern Siberia to the Pacific Ocean contains, even in its southern part—the part best suited to colonization—only comparatively little territory that is suitable for agriculture.

The amount of soil not fit for agriculture—stony, alkaline, and sandy—even in the steppes of Transbaikalia and Minusinsk, is very large. There are still more numerous unsuitable rocky areas in the mountain districts.

AGRICULTURAL SOILS IN WESTERN SIBERIA

Much more room is offered to colonization by the West Siberian lowland, where the chernozem soils extend in an almost uninterrupted strip about 2° of latitude in width from the Ural Mountains to the Altai. But it should be noted that the total area of the chernozem soils of Siberia, even including the degraded chernozems and gray-forest soils of the forest-steppe, amounts only to about 1,000,000 square kilometers. This area is smaller than the area of the chernozems of the European part of the U.S.S.R.

Besides, the West Siberian chernozem steppe abounds in the different kinds of "intrazonal" soils, alkalis, *solodi*, saline meadows, sandy soils, which certainly reduce very much the area suitable for agriculture. Its climate is also less favorable than that of the

European chernozem steppes. To the south the West Siberian lowland passes over into the area of the low, much denuded uplands (such as the Chingiz Ridge, the Kokchetav Mountains, the Ulu-tau, and others), where on the more elevated points chernozems can be found down to about latitude 48° N., but where in great part the soil is stony and interspersed with rocky ledges. But the lower parts of this country are dry steppes with chestnut-brown soils and with an abundance of alkalines. Agriculture without artificial irrigation is possible on the chestnut-brown soils; but it is real "dry farming," always subject to the risk of a bad crop.

Farther to the south in about latitude 47°–48° N. the desert alkaline and stony steppes begin, to which, for example, belongs the great waterless Hunger Steppe (Golodnaya Steppe, Bekpak-dala) between Lake Balkhash and the northern end of the Aral Sea.

NEED FOR MORE DETAILED STUDY OF SIBERIAN SOILS

All that has preceded gives an idea of the difficulties confronting colonization in Siberia. It is quite clear that from now on, as colonization has already exhausted the reserve of the best and most suitable lands, the struggle with these natural obstacles will be more and more persistent and that it will be impossible to wage the battle successfully without a preliminary serious survey of the territory. First of all it is necessary to have good topographical maps; it is necessary also to increase the number of meteorological and agricultural experiment stations and to proceed energetically with soil-botanical explorations. All this is already contemplated. In recent years there have been organized a great many expeditions, and many substantial scientific works have been published about Siberia, as for example the numerous works of the Yakut Commission of the Academy of Science. One of the principal problems for the soil student is that of the northern bogs, their development and extent, in connection with a study of the basic wealth of the North, the forests.

Conditions of exploration in Siberia, especially in the zone of the taiga, are usually very hard; to overcome them it is necessary, in addition to personal energy and the scientific spirit and persistence of the explorers, to call in the aid of modern technology in the form of aviation, wireless, etc., in which matter great help can be provided by international organizations of scientific research.

BIBLIOGRAPHY*

Climate

Köppen, W. Die Klimate der Erde: Grundriss der Klimakunde. Berlin and Leipzig, 1923.

Köppen, W., and R. Geiger. Klimakarte der Erde. Mercator projection, equatorial scale, 1 : 20,000,000. With 19-pp. text. Justus Perthes, Gotha, 1928.

Köppen, W. Typische und Übergangs-Klimate. *Meteorolog. Zeitschr.*, Vol. 46, 1929, pp. 121–126.

Voznesenskii, A. V. Karta klimatov S.S.S.R. (Map of the Climates of the U.S. S.R.). *Trudy po Selsko-khozyaistvennoi Meteorologii*, No. 21, pp. 3–130 (English summary, pp. 111–130), with map in 1 : 10,000,000. Bureau of Agrometeorology, State Institute of Experimental Agronomy, Leningrad, 1930.

Kaminskii, A. A., and E. S. Rubinstein. Klimaticheskii ocherk Uralskoi Oblasti (Climatic Sketch of the Ural Area). Sverdlovsk, 1925.

Shostakovich, V. B. Materialy po klimatu Yakutskoi Respubliki i sopredelnykh s neyu chastei severnoi Azii (Materials about the Climate of the Yakut Republic and the Adjoining Parts of Northern Asia). *Trudy Yakutskoi Komissii Akad. Nauk*, Vol. 6, Leningrad, 1927.

Koloskov, P. I. Klimaticheskie osnovy selskago khozyaistva Amurskoi Oblasti (Climatic Basis of the Agriculture of the Amur Province). Blagoveshchensk, 1925.

Sumgin, M. Vechnaya merzlota pochvy v predelakh S.S.S.R. (Permanent Frozen Soil in the U.S.S.R.). Far Eastern Geophysical Observatory, Vladivostok, 1927. 372 pp.

Physical Geography and Geology

Tanfilev, G. I. Geografiya Rossii i Ukrainy (Geography of Russia and the Ukraine), Part II, No. 2: Relef Aziatskoi Rossii (Relief of Asiatic Russia). 1923.

Berg, L. S. Zona tundr (The Zone of Tundras). *Izvestiya Leningrad. Gos. Univ.*, Vol. 1, 1928, pp. 191–233.

Berg, L. S. Landshaftno-geograficheskie zony S.S.S.R. (Regional Geographical Zones of the U.S.S.R.), Part I: Vvedenie; tundra; lesnaya zona (Introduction; the Tundra; the Forest Zone). *Prilozhenie 42-e k Trudam po Prikladnoi Botaniki, Genetike i Selektsii*. Institute of Plant Breeding, Lenin Acad. of Agric. Sciences, Leningrad, 1930. 401 pp., with soil map in 1 : 10,000,000.

Gorodkov, B. N. Polyarnyi Ural v verkhovyakh rek Voikara, Syny i Lyapina (The Arctic Ural at the Headwaters of the Rivers Voikar, Syn, and Lyapin). *Sbornik "Severnyi Ural," Akad. Nauk*, 1929, pp. 1–32.

Obruchev, V. A. Geologicheskii obzor Sibiri (Geological Outline of Siberia). 1927. [A more complete edition of this work was published in German under the title "Geologie von Sibirien," Berlin, 1926, with the author's name transliterated W. A. Obrutschew.]

Borisyak, A. Geologicheskii ocherk Sibiri (Geological Sketch of Siberia). 1923.

*This list contains mostly recent publications and general syntheses. In them the reader will find references to the whole literature of the subject.

Edelstein, Y. S. Geologicheskii ocherk Zapadnoi Sibirskoi ravniny (Geological Sketch of the West Siberian Plain). *Izvestiya Zapadno Sibirsk. Otdela Russ. Geogr. Obshch.*, Omsk, 1925–1926, pp. 1–75, with map in 1 : 10,000,000.

Yakutiya: Sbornik statei (The Yakut Region: A Collection of Papers). Academy of Sciences, Leningrad, 1927. 744 pp.

Obruchev, S. O nevedomykh gorakh Yakutii (About Unknown Mountains of Yakutia). 1928. [Deals with the discovery of the Cherskii Range.]

Soils

Glinka, K. D. Pochvy Rossii i prilegayushchikh stran (Soils of Russia and Adjacent Countries). 1923.

Predvaritelnye otchety ob organizatsii ispolnenii rabot po issledovaniyu pochv Aziatskoi Rossii pod redaktsiei K. D. Glinki, za 1908–1914 goda (Preliminary Reports about the Organization and Execution of the Works Relating to the Investigation of the Soils of Asiatic Russia during the Years 1908–1914, edited by K. D. Glinka). 7 vols.

Trudy pochvennobotanicheskikh ekspeditsii po issledovaniyu kolonizatsionnykh raionov Aziatskoi Rossii (Memoirs of the Soil-Botanical Expeditions for the Investigation of the Colonization Regions of Asiatic Russia), Part I: Pochvennye issledovaniya (Soil Research), edited by K. D. Glinka. 23 vols.

Pochvennaya karta Evropeiskoi chasti S.S.S.R. pod redaktsiei L. I. Prasolova (Soil Map of the European Part of the U.S.S.R., edited by L. I. Prasolov). Scale, 1 : 2,520,000. Academy of Sciences, Leningrad, 1930. [A reduced edition in 1 : 7,000,000 was published by the Academy of Sciences in 1930.]

Pochvennaya karta Aziatskoi chasti S.S.S.R. pod redaktsiei K. D. Glinki i L. I. Prasolova (Soil Map of the Asiatic Part of U.S.S.R. edited by K. D. Glinka and L. I. Prasolov). Eight sheets on the scale of 1 : 4,200,000. Academy of Sciences, Leningrad, 1926. [A reduced edition in one sheet on the scale of 1 : 10,000,000 and a simplified edition in 1 : 16,000,000, were published by the Academy of Sciences in 1930 and 1929 respectively.]

Krasyuk, A. A. Pochvy Severo-Vostochnoi Oblasti i ikh izuchenie (The Soils of the Northeast Area and Their Study). Archangel, 1925.

Mezenskaya leso-ekonomicheskaya ekspeditsiya 1925 goda: Otchet i karta raionov pochvoveda N.D. Ponagaibo (Mezen Forest-Economy Expedition of 1925: Report and a Map of Regions by the Pedologist N. D. Ponagaibo).

Ognev, G. N. Pochvy yugo-vostochnoi chasti Komi Oblasti (Soils of the Southeastern Part of the Komi Area). *Trudy Leningradskoi Laborat. Inst. Agropochvoved. Akad. Selsko-khozyaistv. Nauk imeni Lenina*, N.S., No. 8, 1930. 165 pp., with soil and geological maps.

Gorodkov, B. N., and S. S. Neustruev. Pochvennye raiony Uralskoi Oblasti (Soil Regions of the Ural Area). 1923.

Malandin, G. A. and V. V. Nikitin: K voprosu o postanovke issledovanii v severnykh raionakh Uralskoi Oblasti (On the Question of the Organization of Exploration in the Northern Regions of the Ural Area). Perm, 1928.

Gorshenin, K. P. Pochvy chernozemnoi polosy Zapadnoi Sibiri (Soils of the Black-Earth Belt of Western Siberia). Omsk, 1927. 374 pp. and map.

Balkashin, M. I. Kazennye lesnye dachi Tarskogo Uezda Tobolskoi Gubernii (State Forest in Tarsky District of Tobolsk Province). 1911. 27 pp.

Dranitsyn, D. A. Vtorichnye podzoly i peremeshchenie podzolistoi zony na severe Ob-Irtyshskogo vodorazdela (Secondary Podzols and Transformation of the Podzol Zone in the Northern Part of the Ob-Irtysh Watershed). *Izvestiya Dokuchaev Pochv. Kom.*, No. 2, 1914.

Dranitsyn, D. A. Materialy po pochvovedeniyu i geologii zapadnoi chasti Narymskogo Kraya (Materials on the Soil and Geology of the Western Part of the Narym Region). *Trudy Pochv. Eksped.* pod redakt. K. D. Glinki, 1911, No. 1.

Ilin, R. S. Priroda Narymskogo Kraya: Relef, geologiya, landshafty, pochvy (Nature of Narymsk Region: Relief, Geology, Natural Regions, Soils). *Materialy po Izucheniyu Sibiri*, Vol. 2, Tomsk, 1930. 349 pp.

Prasolov, L. I. Pochvenno geograficheskii ocherk severo-zapadnoi chasti Minusinskogo Uezda Eniseiskoi Gubernii (Soil-Geographical Sketch of the Northwestern Part of Minusinsk County, Yeniseisk Province). *Trudy Pochv. Eksped.*, 1910, No. 2, with a map.

Khainskii, A. I. Pochvy Baraby i Altaiskogo Okruga vdol levogo berega Obi (Soils of Baraba and Altai Districts Along the Left Bank of the Ob River). *Trudy Pochv. Eksped.*, 1912–1913, No. 1.

Dranitsyn, D. A. Pochvy zapadnogo Zaangarya Eniseiskoi Gubernii (Soils of the Western Transangara Region, Yeniseisk Province). *Ibid.*, 1910, No. 1.

Prasolov, L. I. Yuzhnoe Zabaikale (Southern Transbaikal). Leningrad, 1927. 422 pp.

Abolin, P. I. Geobotanicheskoe i pochvennoe opisanie Leno-Vilyuiskoi ravniny (Geobotanical and Soil Description of the Lena-Vilyui Plain). *Trudy Yakutskoi Komissii Akad. Nauk*, Vol. 10, Leningrad, 1929. 372 pp.

Krasyuk, A. A. Pochvy Leno-Aminskogo vodorazdela (Soils of the Lena-Aminsk Watershed). Leningrad, 1927. 176 pp.

Agriculture

Makarov, I. F. Karta zemledeliya S.S.S.R. (Agricultural Map of U.S.S.R.), *Prilozhenie 28-e k Trudam po Prikladnoi Botanike i Selektsii*, Institute of Applied Botany and New Cultures, Leningrad, 1926. 91 pp. with map in 1 : 12,500,000.

HISTORY, PRESENT POLICIES, AND ORGANIZATION OF INTERNAL COLONIZATION IN THE U.S.S.R.

By V. P. VOSHCHININ

TWENTY-FIVE years ago Professor Kaufman[1], a well-known student of internal migration in old Russia, quite truthfully stated that the so-called "mass" movement of rural population from the European to the Asiatic part of the country does not take place on a large scale and that, among the other aspects of Russian economic life, migration is not an outstanding phenomenon. In fact if the figures of Russian migration are taken in relation to the mass of population, it will be found that, even in the years of greatest movement[2], the number of migrants did not represent more than 0.6–0.7 per cent of the rural population of the already settled territory, whereas at the same time corresponding Italian emigration amounted to almost 2 per cent and even Norwegian to 0.8 per cent. Before the World War the number of Russian migrants had already decreased to 0.2 per cent, while on the contrary emigration increased considerably in other countries. In recent years in the U.S.S.R. the percentage of peasants moving to new lands decreased still further (to almost half), and the total migration from all centers of emigration amounted to not more than 8 per cent of the normal augmentation of the population.

Therefore the common conception of the magnitude of Russian internal migration is based in reality on a misunderstanding arising from the use of *absolute* figures. It is quite true that more than 9,000,000 persons emigrated during the nineteenth century from the European part of Russia[3]—i.e. more than one quarter of the total emigration for the same period from Europe. But only in a few regions of European Russia did this transplantation affect the absolute number of the population, and only a very insignificant part of the land reserve of Asiatic Russia was taken up by the colonists.

[1] A. A. Kaufman: Pereselenie i kolonizatsiya (Migration and Colonization), St. Petersburg, 1905.

[2] For instance, in 1908, 650,000 colonists including their families emigrated from the European part of the country to beyond the Ural Mountains.

[3] Almost in equal parts to Asiatic Russia (properly, internal migration) and to foreign lands (properly, emigration). Basically, both types of transplantation were fed from the same roots.

Unique Character of Russian Internal Colonization

Also, it is wrong to attribute a certain peculiarity of the Russian migration process entirely to the natural or social-economic conditions of pre-revolutionary Russia. Like other countries, Russia in her evolution followed the path of capitalistic progress, and on that course, without her doing anything about it, arose, as everywhere else, the conditions that led to the displacement of the weakest in the population, and that, in the last analysis, was the basic cause of emigration.

The real peculiarity of Russian migration was due and still is due to another factor: the existence in the same country of an enormous amount of reserve land for colonization which, although not in itself capable of relieving the pressure exerted on the Russian peasant by pre-revolutionary conditions, yet was a very real fact and provided a possibility of relief for a certain part of the rural population of the central area. This fact distinguishes the history and actual conditions of colonization in Russia from those of other countries which usually have to deal either mainly with emigration or mainly with immigration, or, if with both together, then with a foreign contingent of colonists in the case of immigration. Russia found herself in that respect in a peculiar condition on two scores— both emigration and immigration involved her own citizens on her own territory. In other words the country always was obliged to take into account simultaneously emigration from the older communities and the colonization of new lands and to shape correspondingly its emigration and immigration policy.

History of Russian Colonization: To the Close of the Eighteenth Century

The history of the mass movement of population in Russia is closely associated with the history of development of the whole country.[4] In Russia lands are still in a state of being occupied, while in Western Europe the corresponding process was completed almost a thousand years ago. But the stimulus to migration, in the real meaning of the word as a phenomenon evoked by definite

[4] The history of pre-Soviet migration and colonization is authoritatively set forth in several papers in Aziatskaya Rossiya (Asiatic Russia), 3 vols. and atlas, Emigration Bureau of the Department of Land Utilization and Agriculture, St. Petersburg, 1914, viz. in Vol. 2: Peasant Emigration and Russian Colonization beyond the Urals, pp. 440–499; New Immigrants in Siberia, pp. 188–199; Land Tenure in Siberia, pp. 532–576. See also the bibliography of these subjects in Vol. 3, especially pp. lxxxiii-xcviii and the atlas, especially Pls. 66–71.—Edit. Note.

social and economic conditions, can be referred in Russia strictly speaking only to the sixteenth and seventeenth centuries, when the principle of serfdom of the peasants received formal sanction and when the Moscow government in the interest of commercial capital began an intensive policy aiming at the political seizure of new territories. It was at that time particularly that the so-called "free" (runaway) colonization of peasants developed which spread partly to Siberia, but mostly to the Don, Volga, Dniepr, and Ural basins, and that the government, either directly through its own agents or indirectly through the class of men in public service, started to put into effect—often by utilizing the "free" movement—the government colonization of the frontiers. In this period, up to the nineteenth century, the policy of the authorities as to settlement generally exhibits two contradictory aspects: on the one hand migration is prohibited in the interest of the landlords, and, on the other, migration is to a certain extent encouraged—because of the necessity, at least in a general way, of consolidating recently acquired territory. At all events migration to new land, notwithstanding the hardship of the process itself, was very popular among the broad mass of the people. Of course, at that time an exact numerical record of the movement was not kept; but, according to the actual results of colonization, the movement must have been considerable. At least the present black-earth belt of the Volga, Samara-Orenburg, Novorossiisk (New Russia), Black Sea, and Azov Sea regions was closely settled at that time and also Western Siberia, where the Russian population surpassed 500,000 persons in 1797. The collision of the Russians, on territory being colonized, with the natives of those regions partook of all the features of manifest violence characteristic of the colonial expansion of that epoch.

During the Nineteenth Century to 1893

The subsequent history of Russian migration exhibits a logical development of events. Thus, in the first half of the nineteenth century, in which industrial capitalism already existed in an embryonic stage, the peasant's labor, as a result of the aim of the landlords to raise its productiveness, was subjected to still more rigid controls, with the result that unlawful migration increased by leaps and bounds, in some years attaining the character of an elemental force. To avoid chaos the government was obliged to prepare land

in Siberia for colonization; thither law breakers of all kinds also
began to be sent in mass. The lawful migration of peasants in
that period is very small, amounting in sixty years to only 216,000
persons (by special permits); but "free" migration was approximately three times as much. The beginning of colonization of
the Far East took place in that period.

The peasants' reform of 1861, giving freedom to the peasants
(with an insignificant amount of land), bound them economically
still more firmly to the landlords as a definitely cheap labor supply.
Insurmountable obstacles were put by law in the way of any migration at all, and by 1866 all agricultural credits for the Transural
region were canceled. In the meantime the annual voluntary
movement of colonists to that area increased to at least twice that
of previous years, and in addition there were twice as many criminal
and political banishments to Siberia. The flow of the peasants
and artisans from the western provinces of Russia to foreign lands,
which was fed from the same roots, greatly increased: in amount
it began to surpass considerably internal migration and banish-
ment. On the whole, migration in the first thirty years after the
liberation of the peasants is characterized by negative influences.
Nevertheless at this time the pressure of the waves of migration
laid the foundation of quite stable colonization in the Amur, Altai,
and Kirghiz Steppe regions (accompanied, however, as before, by
all the manifestations of colonial usurpation) and also in the eastern
part of Siberia (Tomsk and Transbaikal regions).

FROM 1893 TO THE REVOLUTION OF 1917

With the beginning of the construction of the Trans-Siberian
Railway (1893), however, a new era in Russian colonization began,
because the systematic peopling of the strip of land along the railroad obviously became indispensable. On the other hand, in the
center of the country, peasants' households grew poorer and poorer,
because of the attempts of the landlord class to solve through the
same exploitation of the peasants as formerly the inconsistency
between the obsolete forms of their economic system and the severe
requirements of the market. Because of this, especially in the
black-earth region, the pauperism of the peasants developed apace
and the amount of migration correspondingly increased, becoming
125,000 annually, with the same number for foreign emigration.
Because of the lack of organized colonization, from 12 to 31 per

cent of the colonists returned, and that complicated even more the condition of the center of the country.

At the beginning of the present century, because of the extreme crisis in the condition of the peasants, the well-known peasants' revolution of 1905 broke out, and, after its suppression, migration increased to an unprecedented extent.[5] In that period, as a measure to ease the acute class tension, migration was encouraged by the government; but the reserve of easily available land in Asiatic Russia was soon exhausted, and an immense number of colonists returned disappointed.

The government's attempt to bring about the progressive peopling of new land through its gradual improvement did not succeed, because the administrative steps taken were not in keeping with the economic condition of the regions of colonization; and, notwithstanding the comparatively large sums[6] appropriated for settlement, the various measures undertaken appeased the peasants less and less. All the attention of the needy class became centered on the lands of the landlords, and just then the World War broke out.

Nevertheless, it is true that the pre-revolutionary colonization of the border lands yielded noticeable results: the settling of 3,000,000 colonists in the Asiatic part of the country (all within the last decade before the war) greatly increased the sown area and the export from there of grain, meat, and butter; local markets developed considerably—in general, the revivification of the borderlands undoubtedly began. But, if on the other side of the balance sheet are entered such matters as the expropriation of the fundamental means of production and the forcible Russification of many millions of natives of the borderlands (Buryats, Kirghiz, etc.) and the utter disillusionment of many settlers who came back, then the impression of the real effectiveness of Russian pre-revolutionary colonization is on the whole diminished.

Under the Soviet Régime

The February, 1917, revolution did not bring about any essential changes in the principles nor in the status of migration, and colonization, until October, remained in abeyance: on the one hand the

[5] In two years (1908 and 1909) about 1,300,000 individuals.

[6] In 1913, 30,000,000 rubles. [The whole question of pre-Soviet government subsidies and the results they produced in the various regions of the colonization area with their different natural endowment is discussed for the lesson it teaches for the future in B. N. Zhdanov: Ob effektivnosti i trudoemkosti zatrat na pereselenie (On the effectiveness and cost of internal migration), *Severnaya Aziya*, 1928, No. 4, pp. 65–83.—Edit. Note.]

rural population of central Russia were not at that time, as was said before, inclined to move to new lands, and on the other hand the Provisional Government refrained from final decision on the agrarian question until the convocation of the Constituent Assembly. The concrete results of such a waiting policy were that in 1917 only about 6000 colonists crossed the Urals and that the severest measure of the former colonization policy—the expropriation of the land of the border natives—was annulled by the stoppage of all new assignment of land.

The October revolution at once took the colonization-migration problem out of its deadlock. One fact alone, the nationalization of the land and its withdrawal as a commercial commodity, broke up a century-old thésis of Russian emigration: the termination, on that ground, of the serf relation in all its forms and manifestations made possible a broad and free development of colonization processes.

But during the first years of the revolution these processes were on a small scale and did not run smoothly, because at that time new agricultural areas were actually created throughout the country and also because the civil war for a time cut off the main colonization regions—Siberia, the Far East, part of northern European Russia, and the eastern steppe belt (present Kazakstan)—from the center. Only from 1924 on did migration and colonization in the U.S.S.R. become stabilized.

This stabilization was preceded by very interesting steps from the point of view of the novelty of the main principles involved:

1. A period when the "Basic Law of the Socialization of Land" (1918) and the "Statute About Socialistic Land Organization" (1919–1921), which replaced the 1918 law, were in force. In this period it was thought that there should not be any migration of peasants until after a land and population census of the territory of the entire country had been taken and an assigned "norm" of land set aside for each peasant—only after these steps had been carried out, it was believed, would the legal bases be available for shifting population strictly according to a plan. Naturally, in this period, on account of the law, free migration did not develop and was allowed only as an exception.[7]

2. A period when there was in force the "Land Code" (1922–1928), evoked by the transition from "militant communism" (the whole first phase of proletarian dictatorship) to the flexible

[7] For instance, migration of population from a region that had had a poor crop.

forms of the "new economic policy" with its conditional regard for especially industrious peasants and comparative freedom in the domain of land transactions. This period is characterized, on the one hand, by increase in migration (in entire conformity with a certain relapse to capitalism in the village and therefore an inclination of a certain proportion of peasants to emigrate) and, no the other hand, by a greater interest on the part of the government in the occupation of the new lands as the simplest and quickest means of developing the productive forces of the country through the utilization of the initiative of the population.

3. The present period, representing a new step of the revolution, a period of very active socialistic organization in the village (and also in the city) on the basis of a fundamental reconstruction of the obsolete forms of rural economy. In accordance with the technical upheaval in the Soviet villages, the migration processes, of course, will develop new forms and dimensions, and Soviet colonization will be from now on regulated in a distinctive socialistic spirit.

PRINCIPLES OF SOVIET COLONIZATION

The fundamental principles of Soviet colonization, independently of the form of its organization, may be stated to be as follows:

First of all, the point of view of the Soviet authority on migration processes is diametrically opposite to the pre-revolution opinion on that question. The principle of "natural forces" is absolutely excluded, and, just as the whole economic system of the U.S.S.R. in principle and in fact is based on a plan, so the movement of people is conceived to be subordinate to that plan. Such a disposition of the question is real as long as all the fundamental means of production are concentrated in the hands of the state and to the extent that the people's government is able to exert economic and other pressure on every process. It is true that in the U.S.S.R. up to the present time, in addition to the assignment, obligatory for each year, of the available reserve land among the regions from which the migration comes, a deviation from the plan, in the sense of "free" (unregulated) migration, has been taking place; but this phenomenon is diminishing from year to year. However, the chaotic occupation of new lands by the colonists is also gradually dying out. By improving the technical preparation of the land plots and accompanying their peopling by all the economic and cultural means necessary for the beginning of existence, the government now clearly demonstrates that there is no advantage to the colonist in occupying any other land.

Furthermore, the most characteristic feature of Soviet colonization is its relation to the natives of the borderlands. Steps to attract colonists from the center of the Union can be taken only by a special decree of the highest Soviet body, and the movement can be directed only toward the land reserves that had previously been designated as having Federal colonization importance.[8] But, aside from that, no migration whatsoever is allowed to take place unless it is above all in keeping with the interest of the region to be colonized and unless the natives there are already provided for. This principle is adhered to with special scrupulousness in regions of nomadic and semi-nomadic economy.

PLANNING: A CARDINAL PRINCIPLE

Finally, a word about the methods of colonization. Colonization in the U.S.S.R. is considered (like other government activities) as a certain, *scientifically based* system of means to an end, which by way of peopling raises the economically backward regions to the pace and level of the economic development of the whole country. Therefore, the greatest care is taken in the preparation of the organization plans for the development of each region designated for colonization; and before that a most careful calculation and an estimate are made of all its actual and potential resources. To investigate many questions connected with this the U.S.S.R. has opened special research institutions and established university chairs of colonization to train the young forces. In this domain there is gradually arising a new school of specialists who have nothing in common with the colonial scholasticism of the past but who have a concrete knowledge of the present and are firmly imbued with the view that the best organization of mankind in the future cannot be based on the interests of individual groups, classes, or states but ought to reflect the whole rational culture of humanity.

COLONIZATION INTEGRATED WITH OTHER ASPECTS OF STATE SOCIALIZATION

Lately, certain new elements have arisen in the organization of colonization and migration; they are correspondingly changing

---

[8] Besides these reserves, located partly in the present administrative divisions bearing the names of the Siberian Area, the Far Eastern District, and Kazakstan, partly in northern European Russia and other areas, each autonomous national republic can have its own "republican land reserve" and each province its local land fund for settlement.

the technique and methods in this field. The work is now carried out on the principle of not removing population from the over-populated rural regions (area 2 on Fig. 1) but of organizing the unsettled and poorly settled areas as quickly as possible and thus creating new economic complexes whose production type is determined by the general plan of economic development of the country.

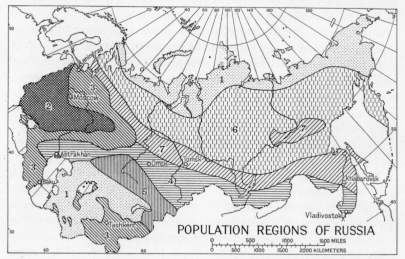

FIG. 1—Population regions of Russia. Scale, 1 : 78,000,000. Key to numbers: 1, areas not suited to agriculture (tundra and desert), 467,000,000 hectares; 2, areas with rural overpopulation, 119,000,000 hectares; 3, fully occupied areas with no excess of population, 303,000,000 hectares; 4, relatively densely populated areas with possibilities for additional settlement, 244,000,000 hectares; 5, sparsely populated areas, 72,000,000 hectares; 6, part of the taiga belt unsuited to agriculture, 613,000,000 hectares; 7, southern border of the taiga belt suited to agriculture, 267,-000,000 hectares; (not shown on the map) irrigable areas in Kazakstan, 7,600,000 hectares. (From Paul Czechowicz: Russland: Die innere Kolonisation in den Jahren 1923 bis 1928, *Wirtschafts-dienst*, Vol. 44, 1929, pp. 1908–1910 and 1954–1959, based on M. A. Bolshakov.)

At the same time this work should help the technical and social reconstruction of the remaining households in the center from which colonists emigrate.

The principle of freedom and voluntary decision in migration remains valid as before for every citizen of the U.S.S.R., but the principle that government help is given only to the type of migration that corresponds to the general policy and real potentialities of the state is being put into operation now more than ever before. Thus, only collective migration is assured all possible help from the state; but those who are willing to go to new lands in this manner are to organize a collective body in their old place of abode.

Furthermore, a system is now being gradually introduced whereby, on the one hand, the localities from which emigration proceeds are correlated with the localities to which it is to go (mainly according to the principle of identity of natural conditions), and, on the other hand, so-called "nests," or places with territorial centralization of related types of activity, are organized in the regions of emigration as well as in the regions of immigration, in order to assure the concentration and effectiveness of work.

But the most outstanding feature of the new organization for the appropriation of new lands is the provision that the immigrants' collectives are not as a mass to create continuous regions of rural economy but will enter as an integral part into the system of government households or into mixed transportational and industrial colonization combinations, i.e. into economic organizations (in both cases) of a type requiring a sufficient foundation of rural economy or a constant reservoir of labor in order to function properly.

Thus, the new principles in the sphere of internal colonization and migration in the U.S.S.R. assign a place to these phenomena secondary to the main pressing problems of the socialization of the state: as long as the state pays its main attention to the industrialization of the country, the migration of farmers is entirely subordinated to the interest of developing industry and natural resources. Therefore, within this subordination, for the immediate future particular attention is given to the colonization of the Far Eastern District and the Siberian Area, with their great possibilities in industry, rational forestry, and useful crops, and also to northern Kazakstan, as a future great grain and cattle center of government farmsteads surrounded by the collective farmsteads of peasants. In the near future there will also be laid the foundation for organized colonization of the northern European part of the Union[9], which, when industrially developed, will absorb several hundred thousand permanent workers.

RECENT REGIONAL TRENDS AND FUTURE PROSPECTS OF THE COLONIZATION MOVEMENT

In conclusion, the migration processes in the U.S.S.R. for four years are summarized in the following table.

[9] See the writer's brief article on "The Bases of Colonization in North European Russia," pp. 236–239 above.

TABLE I—INTERNAL MIGRATION IN THE U.S.S.R., 1926–1929

PROVENANCE IN EUROPEAN RUSSIA		DESTINATION IN ASIATIC RUSSIA	
Administrative Unit	Percentage of Total Emigration	Administrative Unit*	Percentage of Total Emigration
Ukraine	23.1		
White Russia	20.0	Siberian Area . . .	52.1
		Far Eastern District	19.3
Western District (Zapadnaya Oblast)	11.1	Ural District . . .	10.5
Central Black-Earth District	10.1	Kazakstan	6.8
Leningrad District . . .	7.4		
Nizhni Novgorod District	6.4		

*Only those parts of the administrative units come into consideration that are suited to agriculture, i. e. those parts that lie between the limit of agriculture shown in Figure 3, p. 249, above, on the north and, on the south, approximately the 47th parallel and the southern boundary of Asiatic Russia. In Figure I on p. 269 this corresponds approximately to regions 4, 5, and 7.

In this table are shown (1) the proportion of emigrants (in per cent) leaving each of the main emigration regions of the European part of the Union during the four years from 1926 to 1929 inclusive, during which the total emigration amounted to about 750,000 persons, (2) the percentage of immigration absorbed by each of the main colonization regions in the Asiatic part of the Union. From this it is seen that the first place in emigration, as in pre-revolutionary times, is occupied by the Ukraine, and in immigration by the Siberian Area (which in its more important southern part extends roughly from the Irtysh River to Lake Baikal). However, the latter is gradually giving up its historical primacy to the Far Eastern District; while a new social and political formation, Kazakstan, is gradually coming to the fore as a colonization region.

In any case it is necessary to bear in mind that the empirical data of emigration as well as immigration of one region or another, so essential in the past for economic forecasting, do not now, under the conditions of regulation of colonization by the Soviet authorities according to a plan, have the same importance as formerly. Evolutional tendencies in the U.S.S.R. are now subject to revolutionary shifting, and therefore it will not be surprising if the picture of migration processes in the immediate future undergoes a fundamental change under the influence of special measures.

Taking into consideration that of the 2,000,000,000 hectares of the country not more than 400,000,000 (or 20 per cent) are more or less completely appropriated and that in the creative upbuilding of the present time, based on a broad program of railroad expansion and the creation of great industrial centers, all regions are drawn in without exception, even the most backward and far distant, then it will be seen that the range and magnitude of this development are almost limitless.

CHINESE COLONIZATION IN MONGOLIA:
A GENERAL SURVEY

George B. Cressey

THE boundary zone between the agricultural Chinese and the pastoral Mongols has never remained fixed. With vicissitudes of climate and the varying strength or weakness of one people or another it has shifted to the north or south. The Great Wall was built to keep out the nomads of the desert, but during half of the past fifteen hundred years it has failed to do so and China has been ruled by Tatar dynasties. At other times, as for example during the height of the Ming Dynasty, effective Chinese occupation extended to the middle of the Gobi Desert. The present advance of the Chinese farmer is but another of these movements, destined perhaps to be more permanent because of the knowledge of scientific agriculture soon to be available but none the less directly dependent upon climate and subject to its dictates.

The Great Wall is more than a political line. For much of its course it follows a major physiographic boundary that separates the Mongolian Plateau from the lower lands of historic China. It likewise marks a climatic transition, dividing the lands to the south, which receive their rainfall through the monsoon winds, from the Gobi, Ordos, and Alashan Deserts to the north, which are distinctly semi-arid. The Great Wall likewise roughly marks the limit of interior drainage, for, although the Hwang Ho swings outside the wall, it receives scarcely a single tributary from Mongolia. Furthermore, the Great Wall approximately locates a major change in potential land use—the transition from cultivation to grazing. North of the wall are occasional steppe lands with rich grasses and even scattered forests in the mountains, but in general agriculture is only possible under special conditions and with considerably increased risk of failure as compared with the lands to the south.

The absolute desertward limit of possible agriculture will depend upon varying factors, such as improved agricultural methods, cheap transportation, market price, the economic availability of fertilizer, machinery and power, fluctuations in both time and

273

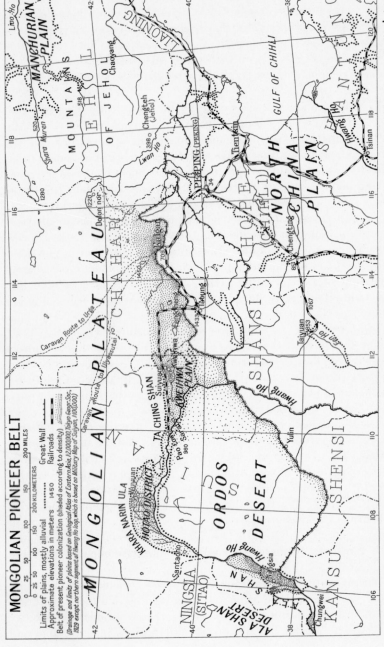

FIG. 1—The Mongolian pioneer belt. Scale, 1 : 8,300,000. The fringe of present pioneer colonization by the Chinese is indicated by stippling, shaded according to density of settlement.

amount of rainfall, the state of public security, and the standards of living the people will accept. Any change in one of these elements will bring an advance or retreat of the desert margin of cultivation and will change the prosperity of the entire zone. Since the permanence of these factors is unpredictable, settlement in these marginal pioneer regions will inevitably be attended with uncertainty.[1]

THE MONGOLIAN PIONEER BELT AS A WHOLE

The present colonization movement affects a belt of country (Fig. 1) outside of the Great Wall running southwestward from the area north of Peiping (Peking) to the northeastern corner of the great loop of the Hwang Ho, whence, to avoid the Ordos Desert, it separates along the flanks of that loop into two prongs which unite south of the city of Ningsia. This movement has been in progress longest in eastern Inner Mongolia in proximity to the crowded lowland plains of China. Huc[2] describes it as commencing in the country north of Peking, in the seventeenth century, whereas Rockhill[3] places the date for the occupation of the area bordering the Ordos Desert on the east as later than 1860. At no time or place has there been any wave of migration similar to that now invading Manchuria. In times of trouble south of the Great Wall, as during the Mohammedan rebellion of 1861–1878, many Chinese have sought security by moving out into the grasslands. At other periods the mere pressure of population, as in Hopei (Chihli) and Shansi, has led people to seek their fortune as pioneers in these new lands. The most important recent stimulus to colonization has probably been the construction of the Peiping-Suiyuan Railway, which was completed to Kalgan in 1909 and to Paotow on the Hwang Ho in 1923. On the other hand, drought has often driven

[1] Paul Wilm: The Agricultural Methods of Chinese Colonists in Mongolia, *Chinese Econ. Journ.*, Vol. 1, 1927, pp. 1023–1043.

Paul Wilm: Wirtschaftsarten in der Mongolei, *Berichte über Landwirtschaft (Zeitschr. herausg. im Reichsministerium für Ernährung und Landwirtschaft*, Berlin), Vol. 7 (N.S.), No. 21, 1928, pp. 266–313.

Paul Wilm: Notes on Mongol Economy and Modern Dairy Farming in Chahar, *Chinese Econ. Monthly*, Vol. 3, 1926, pp. 281–295.

M. T. Volkonsky: Milk Products of Mongolia, *Chinese Econ. Monthly*, Vol. 3, 1926, pp. 540–550.

R. Verbrugge: Les confins sino-mongols: Géographie et ethnographie, *Bull. Soc. Belge d'Études Coloniales*, Vol. 20, 1913, pp. 1–51, 120–135, and 176–216.

[2] E. R. Huc and Joseph Gabet: Travels in Tartary, Thibet and China 1844–1846, edited by Paul Pelliot (in series: The Broadway Travellers, 2 vols., New York and London, 1928), Vol. 1, p. 4.

[3] W. W. Rockhill: Diary of a Journey Through Mongolia and Tibet in 1891 and 1892, Smithsonian Instn., Washington, 1894.

people back from newly occupied regions, or bandits and disorgan-ized soldiers have laid waste the pioneer belt. The penetration of the Chinese has been aided in many cases by the degeneracy of the Mongol princes, many of whom have residences in Peiping, where they have settled down to a life of pleasure and have often sold the rights of colonization to speculators without the knowledge of their tribesmen. No statistics are available as to the number of immigrants to the Mongolian borderlands or as to the extent of the land now under cultivation outside the Great Wall. The number of colonists within the past decade is probably to be counted by the tens of thousands rather than the hundreds of thousands.

CLIMATE, SOIL, CROPS

The climate of the area is sharply continental and semi-arid.[4] The winters are long and bitterly cold, with temperatures down to −30° F., while the summers are short and hot, and the ther-mometer rises to 100° F. Few rainfall records are available for Mongolia, but along the line of the Great Wall the annual precipita-tion averages 15 inches and decreases toward the desert. There is considerable variation in the time of the summer rainy season, and the spring rains are light and often fall so late that plowing cannot be started in time for crops to mature before the early autumn frosts. The growing season is seldom more than 100 days long. In order to conserve the soil moisture by decreasing evapora-tion, the surface of the cultivated fields is usually kept pulverized. In the outer areas nearer the true desert there is usually not enough rain to permit crops to be grown each year, so that fields are allowed to lie fallow every other season or in some cases two years out of three.

The virgin soil is generally fertile, being a mixture of alluvium and loess and containing a relatively high percentage of soluble plant foods. The soils generally belong to the gray-earth group of the pedocals. The soil unfortunately does not retain its pro-ductivity for more than six to eight years without fertilization. Since the pioneer farmers have no dairy cattle and only two or three draft animals, there is a shortage of manure and what dung is available is largely used for fuel. Harvests consequently become smaller and smaller. In the irrigated regions along the Hwang Ho

---

[4] E. Gherzi: Étude sur la pluie en Chine (1873–1925), Zi-ka-wei Observatory, Shanghai, 1928. H. Gauthier: La température en Chine, Zi-ka-wei Observatory, Shanghai, 1918.

where moisture is brought to the surface and evaporated, salts accumulate to excess and render the soil alkaline and thus unfit for cultivation.

The principal crops are oats, barley, wheat, millet, buckwheat, rape, linseed, flax, peas, broad beans, and potatoes. Rape, linseed, and flax are raised only for their oil, and it is an index of the status of civilization of the inhabitants of these regions that the same oil is used for cooking, lighting, and lubricating the wheels of the carts.

THE CHINESE FARMSTEAD

The standard of living of the pioneer farmers is low. The houses are of sun-dried mud bricks or of pounded earth, with a mud roof laid over a mattress of reeds or brush. There are commonly two rooms, one with a crude mud stove with a single circular opening for the large iron pan in which all cooking is done and the other with a raised platform, or *kang*, which serves as a bed and through which circulates the smoke from the adjoining stove. Wood is scarce, and its use is restricted to the roof beams, doors, and windows. Such a house may be built for the cost of the wood and a few days' labor. A few simple dishes and jars for food, together with bedquilts and a chest for extra clothing and supplies, complete the necessary equipment. Farm animals usually include a team of mules or oxen, a riding donkey, a pig or two, a dozen chickens, and one or more mongrel dogs. The animals are kept in a mud structure similar to the house and often adjoining it, and the courtyard is surrounded by a mud wall. In regions where protection is necessary several families, usually from the same ancestral village, build their houses together and erect a veritable fortress with walls ten to twenty feet high. Stones may be placed around the parapet to throw down on bandits.

Some of the farms are large by Chinese standards, but they seldom exceed 300 acres, and the average in the irrigated areas along the Hwang Ho is less than a tenth of that figure. The price of the land varies greatly with its location and fertility, Mex. $2.00 per *mow* being a common figure for undeveloped new land. This is equivalent to U. S. $6.00 per acre and applies only to the poorer land. The cost of good farms or irrigated land is considerably greater, irrigated land west of Kweihwa being valued as high as Mex. $50.00 per mow, or U. S. $150.00 per acre.

Increased Erosion Due to Deforestation
and Cultivation of Marginal Lands

The penetration of the Chinese agriculturist into these desert borderlands has not been without its disastrous effects. The following quotation from Huc,[5] written in 1847, graphically describes some of the consequences in the region to the east of Kalgan.

Towards the middle of the seventeenth century, the Chinese began to penetrate into this district. At that period, the whole landscape was still one of rude grandeur; the mountains were covered with fine forests, and the Mongol tents whitened the valleys, amid rich pasturages. For a very moderate sum the Chinese obtained permission to cultivate the desert, and as cultivation advanced, the Mongols were obliged to retreat, conducting their flocks and herds elsewhere.

From that time forth, the aspect of the country became entirely changed. All the trees were grubbed up, the forests disappeared from the hills, the prairies were cleared by means of fire, and the new cultivators set busily to work in exhausting the fecundity of the soil. Almost the entire region is now in the hands of the Chinese, and it is probably to their system of devastation that we must attribute the extreme irregularity of the seasons which now desolate this unhappy land. Droughts are of almost annual occurrence; the spring winds setting in, dry up the soil; the heavens assume a sinister aspect, and the unfortunate population await, in utter terror, the manifestation of some terrible calamity; the winds by degrees redouble their violence, and sometimes continue to blow far into the summer months. Then the dust rises in clouds, the atmosphere becomes thick and dark; and often, at mid-day, you are environed with the terrors of night, or rather, with an intense and almost palpable blackness, a thousand times more fearful than the most sombre night. Next after these hurricanes comes the rain: but so comes, that instead of being an object of desire, it is an object of dread, for it pours down in furious raging torrents. Sometimes the heavens, suddenly opening, pour forth in, as it were, an immense cascade, all the water with which they are charged in that quarter; and immediately the fields and their crops disappear under a sea of mud, whose enormous waves follow the course of the valleys, and carry everything before them. The torrent rushes on, and in a few hours the earth reappears; but the crops are gone, and worse even than that, the arable soil also has gone with them. Nothing remains but a ramification of deep ruts, filled with gravel, and thenceforward incapable of being ploughed.

While Huc's conception of the relation between deforestation and rainfall is open to question, there can be no doubt that the cultivation of these marginal lands has greatly increased erosion by wind and water. An example of this may be seen in the southern Ordos Desert, where the land was originally covered with a sparse

---

[5] Huc and Gabet, *op. cit.*, Vol. 1, pp. 4–5.

growth of grass and low bushes. Within the memory of Belgian priests living in this area Chinese colonists have attempted to cultivate this region. The result has been that, as soon as the protecting vegetation was destroyed, the strong winds began to erode the soil and piled up great sand dunes, which now cover hundreds of square miles. Cultivation in the region is now declining, and the remaining farms are continually in danger of being engulfed by wandering dunes. Too often the object of the Chinese farmer has been merely to produce enough food to nourish his family at the moment, rather than to increase the productivity of his fields or to look ahead to the future.

IRRIGATED AREAS ALONG THE GREAT BEND OF THE HWANG HO

Along the course of the Hwang Ho in its northward bend through the Ordos Desert there are several areas where irrigation canals have been constructed along the left bank, principally in the vicinity of Chungwei, Ningsia, Santaoho, Wuyuan, and Saratsi (Fig. 1). No canals are in use along the right bank of the river except in the extreme southwest, although the writer found abandoned and grass-grown ditches in the northwestern corner of the river's bend in 1924 and south of Paotow in 1928. Except at Saratsi there are no check gates at the intakes, so that the canals tend to fill up rapidly with silt if neglected. Many of the canals shown on most maps, especially in the Wuyuan area, are so silted as to be no longer usable.

THE NINGSIA AREA

The oldest irrigation works are those around Ningsia. The first canal in this area was dug during the Han Dynasty, two thousand years ago, while others date back to Tang and Ming times. The irrigated area is 85 miles long. Several of the canals are 30 to 40 feet wide and resemble small rivers. Similar irrigation canals have been constructed near Chungwei, while smaller ones encircle Ningan, Ningling, and Lingchow. These canals have transformed their respective areas into productive oases which stand out bright green in an otherwise parched and brown landscape. Many of the canals are lined with willows or poplars which furnish a timber supply for houses or boats. In addition to wheat and other grains, these oases raise delicious apricots, peaches, and melons. Not all of the land served by these canals is under cultivation. Not infrequently desert conditions extend almost to the banks of the canals on both sides. Elsewhere the ditches have become so filled with sediment that they seldom carry water. In places the soil is sandy or alkaline, and there are several swamp areas, particularly east of Ningsia, due to the uncontrolled overflow of the canals. Little effort is made to raise crops on unirrigated land. No reclamation projects or colonization movements are in progress in any of these regions.

THE SANTAOHO AREA

The settlement around Santaoho has been built up by Belgian Catholic missionaries (Scheut Fathers), who have dug an irrigation ditch and established several colonies for their converts. This region is surrounded by barren desert, and the oasis is much smaller and less prosperous than any of those farther south. A few trees have been planted, but cultivation is never very successful. The soil is sandy and poor, with patches of alkali. The rainfall is so low that much of the surface is almost devoid of vegetation. The entire population numbers but a thousand families, and it is doubtful whether the community could sustain itself if outside assistance were withdrawn.

THE WUYUAN AREA

The largest and least prosperous of the irrigated areas in the Ordos Desert lies between the present course of the Hwang Ho and its former bed at the foot of the Kharanarin Ula. This district is known as Hotao, the region of the river, or may better be designated by the name of its principal village, Wuyuan. When Rockhill traveled through the district in 1892 he painted a very dreary picture of the tangle of willow brush, reeds, and spear grass and spoke of the poverty and squalor of the inhabitants. Despite the developments of the past decade the region is still poor and desolate. Historical records, however, refer vaguely to the former prosperity of Hotao. Most maps of China show an extensive system of canals or former river channels in this district. Many no longer carry water, and the area now under cultivation is much smaller than it was at one time.

The Wuyuan region[6] has attracted considerable attention within recent years, and when General Feng Yu-hsiang occupied the northwestern provinces in 1925 he announced ambitious plans for reclamation and colonization. At the request of the Suiyuan government, the China International Famine Relief Commission conducted an engineering survey of the old canals and laid out a program of excavation whereby as much as a million acres might be irrigated. This would be more than six times the area that might be served by the canals now available. Unfortunately political conditions stopped work in the early stages of the project, and nothing further has been done.

The population of Wuyuan *hsien*, or county, was estimated by the Post Office in 1926 as 18,385. This number is augmented during the harvest season by several thousand coolies who come from Shansi, while during the winter many of the residents move to Paotow to escape depredations of bandits. The farmers generally have little or no capital, and many of them are obliged to borrow money at high interest rates, commonly 2 per cent a month, for all of their requirements. To meet these loans they are not infrequently obliged to sell their crops at forced prices, thus suffering a double loss. The number of settlers who have migrated to Wuyuan in recent years in response to General Feng's propaganda is unknown but probably does not exceed 10,000. Since 1926 the region has suffered severely from bands of brigands; and the district has been a favorite point of retreat for defeated soldiers, who have confiscated carts and farm supplies. These misfortunes, combined with the severe famines of 1928 and 1929, have probably reduced the population to a smaller number than for several decades.

One of the chief problems in this area is the soil, which is sandy and tends to be infertile. In many sections the soil is impregnated with alkali, even to the extent of showing a white efflorescence. In areas of excessive evaporation such as this, adding water by irrigation merely increases the amount of water evaporated from the surface and so increases the concentration of these soluble materials in the upper horizons of the soil. The remedy for this situation lies either in expensive subdrainage, whereby the salts are flushed out of the soil, or in growing certain salt-consuming plants which can be cut and removed so that in the course of

[6] Wuyuan, *Chinese Econ. Bull. No. 163*, Chinese Gov. Bur. of Econ. Information, Peking. Annual Reports, China International Famine Relief Commission.

several years the alkalinity is sufficiently reduced for normal cultivation.

The following data, collected by the Suiyuan Industrial Board,[7] apply to 63 farm families in a small village near Linho in the Wuyuan area and give a picture of the use and productivity of the land (Table I). Irrigation is almost essential, although during the more favorable seasons a poor crop may be obtained from the better fields without it.

TABLE I—CROP YIELDS NEAR LINHO

PRODUCT	PERCENTAGE OF CULTIVATED LAND OCCUPIED	AVERAGE YIELD PER MOW	AVERAGE PRICE PER UNIT	AVERAGE VALUE PER MOW
Millets	43.2	5 tou	$3.00 per tan	$1.50
Wheat	35.3	4 "	5.00 " "	2.00
Peas	8.5	4.5 "	6.00 " "	2.70
Linseed	5.9	2 "	6.00 " "	1.20
Beans	4.0	4 "	4.00 " "	1.60
Buckwheat	1.1	3.5 "	3.50 " "	1.23
Potatoes	0.6	2000 catties		
Kaoliang	0.3	5 tou	4.00 " "	2.00
Melons	0.3			
Vegetables	0.3			
Others	0.4			
Total	100.0			

6 mow = 1 acre; 1 tou = about ¼ bushel; 1 catty = 1⅓ pounds; 10 tou = 1 tan.
Values in Chinese (Mex.) currency, par value Mex. $1.00 = U. S. $0.50.

SARATSI IRRIGATION PROJECT

South of Saratsi a large irrigation project is being constructed under the supervision of the China International Famine Relief Commission and the Suiyuan government which will utilize the water of the Hwang Ho to irrigate about 335,000 acres.[8] Work was started on the undertaking in 1929 and is now (1931) in process of completion. The main canal, 40 miles long, has a bottom width of 60 feet at the intake, decreasing to 45 feet in the east, while the 14 laterals are 10 feet wide at the base. The canals have been dug by hand at a cost of U. S. $0.02 per cubic yard, from 1000 to 5000 laborers being employed according to the season. The entire proj-

[7] Agricultural Conditions in Suiyuan, *Chinese Econ. Monthly*, Vol. 3, 1926, pp. 413–417.
[8] O. J. Todd: Getting Yellow River Water on the Saratsi Plain, *Journ. Assn. of Chinese and American Engineers*, Vol. 11, No. 11, Nov. 1930, pp. 1–11.

ect, including a submerged wire across the river, is estimated to cost Mex. $800,000, a considerable part of which is being advanced from American relief funds. This project, when completed, should materially add to the prosperity of the district and should make famine from drought unlikely. The real problem in this and similar situations, however, is to keep the population from expanding up to the new productive capacity of the land. It is surely of no use to quadruple the amount of food produced if the number of mouths to be fed is increased in the same proportion.

Irrigation projects similar to that at Saratsi are probably feasible at several other points along the Hwang Ho in its course through the Ordos, and engineering advice might materially extend the irrigated areas in the regions of existing canals such as Ningsia. It is even conceivable that the Ordos might be transformed in a manner similar to the Indus valley in northwestern India. Such a condition, if ever to be attained, must await a stable and rich government and improved transportation.

The Agricultural Area of the Kweihwa Plain

Around the city of Kweihwa is a broad plain which extends from the foot of the Taching Shan to the Hwang Ho.[9] This is one of the few good agricultural areas not enclosed within the Great Wall and for centuries has been a grain-growing and supply area for the nomads of the desert. The best portion of the plain lies between Kweihwa and Saratsi, but lesser agricultural occupation extends to Paotow on the west and to longitude 112° E. on the east. Much of the area is too high to be irrigated from the Hwang Ho, but several small streams flow out from the mountains and provide some water for near-by fields. The rainfall is more abundant than farther west, and dry farming is possible with considerable success. The cultivated area amounts to something over a thousand square miles, although only a small part is used at all intensively.

Portions of the Kweihwa Plain have been occupied by the Chinese for several centuries, and the Tumet tribes that held the land before them carried on some agriculture. With the construction of the Peiping-Suiyuan Railway a considerable number of new colonists have migrated to the region and settled on the lands to the south of the railroad. Unfortunately, the railroad has been cut by military operations several times and has not been operating

---

[9] R. Verbrugge: Hinterland mongol: Le pays au delà de Koei-hoa-tch'eng, *Bull. Soc. Belge d'Études Coloniales*, Vol. 29, 1922, pp. 99–168 and 221–274.

effectively as a freight carrier for more than half of its history, so that there has been no real opportunity to test the productive capacity of the region. Kweihwa and Paotow are outposts of Chinese business in the caravan trade with Mongolia and thus furnish a large market for agricultural products.

The Chinese Government Bureau of Economic Information has studied[10] conditions in an area of some 300 square miles to the

TABLE II—CROP YIELDS NEAR PIKECHI

PRODUCT	PERCENTAGE OF CULTI-VATED LAND	AVERAGE YIELD PER MOW	AVERAGE PRICE PER UNIT	AVERAGE VALUE PER MOW
Millets . . .	35.7	8 tou	$6.00 per tan	$4.80
Kaoliang . . .	20.5	7 "	6.00 " "	4.20
Hemp . . .	11.0	80 catties	17.00 per 100 catties	13.60
Wheat . . .	7.0	7 tou	8.00 per tan	5.60
Green peppers	4.4	20 catties	4.00 per 100 catties	.80
Potatoes . .	4.3	2000 catties	.33 " " "	6.60
Tobacco . .	3.4	100 "	12.00 " " "	12.00
Onions . . .	3.0	900 "	.80 " " "	7.20
Wild oats . .	2.7	3.6 tou	6.60 " tan	2.37
Barley . . .	2.0	8 "	6.00 " "	4.80
Vegetables .	1.6	2000 catties	.50 per 100 catties	10.00
Buckwheat .	1.4	5 tou	3.70 per tan	1.85
Garlic . . .	1.3	400 catties	3.20 per 100 catties	12.80
Others . . .	1.7			
Total . . .	100.00			

west of Kweihwa thought to be representative of the better parts of the district. In this locality there are 108 villages containing 10,247 families with a total population of 54,577. The area under cultivation amounts to about 480,000 mow, or nearly 80,000 acres, which is 40 per cent of the area. The population density is 182 per square mile, and the area of cultivated land per person is 8.8 mow, or nearly an acre and a half. The productivity of the land depends to a considerable extent on irrigation. Where there are canals, the yield may be as much as twice that of fields dependent on rainfall alone.

Agricultural conditions have been studied in particular detail in the community of Pikechi, a village near Saratsi. In this village dwell 1101 families, of whom 836, or 76 per cent, are engaged in

[10] Agricultural Conditions in Suiyuan, *Chinese Econ. Monthly*, Vol. 3, 1926, pp. 413-417.

farming. Landholdings are smaller than in most other districts, for the average family, with nearly six members, has but 12.9 mow of land. Ninety-five per cent of the farms are smaller than 50 mow, and only three farmers own their own farms. A detailed survey of the crops of 73 farm families in the Pikechi district is shown in Table II.

EASTERN ORDOS AREA

In the eastern Ordos there is another region of Chinese colonization along the line of the Great Wall. The agricultural population is everywhere sparse and thins out toward the west. The German explorer Tafel[11] traveled south from Paotow to Yulin in 1908 and reported Chinese farmers scattered all along his route, although the cultivated land amounted to only a small portion of the area. The best agricultural sections are in the extreme south of the Ordos north of Chingpien, in the north opposite Paotow, and in the east near the Hwang Ho. In some of these areas the Mongols have settled down to a sedentary life after the Chinese manner and have combined stock raising with farming.

AREA NORTH OF KALGAN

The area of Mongolian colonization that has received most frequent mention is the area lying outside the outer line of the Great Wall north of Kalgan. This is nearest to the overcrowded North China Plain and is thus most accessible both to the prospective pioneer and to foreign observers. The region is separated from the lands of historic China by a belt of rugged mountains, but on the plateau there are broad rolling plains covered with short grass and known to the Chinese as the *tsao ti* (land of grass), or as *kou wei* (outside the gate). The land has traditionally been occupied by Mongolian nomads and their flocks, but on several occasions the Chinese agriculturist has advanced into these fertile plains with his plow. The soil is rich, and good crops can be secured if the rains come at the right season and in sufficient quantities. On the north this grassland passes gradually into the dry desert without possibilities of cultivation. The belt in which agriculture of any sort is possible probably does not extend more than 100 miles beyond the Great Wall, and the outer margin is of

[11] Albert Tafel: Meine Tibetreise (2 vols., Stuttgart, etc., 1914), Vol. 1, pp. 96–105.

questionable value. Berkey and Morris[12] state that the width of the grassland along the southern border of the desert is less than 80 miles.

The penetration of the Chinese colonists into this district has been summarized by Buxton,[13] who concludes that there has been a northward movement of the frontier amounting to 50 miles in about fifty years. In 1922 he reports the limit of settlement along the road to Urga as 70 miles from Kalgan. This penetration has not been a steady advance of a mile or so a year, but the frontier of settlement has shifted backward and forward in response to political, economic, and climatic factors. With the varying fortunes of life in old China colonists have been willing to hold on in the pioneer fringe under differing standards of livelihood. Berkey and Morris describe the situation in 1922 northwest of Kalgan as follows: "The outermost patches under cultivation are scattered and clearly represent a pioneering experience, but within a very short distance there appear extensive well-cultivated fields of grain with ripening barley, oats, flax, and millet." The outermost fringe of cultivation is at about latitude 42° N. and longitude 113° E., while the limits of prosperous agriculture and Chinese villages are placed at 41° 30' N. Chinese penetration has extended farther along the main highways than in the inter-trail regions, which in many cases are drier or more hilly. Some of the broad valleys owe their relative prosperity to the presence of ground water near the surface; elsewhere wells need to be 50 and 75 feet deep. There are no possibilities of irrigation, for there are no rivers and the few mountains are not high enough to receive extra moisture. Temperatures on the plateau north of Kalgan are more rigorous than in the regions to the west because of the altitude, but the proximity to the sea makes the summer rainfall somewhat greater. Much of the surface is naturally covered with a continuous spread of vegetation.

PROVINCE OF JEHOL

The province of Jehol lies outside the Great Wall and is the easternmost portion of Inner Mongolia. It is largely mountainous, and the few valleys have been occupied by Chinese farmers for some decades. It does not form a part of geographic Mongolia.

[12] C. P. Berkey and F. K. Morris: Geology of Mongolia (Natural History of Central Asia, Vol. 2), Amer. Museum of Natural History, New York, 1927, p. 396.

[13] L. H. Dudley Buxton: Present Conditions in Inner Mongolia, *Geogr. Journ.*, Vol. 61, 1923, pp. 393–413; *idem:* The Eastern Road, London and New York, 1924, pp. 144–145.

Outer Mongolia: Between Urga and Kiakhta

In addition to settlement in Inner Mongolia outside the Great Wall, Chinese farmers have penetrated to Outer Mongolia north of the Gobi Desert. In 1923 the writer noted several groups of farmhouses in the fertile valleys of the Iro Gol, Chara Gol, and other rivers along the road between Kiakhta and Urga. The region is well watered and should have considerable possibilities, although the growing season is short. The area along the road which was under cultivation amounted to several thousand acres, with areas of unknown size reported on each side. Russian and Buryat colonists have also pushed into this country from Siberia but are more often engaged in cattle raising than in farming.

Conclusion

The entire Mongolian borderland is an area of precarious agriculture. Irrigation can modify but one of the unfavorable factors of the environment, and on unirrigated fields harvests will always be conditioned upon favorable precipitation. Except for the areas along the Hwang Ho the agricultural possibilities of the region are rigorously limited. At the utmost it seems unlikely that Inner Mongolia can ever absorb an additional population of more than, say, 2,000,000 or 3,000,000, which is but a small fraction of China's surplus. The roseate hopes often held out that Mongolia may be able to absorb great numbers of settlers from south of the Great Wall are without foundation. So long as the physical environment remains as now, the bulk of Mongolia is not a land for the farmer.

CHINESE COLONIZATION IN INNER MONGOLIA: ITS HISTORY AND PRESENT DEVELOPMENT*

Owen Lattimore

CHINESE colonization in Inner Mongolia is not by any means a new phenomenon. Indeed, it might well be defined as the contemporary phase of a cyclical process originating in the remote past and operating during a period of at least twenty centuries of which we have some sort of knowledge, historical or archeological. To sketch in the background of even the modern phase would require a study of all the Imperial Edicts relating to this region promulgated during nearly three centuries of Manchu rule in China (1644–1911) and of the records of the Imperial Board of Mongolian and Tibetan Affairs, as well as a study of the city records of the many townships of ancient origin situated in or near the traditional frontier area. Information could undoubtedly be secured also from records of the Catholic missions, especially at the period after the expulsion of the Jesuits from Peking, when work was renewed under the Lazarists, who gathered together along the Mongolian frontier remnants of old Christian communities and began to build afresh. In such an article as this, however, it would be vain to attempt to do more than indicate the nature of some of the principal forces at work, in order to clear the ground somewhat for future study.

The "pioneer belt" of Inner Mongolia (see map, Fig. 1, on p. 274 of the preceding article) can be readily defined on the south by the escarpment of the Mongolian Plateau, overlooking the plains of North China, and on the north by the Gobi Desert. The western limit may be set at the Kharanarin Ula (107° W.), north and west of which range the country becomes too arid for agricultural colonization. The eastern boundaries, topographical and climatic,

*A great part of the information in the present article is derived from the writer's conversations with traders, petty officials, soldiers, pioneer settlers, caravan men, and Mongols in the Kweihwa-Paotow zone. It is obvious that no claim to absolute accuracy can be made for such information. Still less can there be any pretension to having catalogued the whole of all the facts. It should be said, however, that the region is an excellent area for type studies, because the sharp physical cleavage here between the plateau country and the country below the plateau favors equally sharp social cleavages. These have to a great extent been clearly preserved during the modern period of rapid change, owing to the remoteness of the area from the coast of China and its protection from extraneous influences.

288

are much more vague; they merge gradually into Manchuria and the northeastern part of Hopei (Chihli) Province. Because in the east the physical division is not sharply marked, there is a corresponding lack of contrast in social divisions.

The Mongolian Plateau As a Nomad Habitat

The rolling topography and steppe climate of the plateau have in the past favored the development of a nomadic and pastoral rather than a settled and agricultural society. The tribes living on the plateau have tended to develop a vivid sense of the outer boundaries of the plateau but not of any internal boundaries. With this has gone a strong race consciousness but no very strong group consciousness or attachment to particular localities. There has been, instead, simply a tendency to break into what might be called vortical movements, or to camp and move and camp again round the periphery of the different groups of low hills which occasionally project from the general level of the plateau and which act as the conservators of what little water supply there is. At the same time there is nothing to obstruct free lateral movement, as the country generally is open and easy to traverse.

The ancient prevalence of nomadic society does not mean that agriculture is impossible. The climate is rigorous, with a long, cold winter and a hot summer. The shortness of the growing season precludes the cultivation of wheat or even kaoliang (sorghum, or giant millet) or Indian corn, which are among the staple crops of North China. Oats, buckwheat, and peas all flourish, and potatoes can be grown, though they are not a favorite crop. In specially sheltered places even opium poppies can be raised; and of garden produce (though in point of fact gardens are almost totally neglected by the Chinese colonists) Chinese cabbages, onions, garlic, and a plant called *chiutsai*, which may be of the leek family, all grow well. Along the flanks of hills on the plateau, at the level where water appears most freely, farming is relatively easy. At lower levels, where the characteristic growth is rich pasture and there is subsoil drainage, farming, aided to a certain extent by the moderate summer rainfall, is also practicable. Even where the natural browse is thinner, the soil more sandy, and the *shatsung* ("sand-onion," i.e. wild garlic) flourishes better than grass, crops can be raised successfully by the methods of dry farming traditionally known and practiced by the peasants of North China.

Indeed there is archeological evidence that agriculture and settled habitation have been attempted on the plateau at many different times, in many different places. Until the beginning of the modern phase, however, the main tide of history favored the nomad against the settled peasant, for a number of reasons. Of these the chief, geographically, was the following. The nomad shepherd who chose to stake out a personal claim to a definite tract of land and occupy it permanently would naturally pitch on a region of fertility and good water supply as being the most favorable to his altered way of life. In times of drought, pressure of population, or warfare among the tribes this man and any of his fellows who had joined with him in making a settled community would be at the disadvantage of holding a weak, immobile position, open on all sides to the attack of nomad tribesmen. His crops could be burned and his cattle driven off, while his assailants, holding the advantage of mobility, would be able to move to a safe distance the cattle and tents that comprised all their wealth, so that even if driven off they would suffer no permanent loss. This reason was fortified by a political reason. In the warfare of nomadic tribes mobility counts for as much as virility, if not for more. Granted the prevalence of a nomadic society on the plateau of Inner Mongolia, the most powerful chiefs would be those who could not only summon a host of warriors but could man them freely without the embarrassment of a fixed base. This appears to be a universal condition of nomadic warfare, holding good for such people as the Arabs as well as for the Mongols. The women and children of such tribesmen must be fit to handle their heavy transport and commissariat, must be able to follow the warriors with fresh mounts and able to move the tents, gear, and flocks out of harm's way. Any chief who jeopardized his military power for the sake of a few years of prosperous farming during an interlude of peace would soon be shorn of that power. This goes far to explain why the Mongol chiefs show no tendency to appropriate land to themselves but are wholly in favor of the central nomadic tradition that all land belongs to the tribe and should not be alienated to any individual, the title to it not being even nominally vested in the chief as the head of his tribe; and also why they are solidly opposed (as will be more fully shown later) to any tendency among their tribesmen to abandon the nomadic way of life for permanent individual holdings.

THE EARLIER OSCILLATIONS OF THE MONGOL-CHINESE FRONTIER

Enough has been said of the physical border between China and the Mongolian Plateau to show that it accounts for a marked climatic difference between the cultures of the pastoral nomads on the plateau and the agricultural peasants to the south. Yet the physical boundary, though abrupt and striking enough to account for such contrasts, is not at all difficult of passage, so that the peoples on either side of it have been in frequent contact during a long, eventful history. Looking north from Kweihwa, at a typical point on the frontier, the Ta Ching Shan, as this part of the plateau escarpment is known, appears as a formidable range of mountains. Ascending through them for some 30 miles, by a road practicable for carts although attaining a maximum elevation of over 5000 feet, it is found that on the northern side there is no compensating drop but that the surface of the plateau opens out—somewhat broken and irregular, but easy to traverse. The southern face of the hills attests the fact that the escarpment is a climatic frontier, for it is the northern limit of forest growth. The forests have been almost entirely destroyed by reckless cutting, but enough vestiges remain to prove the ancient growth; whereas on the plateau itself there is no sign that forests ever existed within the historical period, except many hundred miles to the north where the Siberian climatic zone is approached.

Although the geographical conditions north and south of the rim of the plateau are so different as to have encouraged during the past different types of social culture, communication between the peoples of the two cultures has always been feasible. It has more usually been hostile than amicable. The savagery of the nomad tribes led them to prefer robbery to trading. They had the advantage of position, it being easy for them to raid down from the plateau and subsequently defend the edge of the plateau against counterattack. They had the advantage of mobility, it being easy for them to harry settled farmers and hard for the settled farmers to pursue them. Thus in the past the effective frontier of Mongolia was more often than not south of the physical frontier marked by the plateau escarpment. The savage tribes being the aggressors, it was difficult for the Chinese to hold the rim of the plateau; they had to retire well to the south before finding terrain on which they could align a permanent defense.

The Real Frontier (Great Wall) Lay Below the Plateau Scarp

The ancient political frontier, as distinct from the physical frontier, is therefore to be sought along the line of the Great Wall— an immense frontier work that, despite its superficial unity, represents in reality the linking up of numerous local defenses. This is decisively proved by the fact that, in several sections of its enormous length, there are northern and southern variants of the Wall. In what is now northern Shansi and Hopei the northern and southern courses of the Great Wall are, for much of their length, over 100 miles apart, so that the whole of this great territory must have been stoutly disputed between the forces of China and the northern barbarians.

The structure of the Great Wall system is, however, in itself a witness to the fact that the Chinese, though the relief of the land was against them in coping aggressively with the mobile nomads, were capable of a formidable resistance. This power of resistance, in point of fact, was occasionally translated into active aggression, when the Chinese endeavored to penetrate into the Mongolian hinterland and even to establish permanent colonies, in order to replace the recurrently hostile nomad population with one more germane to the central Chinese culture. Thus, in the typical frontier area of Kweihwa, I noticed in 1926 the line of an ancient earthwork at a point well to the north of the edge of the plateau. The same earthwork seems to have been noticed, at another point, by Przhevalskii,[1] so that it must be of considerable extent. Such an earthwork, by the testimony of its position, could never have been constructed by people of the plateau wishing to defend themselves against aggression from the south. It must have been built by people holding the Kweihwa valley and wishing to keep nomad tribes away from the hills overlooking them.

Such evidence as we have, however, all points to the conclusion that the Chinese were usually the defenders and the nomad tribes the aggressors. Tribes from the plateau time and again pushed down into North China and conquered kingdoms for themselves, at different times ruling all North China and dominating the south. Invaders from the north had the advantage of winning their way into a higher form of civilization; in which, in fact, they invariably merged themselves, to be succeeded as rulers, after a lapse of time,

---

[1] N. M. Prjevalsky: Mongolia, the Tangut Country and the Solitudes of Northern Tibet, transl. by E. D. Morgan, 2 vols., London, 1876.

by fresh barbarians from the plateau. The Chinese, on the contrary, whenever during an access of power they were able to reach the plateau, were handicapped by having to modify in a retrogressive sense the civilization they brought with them, in accommodating themselves to a terrain and a climate that favored the more primitive social order of the pastoral nomad.

INTRODUCTION OF LAMAISM WEAKENS POWER OF MONGOLS

So far as can be determined, the chief agent in interrupting the age-long succession of barbarian conquests that swept from the plateau down into China was the introduction among the Mongols of the Lamaist, or Tibetan, form of Buddhism. The lamas, with their creed of quietism, sapped the energy and virility of the Mongol race. The large communities of lama monks, recruited from among young men who would in the older tradition have become warriors, were even more potent in degrading the race; for, producing nothing themselves, they demanded the best produced by the nation for their support and the embellishment of their monasteries, thus draining the common wealth.

Lamaism had already been introduced into Mongolia but had not gained an overpowering hold, when the Manchus entered and conquered China in the seventeenth century. There was even at first some danger that the Manchu conquests might be challenged from Mongolia. The Manchus, therefore, in order to prevent a recurrence of barbarian invasions from the north, adopted from the beginning of their rule in China a strong and calculated Mongolian policy. In the first place they fostered the lama church in order to weaken the Mongols. In the second place they altered the Mongol tribal system and increased the number of chieftains, whom they required to visit Peking periodically. Thus the chiefs, owing their positions to the Manchu overlordship, were drawn to the side of their rulers. The Mongols generally were impoverished by the increased demands both of the church and the princes, while the princes were prevented from gaining too much power by the required periodical visits to Peking, entailing heavy expenses both to keep up their appearance and to purchase honors at the court, not to mention the extraordinary disbursements made to courtiers and eunuchs, every time that a chieftain died, by rival claimants to his title.

On top of these measures the Manchus encouraged the advance

of Chinese colonists into Mongolia. To the early Manchu emperors, holding the positions of sovereigns over both Chinese and Mongols, were due the first decrees that gave a legal and orderly basis for the taking over by Chinese colonists of Mongol tribal land. This is a matter of the highest importance, for it establishes an epochal date—the change from the long-drawn-out military process of invasion and counterinvasion to the civil process of colonization.

COLONIZATION UNDER THE MANCHUS (1644-1911)

The colonization of Inner Mongolia, while China was a Manchu empire and Mongolia a Manchu appanage, proceeded from the middle of the seventeenth century until the Chinese Revolution in 1911, or say for 250 years. The forward movement of colonists appears to have diminished steadily in velocity. Like many of the projects set on foot in the first vigor of the Manchu conquest it was ably conceived; but as the Manchus, from the court downwards, began to lose their barbarian energy, official enthusiasm for such projects waned. Moreover, with the rapid expansion of the lama church in Mongolia and the concurrent decay of the Mongols, the need for a bold frontier policy became less urgent. Thus the flow of Chinese colonists toward Mongolia became largely a matter of dead-weight pressure, representing little but the onward movement of the slowly increasing population of regions contiguous to the border.

What was actually accomplished was a comparatively rapid reclamation by Chinese settlers of the old debatable lands between the ancient Great Wall frontier and the escarpment of the plateau, succeeded by a comparatively slow advance into the plateau itself. Once the plateau was reached, the Chinese advance became largely a matter of economic distance from centers of trade. Economic distance was controlled by the factor of transport, which hundreds of years before had been brought, in China proper, to a level above which it could hardly be raised without the introduction of mechanical methods and appliances quite alien to the ancient indigenous Chinese civilization. The trade of that part of China toward which the produce of Inner Mongolia would naturally be despatched was dominated by inland waterways. North China was itself almost wholly agricultural. Extra food supplies for the metropolis of Peking were brought up as tribute from the south, by the Grand Canal. Agricultural settlers on the plateau, unable to market grain except by sending it for a great distance along difficult hilly tracks by pack trains or camel caravans, were unable to compete with the cheap food supply of North China. Thus colonization became in the main an affair of simple peasants tilling enough soil for their own support, unconcerned with the marketing of an export surplus. This condition was modified only in the second half of the nineteenth century, when the growth of opium became profitable. The border country, being comparatively free from official supervision and therefore lightly taxed, then became interested in the sale of opium, which represents a high value for a small bulk and weight and could therefore be profitably transported over difficult roads for long distances.

Mode of This Colonization toward End of the Period

Our accounts of Inner Mongolia under the Manchu empire are comparatively rare and sketchy; nor were any of the travelers to whom we owe the accounts especially interested in Chinese colonization. Occasional remarks, however, can be picked out, none the less illuminating for having been casually made. Among accounts which may be cited from the last period of Manchu decay are those of Huc in 1844,[2] Elias in 1872,[3] and Hedley in 1905.[4] The ingenuous records of Hedley are especially valuable as giving an account of the state of affairs in northern Chihli, eastern Inner Mongolia, and southern Manchuria a few years before the downfall of the Manchu Dynasty.

From these accounts and from the physical geography of the region (which remains the best guide of all) the salient facts emerge.

Different Pattern of Colonization Northeast and West of Kalgan

North of the line from Kalgan eastward through Chengteh (Jehol) to Chaoyang and east of the line from Kalgan northeast-ward to Dolon Nor and beyond (Fig. 1, p. 274), colonization was more rapid and went much farther than west of the Kalgan-Dolon Nor line and north of the line from Kalgan westward through Kweihwa to Paotow. This is explained by the fact that in the

[2] The most recent and handiest edition of the "Travels in Tartary, Thibet and China" of Huc and Gabet is that edited by Professor Paul Pelliot in the series "The Broadway Travellers," edited by Sir E. Denison Ross and Eileen Power, 2 vols., New York and London, 1928.

[3] Ney Elias: On a Journey Through Western Mongolia, *Proc. Royal Geogr. Soc.*, Vol. 17, 1872–1873, pp. 184–192.

[4] John Hedley: Tramps in Dark Mongolia, London, 1910.

western area the plateau breaks down sharply, clearly defining the traditional nomad lands on the north; while in the eastern area there is no simple escarpment, but a gradual descent to wide, irregular, and rough hilly tracts, with valleys forming deep reentrants into the plateau. Thus the western terrain postulates that any racial advance, whether to the north or south, must be on a comparatively regular, unbroken front; whereas the eastern area admits of a great deal of interpenetration between Mongols and Chinese, and the reëntrant valleys, forming climatic avenues leading into Mongolia, permit the distribution of a good rainfall far inland and accordingly favor the advance of agricultural colonists.

These same valleys in time past had facilitated the advance of Mongols coming down from the plateau. Thus, when the great Chinese advance began, Mongol communities would be left in some of the valleys while the Chinese were pushing up other valleys parallel to them. This interdigitation of Chinese and Mongols in the hilly country made possible a far greater mingling of cultures than is elsewhere noticeable in Mongolia and explains the phenomenon noted by Hedley of Mongol communities well within the fringe of the Chinese advance. Many of these Mongols, left behind by the general retreat of their race, adapted themselves to the new Chinese way of life, until whole communities are found that have forgotten their own language, speak Chinese exclusively, have settled on the land exactly like the Chinese, and can be identified as Mongols only by their own traditions and by certain remaining customs and, frequently, by the unbound feet of the women and their way of doing up their hair.

West of Pingtichuan (113° W.), as the escarpment becomes more simple and the line of racial cleavage correspondingly sharp, this phenomenon is not nearly so common, but it can also be traced in some of the valleys of the escarpment north of Kweihwa and Paotow. In the Pingtichuan region this process must be comparatively recent, as the Mongol language has not been entirely obliterated and men as well as women retain for the most part Mongol costume, including even the boots with upturned toes which are designed more for the horseman than the husbandman.

LITTLE OFFICIAL CONTROL OF FRONTIER AREAS

Official interest in colonization was half-hearted, and official control, supervision, and administration were almost entirely lacking. Frontier officials, who interested themselves almost entirely in taxation, were largely not of the ordinary civil service but of a special service, semi-military in character, whose heads were the "Tatar Generals" of such places as Suiyuan (Kweihwa). The military establishments were commonly cut down to a bare skeleton, that the officials might support themselves on the pay of non-existing troops. Thus they were not eager to use what troops they had for the suppression of banditry. Colonists largely administered themselves under "village elders." Lawsuits, owing to venial officials, were rarely brought into court but settled before village headmen. On the fringe of Mongol-occupied country the anomalous situation might even arise of Chinese going before the nearest Mongol chieftain for a comparatively impartial settlement of their disputes (Hedley).

In such cases as were brought before Chinese officials Mongols were treated as admittedly the subject race. Discrimination against the Mongols, however, was not so much racial as social, being directed against their status as nomad barbarians. Mongols who had formed village communities on the Chinese model, and so passed within the fringe of the Chinese advance, automatically passed out of the tribal system and seem to have been recognized as Chinese to all intents and purposes. In the older settled Mongol communities there came even to be mixed communities of Chinese and Mongols, living side by side but not intermarrying very freely, such intermarriage as took place being of Mongol women to Chinese men, not of Chinese women to Mongol men.

The Intermediary Rôle of the Mongol Princes

Lack of friction on the edge of the advance between Chinese and Mongols must have been attributable not to good administration but, in the first place, to the decline of the military tradition among the Mongols and, in the second place, to the large measure of local power left in the hands of Mongol princes by high Manchu-Chinese (Imperial) policy. The Mongols as a race were treated as inferiors; their princes were kept in political favor. Thus the princes, or chiefs, being in absolute local authority over their own tribesmen and anxious to maintain their privileges, became to a great extent intermediaries between Chinese and Mongols. From this period dates the practice of dealing through the princes when taking over Mongol tribal land for the settlement of Chinese colonists. The Mongol princes guaranteed the good faith of their subjects and as a general rule seem to have reserved for themselves whatever money they received from the Chinese for the purchase of land. Also, to increase the prestige of the princes, Mongol delinquents, when taken anywhere near the edge of Mongol-occupied country, were turned over to the princes for trial and judgment, though Mongols taken well within the line of Chinese advance were brought before Chinese courts.

The new authority of the princes in matters of land tenure and land transfer fortified their reluctance (anciently based on the conditions of nomad life) to allow their own subjects to cultivate the land. Thus it was, commonly speaking, only Mongol communities that had been "pinched out" or isolated by the Chinese advance that settled on the land. For land still under their own jurisdiction the princes preferred to take in cash the profit on sale to the Chinese rather than allow cultivation by their own subjects; for, as soon as such land had been overpassed by the Chinese, those subjects would pass out of their control. Thus Hedley notes that in a district north of Jehol the Mongols were allowed by the local chief to grow a little millet for winter supplies; but no land might be farmed for more than two years in succession, and thus the evolution of a farmer class was prevented.

The Rôle of the Chinese Trader

During this late-Manchu period, the officials being lethargic, Chinese traders[5] appear to have been in the forefront of the advance. The trader would move out well in advance of the Chinese line of holdings and establish himself—of course by arrangement—either near the headquarters of a prince or near a monastery. At either place there would be a coming and going of Mongols conducive to trade. All trade, then as now, was on credit, with heavy interest, and the local Mongols would soon be in debt, the prince more heavily than any of the rest. The trader would also act as agent of the prince in disposing of the dues collected from tribesmen in the form of livestock, wool, pelts, etc. Having thus firmly established himself, the trader, on the gradual approach of the line of colonization, would act as intermediary between the prospective settler on the Chinese side and the prince on the Mongol side, in the transfer of land. There is no doubt that a good deal of land came into private ownership in this manner.

[5] The trader, now as then, never carries his family with him. He goes out to a "post" for a period of years, during which he usually has temporary relations with Mongol women but does not recognize the offspring, and revisits his family on furlough.

Forms of Land Acquisition

At times land was taken over from the Mongols at rental instead of by purchase, a low ground rent being paid to the chief as representing the tribe. In that event the rental might be taken over by a Chinese trader as security for debts. In the trading quarter of Kweihwa, a town now purely Chinese except for the lama monasteries, ground rent on certain land is still paid to the Mongols, out of whose title it has never passed, although the tribe of that area, the Tumets, are now practically non-existent and the nearest Mongols, except for a very few remnants, are to be sought at fifty or sixty miles' distance on the plateau. It is almost certain that in such a case as this the Mongol title to the land has been preserved through its having passed into the ownership or under the protection of a lama monastery. Under the native Mongol system monastery land is the only exception to the rule of tribal ownership. Nor, even when they have become isolated in purely Chinese communities, are the monasteries disturbed. In the first place, the "magical" powers of the lamas are respected. As members of the race originating from the soil they are supposed to be in closer spiritual relationship with the powers of wind, rain, and climate and better able than Chinese priests to induce good harvests and prosperity. In the second place, Mongols will ride through wide belts of Chinese cultivation to reach a celebrated temple or monastery, and at seasonal festivals great concourses gather which give occasion for fairs and not a little trade. In the third place, the lamas are so much venerated by the Mongols, especially abbots of high rank and "Living Buddhas," that their presence in the midst of the Chinese becomes a surety of a certain value for the good behavior of the Mongols generally.

CONTEMPORARY COLONIZATION [6]

Effect of the Introduction of New Instruments of Power

A great many of the conditions of contemporary colonization derive directly from the conditions just described; but others, of

[6] Among the sources of information is the valuable *Chinese Economic Journal*, formerly (1924–1926) the *Chinese Economic Monthly*, published monthly since 1927 by the Chinese Government Bureau of Economic Information (a non-political organization) under the direction of Mr. W. H. Donald, in which appear articles and statistics gathered by trained Chinese workers. Valuable notices appear on colonization in Manchuria and more rarely on economic affairs in the Inner Mongolian area. Information could also be sought from the Catholic missions and from the Protestant mission at Patsebolong (northwest of Paotow), which is supported partly by American Boxer Indemnity funds and of which a main object is the "reclamation" of Mongols as agriculturists.

the greatest importance, remain to be indicated. These chiefly concern new "instruments of power," as they have been called—the new mechanical factors that have been introduced into China from the West. Most of these new instruments of power have been developed in the West during the past century; in the course of their development the civilization of the West has been adapted to them *pari passu*, so that for the most part they have been used constructively, except during periods of warfare. In China they have been introduced already fully developed, only within the last thirty years, so that their introduction has had the force of a sudden impact and has often had a disruptive rather than a constructive effect.

The most important of the new instruments of power in China is the railway. Transport is one of the basic sources of political, social, and economic control. In China all these functions have for centuries been geared down to accommodate a high civilization to primitive methods of transport. The sudden introduction of the railway has been especially disruptive because the power concentrated in it has tended to fall into the hands of able and ambitious individuals instead of being harnessed to an orderly national expansion. Railways have not yet linked up China in a unified system of transport. Their more obvious effect, especially in the recent past, has been to divide the country into zones, each zone centering on a railway which enables a local military power to transport troops to maintain his authority and by combined use of troops and railway to exploit for his own benefit the region under his control.

THE PEIPING-SUIYUAN-PAOTOW RAILWAY

The completion, since the Republic, of a railway passing from Peiping (Peking) through Kalgan to Kweihwa and then to Paotow on the Hwang Ho, has completely transformed the question of colonization in Inner Mongolia. The most obvious effect of the railway is the way in which it has altered the factor of economic distance. Formerly the basis for the calculation of all trade, including the produce of colonists, was the distance, time, and cost involved in transport between North China proper (within the Great Wall) and the front of advance at or beyond the plateau escarpment. Now the base of calculation has been moved up, so that each point like Kalgan, Fengchen, Kweihwa, and Paotow has become railhead for that segment of the pioneer belt that lies to the north of it; and the railway, moreover, provides a freedom of lateral communication formerly unknown.

The political significance of the railway goes even deeper. Formerly the Chinese were never able to take the initiative along the plateau unless backed by a strong power in China proper, within the Wall; and strong power in North China seems to have depended, paradoxically, on the rate at which the Chinese could absorb and give a Chinese veneer to fighting barbarian invaders from the north. On the whole, the normal state of affairs for many centuries was for the initiative to rest with the nomadic barbarians, of whom the Mongols are the final representatives. Even under the powerful Manchu empire in China it would not have been so easy for the Chinese to take the initiative had not the Mongols themselves lost the initiative through their decay after the introduction of Lamaism.

As affairs now stand, the railway, with the influx of other related instruments of power, places the advantage wholly and finally with the Chinese, at least in Inner Mongolia; though in Outer Mongolia the Mongols may be armed with the pseudo-initiative of power borrowed from the Russians.

Political conditions in modern China are in such a state of flux that it is impossible to speak absolutely. Still, it may be said that in recent years the railway along the frontier has not represented national interests so much as the personal interests of the locally dominant military power. Even so, a new point of view is predicated for the Chinese official. New lands taken over from the Mongols mean increased revenue in land taxes, in taxes on trade and transport, and in the operation of the railway, also in increased man power available by conscription from the growing Chinese population. The officials are now supporting and directing colonization as never before.

Method of Land Expropriation

Whether or not, under the laissez-faire rule of the Manchus, land was taken over more by the dead-weight force of the encroachment of Chinese traders, followed by colonists, than by planned and directed official authority, it is now taken over entirely under official supervision. Delegated officials negotiate with the nearest Mongol ruler when more land is needed. Land is assessed at a

flat rate.   It is reported that commonly the purchase money
dwindles as it passes through the hands of the negotiating officials.
What remains is not distributed to the tribe, who are the owners
in common of the land, but is usually retained by the chief or
"prince."   The policy of according official recognition and open
honor and favor to chiefs is continued.   Thus the chiefs, though
responsible for tribal dues to the paramount Chinese authority,
are left in well-nigh absolute authority in the territory remaining
to them.   Chinese colonists are excluded absolutely from land still
recognized as tribal, and even traders are not allowed to enter
except with Mongol permission.   Trading caravans passing through
Mongol territory pay dues for grazing and water.   This enables
the Chinese authorities to keep a check on movements along the
border and prevents to a certain extent the escape of disaffected
Chinese into tribal territory, where as brigands or leaders of
disgruntled Mongols they might (and sporadically do) embarrass
the officials.

The Mongol princes do not relish any more than their tribesmen
the forced retreat of their race; but, as they are supported in what
power remains to them and can take a share in the profit on land
transactions, they perforce make the best of a bad business.

RACIAL AND SOCIAL CHARACTERISTICS OF THE SETTLERS

The type of colonist varies in general according to the region
within the Great Wall from which he has come.   In the east, where
the Great Wall approaches the sea and the North China Plain,
the colonists are largely drawn from the same reservoir that
supplies Manchuria—the plains-dwelling people of Hopei and
Shantung, of the true North China stock, hardy, energetic, and
capable.   In the western area it will be seen at once (Fig. 1 on
p. 274) that there is a wide belt of country between the outer and
the inner Great Wall, and a still wider belt between the plateau
escarpment and the inner Great Wall.   All of this is country
that for centuries was invaded and harried by barbarians from the
north.   By way of illustration it may be pointed out that Tatungfu
was the seat, in the fourth and fifth centuries, of the kingdom of
the Wei Tatars, who in the sixth century were able to move their
capital as far south as Loyang in Honan.   At the present day, at
Wutaishan in northern Shansi, within the inner Wall, there is a
great religious center of Mongol and Tibetan lamas (together with

Chinese Buddhist temples) visited yearly by thousands of Mongol pilgrims, who, in order to reach it, travel for hundreds of miles through districts now held solely by Chinese.

Northern Shansi supplies the majority of colonists taking up land north of Kweihwa and Paotow. The people show signs of much racial admixture, in physical and especially cranial, type, not to mention dialect. They are the product of a long border history; in all their traditions the record of conflict between Chinese and "Tatze" ("Tatars," or Mongols and pre-Mongols) is very vivid. They are in many ways an admirable type of colonist, but they are inferior in civilization, judged from the Chinese point of view, to the men of Hopei and Shantung and, being remote from the coast, are much less familiar with the new forces introduced into China by Western civilization. Their best characteristic is the readiness with which they adapt themselves, through their heredity and traditions, to the most arduous pioneer life.

The average age of pioneers, at least in the western area, is low. It is a community of younger sons. On inquiry it is constantly found that, on account of hard times in northern Shansi, fathers and elder brothers have been left on the family holdings, and groups of younger brothers, banded together, have trekked north. On the plateau, in the forefront of colonization, the typical "village elder" is a man not past his thirties. (It is characteristic that "hard times"—the failure or insufficiency of crops—is always given as the cause of emigration; it is doubtful if the increase and pressure of population are understood as we understand them.)

Land Tenure

After land has been taken over from the Mongols at a flat rate, it is re-assessed and made available to settlers at rates varying according to the productive capacity of the soil. The first demand is always for the higher-priced bottom land. Generally the land is vacated by the Mongols in the summer; the pioneers move in during the autumn. They bring with them supplies for the winter, build mud huts, and as it were entrench themselves until the spring, when the ground is first broken. An autumn sowing for an early crop is, so far as my observation goes, rare, late spring frosts being too severe. Usually by the second harvest good land is producing full crops. Occasionally the settlement is opened by young men, who go back after the first harvest to fetch their

women and children. Social ties, especially in the first years of
settlement, are loose, the state of affairs appearing barbarous to
Chinese from within the Wall. Men fail or become discouraged
and abscond, and their wives go to other men. Young men drift
away for a season of caravan work, and their wives "lean," as the
expression goes, on other men. Parentage of children is often
doubtful, and filial piety is not comparable, as a social force, to
filial piety in China proper.

The staple crops are oats and "small" millet. Village gardens,
even for home supply, are almost non-existent. The staple diet
is oat flour, made into dough, rolled into hollow cylinders, and
steamed in a sieve over boiling water. It is varied only with
millet porridge. In the eastern area, in sheltered parts of the western
area, and everywhere below the rim of the plateau opium is an
important crop. It is everywhere under a nominal ban but everywhere unofficially countenanced. In some districts land is taxed
on the basis of potential opium yield; as the tax cannot possibly
be met by a food crop, this in effect makes poppy-growing compulsory. The ban on opium merely puts up the market value and
the tax revenue.

The land taken up by colonists is, so far as I know, always paid
for in cash. The government, or rather the provincial authority,
makes a profit of 200 or 300 per cent over the low cost of purchase
from the Mongols, although the inferior land is sold much lower
than the good bottom land. Even so, the selling price to the
colonist is not high; it is far lower than in China proper, and,
once the line of advance has passed beyond land in cultivation,
that land increases rapidly in value. Land may rise to six or eight
times its purchase cost within the lifetime of the pioneer—even
though the reservation be made that figures given in conversation
with a peasant cannot be considered statistically accurate.

The only governmental credit allowed in general practice is
the remission of land taxes for a period of years varying with the
value of the land and its situation relative to actual or potential
markets. Land taxes thereafter rise conformably to the price
of land. This credit is supplemented by the credit given by traders
and especially grain buyers, who carry the heaviest finance of
colonization. The purchase price of the land may even be advanced
to the pioneer, the deeds for the land being endorsed over to the
grain buyer. Once indebted to the grain buyer, the colonist seldom
wins his freedom entirely. Crops are contracted for in advance,

the essence of the bargain being a cash advance to the farmer in the spring, against a contract for his harvest in the autumn, at a low price. This form of interest, like all others, is very high and is computed monthly, 1.2 per cent a month being considered fair interest when good average security is offered.

Mingling of Cultures

There are two common forms of racial admixture on the pioneer front. The first is the introduction of Chinese blood among the Mongols, by traders, peddlers, and caravan men. The Mongols, owing to the nomadic tradition of hospitality, are indifferent to the chastity of either married or unmarried women. Thus there are many half-Chinese children among the Mongols, the offspring of casual intercourse. These children grow up as Mongols. The second class of admixture results from the taking of Mongol women into Chinese communities where there is a surplus of young men. These children grow up as Chinese.

Another Mongol element in the population, more important culturally, results from the "stranding" of small groups of Mongols behind the line of the Chinese advance, to which reference has already been made (p. 296). Even in the western area, where the line of advance is comparatively even, small local salients occur, owing to the choice of particularly good land for expropriation. Somtimes Chinese communities are found like islets out beyond a belt of land still occupied by Mongols living in the traditional Mongol manner. This occurs either when the intervening land is too poor for anything but grazing and has not been claimed by settlers and Mongols filter back into it to escape their heavy tribal dues, or when a belt of monastery land has been overpassed without expropriation. The result is a gradual merging of Chinese and Mongol. The pioneers frequently hand over their draft ponies and plow cattle (oxen and ponies) to be herded by these Mongols during the season when they are not in use. A small fee per head is paid, and the increase is kept by the herdsmen. Such Mongols also keep milch cows and do a small business in selling milk cake. This is made by simmering milk slowly in a caldron until a thin, rich, buttery pancake is left. It becomes rancid if kept but remains edible. Hard cheese is also made as a winter provision. It is worthy of remark that the Chinese eat this milk cake and cheese, as they are considered unclean in China proper.

Among these isolated Mongols the first step toward the Chinese way of life is to abandon the felt *yurt* and move into a mud cabin. At this stage they continue to speak Mongolian, though some of the young men speak broken Chinese. The next generation is bilingual. The third generation speaks Chinese only or at least Chinese more fluently than Mongolian. At about this time there is a tendency to attempt farming and to claim permanently the land held by the little community as squatters. It takes, however, at least another generation or two before the Mongols can compete with the Chinese as farmers.

A concession on the part of the Chinese toward the Mongols may be observed when the children of very poor parents are turned over by them to Mongols. These children live a hard life, earning their keep by herding flocks. When grown, they are supposed to return to their parents and to share in farming the family land. Many of them, however, find farming tedious after the Mongol life and drift away to join the great trading caravans, where they are especially useful through their fluent knowledge of Mongolian. The more capable enter the service of trading firms as interpreters. The relinquishment of children by poor parents, however, is uncommon in the Kweihwa area. It occurs much more frequently farther to the west, on the borders of Kansu and Mongolia.

Still another form of compromise, almost never found in the Kweihwa region, is fairly common in parts of Chinese Turkestan. This is the turning native, as it may be called, of adult Chinese, who go among the Mongols, take Mongol wives, and settle down to live in the Mongol manner. The children of such unions are known as *erh-hun-tze*, or bastards. They are a valuable class, being more thrifty and capable than the Mongols. They tend to become cattle breeders and cattle sellers rather than mere cattle owners, like the Mongols. They make important concessions to Chinese ideas of propriety in their customs of marriage and burial, both of which relate to the respect for ancestry. The originators of this class are almost all men who have come from the region of Kweihwa, having originally been caravan men. If similar cases do occur near Kweihwa itself, the men are probably also ex-caravan men.

RELIGION

Religion may also be classed with the contact and fusion of cultures. The original pioneers almost never bring priests of their own with them; all the pioneer men are able-bodied workers, unless aged parents happen to have been brought along. In the first place they show a great deal of respect to the lamas. The first sign of Chinese religion in the villages is the appearance of a small shrine, usually empty except for strips of paper bearing in Chinese characters the name of a god or spirit. The first sign of active religion, other than this sort of respect, is usually magical and relates to the need for rain. In a season of drought there may be undertaken a circumambulation of the fields, by young men carrying a "chair of honor" in which there is a tablet inscribed with the name of the God of Rain (Lungwang, Dragon King). A goat or sheep may be led before the little procession. The Chinese, however, also make gifts to lama monasteries for services to invoke rain. Later, as local Chinese shrines come to acquire a measure of reputation, they may be occupied by one or two Taoist priests. At such places theatrical performances are given in honor of the God of Rain. The Taoist priests are the first to appear, Taoism, as the residuum of superstitions believed to control the elements and the weather, being more readily appreciated by the pioneers. It has also many rites cognate to the magical practices of the lamas. True Chinese Buddhism is practically non-existent.

Of the Christian religions Protestantism is not a strong social factor, though recently, when the "Christian army" of Feng Yü-hsiang occupied the frontier area, it was important politically. On the whole, its converts are as negligible in quality as they are in numbers. The Protestant missions, however, render important services to the community in providing medical treatment and elementary education. Catholicism, under the direction of missions staffed by Belgian fathers, is much more important. Catholic work in the border area goes back beyond the middle of the last century and is in many ways closely associated with colonization. The common practice is not to accept a man as a convert unless his whole family is admitted to the church. The Catholic Chinese are gathered into village communities, each presided over, where possible, by a priest. Marriage in the younger generation must always be with Catholics. The priests, as heads of the community, give a focus of authority and a continuity of tradition and policy not found in other Chinese communities. They organize the resources of the community to provide for the collective financing and marketing of crops, thus keeping their charges out of the hands of usurers and grain dealers. The average Catholic village is comparatively prosperous, energetic, and enterprising.

TRADE

In the Kweihwa area there are two kinds of trade that have been of long-standing importance—local trade with the Mongols and the caravan or carrying trade with distant parts of Mongolia and through Mongolia with Chinese Turkestan and Russia. The advent of the railway has increased both kinds of trade and added the export of foodstuffs to China proper.

For the export of grain and flour the problem of economic distance from the railway is partially solved by a double transaction. The more valuable grains, such as wheat and kaoliang (giant millet) grown below the plateau, are sent down by rail to North China. The farmers who grow these grains do not reserve even enough for their own consumption but bring down the cheaper oatmeal and small millet from the plateau for their own use. Near Kweihwa the surplus of wheat and the other more valuable cereals was formerly sold to the Mongols of the plateau for winter supplies. This trade has now passed to the oatmeal and small millet of the plateau, white flour being more than ever a luxury among the Mongols.

Grain grown on the plateau at too great a distance to be brought profitably to market and in too great quantity to be disposed of to the Mongols is made economically portable by distilling it into grain alcohol. This is an important article of sale to the Mongols and can also be exported to China. It is distilled at great strength, in order to give value for bulk, and is progressively diluted as it is transported farther and farther from the distillery.

The trade in grain and grain alcohol is supplemented by the introduction of flour mills. These are equipped almost exclusively with American machinery. The further extension of flour-milling is entirely a question of local credit and relief from civil war. The flour is ground rather coarsely and, for sale among the Chinese, with whom white flour is becoming fashionable, is afterwards "dusted" with imported American flour. Grain warehouses, even more than flour mills, represent capital and are actively engaged in all kinds of external finance, in extending the area of the crop and manipulating the control of it.

The trade in cattle and sheep to be butchered at Peiping and Tientsin is one that has existed for a long time but has grown enormously since the advent of the railway. The cattle and sheep are bought on the hoof far out in Mongolia and herded down to points near the plateau escarpment. They usually arrive during the winter and are held over until the spring, to be fattened somewhat on the first growth of grass before rail shipment. This allows also of sheep being combed (not shorn) for the first or more valuable crop of wool. Herds are frequently split into smaller lots and parceled out through thinly colonized areas, where they can graze on the stubble and so afford a supplementary income to farmers.

Points like Kweihwa and Kalgan are centers of the traditional caravan trade, which formerly had a double direction, down toward China and out toward Mongolia. It might be thought that this trade would have been superseded almost entirely by the railway, but, although practically no caravan trade now exists in the direction of China (except for such very cheap cargoes as lime), this has been more than compensated by the expansion of the trade into and through Mongolia, which now employs far more camels than at the most flourishing periods of the past.

Travelers like Ney Elias and Sir Francis Younghusband[7] testify that in the seventies and eighties of the last century negligible return cargoes were brought back by caravans going into Mongolia. Their outward freight consisted entirely of cloth, saddlery, boots, pipes, tobacco, and trinkets for the Mongols. These were bartered against valuable furs and against ponies, sheep, and cattle; but these were brought back on the hoof, the camels returning practically unladen, although homeward-bound caravans from Chinese Turkestan might bring small quantities of gold, silver, and jade and medicinal articles like elk horns and the horns of the *saiga* antelope.

The trade has been revolutionized by the railway, which transmits far into the interior the stimulus of foreign trade at the seaports of China. The basis of this trade is the demand abroad for raw materials, especially wool, lambskins, and camel hair from Mongolia, and wool, lambskins, and cotton from Chinese Turkestan. The difficulty now is to transport outward enough merchandise to obtain the raw produce by barter without being forced to carry silver, which is a dangerous temptation to bandits; and in fact a great deal of silver thus enters Mongolia, where it is either hoarded or used for ornaments.

The caravan trade is an important factor in the economy of the frontier, both because of the earnings of the men engaged

[7] F. E. Younghusband: The Heart of a Continent, 2nd edit., London, 1896.

and the demand for provisions required for long desert journeys. Between journeys the camels are pastured on Mongol land at a small fee per head. The provisions required are white flour, oatmeal, and millet for the men and dried peas for the camels. It is noteworthy that peas, which are for this reason an important crop on the plateau, are not considered, by men whose staple diet is oatmeal, as fit food for human consumption.

Young men from among the colonists on the plateau are constantly recruited into the caravan trade, from which they are frequently able to retire after they have earned enough to purchase land of their own. Many small villages also send out lots of a few camels at a time, which are organized into large caravans under a single caravan master, the profits on the venture representing an important source of income.

Many of the firms in the caravan trade and in all other forms of transport are Mohammedans. In all the border towns there are strong communities of Mohammedans, who make keen traders and are usually prosperous. The caravan connection with Chinese Turkestan probably accounts in some measure for the origin of these communities. The fact that Mohammedans are so active in transport accounts for the fact that they are always noticed by travelers. Mohammedan villagers and farmers are also found, but as pioneers taking up land they do not compare in numbers, at least not in the Kweihwa area, with ordinary Chinese.

In the Kweihwa area the old border stock, which preponderates among the pioneer settlers, is not so well represented among the petty traders. In all forms of trade the Hopei men show to advantage, because they come from a province more in touch with all the new forces operating in China. A large class of peddlers traveling on foot from village to village on the plateau is composed almost entirely of Hopei men. They are the news bearers and commission agents of the remoter frontier and prosper exceedingly. After a few years they are usually able to set up a small business in a town such as Kweihwa. Not only peddlers but craftsmen and artisans such as carpenters and tinkers also travel widely, moving about between large villages and congregating at seasonal fairs and the festivals at Mongol lamaseries.

Economic Handicaps

In the colonization of such territories as North America or Australia the most striking phenomenon is the replacement of the low standards of living of the indigenous races by the higher standard of living of the intruding races. The parallel does not entirely hold in Inner Mongolia, where the success of the Chinese represents, in effect, their power to underlive the Mongols by maintaining a larger population at the bare level of survival on a given terrain. It is necessary to state this, as the mere recital of Chinese expansion into the plateau may give a false impression of material progress. By our standards of the history of society the Mongol way of life is more primitive than that of the Chinese. At the same time, it is difficult to draw a true comparison between, say, the highest development of the nomad life and the most primitive form of the Chinese agricultural life.

In the contemporary state of affairs it is demonstrably true to say that the Chinaman, pushed out of his old country by pressure of population and grinding poverty, does not win his way into a better world by emigrating to Mongolia as a pioneer. He does not even have the opportunity of permanent betterment. For the first few years he may have more food for his own immediate needs; but, as he carries with him the standards and traditions of his people, the old conditions are reproduced within a few generations.   There is no enlargement of opportunity.

The reasons must be sought in China, not in Mongolia, and the possibility of amelioration rests on the possibility of a revision of customs and standards in China.   The reasons are:

1)   Excessive regard for the family, leading to early marriage of sons in order to provide grandsons.   In order to hasten marriage the family will contract debts from which it is often impossible to recover.

2)   Lack of credit, lack of investment facilities, lack of a stable currency.   There is no such thing as a safe Chinese paper currency or a safe Chinese bank.   Banks may be ruined and their paper currency rendered valueless by a political upheaval or a civil war. Joint-stock companies are unknown throughout the pioneer area. Every business is a family business and tends to be overstaffed with the relatives of the family concerned.   There is no machinery for treating and distributing credit as the accumulated reserve energy of the community.   Thus silver, the only approximately reliable standard of value, tends to be hoarded without drawing interest; and in time of emergency it cannot be produced for fear that it will be taken away by violence.   The pioneer farmer who has had a successful year must either bury his silver or lay it out in

arranging the marriage of another son—in which case provision for that son's future family depends entirely on the success of future crops. Generally speaking, the pioneer farmer is successful if he has enough food for the year, enough seed for the next year, and enough cash in hand to buy winter clothing and a new draft animal; and it is exceedingly difficult for the son of a farmer to become anything but a farmer, owing to lack of education and opportunity.

Thus there is no predictable future in the pioneer belt of Inner Mongolia except the disappearance of nomads and their grazing grounds and their replacement by the social and economic conditions known to exist at the present time practically throughout China and known to be, economically at least, unsound.

MANCHURIA AS A REGION OF PIONEER SETTLEMENT: ITS NATURAL CONDITIONS AND AGRICULTURAL POSSIBILITIES

E. E. AHNERT

ALTHOUGH Manchuria is a land of old civilization, dating back more than a thousand years, the greater part of the country has until recently been sparsely populated and has remained almost a wilderness. Only toward the end of the last century (1880) did settlement of the unoccupied land begin in any marked degree. Since the building of railroads (1900) colonization has continued at an ever increasing pace. The suitability of a country for settlement depends, of course, on its agricultural possibilities. These depend primarily on climate and soils; and these in turn are based on location, surface configuration, and geology.

SURFACE CONFIGURATION AND GEOLOGY

Manchuria is essentially the lowland area enclosed between the eastern edge of the Mongolian Plateau and the belt of mountains that border the Pacific. But, as its political boundaries[1] lie on these bordering mountains or even extend beyond them, the surface configuration of the country is, on the whole, quite diversi-

[1] For a correct representation see the map of the political divisions of China by G. B. Cressey, *Geogr. Rev.*, Vol. 20, 1930, p. 653 (followed in our Fig. 1). Many maps still show a sizable area east of the central Great Khingan Range as belonging to Mongolia. Since the revolution of 1911, however, this area has been assigned to one of the three provinces that constitute Manchuria. These three provinces are Heilungkiang, Kirin, Liaoning (so named in 1928 by the Nationalist government in Nanking; formerly Fengtien). In the note accompanying his map Cressey gives the areas in square miles of these provinces within the new boundaries as follows (based on planimetric measurement of a map in 1:5,000,000): Heilungkiang, 219,274; Kirin, 105,003; Liaoning, 100,246. This gives a total for Manchuria of 424,523 square miles. These figures should, it would seem, supersede the estimates, necessarily based on less reliable material, cited by Chu Hsiao on pp. 381–382 of "Problems of the Pacific, 1929: Proceedings of the Third Conference of the Institute of Pacific Relations," edited by J. B. Condliffe, Chicago, 1930.

In defining Manchuria above as the "Three Eastern Provinces," to use its Chinese name, it is not necessary to take into account the reported enlargement of the territory into the "Four Northeastern Provinces" by the addition of Jehol province (Second Report on Progress in Manchuria—to 1930, South Manchuria Ry., Dairen, 1931, pp. 15, 59, and map), as the data and maps of the present paper relate to the three provinces only, nor is it necessary to consider the new independent state proclaimed in February, 1932. It may be pointed out, however, that the inclusion of Jehol, physically oriented rather toward the Manchurian Plain than toward the Mongolian Plateau (Fig. 2), would increase the area of Manchuria by 72,008 square miles (Cressey, *op. cit.*, p. 654) to nearly 500,000 square miles.

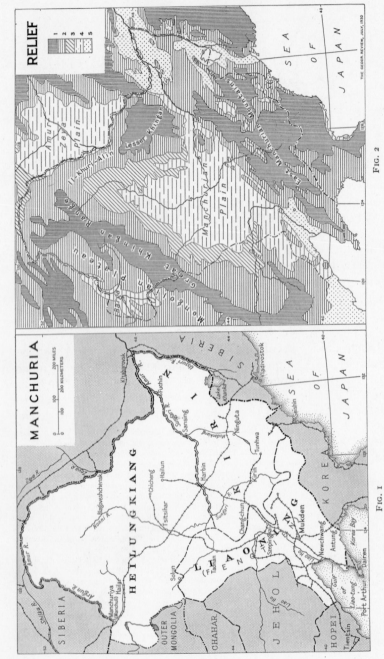

FIG. 1—General locational map of Manchuria showing the provincial divisions and chief towns and railroads.   Scale of Figures 1–12, 1 : 17,500,000.   On the boundaries of Manchuria see footnote 1.

FIG. 2—Elements of relief.   (Based on the orographical sketch map in the author's "Poleznye iskopaemye Severnoi Manchzhurii" (Useful Minerals of Northern Manchuria), Manchuria Research Society, Harbin, 1926; see also footnote 2.)   Key to numerals: 1, mountains; 2, uplands and higher foothills; 3, lower foothills; 4, plains; 5, lowlands.

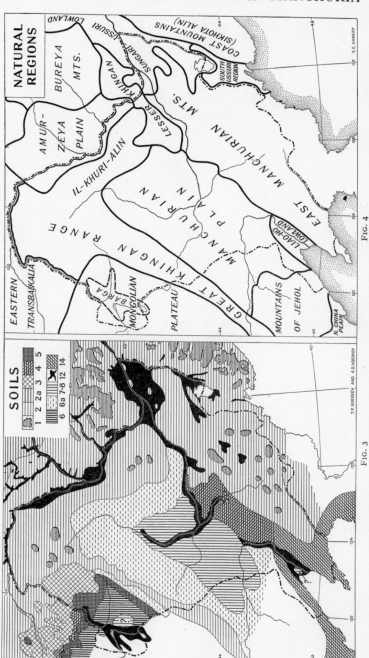

FIG. 3.—Sketch map of the soils of Manchuria. Prepared for this paper by T. P. Gordeëv and, south of 42° N., by A. D. Voeikov. Soils in Asiatic part of U. S. S. R. added from map of that territory on the scale of 1 : 4,200,000 referred to in footnote 4. The numerals in the key correspond to the numbers in the description of the soils in the text, pp. 322–323 and 326, except the following: 2a, podzolized soils of the Okhotsk Basin (see 2c, Fig. 2, p. 248); 6a, complex consisting of soils 2, 3, 4, 5, 10, and 11.

FIG. 4.—Natural regions. (Based on the author's maps in "Practical Hints to Scientific Travellers," Vol. 5, The Hague, 1927, p. 122, and *Rev. of the Manchuria Research Soc.*, Harbin, March, 1928, Map 2.) Correlate with Figure 2.

fied (see relief map, Fig. 2[2]). Four major relief elements, trending southwest-northeast, may be distinguished. From west to east these are: The Mongolian Plateau, with an average elevation of 630–680 meters above sea level; its dissected scarp margin, the Great Khingan Range (700–1500 meters); the Manchurian Plain (140–170 meters); and finally the East Manchurian Mountains (200–1200–2300 meters). In addition there are a number of less important elements in the relief: the northwest-trending Il-Khuri-Alin, a mountain range much worn down to its present condition of an upland peneplain separating the Manchurian Plain from the Amur lowland and merging at its southeastern end with the foothills of the Lesser Khingan; secondly, the small ranges that separate the Manchurian Plain from the lowland at the head of the Gulf of Liaotung; and, finally, the great lowland at the mouths of the Sungari and Ussuri Rivers and the lowland of Lake Khanka. In the Great Khingan the main valleys are transverse valleys; in the East Manchurian Mountains they are longitudinal valleys, partly coinciding with down-dropped blocks.

The Manchurian Plain, the most important physical unit from the standpoint of settlement, is bordered by a broad belt of very thick stratified clays consisting partly of loess deposits and to a lesser extent of sandstones and marls, which are overlain toward the middle of the plain by stratified sands intercalated with clays. In the center and in the southwestern part of the plain saline and alkaline soils occur, likewise drifting sand and sand dunes (barkhans). Along the margin of the plain lie isolated hills consisting of recent effusives, tuffs, or granites.

[2] The best relief map of the area is the new Topographic Map of Manchuria and Bordering Countries, 1 : 2,000,000, published by the geological bureau of the South Manchuria Railway, 1931, with relief in altitude tints. This map, which has just become available as the present volume is going to press, has the same drainage base as the sheets of the geological atlas in 1 : 2,000,000 mentioned below. Northeast of the Seishin-Barga line (Figs. 1–2) it appears to incorporate E. E. Ahnert's Carte Hypsométrique du Bassin de l'Amour, 1:1,680,000, St. Petersburg, 1913.

The standard map representation of the geology of the region is on Sheets 2, 3, 7, and 8 of the Geological Atlas of Eastern Asia, 1 : 2,000,000, edited by the Tokyo Geographical Society and published by the Association for Mineralogical and Geological Research, Tokyo, 1929. The status and degree of accuracy of our geological knowledge of Manchuria and adjoining territory is shown in a map published by E. E. Ahnert in two places (Die Nord-Mandschurei, das Amur- und Küstenland im Fernen Osten Asiens: Mitteilungen und Praktische Ratschläge für Untersuchungsreisende, in "Practical Hints to Scientific Travellers," edited by H. A. Brouwer, Vol. 5, The Hague, 1927, pp. 99–161, map on p. 103; and Northern Manchuria, One of the Least Investigated Countries in the World, *Rev. of the Manchurian Research Soc.*, Harbin, March, 1928, pp. 16–22, Map 4). All of the areas shown as geologically unsurveyed on Ahnert's map are geologically colored in the Geological Atlas of Eastern Asia. This may be due to a certain amount of generalization in the atlas and the incorporation of Japanese data not generally available, such as the work of the geological expedition in Siberia and Manchuria under the direction of K. Inouye. In any case the use of Ahnert's map in connection with the atlas gives a clue as to the relative reliability of the information.—EDIT. NOTE.

The rivers of the larger, northern part of Manchuria belong to the Amur system. The smaller, southern part of the country is drained by a number of river systems of secondary importance to transportation which empty into the gulfs of the Yellow Sea, among which the largest is the Liao-ho system. The Amur with its tributaries comprises a network of transportation lanes more than 15,000 kilometers long, of which about 10,000 kilometers are navigable for steamboats. The other rivers, even the Liao-ho, are of use as waterways in their lower courses alone. As the roads are generally impassable in summer on account of the heavy rains of that season, the waterways take on added importance, especially for the areas not yet settled. High water in the rivers is characteristic not of spring but of late summer, because little snow falls in winter and spring is cold and dry, whereas the late summer is rainy.

Climate

The climate of the country during the six months of the year when winter conditions predominate is markedly continental. During the four months when summer conditions prevail it is, as a result of the summer monsoon, humid and less subject to abrupt changes, i. e. it exhibits oceanic influence.

Manchuria, together with the whole Amur basin, has a monsoonal climatic régime. Cold northwest winds generally dominate during the winter half of the year, whereas the warm southeast winds of summer usually make themselves less definitely felt. The contrast between the two seasons is less marked on the Manchurian Plain and in the Amur lowland than on the high plateaus to the west and east of the country where no near-by mountain areas can deflect the direction of the air currents. In keeping with the direction of these air currents, the winters in Manchuria are very cold and dry, i.e. free from snow, the summers hot and rainy, the other two seasons cold and deficient in rainfall. As shown by Table I, the amount of rainfall during the growing season is about four to five times as much as during the rest of the year.

In regard to temperature, however, the country, except for the previous general characterization, cannot be considered a unit because temperatures vary greatly as a result of its wide extent north and south and the considerable differences of altitude. In the extreme northwestern part of the area, near the boundary along the Amur and Argun Rivers and on the upland plains of Barga and

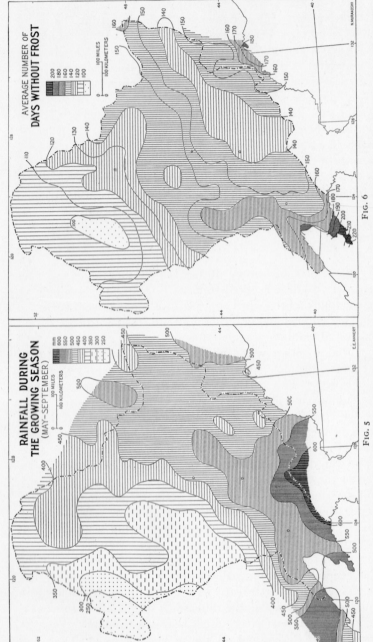

FIG. 5—Average precipitation during the growing season, May to September inclusive. Prepared by the author on the basis of data kindly supplied by P. A. Pavlov, lately director of the meteorological service of Northern Manchuria.

FIG. 6—Average number of days without frost. (Reproduced from the map by N. Murakoshi, agronomist of the Kungchuling agricultural experiment station, Southern Manchuria, in the *Geogr. Rev.*, Vol. 20, 1930, p. 485.)

Table I—Climatic Data of Manchuria Bearing on Agriculture

Natural Region (see Fig. 4)	Station	Position N. Lat.	Position E. Long.	Altitude (meters)	Mean Seasonal Temperatures (C°) Winter	Spring	Summer	Autumn	Warm Season Rainfall (mm.) May–Sept. inc. (see Fig. 5)	Per Cent of Annual Rainfall	Growing Season From	To	Days	Days Without Frost (see Fig. 6) Last Frost in Spring	First Frost in Autumn	Number of Days
Barga	Nerchinski Zavod	51° 19'	119° 37'	629	−26.3	−1.6	+17.1	−2.5	355	88	May 16	Oct. 5	142	May 27	Sept. 26	121
	Manchuriya	49° 35'	117° 26'	661	−24.0	−1.1	+18.7	−1.9	227	90	May 1	Oct. 1	154	May 24	Sept. 13	111
Mongolian Plateau	Hailar	49° 13'	119° 44'	632	−26.2	−1.6	+18.6	−1.7	273	86	May 9	Oct. 1	152	May 22	Sept. 13	103
Great Khingan	Mientuho	48° 59'	121° 12'	721	−25.5	−2.4	+17.0	−2.3	318	88	May 20	Sept. 18	121	June 2	Sept. 1	94
	Puhotu	48° 46'	121° 55'	693	−20.3	−0.6	+16.8	−0.9	354	91	May 10	Oct. 5	146	May 25	Sept. 10	107
	Chalantun	48° 01'	122° 44'	339	−16.8	+3.1	+19.7	+2.1	401	88	......	......	......	......	......	......
Amur-Zeya Plain	Ulanga	53° 22'	126° 32'	427	−26.0	−2.0	+16.6	−4.2	374	89	May 9	Sept. 31	146	May 27	Sept. 17	112
	Blagoveshchensk	50° 16'	127° 30'	241	−21.8	+4.4	+19.4	−0.5	439	88	April 26	Oct. 4	161	May 16	Sept. 21	127
Manchurian Plain	Tsitsihar	47° 21'	123° 57'	164	−17.9	+3.6	+20.8	+3.0	301	88	April 18	Oct. 25	190	May 14	Oct. 1	139
	Anta	46° 48'	126° 49'	164	−19.3	+3.7	+21.5	+2.8	386	92	April 14	Oct. 27	196	May 5	Oct. 3	150
	Harbin	45° 45'	126° 38'	142	−17.2	+4.6	+21.3	+4.1	441	84	......	......	......	......	......	......
	Yaomen	44° 32'	125° 43'	192	−15.6	+5.0	+21.9	+4.7	460	87	......	......	......	......	......	......
	Changchun	43° 55'	125° 18'	226	−15.5	+7.7	+21.7	+5.8	581	85	......	......	......	......	......	......
South Manchurian Lowland	Mukden	41° 48'	123° 23'	44	−11.3	+6.5	+23.6	+8.2	510	82	......	......	......	......	......	......
	Yingkow	40° 40'	122° 14'	12	−8.5	+8.3	+23.5	+10.0	491	82	......	......	......	......	......	......
Sungari-Ussuri Lowland	Khabarovsk	48° 28'	135° 03'	50	−19.0	+2.4	+19.7	+3.2	422	80	April 24	Oct. 15	174	May 28	Sept. 20	109
	Muraviev-Amurski	45° 52'	133° 38'	67	−18.6	+2.7	+19.8	+3.9	533	74	April 20	Oct. 17	181	May 14	Sept. 16	124
East Manchurian Mountains	Imienpo	45° 04'	128° 05'	233	−16.9	+4.0	+20.1	+3.9	554	81	......	......	......	......	......	......
	Mutanchiang	44° 36'	129° 36'	259	−17.8	+3.6	+20.1	+3.5	436	84	April 19	Oct. 18	183	May 16	Sept. 23	129
	Taipingling	44° 33'	130° 36'	563	−16.2	+2.0	+18.2	+3.0	457	82	......	......	......	......	......	......
	Yantze	42° 54'	129° 31'	234	−10.8	+7.4	+20.8	+7.2	400	81	......	......	......	......	......	......
Coast	Vladivostok	43° 07'	131° 55'	29	−10.8	+3.9	+18.3	+8.5	421	73	April 16	Oct. 20	188	May 5	Sept. 27	144
	Cape Gamov	42° 33'	131° 13'	50	−7.7	+2.9	+17.2	+9.4	...	...	......	......	......	......	......	......

TABLE II—SOIL TEMPERATURES AND DURATION OF FROST AT THE SURFACE AND IN VARIOUS DEPTHS AT SELECTED STATIONS IN MANCHURIA

STATION	LAST AND FIRST FROSTS AT A DEPTH OF							MAXIMUM DEPTH OF FROST (in meters)
	0 cm.	10 cm.	20 cm.	40 cm.	80 cm.	1.6 m.	3.2 m.	
Ulanga (Agric. Exper. Sta.)	Mid May / End Sept.	End May / Mid Oct.	Beg. June / End Oct.	Mid June / Beg. Nov.	Beg. July / Mid Nov.	End July / Mid Dec.	.... / End March	Permanently frozen soil at a depth of 2 meters and more
Amur Agric. Exper. Sta. near Blagoveshchensk	Beg. Apr. / Mid to end Oct.	End Apr. / End Oct.	Mid Apr. / Beg. Nov.	Mid to end Apr. / Mid Oct.	Beg. May / Beg. Dec.	Mid to end May / Beg. Jan.	.... /	2.5
Manchuriya*	Beg. June / End Aug.	End Apr. / Beg. Oct.	End Apr. / Mid Oct.	End Apr. / End Oct.	Beg. May / End Oct.	Mid May / Mid Nov.	Mid July / End Jan.	4.0
Harbin	End May / Mid Sept.	Mid Apr. / End Oct.	Mid Apr. / Beg. Nov.	End Apr. / Mid Nov.	Beg. May / Beg. Dec.	Beg. June / End Jan.	No frost / No frost	2.5–3.0

STATION	DURATION OF TEMPERATURE HIGHER THAN 10° C. AT A DEPTH OF						
	0 cm.	10 cm.	20 cm.	40 cm.	80 cm.	1.6 m.	3.2 m.
Ulanga (Agric. Exper. Sta.)	Beg. May / Beg. Aug.	Mid May / Beg. Aug.	Mid May / Beg. Aug.	Mid June / End July	Beg. to mid July / Mid July	....	Lower than 10° C.
Amur Agric. Exper. Sta. near Blagoveshchensk	Mid Apr. / Mid to end Aug.	Mid to end June / Mid to end Aug.	End Apr. / Mid to end Aug.	Mid May / Mid to end Aug.	Mid June / Mid Aug.	Mid July / Beg. Aug.	" " "
Manchuriya*	No records available						" " "
Harbin							3.2 m.

*In Manchuriya the soil froze to a depth of 4 meters only in three years out of seven; in the other four years frost did not penetrate so far. However, as indicated by observations at the Chalainor coal mines, there is farther below, under a layer of soil permanently not frozen, a stratum of permanently frozen ground 3–5 meters thick which begins 5.5 to 8.5 meters below the surface and lies 6–10 meters above the coal beds.

Mongolia as well as in the Great Khingan Range, the frostless period amounts to only 80–120 days a year (even so, the probability of night frosts during this period does not go below 30 per cent), the growing season varies between 120 and 150 days, the soil freezes to a depth of 4 meters and generally is permanently frozen below that depth, and even relatively large rivers freeze up completely. By contrast, in the rest of the area, the period entirely devoid of frost increases to 112–180 days (the former figure holds for an upland plateau in the eastern mountains) and the growing season to 160–190 days; but here, too, as a result of the long, cold, and snowless winters, the ground freezes to a depth of 1 ½ to 2 ½ meters and thaws out completely only in April to June (cf. Table II). In keeping with these facts and those shown in the accompanying tables, the area might be subdivided climatically in the following way: Amur-Argun region, northern Barga, and a southward strip along the inner side of the Great Khingan, moderately warm, semi-arid; southern Barga and the adjoining part of Mongolia, moderately warm, arid; the northern part of the Manchurian Plain, warm, semi-arid; the southern part of the Manchurian Plain, hot, semi-arid to arid; the northeastern corner of Manchuria, warm, humid; and east-central and southern Manchuria, hot, humid.

VEGETATION

Let us now turn to the native vegetation and the soils,[3] both of which are the result of the interaction of the climatic conditions just described with the geology and the relief of the area.

The sporadic occurrence of typical steppe plants as far south as the southern Ussuri region and, on the other hand, the existence of forests in eastern Manchuria (and probably also along the Great Khingan) several centuries ago as far south as Mukden and even beyond, show how greatly the climate has varied in the past and explain the origin of the present soil-determined plant associations as well as the special conditions and possibilities of agriculture. In this connection it should also be stated that there was no ice age in this region.

In Manchuria and the adjoining territory plant life as a rule

[3] For the information on which the sections on vegetation and soils and the soil map (Fig. 3) are based the writer is indebted to Messrs. T. P. Gordeëv and A. D. Voeikov, agronomists, each of whom specially prepared for him a statement of five to six pages, the former dealing with the vegetation and soils of Northern Manchuria, the latter with the vegetation, soils, and food plants of Manchuria as a whole. Mr. Voeikov is a nephew of the eminent Russian climatologist Alexander Voeikov (Woeikof), author of "Die Klimate der Erde," 2 vols., Jena, 1887.

is almost wholly independent of mean climatic conditions, including the extremely cold and dry winters; rather, it is related to the amount of heat and rain received during the growing season. But these two elements are so great that, except for the Mongolian Plateau, the Barga region, and the high mountains, the natural flora and fauna take on an aspect markedly subtropical and are in part characterized by surviving Tertiary forms.

In the parts of the country that have sufficient warmth during the vegetational period and where the annual precipitation amounts to more than 450 millimeters the Manchurian-Korean flora predominates (with *Pinus koraiensis* and a number of lianas, resembling the flora of the Atlantic states of the United States). The parts of the country that are colder but not much drier have a flora (with *Picea ajanensis* and *Abies nephrolepis*) closely related to the Dahurian-Okhotsk, or East Siberian, flora. Finally, the drier parts of the country have an out-and-out steppe flora in the areas where chernozems or diversified soils predominate and a semi-steppe flora where chestnut-brown or gray steppe soils preponderate.

At the present time, the country, except for its semi-deserts, is agriculturally exploited or exploitable up to the limit to which the forests have been pushed back into the highest parts of the mountains and out-of-the-way places. Even so, the steppe and semi-desert areas are well adapted to stock raising.

Soils

In accordance with the conditions that have been described, the following soils may be distinguished in Manchuria (see Fig. 3;[4] this is of course necessarily a sketch map, as only very few investigations have been made):

1. Peaty podzolized soils and silty bog soils of the higher mountain slopes.

[4] Since the present paper was written there has appeared V. A. Boltz and B. B. Polynov: On the Soils of Manchuria (Contributions to the Knowledge of the Soils of Asia, No. 1, pp. 31–44, with separate table and soil map in 1 : 8,000,000), Dokuchaiev Inst. of Soil Science, Acad. of Sci. of U. S. S. R., Leningrad, 1930. On the basis of Ahnert's relief map facing p. 18 of his "Poleznye isko-paemye Severnoi Manchzhurii" (Useful Minerals of Northern Manchuria), Manchuria Research Society, Harbin, 1926, Manchuria is divided into seven physico-geographical regions and the soils in each region, where precise information is lacking, deduced by comparison with known soils in similar regions elsewhere. The accompanying soils map, which is avowedly sketchy, while broadly resembling the present map, of course differs from it in detail. For the soils of Russian territory adjacent to Manchuria see Sheets 7 and 8 of the "Soils Map of the Asiatic Part of U. S. S. R.," 1 : 4,200,000, by S. S. Neustruev, B. B. Polynov, L. I. Prasolov, and N. I. Prokhorov, under the direction of K. D. Glinka and L. I. Prasolov, Dokuchaiev Inst. of Soils, Acad. of Sci. of U. S. S. R., Leningrad, 1926 (simplified one-sheet editions in 1:16,000,000, by L. I. Prasolov, 1929, and in 1:10,000,000, by K. D. Glinka and L. I. Prasolov, 1930).—Edit. Note.

2. Lightly podzolized mountain soils of clay or loam, sometimes silty.

3. Gray forest soils that border the foot of the mountains facing the plains. They also occur in the hilly area of the Barga upland plain (on Fig. 3 they are shown only in this area).

    (Soils 1, 2, and 3 are derived from rock weathering in the mountains under the influence of a former forest cover and make good farming land. On the steeper slopes, however, they tend to gully and to erode rapidly.)

4. Leached or degraded chernozems.

5. Chernozems.

    (Soils 4 and 5 are typical of the Manchurian Plain, the hill country, and a number of mountain valleys of the Great Khingan Range, etc. They have developed on loess or loess-like clays under the influence of the steppe flora of the more or less level areas. In the present steppe areas, where forests formerly occurred, the chernozems have been degraded; east of the middle Sungari they contain podzolized horizons and *ortstein* concretions (see above p. 247). These two soils are by far the best agricultural soils in Manchuria. The area of the middle Sungari chernozems is densely populated and thoroughly cultivated.)

6. Chestnut-brown soils, mostly alkaline. These have so far been found only on the Barga upland, specifically next to the railroad station Manchuriya, where they rest on a loess-like sandy or weathered stony subsoil, and farther east on the Hailar plains, where they have developed on a sandy subsoil. The chestnut-brown soils are not suited to cultivation and produce only a sparse growth of semi-desert and steppe grasses.

7. Gray steppe soils (serozems), mostly alkaline. They are especially characteristic of northern Manchuria; they are the soils par excellence of the central part of the Manchurian Plain. These soils have a thin layer of humus, and the effervescence of top samples when hydrochloric acid is applied indicates their alkalinity. Their lower horizons consist of loess-like, often very sandy material. Within the distribution area of these soils lie the alkali steppes of Tsitsihar-Anta, Potuno, and Taonan (and probably also farther south) with their soda, alkali, and salt lakes in the shallow depressions of the gray-soil steppes.

8. Alkaline and saline soils. These do not constitute large areas; they occur within the gray steppe soils and sometimes within the chestnut-brown soils (the alkali and salt steppes of the Barga region). They are generally bordered by good meadowland.

9. Rendzina soils (dark carbonate soils). These develop from the weathering of limestones and therefore in Manchuria occur only in very small patches.

10. Coarse undeveloped detrital (gravelly) soils. These occur on many mountain slopes, especially on the sunward slopes of the Great Khingan Range.

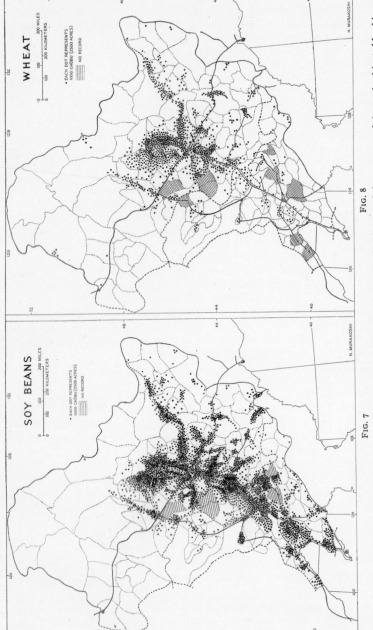

Fig. 7—Soy bean crop area in 1927. The soy bean, the most important cash crop of Manchuria, occupied 25 per cent of the total cultivated land in 1927. The crop is put to three primary uses: food for animals and man, oil, and fertilizer in the form of bean cake. The soy bean crop reaches its greatest relative and absolute importance in the north, reflecting an ability to mature in a somewhat cooler climate with shorter frost-free season than is true of kaoliang (Fig. 9).

Fig. 8—Wheat, occupying 11 per cent of the cultivated area in 1927, is the fourth-ranking crop. It is emphatically a crop of the north. Eighty per cent of the crop is spring-sown. (Figures 7–10 are reproduced from the maps by N. Murakoshi in the *Geogr. Rev.*, Vol. 20, 1930, pp. 487, 490, 488, 491.)

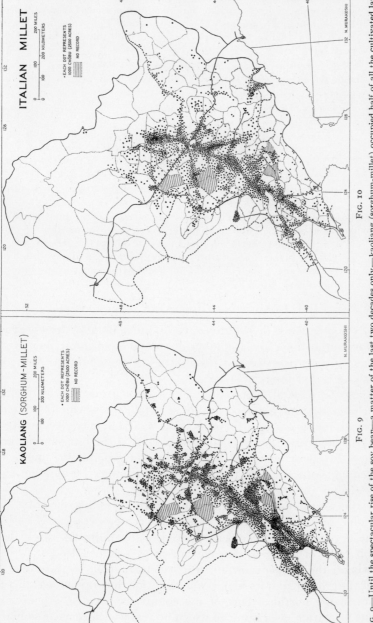

FIG. 9.—Until the spectacular rise of the soy bean—a matter of the last two decades only—kaoliang (sorghum-millet) occupied half of all the cultivated land in Manchuria. For its best growth it requires at least 150 days without killing frost; hence the crop reaches its greatest importance in Southern Manchuria. FIG. 10.—Italian millet, occupying 16 per cent of the cultivated area in 1927, ranks third among Manchurian crops. Being deep-rooted and tolerant of drought conditions, it attains its greatest relative importance in the semi-arid western lands.

11. Bog soils and meadow bog soils. These develop within all the other soil groups under favorable circumstances, almost always only as small separate patches. But in the case of wide valleys or large river flood plains, where they occur within the alluvium, they may often occupy quite large areas.

12. Alluvial soils of the river and lake basins and their terraces. These soils are a complex of successive sand, loam, clay, peat, and similar layers.

13. A number of present geological formations.
    a. Peat, moss, and similar soils.
    b. Loose sand of the dunes in the large river valleys and the barkhans of the semi-deserts (within the domain of the chestnut-brown soils of the Barga region and the gray steppe soils of the Manchurian Plain).
    c. Deep humus on the sand ridges along the western margin of the alkali steppe.

14. Laterite-like (?) soils. These are observed only at the 42nd parallel and southward. They form more or less the continuation of the belt of degraded chernozems and have developed under the influence of the higher temperature, greater humidity, and vegetational decomposition. These soils do not yield satisfactory crops unless well fertilized.

Special Conditions Governing Agriculture

As a consequence of the diversity of the soils and the climate of Manchuria, there are a number of special conditions governing the agricultural practice and possibilities of the country. Let us consider a few of them.

Except in several mountain valleys of central and southern Manchuria that have a good deal of snowfall, the sowing of winter cereals is not possible. In order that the soil may accumulate sufficient moisture, the fields must be plowed in the late summer or autumn. Oats, which must be sown on wet ground (in "mud"), here cannot be sown until the beginning of summer because spring is too dry.

In the northern part of the country the grinding of grain is restricted by the fact that all water mills cease operation as early as the beginning of December. Indeed, water mills can rarely be used because of the great damage caused by summer floods.

Owing to the meager snowfall, deep penetration of frost, late thawing of the ground, and its highly wet condition during summer, there occurs in the northern part of the country a peculiar process of humus formation, as a result of which no real chernozems or similar soils can develop; rather, there is formed a type of bog soil, especially farther south, in the Manchurian Plain and the lowland of Lake Khanka.

In these two regions the excessive summer humidity accompanied by high temperature produces an extremely rapid growth both of native and cultivated plants; also it frequently causes damage, especially to wheat, in the form of rust, Fusarium wilt, and other fungous diseases, and also to sugar beets in lowering their sugar content.

The cold and dryness of spring retard the beginning of plant growth; but the dryness fosters grass and forest fires in spring and autumn. These have occurred regularly since civilized man has lived in this region;[5] they generally not only destroy the forest but also burn the forest and steppe soils, as they consist of decomposed vegetable matter. This phenomenon has had a marked influence on soil temperature, to such an extent that where the soil has been burnt its temperature in the following summer at a depth of 5–6 centimeters has proved to be 4° C. higher than the temperature of soil near by that has not been subjected to fire. The plowing of virgin soil whose upper layer has been destroyed by fire is said to bring about an increase of temperature of as much as 9°. In a number of mountain valleys in the north the permanently frozen layer previously there observed is said to have disappeared completely after the removal of the moss or bog soil by fire or gold-mining operations. Thus, in many cases, the activity of civilized man may produce a number of changes usually only produced by a different climate.

Suitable Food Plants[6]

The food plants climatically best suited to cultivation are: certain native millets, such as hsia-mi-tsa, pai-tsa, and others; kaoliang (*Sorghum vulgare*) to latitude 48° N.; many species of beans, among

[5] The author's collaborator, Mr. T. P. Gordeëv, suggests that the protection of nature in pioneer regions might well be included in any rational scheme of scientific as against haphazard settlement. While it is recognized that the taming of the wilderness is the pioneer's primary preoccupation, nevertheless, in his own interest it would be desirable to have some measure of control to prevent the ruthless destruction of plant and animal life and the abuse of the aborigines that often accompany the opening up to settlement of a new area. Based on his observations in the Maritime Province of the Siberian Far East, northern Korea, and northern Manchuria, Mr. Gordeëv urges the establishment of national parks, game preserves, natural environment plots, etc., which would preserve for future generations the aspect of primitive nature without detriment to the colonization of a given area in the present.

[6] B. V. Skvortsov (B. W. Skwortzow): Polevye kulturnye rasteniya Severnoi Manchzhurii: Kratkii ocherk (Field Crops of Northern Manchuria: Abridged Sketch), *Publs. Manchuria Research Soc.: Nat. Hist. Sect.*, Ser. A, No. 14, Harbin, 1926 (reprinted from *Manchuria Monitor*, No. 10, Harbin, 1926).

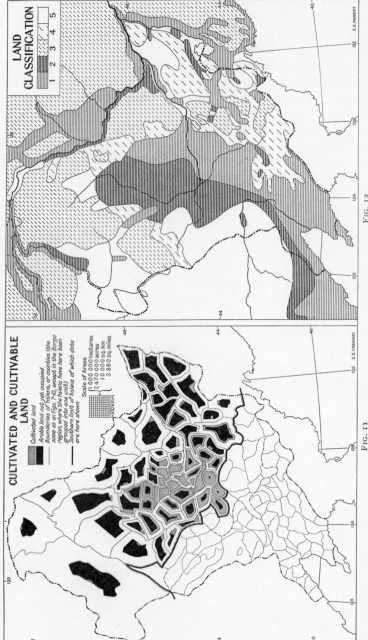

FIG. 11

FIG. 12

FIG. 11—Cartogram showing the cultivated land and the land still open to agricultural settlement in Northern Manchuria. (Based on and modified from E. E. Yashnov: Kitaiskaya kolonizatsiya Severnoi Manchzhurii i eë perspectivy (Chinese Colonization in Northern Manchuria and Its Prospects), Chinese Eastern Railway, Harbin, 1928, tables on pp. 95, 110, 118, 152, 161, 176, 204, 229, 235, 248, and map.) The polygons are drawn to scale and hence correctly represent the estimated amount of cultivated and cultivable land within each *hsien*, or county. The method of representation being diagrammatic in centering each polygon within its county, the two types of land are not shown in their actual positions. As a rule the cultivated land is represented as the "core" of its polygon; in the northern riverine counties, however, an attempt has been made to show the side on which the cultivated land actually lies. — The area left blank in each county north of the bold line inferentially represents the amount of non-agricultural land.

FIG. 12—Land classification and utilization. Prepared by the author. Key: 1, land long cultivated; 2, land recently brought under cultivation; 3, areas of which more than 25 per cent are forest-covered; 4, areas of which less than 25 per cent are forest-covered; 5 (within Manchuria), non-forested areas.

them the soy bean,[7] the most important cash crop of Manchuria and its largest export item; Indian corn, or maize (flint corn, dent corn, etc.); and wheat.[8] The extent and quantity of some of these crops is indicated in the accompanying maps (Figs. 7–10) by N. Murakoshi, agronomist of the Kungchuling agricultural experiment station, South Manchuria, which have already been published in the *Geographical Review*.[9] Cotton is grown as far north as latitude 43°. The experience of recent years has shown that east of the Great Khingan Range, as far north as 51° N., in suitable valleys and lowlands a number of species of rice, specifically water rice, which were formerly cultivated in northern and central Manchuria, grow very well. It has also recently been demonstrated that the fiber flax does well here on the podzol soils.

DISTRIBUTION OF POTENTIAL AGRICULTURAL LANDS

The conditions set forth above as regards soils and suitable food plants determine the agricultural possibilities in the areas not yet settled. The areas of cultivated and uncultivated but cultivable land in each district of Northern Manchuria are shown on the accompanying map (Fig. 11), which is of course diagrammatic and approximate only.

As to the location of pioneer lands still open to colonization (see Fig. 12), the large areas are in northern Barga, in the northern and western part of the Manchurian Plain, and in the extreme northeast of the country, between the lower Sungari and Ussuri Rivers. In the eastern and southeastern part of the country there is less vacant land; in the center, i.e. in the southeastern belt of the Manchurian Plain and the adjoining part of Liaoning Province, all land is occupied and cultivated.

From the foregoing description it is evident that the pioneer region discussed in this article, as regards its natural conditions and agricultural possibilities, is very promising in every respect.

[7] B. V. Skvortsov: The Soy Bean—Wild and Cultivated in Eastern Asia, *Publs. Manchuria Research Soc.: Nat. Hist. Sect.*, Ser. A, No. 22, Harbin, 1927. [In Russian.]

A. A. Horvath: The Soy Bean as Human Food, *Chinese Govt. Bureau of Econ. Information Booklet Series No. 3*, Peiping.

C. V. Piper and W. J. Morse: The Soybean, New York, 1923.

[8] B. V. Skvortsov: Manchurian Wheat: Abridged Sketch, *Publs. Manchuria Research Soc.: Commercial and Industrial Sect.*, Ser. A, No. 18, Harbin, 1927 (reprinted from *Manchuria Monitor*, Nos. 4, 5, 1927). [In Russian.]

[9] Nobuo Murakoshi and G. T. Trewartha: Land Utilization Maps of Manchuria, *Geogr. Rev.*, Vol. 20, 1930, pp. 480–493.

CHINESE IMMIGRATION AND COLONIZATION IN MANCHURIA

C. WALTER YOUNG

THE subject of settlement in Manchuria is so intimately associated with the prevailing political conditions in China that any attempt to substitute a scientific and comprehensive program for the generally haphazard and uncontrolled flooding of Chinese immigrants over the Manchurian Plain must meet with serious obstacles. Of hardly less significance are the facts that under present conditions this migration movement is spontaneous rather than induced and that the combination of causes that give rise to periodic famines in China, latterly more especially in Shantung Province, together with complementary factors that make the struggle for existence there especially severe, present a problem whose solution alone may operate to stem the tide of emigration to Manchuria and elsewhere. The problem of settlement in Manchuria is rather one of taking care of a vast horde of immigrants than of inducing them to come from their homeland.

Since the overthrow of the Manchu Dynasty in 1911 the somewhat tenuous administrative ties which bound to the national capital the "Three Eastern Provinces" constituting Manchuria (Liaoning—called Fengtien before 1928—Kirin, and Heilungkiang) have often been strained, concealed, or even broken on occasion, as, for example, during January, 1926, when the Manchurian local régime declared their complete independence of Peking. South of the Great Wall and within the part of China from which these immigrants have come, the more urgent demands of civil war and the lack of any stable government caused the nominal political authorities in Peking to be generally disinterested or powerless to control the movement of emigrants from Shantung. The capitulation of Peking to the Nationalists in July, 1928, has established the National government at Nanking as the present nominal central authority of China. But the responsibility of Nanking for political administration in Manchuria is more nominal than real. Manchuria, therefore, remains, for purposes of overseeing colonization enterprises, under the control of the Mukden government. The preoccupation of the Nanking governmental authorities

330

with the more pressing problems of obtaining political power, and of maintaining it, in the next few years at least may perhaps afford little opportunity, whatever their inclination, for them to give anything but incidental attention to a studied program for settlement of Chinese in Manchuria.

Sanguine as it may be to expect more than sympathetic coöperation from Chinese authorities, either in Nanking or Mukden, and difficult as it must be to control either the forced exodus from Shantung and Hopei (former Chihli) or the dispersion and settlement in Manchuria, there remain certain cogent reasons why the phenomenon of the present migration of Chinese to Manchuria should be the subject of scientific study. A reliable body of data pertaining thereto is desirable; and certain non-political problems affecting the livelihood of the hundreds of thousands of near-destitutes who annually find their way into Manchuria must be met.

It would seem, then, that the problem of settlement in Manchuria, so far as scientific organizations may be connected therewith, would resolve itself into two parts: (1) a thorough study of the pioneer belt in Manchuria, characterized by an analysis of the fundamental natural conditions of the region, the history of settlement, and the unique phases of the economic and social structure of Chinese agricultural society, both in the homeland and in the pioneer area, and (2), subsequently, concentrated attention on such phases of the problem as can be influenced by this information, along with recommendations and material assistance from those who would avoid "the waste of life and capital that characterizes pioneer settlement."

Certain facts about this particular migration of Chinese into Manchuria should counsel careful and immediate attention to it. The most recent reliable figures from the only competent sources indicate that upwards of 1,000,000 Chinese immigrants entered Manchuria from other parts of North China, principally from Shantung, during the immigration year 1927 and nearly as many during 1928. The next year, 1929, showed a slight increase.[1]

[1] Immigrants in 1927 (i.e. immigration year, Nov. 1926–Oct. 1927 incl.) 1,065,000, in 1928 938,000, according to *Chinese Econ. Bull.*, published by Bureau of Industrial and Commercial Information, Peking, Vol. 1, No. 11 (June 1, 1929), p. 2 (cited by Hsiao, p. 419). According to the South Manchuria Railway Co. (Report, Second, on Progress in Manchuria, p. 14) 1,178,254 entered in 1927, 938,472 in 1928, and 1,046,291 in 1929.

On the topic of the present paper see also the publications of the writer, except the first, listed in the bibliography. The second, third, and fifth publications contain more detailed figures on immigration to 1928.

(References that are abbreviated in these footnotes are given in full in the bibliography at the end of the present article, where they are grouped alphabetically under each of the two headings there used.)

According to the South Manchuria Railway Company about 750,000 Chinese immigrants arrived in Manchuria in 1930. The magnitude of this migration, perhaps unprecedented in modern history and assuredly unparalleled today, combined with its continuous character, especially since 1925, makes it a matter of international importance. Its effect on the population problem in Shantung, its bearing on the settlement especially of northern Kirin and sparsely populated Heilungkiang, and its effect on the immigrants themselves warrant attention to the movement both for scientific and immediately practical purposes.

SCOPE OF THE PRESENT STUDY

The subject of Chinese immigration and colonization in Manchuria logically divides itself into three parts, the investigation of each of which is capable of separate if coöperative effort: (1) the source of immigration in Shantung, which comprises the population problem and the periodic causes of increased exodus, such as famines or local disturbances; (2) the volume and character of the migration to and through South Manchuria, including the steamship and railway facilities, the characteristics of the immigrants, and their problems on the way; and (3) the dispersion and settlement in the areas of pioneer colonization, especially in North Manchuria, which comprehends the study of the physical characteristics of the areas of settlement, of the land and its potential productivity, of land utilization and potential capacity for settlement, of the economic and social characteristics of the Chinese colonizing society, and of the relation of these areas of settlement to the general economy and future of Manchuria. Of these three groups of topics the last is the one that should receive most attention, as the factual material concerning the second is available in reasonably accurate data and much has already been done by way of scientific study of the first, especially of the causes of famine in Shantung.

SOURCE OF IMMIGRATION IN SHANTUNG AND HOPEI

With certain exceptions, such as the larger size of landholdings in Heilungkiang than in Shantung, the agricultural society from which these colonists have come in Shantung is in the main not dissimilar to that of the pioneer society in Manchuria. The communal element in Chinese society is of first importance. This, which is the master key to so much of Chinese economics and politics, serves to explain how, with the family system as the central substance and with the force of custom and tradition as reënforcing materials, these Chinese colonists in Manchuria establish communities strikingly like those in the land from which they have migrated. What H. G. Wells has called the "enormous powers of permeation and extension" of the "cultivating civilization of China" has enabled these colonists not only to transport their own mode of life almost intact to whatever area they may have gone but also to displace or absorb the weaker peoples, as the Mongols or Tungus and related tribes in Manchuria.[2]   This factor is emphasized here because it points to the unique character of the Chinese agricultural society, whether it be studied in the ancestral land or in the colonized area, and because he who would understand the life of the pioneer society must first appreciate the essential facts of agricultural life as it exists in Shantung.

The normal condition of the Chinese farmer in Shantung and the abnormal condition prevailing during famine times—though famines have occurred in Shantung and elsewhere in China with a periodicity that almost justifies characterizing them as part of a normal condition—determine the volume of exodus more than the economic magnetism of Manchuria itself   This suggests that with temporary subsidence of the famine the volume of emigration from Shantung may be expected to decrease, to increase anew when conditions again become unlivable. But as the normal condition of the average Chinese farmer family in Shantung, from which province the great majority of the immigrants now come, is one of constant struggle to keep enough of the family alive to tend the ancestral tablets, there exists a condition that will in the future, as in the long past, cause large numbers to migrate annually to Manchuria.[3]

Militating against migration, however, is the fundamental fact that the attachment of the Chinese farmer to the ancestral soil is profound.[4] If to undertake "grievous toil in the wilds,"

[2] Young, Current History, p. 532; Gapanovich; F. G. Kramp: De grenslanden van China, in het bijzonder Mandsjoerie, Tijdschr. Kon. Nederl. Aardrijksk. Genoot., Vol. 18, 1901 (Ser. 2), pp. 343–366; reference on p. 358.

[3] "Famines in Shantung"; Mallory, China: Land of Famine.

[4] Young, Current History, p. 530. Count Keyserling has understandingly written: "There is no other peasantry in the world which gives such an impression of absolute genuineness and of belonging so much to the soil . . . However much they may increase in number, they remain upon it, wringing from Nature her scanty gifts by ever more assiduous labor; and when they are dead, they return in childlike confidence to what is to them the real womb of their mother . . . the inherited fields are at the same time his history, his memory, his reminiscences" (The Travel Diary of a Philosopher, transl. by J. H. Reece, 2 vols., New York, 1925; Vol. 2, p. 71).

to use a Chinese classical phrase, is to disassociate himself from his family and its obligations, then to pioneer is to be un-Chinese, than which for a Chinese there is no greater crime. The fact that over a million Chinese left for Manchuria in a single year, of whom perhaps half will not return at least for many months, many of them never, suggests that there must be very urgent reasons for the migration to Manchuria. Reasons there are in the condition of famine, caused by a combination of factors, economic, social, and political.

RURAL ECONOMY IN NORTH CHINA

Some excellent work has recently been done on Chinese rural economy in North China south of the Great Wall, and this in spite of the herculean task in China of obtaining accurate statistical data on such subjects as density of population. Valuable materials have recently been published on population density in Shantung, land utilization, size of land holdings, methods of cultivation, relation of family income to expenditures, standard of living of farmers, and especially on the causes of periodic famines.[5] What is needed is a coördination of these materials for obtaining a background for the study of Chinese pioneer society in Manchuria. More attention should be given also to such phases of the agrarian situation in Shantung as have special bearing on the study in Manchuria, for example, (1) the population problem in North China in relation to emigration, (2) the relation of periodic famines to emigration to Manchuria, and (3) Chinese farming methods, including the colonists' familiarity with specific crops, farm implements, and utilization of labor. Perhaps the only materials available in English on the emigration movement from the ports of departure in Shantung to the place of debarkation in Manchuria, including such subjects as competition among steamship lines for the carrying trade and facilities offered the immigrants upon landing, are those in the writer's report to the Chinese Government Bureau of Economic Information, Peking, and his subsequent articles.[6]

HISTORY OF SETTLEMENT IN MANCHURIA

Prefatory to an analysis of the contemporary volume and character of the Chinese migration to Manchuria it is essential to

[5] Books and articles by the following cited in the bibliography: Mallory (China: Land of Famine), Lieu, O. E. Baker, Buck, J. B. Tayler, and J. E. Baker.

[6] Young, *Current History*, pp. 532–533; *Chinese Econ. Journ.*, Vol. I, 1927, pp. 621 ff.; *Far Eastern Rev.*, pp. 246 ff.

appreciate two facts: (1) that Chinese settlement in Manchuria is not a new phenomenon but that, particularly after the middle of the past century, the displacement of the aboriginal tribes and the Manchus, which went hand in hand with this movement, was well on the way to completion, and (2) that the present tendency toward increased colonization and settlement on the land was preceded for many years by a migration movement which, in the main, was seasonal. The successive stages in the migration of Chinese to Manchuria and the absorption or the displacement of the native peoples have been discussed by the writer in some detail in an article[7] of which the following statements are a part.

The first significant period of widespread Chinese settlement in Manchuria corresponds almost exactly with the colonial period in American history. Efforts of the Manchu Dynasty to prevent the settlement of their homeland by Chinese were generally unsuccessful, and the slow seepage of Chinese, especially from Shantung, continued. The valleys of the Liao and Sungari Rivers were settled in part by Chinese at the beginning of Tao Kuang's reign (1821–1851). Then followed a period of thirty years during which vast tracts north of the present Harbin were opened. The disorders created by the Taiping rebellion (1854–1860), during which 20,000,000 persons are thought to have lost their lives, drove others into Manchuria, access to which was favored by the weakening of the imperial power. Finally, in 1878 the official barrier to immigration to parts of Manchuria was removed and a steady stream of Chinese flowed into the Three Eastern Provinces. Subsequent periods of political unsettlement in China have given rise to repeated waves of migration, until today of the estimated population of Manchuria perhaps ninety per cent are Chinese.[8] Manchuria thus presents no problem of competition or conflict in any form with aboriginal peoples, and the economic competition with the Korean immigrants is of minor significance.[9]

FORMER SEASONAL MIGRATION OF CHINESE LABORERS

Until 1925 the migration of Chinese to Manchuria from Shantung, Chihli (now Hopei), and other provinces had been rather in the form

[7] Young, *Current History*, pp. 531 ff.

[8] *Manchuria-Mongolia Year Book*, 1927, p. 9. (Hsiao, p. 410, cites 95 per cent as the accepted figure.) Population estimates of Manchuria as of China, are necessarily approximate. The figure of 27,000,000 for Manchuria is considered a reliable approximation.

[9] Korean immigration to Manchuria is given no attention in this report, though there are aspects of the subject which do relate themselves in certain areas to competition with the Chinese. There are probably about 800,000 Koreans in Manchuria (Lee, p. 200).

of a seasonal labor movement than one of intending colonists. There were, of course, numerous exceptions. Certainly the most striking fact about this whole movement before 1925 was its "spring come, autumn go" character. This phenomenon was the result of a combination of influences, chief of which were the seasonal character of the employment (much of which persists) during the growing season on the Manchurian farms, the seasonal demand for laborers in mines and in railway construction (now supplied mainly within Manchuria), together with the Chinese farmers' necessity for increasing the family income outside of the home farm community (Manchuria being especially desirable as a destination because of the high wage scale prevailing there) and the potent influence of his desire, if he has left home, to return and spend the meaningful festive season of the Chinese New Year in his ancestral abode. Hence, during December and January the return movement was usually almost as great as the egress to Manchuria in March, April, and May.[10] As a matter of course these labor migrants left their families behind them in Shantung. However significant the recent change, it should be noted that a very important purely seasonal migration still persists, as likewise in so-called Inner Mongolia (Suiyuan, Chahar, Jehol, etc.).

VOLUME AND CHARACTER OF PRESENT MIGRATION

Before 1925 the maximum annual totals of Chinese immigrants to Manchuria never exceeded 500,000. In 1925 about the same number came by land and sea from Shantung, Chihli, and other provinces. The year 1926 marked a notable change with the coming of 600,000, but the momentum of the increase developed even more markedly in 1927 and 1928, so much so, in fact, that those unfamiliar with the movement have questioned the capacity of transport facilities to carry the increase. When it is realized, however, that the great majority of the immigrants landing at Dairen, for example, actually proceed north into Manchuria on foot and not by rail, and when it is realized that the South Manchuria Railway has placed special trains on the line to accommodate the immigrants during the crest of the movement, it is evident that the figures presented, besides having been tested for accuracy at their source, are quite within reasonable bounds.[11] Of the million Chinese

[10] Figures of ingress and egress for each month of 1924, 1925, and 1926 are given in the writer's report in the *Chinese Econ. Journ.*, Tables 1 and 5, pp. 631–632.

[11] The writer's figures are cited by Mallory, *Foreign Affairs*, p. 79, and by J. E. Orchard in "The Pressure of Population in Japan" (*Geogr. Rev.*, Vol. 18, 1928, pp. 374–401), p. 397.

immigrants into Manchuria in 1927 more than 600,000 arrived during the months from January to June inclusive and a out 450,000 entered through Dairen, the principal receiving port.[12]

EFFECT ON PERMANENT SETTLEMENT IN MANCHURIA

It would seem quite impossible to state accurately the percentage of Chinese immigrants who before 1925 remained in Manchuria more or less permanently. Probably, however, more than 75 per cent of the number who entered in a given year returned eventually to their homes. During 1924 and 1925, of the number entering through Dairen 65 and 49 per cent, respectively, departed for Shantung from the same port. In 1927 it appeared that less than 50 per cent of the number entering through Dairen returned through the same port. If these ratios should prove to be fairly indicative of the migration movement generally, which is not unlikely, for example, from the fact of a similar situation on the Peking-Mukden line, it would seem that during the five-year period from and including 1925 at least 2,000,000 Chinese have settled in Manchuria more or less permanently.[13] That there will be a tendency even for many of these recent immigrants to return if and when conditions improve in Shantung is to be expected. Nevertheless there is an obvious tendency toward settlement on the land, especially in North Manchuria, evidenced by these figures and by the more eloquent testimony of the migrating mass to be observed en route to Manchuria. There has been a distinct increase in the percentage of women and children of all ages.[14] This is evidence of an intention to settle on the land, as are also the actual occupation of lands in certain localities and the employment of the migrants as tenants in already fairly well-settled regions. In the main, the migrants are settling on the land, though a few still continue to find employment in new railway construction, at the mines of Fushun, and elsewhere.[15]

The volume of this mass migration raises a serious question

[12] Futamura, pp. 1–3. "Report on Progress in Manchuria, 1907–1928," pp. 13–14, gives 600,000 as number of arrivals through Dairen in 1927.

[13] The figures gathered by the Chinese Eastern Railway (Harbin, Manchuria) seem also to bear out this statement based primarily on figures derived from Japanese sources [subsequently confirmed in "Report, Second, on Progress in Manchuria," p. 14, which gives 2,383,596]; see Yashnov, *Manchuria Monitor*, 1928, No. 6, pp. 15–21; Young, *Far Eastern Rev.*, p. 244. J. L. Buck of the University of Nanking reports (p. 82) that in a district of Chihli province (Yenshan) 13.5 per cent of the population of a certain village have migrated, mostly to Manchuria.

[14] Young, *Far Eastern Rev.*, section entitled "Increase of Women and Children," p. 244.

[15] For a statement of various occupations of immigrants in the environs of Mukden see: "Shantung Immigrants in Mukden," *Chinese Econ. Journ.*, Vol. 1, 1927, pp. 802–803.

whether even Manchuria can absorb the newcomers in productive pursuits. No longer is it necessary for the Japanese, for example, to recruit unskilled laborers for work in the Fushun coal mines, as Chinese immigrants seeking employment at the mines actually have had to be rejected. Nor is there enough profitable employment elsewhere in Manchuria, other than on the land, to take care of so large an influx, and this in spite of phenomenal development as evidenced by railway construction. Actually Manchuria is occasionally faced with the fact of a temporary oversupply of cheap labor, notwithstanding the fact that there are undeveloped lands still available in North Manchuria. It is entirely possible, however, that, with a change in the economic life of Shantung—cessation of civil war, for example—the seasonal movement will tend to return.

Relief for Temporarily Destitute Migrants

That many of the present immigrants on arrival in Dairen, and more of them on arrival in Changchun, perhaps after 400 miles on foot, are in a sorry state and become charges of the charities, such as the Shantung Provincial Guild, suggests the need of relieving their distress and assisting them in their journey northward. The criticism heard with respect to the placing of sums of money at the disposal of the famine relief organizations in Shantung and elsewhere in China on the ground that such disposition of funds may actually subsidize disorder or be at best but palliative, whatever may be its general tenability, would have little or no application in Manchuria. It would seem to be difficult to imagine a more concrete and at once immediately and permanently practical result than that which might come from assisting the Chinese immigrants actually to proceed to their new fields of endeavor. This relief might well begin at Dairen and should be applied in particular at Changchun, the focal point from which dispersion to the settlement areas takes place. Local Chinese organizations in Manchuria and the Japanese and Russians, principally those connected with the railway, have done commendable work in this respect.

Railways and Communications with Settlement Areas

Three factors have been characterized elsewhere by the writer as primary in contributing to the economic magnetism of Manchuria: (1) the relatively sparse population of the country, especially of northern Kirin and of Heilungkiang, and the consequent availability of cultivable land or of employment on cultivated lands; (2) the comparative peace and order that prevails, in part owing to the fact that the South Manchuria Railway is controlled by the Japanese and no interruptions to traffic have ever been countenanced; and (3) the existence of a network of railways which, with navigable rivers like the Sungari, afford easy access to the pioneer areas.[16]   The communications with and in Manchuria are far superior to those with Mongolia or other areas to the northwest of Shantung.   Manchuria today has nearly 4000 miles of railways, or about half the total mileage of all China (including Manchuria); Liaoning (formerly Fengtien) Province is better served by railways than Kiangsu, the province of Shanghai.   More railways were constructed in Manchuria between 1924 and 1929 than in all the rest of China put together.   It is, therefore, of much importance in considering the relation of railways to Chinese immigration and settlement in Manchuria to realize that there is no one of the several pioneer areas, with the exception of the one in the lower Sungari valley, which can be reached by river, that is not readily accessible from railways already built or building[17] (Fig. 1).   Actual procedure to the places of settlement in certain areas, as in parts of Heilungkiang, is, of course, made difficult at times by the lack or the inadequacy of roads.   But the problem of road communication in Manchuria bears rather on the communication of the pioneer society with trade marts than on the subject of railways.

LAND DISTRIBUTION AND SETTLEMENT

With the passing of the necessity for induced immigration to Manchuria the system of labor recruitment maintained by the Japanese-owned Fushun coal mines has lost its significance.[18] The present Chinese migration to Manchuria has for its chief characteristic agricultural settlement of the immigrants or at least agricultural development.   Although it is evident that the great majority actually become farmers, it is very difficult to indicate what percentage of them work for wages, till the soil on crop-contract, lease land of their own accord, obtain land in freehold, or reclaim waste lands on one or another of these bases.[19]

[16] The first two of these criteria have been developed in Young, *Far Eastern Rev.*, pp. 241–250.

[17] Young, *Chinese Econ. Journ.*, pp. 324–335; Hsiao, pp. 406–409, section on railways.

[18] Young, *Chinese Econ. Journ.*, pp. 629 ff., section entitled "Labor Recruiting System in Shantung and Chihli."

[19] Young, *Far Eastern Rev.*, p. 247, section entitled "Official Encouragement of Immigration."

Much of the land which has been available for distribution in Manchuria has long been held by Chinese official bodies, provincial or district, or by private Chinese companies, usually of a semi-official character, or by individual owners of large estates. For the Chinese immigrants no land is available from the South Manchuria Railway or the Chinese Eastern Railway companies, except within their respective "zones," neither of which can have any great bearing on this colonization movement, as these areas are both insignificant in size and in land available for settlement. Because the pioneer areas, where potential absorption of agricultural settlers is the greatest, are entirely under Chinese jurisdiction, as is the lower Sungari River zone, it is evident that one must look in this connection to the methods followed by Chinese officials and private companies.

Alternately or contemporaneously the Peking government, especially through the Ministry of Communications, the provincial governments in the Three Eastern Provinces, and the local officials in the provinces have taken steps, nominally or with sincere desire to secure results, toward fostering settlement on the land. In 1910, for example, the then president of the Board of Finance in Peking sought to have funds drawn from the national treasury to defray half the expenditure required for transportation of intending settlers to Manchuria.[20] During 1909 and 1910 the provincial authorities in Manchuria, especially under Viceroy Hsi-liang, sought to encourage such settlement. Later, in 1922, the Peking government took a new interest in a similar project, and in 1925 the Ministry of Communications promulgated regulations to facilitate emigration to Manchuria. Since then nothing of any great importance has been done by the Peking or central Chinese authorities toward facilitating such emigration.

For twenty years proclamations of provincial and district authorities in Manchuria have been posted there and in Shantung and Chihli purporting to announce lands available almost for the asking, together with offers of financial assistance, food, and implements. The civil governor of Fengtien announced the opening of virgin lands to such settlement during the summer of 1927. Later the district magistrates in Taonan and Lo-pei districts made such offers. Land settlement companies exist with offices in Harbin which purport to offer land to settlers free or on extravagantly liberal terms.

[20] Young, *Far Eastern Rev.*, p. 247, section entitled "Official Encouragement of Immigration."

Enough has been said to indicate that the character of these land settlement companies and their methods, as well as those of Chinese officialdom, should have the most careful scrutiny. Tentatively, it may be said that, while there are to be found numerous instances where the officials and promotion companies have taken mean advantage of the destitute immigrants, there are, on the contrary, others where real opportunities have been offered them.   It is evident that much of the land advertised as available for the asking is actually held by Manchurian officials or semi-official colonization companies for the unprincipled exploitation of the helpless immigrants.   While it is undoubtedly true that the immigrants rarely are able to obtain free land or even lands in lease for themselves and that vast tracts in North Manchuria are held by speculators, it does not follow that in northern Kirin and Heilungkiang, as in the Lo-pei or Hulan districts, no more land is available in one form or another on terms that will enable destitute Chinese to live better than in suffering Shantung from which they have come.[21]   Right here, however, is the greatest practical problem to be met by those who would seek to substitute for haphazard and selfish exploitation a scientific program of colonization: it is the problem of dealing with an avaricious and parasitic Chinese officialdom living on the lifeblood of its own kind.   There are honest and public-spirited local officials in Manchuria, and through them it may not be impossible to obtain practical results.

THE PIONEER AREAS

Turning, finally, to the third category of study, the characteristics of the pioneer areas themselves, the investigator is confronted with a group of problems of a nature to caution against even such tentatively conclusive statements as have so far been suggested. An initial effort was made by the writer while in Manchuria during 1926 and 1927 to ascertain in what specific areas, and in what numbers, the Chinese colonists have settled. Although the results of that study must be taken as but tentative, because of the inadequacy of the statistical data then available, it was possible to trace the progress of the 600,000 immigrants who entered Manchuria during the first half of 1927. This study disclosed that Manchuria, as a whole, treated as one great pioneer region, may be divided

[21] There would seem to be insufficient bases for the statement that in the winter of 1927–1928 "all of the unoccupied land in Manchuria was parceled out by scrip to favorites of the Government or sold in huge tracts to syndicates of wealthy Chinese" (Hallett Abend in "Manchuria Entraps a Tragic Migration," *New York Times Magazine*, June 24, 1928, p. 9).

for purposes of convenient study into no less than nine separate
settlement areas (Fig. 1). A general description of each of these
zones has been given in the articles in which they are defined.[22]

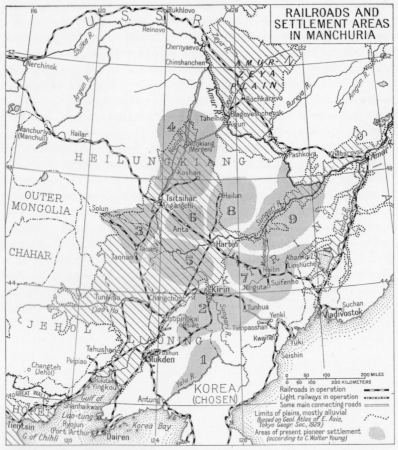

FIG. 1—Railroads and settlement areas in Manchuria. Scale, 1 : 14,700,000. These areas, to
which Chinese migration is chiefly directed, may be designated as follows: 1, Yalu River area;
2, Upper Sungari River area; 3, Taonan area; 4, Upper Nonni River area; 5, Changchun northern
area; 6, western zone of the Chinese Eastern Railway; 7, eastern zone of the Chinese Eastern
Railway; 8, Hulan River area; 9, Lower Sungari River area.

Each has its own characteristics, determined in part by the means
of access by rail or water, the economic geography of the area,
the population characteristics, and the stage of development and
relation to markets.

[22] Young, *Current History*, p. 533; *Far Eastern Rev.*, pp. 296–303; *Problems of the Pacific*, 1929,
pp. 444–459, with map.

At present, difficulties arise from the inadequacy of materials on such fundamental subjects as the following: (1) the distribution of present population in northern Kirin and Heilungkiang, (2) the amount and character of cultivable land that is available and that could be made available, under certain conditions, for settlement, (3) the productivity per unit of labor of lands of various grades in relation to present utilization, (4) the system of land tenure and the manner of exploitation of the land by Chinese official, semi-official, or private land companies or syndicates, (5) Chinese coöperative credit, marketing, and mutual aid societies in the pioneer areas, and, finally, (6) what might be characterized as intensive case studies, covering the points mentioned, in one or more special pioneer areas (*hsien* study rather than a village study), as, for example, that of the Hulan Valley previously referred to.

On the first two of these subjects much of value has already been made readily available even in English. More is now available in Russian, Chinese, and Japanese.[23] Very much more perhaps might be obtained by competent investigators from the research and economic bureaus of the Manchurian railway companies. On the next three subjects material is available for more than one area, but nothing complete enough to permit of adequate conclusions. Hence the need of an intensive study of a selected area, such as the Hulan Valley region north of Harbin, is evident.

ECONOMIC STRUCTURE OF THE PIONEER AREAS

Reference has been made to the fact that in the Manchurian pioneer region most of the present areas of settlement are accessible from the railways. The exception is the lower Sungari River area, which as a region of potential settlement is the most important in Manchuria.[24] Branch lines north from the main line of the Chinese Eastern Railway, however, are contemplated which will eventually make the whole of northern Kirin accessible even to the banks of the Sungari at Sanhsing.[25]

Some road construction under the direction of the Chinese

[23] See bibliography in particular for the work of K. Futamura of the South Manchuria Railway (Dairen) and of E. E. Yashnov of the Chinese Eastern Railway (Harbin). [Yashnov's cartogram of cultivated and cultivable areas in each *hsien* in northern Manchuria from his "Chinese Colonization of North Manchuria and Its Prospects" is reproduced in the preceding article by Ahnert, p. 328. For figures of these two categories of land by province totals for the whole of Manchuria, see *Geogr. Rev.*, Vol. 20, 1930, p. 480.—EDIT. NOTE.]

[24] Young, *Far Eastern Rev.*, pp. 302–303, section entitled "The Lower Sungari Settlement Zone," and Problems of the Pacific, 1929, pp. 456–459; Lubimov and Gorlanov.

[25] Yashnov, *Manchuria Monitor*, p. 19; Young, *Chinese Econ. Journ.*, pp. 334–335.

Eastern Railway is progressing, and roads occasionally have been built to follow the timber concession railways east of Harbin and thus pierce the forests to the Sungari River. Generally, however, Chinese roads in Manchuria, as in most parts of northern China, are often impassable during all but the winter months, when by freezing they become capable of carrying heavy two-wheeled cart traffic. But, as the Chinese are accustomed to the inconvenience of poor roads and as the movement of cereals to market takes place during the winter months, it may be said that generally the Manchurian pioneer region presents no exceptional handicaps in this respect, except where the primitive character of the country is preserved in standing timber, or when traffic is impeded by roving *hunghutzu*, the Chinese bandits. This latter is no inconsequential factor in northern Manchuria, both in Kirin and Heilungkiang.

POPULATION DENSITY OF THE PIONEER REGION

The Manchurian pioneer region, by and large, may be said to lie principally in what is termed North Manchuria (north of the 44th parallel), including the whole of Heilungkiang and the northern part of Kirin. To this area approximately two-thirds of the immigrants have recently gone. The present population of the area appears to be between 10,000,000 and 13,000,000, though some authorities give a larger figure.[26] But the population is not uniform in distribution. That of Heilungkiang appears to have about doubled in the ten years from 1919 to 1928 and is now about 25 to the square mile, or less than one-fourth the density of Kirin, and about one-seventh that of Liaoning. The average population for the whole of Manchuria would appear to be nearly three times that of Heilungkiang and about the same as that of the Anta district in North Manchuria, i.e. about 75 to the square mile. Shantung, from which so many of the immigrants come, is about seven times more densely populated than is Manchuria. It should also be noted that even within Heilungkiang, for example, the density varies widely, e.g. from less than one per square mile in the Barga district to over 300 in the environs of Harbin.

LAND UTILIZATION AND THE COLONIZATION RESERVE

Turning to land utilization and the reserve of profitably cultivable land, it is estimated that at present over 20,000,000 acres are

[26] Yashnov, *Manchuria Monitor*, p. 16; "North Manchuria and the Chinese Eastern Railway," pp. 10 ff.; Young, *Far Eastern Rev.*, p. 299.

under cultivation in North Manchuria and that this amount can be trebled, the reserve available being thus twice that now under cultivation, though the uality of these virgin lands is by no means uniformly good.[27] What effect this may have on the capacity to absorb future Chinese settlers is somewhat problematic, but it would seem theoretically that some 30,000,000 immigrants can be absorbed in North Manchuria.[28] It is estimated that the cultivated area in North Manchuria is at present increasing at the rate of about five per cent annually, a very high figure.[29] What is needed is available material on the extent and classification of uncultivated arable land for particular districts. About Harbin and to the south, as well as about Anta, the land that in future can be brought under profitable cultivation is less than that already under the plow, while in the lower Sungari valley one fourth of the arable land is actually cultivated. Of the cultivable land not yet under the plow the greater part is now officially registered and in private hands.

REGIONAL DISTRIBUTION OF DOMINANT TYPES OF ECONOMY[30]

The economic characteristics of pioneer communities in Manchuria naturally vary according to whether agriculture (soil cultivation), grazing (cattle breeding on wild grass), or forestry

[27] North Manchuria and the Chinese Eastern Railway, pp. 45 ff.; Yashnov, *Manchuria Monitor*, p. 21. Mr. Yashnov concludes with this opinion his valuable summary of the facts published originally in Russian: "Thus there is reason to expect that within a maximum period of forty years —evidently even earlier—North Manchuria may have a population of from 35,000,000 to 40,000,-000, a cultivated area of from 35,000,000 to 40,000,000 *shan* (27,000,000 hectares or 25,000,000 desiatins) and produce annually a grain surplus of from 9,000,000 to 10,000,000 tons. By that time the population of all of the Three Eastern Provinces (Heilungkiang, Kirin, and Fengtien) promises to have grown to 75,000,000." (1 *shan* equals 1.8 acres.) [Figures for the cultivated and cultivable land in each of the three provinces are also cited by Hsiao, p. 383, from a publication of the Statistical Society of Japan. The figures in the *Geogr. Rev.*, Vol. 20, 1930, p. 480, appear to be from the same source.—EDIT. NOTE.]

[28] Dr. O. E. Baker of the Bureau of Agricultural Economics of the U. S. Department of Agriculture, having made independent studies of land utilization in Manchuria, expressed the view at the Institute of Politics, Williamstown, 1928, that somewhat over twice the present acreage can be brought under cultivation in North Manchuria. A committee of the round table on Problems of the Pacific at the Institute in August, 1928, of which the writer was a member, was appointed to investigate and report on the potentiality of Manchuria for absorption of population. It reported tentatively that Manchuria "will support a Chinese population of about 100,000,000 on the strength of living comparable with the existing standard in China." To this report the writer demurred on the ground that there were not sufficient data on which to base such conclusion, submitting instead the statement that "for several decades Manchuria will supply ample room for any excess Chinese population, inasmuch as the Chinese seem disposed to move only under pressure of famine or civil war" and North Manchuria is theoretically capable of absorbing from double to three times its present population, or an additional 25,000,000 to 50,000,000 without the change which industrialization would bring about on capacity for absorption and on standard of living (Report of the Conference, Institute of Politics, Williamstown, Mass., 1928, p. 194).

[29] Yashnov, *Manchuria Monitor*, p. 20. Hsiao, p. 384, gives figures for all of Manchuria, indicating an increase of a little over one per cent a year from 1922 to 1927.

[30] North Manchuria and the Chinese Eastern Railway, pp. 14–25 and Map 2.

is the principal occupation. Moreover, a form of intensive farming often is supplemented by stock raising, as in the region south and west of Harbin, which produces grain and soy beans for the outside market and is also the principal area where horses, meat, and hides are produced. Again, in the lower Sungari area, for example, lumbering, or at least fuel cutting, is an important subsidiary industry for the farmer who tills the soil during the growing season. In the main, however, in the environs of Harbin and the lower Sungari region agriculture predominates, while grazing extends from Harbin and Changchun west, across the line of the newly constructed Taonan-Angangchi railway into the western part of the Manchurian Plain in northern Liaoning Province. Generally, too, the whole valley of the Sungari may be characterized as one of agricultural settlement; and, as this region has the greatest potentialities for absorption of Chinese colonists, attention should be given to it along with that which lies immediately north of Harbin, the Hulan area.

SIZE OF THE FARM UNITS

Neither is it tenable to assume that because the average land-holding per household in China proper is small a similar situation prevails in Manchuria, nor that because there is a large reserve of uncultivated land in Manchuria the landholdings are large. As a matter of fact, there is a wide variation in the size of land-holdings in the different parts. In Liaoning individual holdings are but slightly larger than in Hopei and Shantung.[31] But in North Manchuria, while the tendency is for larger holdings per household, there is a wide variation from farms of a *mou* or two to estates covering several thousands of *shan* (one *mou* equals 0.1 *shan*, one *shan* equals 1.8 acres).

LAND TENURE IN THE PIONEER AREAS

Of the farming population of North Manchuria one-fourth is estimated to be entirely landless, i.e. working on rented land, while about the same proportion have holdings so small as to require renting of additional land, a situation paralleled in Shantung whence the colonists may have come. What portion of the present annual totals of Chinese immigrants actually are able to obtain some land for themselves in freehold is a subject on which informa-

[31] Lieu and Chen; O. E. Baker, in Problems of the Pacific, 1927.

tion is not obtainable, but the number must be very small. The availability of virgin lands naturally tends to diminish from year to year, and the tendency for an increase in the number of colonists settling on rented lands is evident. Whether certain large land-holdings of speculators or absentee landlords can be broken up and distributed on productive terms to intending settlers is a problem for investigation. During October and November, 1929, the writer spent several weeks investigating the subject of large landholdings with Harbin as a base. He visited two estates within 25 miles of Harbin, each over 1000 acres in area, of which approximately half was under cultivation. He found several land companies in Harbin, formed principally of officials and ex-officials, each of which held virgin cultivable land in Heilungkiang Province in as many as ten separate estates, the estates varying from 100 to 10,000 acres. One official showed maps of no less than ten estates which he himself owned in the Hulan Valley north of Harbin, estates varying from 200 to 1000 acres in area, almost none of them touched with the plow. Many of these estates were only partly covered by timber, vast areas being covered by varieties of grasses that grow only on soil that is good to excellent. The non-development of these estates was as much due to inertia and general unfamiliarity with Western agricultural machinery as to lack of capital and a hesitancy to open tracts where the local political authorities had not yet stabilized the country through exterminating or placating the bandits, who are as often destitute farmers as professional robbers. That at present the tenants are kept in stringent financial circumstances by their obligations to the landlords and are compelled to pay usurious interest rates (usually high in China) on necessary loans points to a most acute problem.

Lease of lands by foreigners in North Manchuria, as elsewhere in China, is restricted by legal barriers, and political unsettlement has so far made foreign participation in nominally Chinese projects difficult. The experiment of the late Major Morgan Palmer near Sanhsing on the Sungari and the present participation of a missionary society in settling Chinese in the Hulan Valley offer interesting examples for study.

Of the land not held in freehold or lease by the settlers the greater part is tilled by tenants on some form of crop-contract basis. Even when land is held in leasehold the annual fee may be in kind rather than cash, except when the leased land remains a part of the public domain. Virgin lands may be offered a tenant on condition that a like amount be brought under the plow for the landlord, but usually the landlord shares in the annual crop on a crop-contract or profit-sharing basis, somewhat as follows: (1) equal division of the crop, the owner furnishing the tenant with the land, living quarters, livestock, implements, and seed, or (2) unequal division of the crop, the owner receiving the smaller share, the tenant supplying livestock and implements, the owner the land and the living quarters, or (3) unequal division of the crop (in rarer cases monetary rental), the owner receiving a still smaller share, in which the tenant receives nothing but the land from the owner for use. Variations of these forms are to be found according to availability of land, distance to railroads, prevalence of fuel, quality of soil, and labor supply.[32] Major Palmer's departure from the usual custom of obtaining farm laborers on a crop-contract basis and paying them a wage for their services instead proved a failure. In summary, it may be said that the condition of the average Chinese tenant farmer in North Manchuria is far from happy but that it is far better than that of the farmers, even on their own land, in Shantung. The same problem of confronting avaricious local officials and "land hogs" suggests the principal obstacle to an improvement in this condition. Nor is this situation unparalleled elsewhere in China.

Systems of Farming and Farm Implements

In the Chinese agricultural community in North Manchuria the raising of livestock is less for market or even for food than for draft purposes. Horses, mules, donkeys, oxen, ordinary cattle and nondescript equestrian animals supplement the manual labor that is applied so industriously to the tilling of the soil. The disinclination of the Chinese farmer to raise livestock for market may prove a future problem in North Manchuria as it is now in Inner Mongolia, the drawback being the lack of manure for fertilizer, though in North Manchuria it may generally be said that the soil does not require fertilizer in the same manner as in the western part of Manchuria bordering on Mongolia.[33]

Crops suitable to short seasons, generally usable for the family

---

[32] North Manchuria and the Chinese Eastern Railway, p. 49; Agriculture in Manchuria and Mongolia, *Chinese Econ. Journ.*, pp. 1044–1047. For a comparison with land tenancy elsewhere in China see Lieu, Land Tenure Systems in China.

[33] Wilm, English and German articles.

food supply, as millet and kaoliang (a kind of sorghum) and vegetables and maize (especially in the south), or for outside market, as soy beans (the leading money crop) and wheat and, to a lesser degree, rice, are grown in North Manchuria.[34] The experience of the Shantung colonists with all but rice cultivation usually enables them to adjust themselves readily to the local conditions, somewhat contrary to the situation in Mongolia. It naturally follows that the farm implements are, likewise, in the main, either replicas or slight variations of those used in Shantung. These implements are by no means few, though comparatively simple of construction, and owing to the necessity of obtaining iron and stone parts for plows and harrows away from the farm itself, and to the expense of a full equipment, the colonists resort to the well-established Chinese communal practice of borrowing. Utilization of Western farm machinery, while occasional on certain large estates, is but in its initial stage in North Manchuria, but several enterprising Chinese landowners have already invested in a full line of American farm machinery, including tractors, harvesters, and threshers. But native Chinese agriculture has at least the merit of providing food and labor for a large population and of being adjustable to the Chinese social system.

Chinese farming methods in North Manchuria are in general strikingly similar to those in Shantung and are characterized by the use of extremely simple farm implements, the relatively great share of manual labor as opposed to that of draft animals or machines, the absence of the practice of allowing lands to lie fallow periodically, and an inadequate system of crop rotation. The agricultural experiment stations of the South Manchuria Railway and the Chinese Eastern Railway companies have already done much toward the improvement of the quality of seeds, the introduction of varieties more suitable to the climate and needs of crop rotation, and the improvement of farming methods.

SOCIAL STRUCTURE OF THE CHINESE PIONEER SOCIETY

The solidarity of the Chinese agricultural community of Shantung, the communal basis of organization centered in the family system, and the persistence of long-accepted standards of value and of social institutions are likewise characteristic of the pioneer society in North Manchuria. The pronunciation and idiom of

[34] See the dot maps of the leading crops in preceding article by Ahnert.

the Shantung farmer's *patois* (a slight variation from the Peking dialect), his four-walled living compound, his simple farming implements, and, above all, his predisposition to live in Manchuria much as he and his ancestors in Shantung have lived, these are transplanted to North Manchurian soil. The process of this colonization has aptly been described as that of "transplantation of the entire Chinese social complex into new soil."[35]

The tendency of Chinese farmers to congregate in or near villages, and for these population clusters in turn to congest in river valleys or in the environs of large centers of population, is likewise expressed in similar tendencies in North Manchuria. Tradition and the practical need of protection from banditry combine with lesser motives, such as the economic interdependence of the settlers, to cause the Chinese colonists to congregate in hamlets, these in turn tending to spring up along the navigable rivers and more especially along the Sungari, which has played so important a rôle in the colonization of North Manchuria.[36] Intensiveness of cultivation and dependence upon cities are characteristics of Chinese colonization in Manchuria that differ strikingly from those of the Russians in Siberia. The deep-grained Chinese tendency to settle only in groups militates against rapid absorption of outlying areas. But the pressure of such numbers as have recently migrated to Manchuria in a measure counterbalances this characteristic, though the land annually converted to cultivation naturally expands but slowly away from the population, market, and communication centers.

CHINESE ASSOCIATION GROUPS AND SERVICES IN THE PIONEER COMMUNITY

The paragraph quoted below lays emphasis very properly on "the spirit of association" in Chinese life—a force which must be appreciated by the student of Chinese colonization.

Cet esprit d'association est vraiment caractéristique de la mentalité du peuple chinois. Il révèle chez lui le besoin de se grouper. C'est comme un instinct de conservation qui l'y pousse. S'il est seul, le Chinois se sent faible, exposé à toutes sortes de dangers, en butte à l'oppression des puissants, des gens d'autres provinces. Il voit dans l'association le seul remède efficace, l'arme défensive et même offensive, lorsqu'il a quelque danger à redouter. S'il quitte sa province, il s'unit à ses compatriotes dans la ville de sa nouvelle résidence et, dans l'associa-

---

[35] North Manchuria and the Chinese Eastern Railway, p. 68.
[36] Lubimov and Gorlanov.

tion provinciale, il retrouve sa petite patrie, avec son culte et ses traditions; il y trouve aussi l'affection, le bon conseil, l'aide morale ou pécuniare.[37]

This spirit of group action, of union in various forms to secure specific ends, so characteristic of the Chinese in all phases of their social life, manifests itself markedly in Manchuria among the colonists.

One finds whole communities in North Manchuria that, while inevitably revealing the results of admixture of extraneous elements, yet are, in the main, but transplanted organisms that grew to a maturity in the homeland of the immigrants. The same mutual aid associations exist in the pioneer communities for the multifarious purposes of physical protection and police, financial coöperation and assistance, professional coöperation, and other social utilities. I have found in Manchuria in a pioneer community the ancient Chinese institution called *Pao Chia*, a sort of volunteer vigilantes organization which is formed in the community, locally selected and supported, for the purpose of protection against bandits in the "season of ripe kaoliang"—when the tall sorghum affords conceal-ment for the brigands, who may be but impecunious farmers. But the function of Chinese associations in assisting colonization begins long before the arrival of the colonists at their destinations. The Shantung Provincial Guild, especially at Dairen, continues to render commendable assistance to the migrating thousands in the form of food and cash.[38] The consciousness of provincial solidarity main-tains itself in the pioneer areas. Professional guilds and chambers of commerce perform for some groups what in another way is done for the farmers by their agricultural or communal societies for mutual aid. Coöperative loan associations, like those in Shantung and elsewhere in China, do assist the immigrants to evade the usu-rious terms of professional credit agencies and pawnshops, though the latter are as conspicuous in North Manchuria as elsewhere in China.[39] Low valuations on deposited property and excessive interest charges are characteristic of these pawnshops, which in many localities are a principal source of ready cash for the settlers. But of the associations that in the pioneer areas have great im-portance one is all-pervading, the family itself. The family in

[37] Batiste-Maybon, p. 6. For references on the associational factor in Chinese social life see the first section of the bibliography.

[38] Young, *Far Eastern Rev.*, p. 250, section entitled "The Shantung Guild and Immigration to Manchuria."

[39] North Manchuria and the Chinese Eastern Railway, p. 352. On pawnshops elsewhere in China see Chi-lien Hsu, pp. 13 ff. For an illustrative study of local mutual aid and defense associa-tions in a district of northeastern Kirin province see the paper by A. P. Chien.

China is not limited to man, wife, and a possible offspring or two. In its expansiveness it includes "the greater family," the living and the dead. Each new home in the pioneer community includes the *lares* and *penates* of the former abode: in cases, even the material images by which these spirits are invoked in Manchuria are those brought by them from Shantung. And over every community hovers the memory of the ancestral village, to which many will return eventually—some, however, only in wooden boxes by the ancient cart road south through the pass at Shanhaikwan.

Suggestions As to Research Methods and Source Materials for the Study of Problems of Pioneer Settlement in Manchuria

In the introduction to this paper the writer has presented his opinion as to the part which scientific organizations can assume in connection with the study of Chinese colonization in Manchuria, characterizing this service as twofold. In pursuance of the first objective (scientific study of the pioneer belt) and as an indispensable foundation for the second (concentrated attention to such phases of the problem as are capable of being influenced by this study) the following suggestions as to agencies and materials in Manchuria and elsewhere with which to work may have value.

At least sympathetic interest may be expected from the Nanking government, particularly as to the population and famine problems in Shantung, however incapable the government may be of giving more than nominal attention to the areas that, like Manchuria, are now beyond its direct political control. A certain amount of coöperation may be anticipated from the Mukden authorities, qualified by the degree to which they are themselves otherwise preoccupied or by the manner in which they themselves are interested in settlement syndicates for exploiting the colonists. Whole-hearted coöperation may perhaps be expected from the authorities in Manchuria of the two principal railways, the South Manchuria Railway Company in Dairen and the Chinese Eastern Railway Company in Harbin, the former under Japanese and the latter under joint Sino-Russian control. Both of these agencies, through their scientific and research sections, have already accomplished much toward assembling data relating to the Chinese immigration. Both have departments that have at once a scientific and commercial interest in the subject. With directors and technical experts of both these railway companies the writer has had sufficient contacts to justify the statement that, granted a complete understanding on their part of the nature of the work to be undertaken, it is highly probable that the very valuable information in their possession and the assistance of their experts familiar with the field may be placed at the disposal of whoever is entrusted with the task of correlating these data and directing the study in Manchuria or elsewhere. Without the coöperation of both these companies the task would be undertaken under considerable obstacles. The former is possessed, in the main, of much of the necessary data on the current volume and character of the Chinese immigration through South Manchuria. The latter has much of the material pertaining to North Manchuria (of the immigration movement as it leaves the jurisdiction of the South Manchuria Railway authorities at Changchun), though the nature of the information pertaining to settlement in North Manchuria (whither two-thirds of the immigrants proceeded in 1927), which has particular bearing on the exact character and problems of the colonists themselves in the pioneer area, is such that the task of supplying necessary data is far greater than that of supplying mere statistical tables.

Contact with the settlers and the conditions of settlement in outlying pioneer pockets, as, for example, in the Lo-pei district near the confluence of the Sungari and the Amur Rivers far north in Heilungkiang Province, is essential to scientific deductions. Only after such studies of separate settlement areas in the Hulan Valley north of Harbin, in northern Kirin, or in the Lo-pei district, would it be possible to present findings both of scientific and immediately practical value. In spite of local political disorders and occasional banditry in these areas such a study might well be made in the Hulan Valley, which has recently been made readily accessible from Harbin. In fact, as to this area, the writer's past contacts with the management of the Hulan-Hailun Railway suggest that the coöperation of these executives would be of great value.

Bearing on sources of information from agencies in the field, four additional types of organization or officials may be mentioned. Chinese district magistrates, as in the Lo-pei and Taonan districts, have shown a special interest in the problem of reclaiming waste lands. Chinese civil officials of this type may be prevailed upon by proper methods to coöperate with field investigators. Some knowledge of the Chinese language and the assistance of an interpreter would be, of course, essential to the investigator. In Harbin and to a lesser degree in Mukden settlement promotion companies or syndicates have been formed to foster colonization projects particularly for the purpose of bringing virgin lands under cultivation. Certain of these are of a semi-official character or are intimately related to the political authorities, a factor which, with the business nature of their interest, suggests the difficulty of securing their coöperation, especially when it may appear that their interests would suffer by divulgence of information. Tact and knowledge of the "local situation" must be presumed in those who would be expected to approach them. In Harbin, too, is another very valuable source of essential information, the representatives of commercial companies, as, for example, American, Russian, and German field agents of companies that handle foreign agricultural machinery, such as plows, some of whom have had most intimate contacts with the settlers.

Finally, there are certain non-commercial or non-official organizations fostering individual colonization projects, somewhat similar to that of the late Major Morgan Palmer in the lower Sungari valley. A most interesting effort has been made by a Shantung missionary association, from whose members the writer has had information. This society has obtained in the name of certain Chinese a grant of land in the Hulan Valley north of Harbin and has attempted to send several hundred immigrants from unfortunate Shantung to Manchuria. If an intensive field study were to be undertaken of a limited local area this interesting development in the Hulan district, however meager, would be an additional reason why attention might first be given to this settlement district.

BIBLIOGRAPHY

Chinese Rural Economy and Social Organization

Baker, J. E.   Economic Value of Railroad Transport.   *China Weekly Rev.*, Vol. 32, Shanghai, 1925, pp. 43–50.

Baker, J. E.   Report on the Shantung Famine [1928].   *China Weekly Rev.*, Vol. 46, Shanghai, 1928, pp. 182–183.

Baker, O. E.   Agriculture and the Future of China.   *Foreign Affairs*, Vol. 6, New York, 1927–28, pp. 483–497.

Baker, O. E.   Land Utilization in China, pp. 324–338 in "Problems of the Pacific, 1927: Proceedings of the Second Conference of the Institute of Pacific Relations . . . ," edited by J. B. Condliffe, Chicago, 1928.   [A "data paper" prepared for the conference.]

Baker, O. E.   The Progress of Population.   *Mid-Pacific Mag.*, Vol. 35, Honolulu, 1928, pp. 41–48.

Bard, Emile.   Chinese Life in Town and Country.   Adapted from the French by H. Twitchell.   New York, 1905.

Batiste-Maybon, Pierre.   Essai sur les associations en Chine.   Paris, 1925.

Bishop, C. W.   The Geographical Factor in the Development of Chinese Civilization.   *Geogr. Rev.*, Vol. 12, 1922, pp. 19–41.

Buck, J. L.   An Economic and Social Survey of 150 Farms in Yenshan County, Chihli Province, China.   *Publs. Univ. of Nanking, College of Agric. and Forestry Bull. No. 13*, Nanking, 1926.

Chen.   See Lieu.

Christie, Dugald.   Manchuria Half a Century Ago and Today.   *Scottish Geogr. Mag.*, Vol. 46, 1930, pp. 193–210.

Courant, Maurice.   Les associations en Chine.   *Annales des Sci. Politiques*, Vol. 14, 1899, pp. 68–94.

Dittmer, C. G.   An Estimate of the Chinese Standard of Living.   *Quart. Journ. of Economics*, Vol. 33, 1918–19, pp. 107–128.

Doolittle, Justus.   Social Life of the Chinese.   2 vols.   New York, 1865.

Famines in Shantung.   *Chinese Econ. Journ.*, Vol. 2, Peking, 1928, pp. 36–43.

Hosie, Alexander.   Droughts in China (620 to 1643).   *Journ. North-China Branch of the Royal Asiatic Society*, Vol. 12, 1878, pp. 51–89.

Hsu, Chi-lien.   Rural Credit in China.   *Chinese Soc. and Polit. Sci. Rev.*, Vol. 12, Peking, 1928, pp. 1–15 and 273–286.

Impey, Lawrence.   Chinese Rural Economics and Their Relations to Famine.   *China Weekly Rev.*, Vol. 30, Shanghai, 1924, pp. 245–249.   [Reprinted in *Chinese Students Monthly*, Vol. 20, No. 3, Ann Arbor, Mich., 1925, pp. 9–13.]

King, F. H.   Farmers of Forty Centuries.   Madison, Wis., 1911.

Leong, Y. K., and L. K. Tao.   Village and Town Life in China.   London, 1915.

Lieu, D. K.   Land Tenure Systems in China.   *Chinese Econ. Journ.*, Vol. 2, Peking, 1928, pp. 457–474.

Lieu, D. K., and Chung-min Chen.   Statistics of Farm Land in China.   *Chinese Econ. Journ.*, Vol. 2, Peking, 1928, pp. 181–213.

Lowdermilk, W. C.   Erosion and Floods in the Yellow River Watershed.   *Journ. of Forestry*, Vol. 22, 1924, No. 6, pp. 11–18.

Lowdermilk, W. C.   Forest Destruction and Slope Denudation in the Province of Shansi.   *China Journ. of Sci. and Arts* (now *The China Journal*), Vol. 4, Shanghai, 1926, pp. 127–135.

Mallory, W. H.   China: Land of Famine.   *Amer. Geogr. Soc. Special Publ. No. 6*, New York, 1926.   [The definitive work on the causes and cures of famines in China.]

Malone, C. B., and J. B. Tayler.   The Study of Chinese Rural Economy.   *Publs. China Internatl. Famine Relief Commission*, Ser. B, No. 10, Peking, 1924.

Maybon.   See Batiste-Maybon.

Moellendorff, P. G. von.   Le droit de famille chinois.   Paris, 1896.   Also a transl. from the German into English, "The Family Law of the Chinese," by Mrs. S. M. Broadbent, Rangoon, 1920.   [A lecture delivered in 1878, printed in *Journ. North-China Branch of the Royal Asiatic Soc.*, Vol. 13 (N.S.), Shanghai, 1879, pp. 99–121, partly rewritten.]

Otte, Friedrich.   China: Wirtschaftspolitische Länderkunde.   *Ergänzungsheft No. 194 zu Petermanns Mitt.*, Gotha, 1927.   [Pages 25–46 deal with agriculture.]

Otte, Friedrich.   Sketch of Chinese Agricultural Policy.   *Chinese Econ. Journ.*, Vol. 2, Peking, 1928, pp. 361–372.

Report of the China Famine Relief, American Red Cross, October, 1920–September, 1921.   Shanghai, n.d.

Rockhill, W. W.   Inquiry into the Population of China.   *Smithsonian Misc. Colls.*, Vol. 47, 1904, pp. 303–321.

Rockhill, W. W.   The 1910 Census of the Population of China.   *Bull. Amer. Geogr. Soc.*, Vol. 44, 1912, pp. 668–673.

Ross, E. A.   The Changing Chinese.   New York, 1911.   [Chapter 4 is entitled The Struggle for Existence in China.]

Roxby, P. M.   The Distribution of Population in China: Economic and Political Significance.   *Geogr. Rev.*, Vol. 15, 1925, pp. 1–24.   [Based on the China Continuation Committee's volume entitled "The Christian Occupation of China."]

Smith, Arthur H.   Village Life in China.   New York, 1899.

Tao.   See Leong.

Tayler, J. B.   Denmark and Rural China.   *Chinese Soc. and Polit. Sci. Rev.*, Vol. 12, Peking, 1928, pp. 116–129.

Tayler, J. B., and C. B. Malone.   See Malone, C. B.

Twitchell.   See Bard.

Wagner, Wilhelm. Die chinesische Landwirtschaft. Berlin, 1926.

Williams, S. Wells. The Middle Kingdom. 2 vols. New York, 1883.

Wittfogel, K. A. Wirtschaft und Gesellschaft Chinas: Versuch der wissenschaft-
lichen Analyse einer grossen asiatischen Agrargesellschaft. Teil I: Produktiv-
kräfte, Produktions- und Zirkulationsprozess. Leipzig, 1931.

Yü, Tseh-tang. Systems of Land Tenure in China. *Chinese Soc. and Polit.
Sci. Rev.*, Vol. 12, Peking, 1928, pp. 597–613.

Chinese Immigration and Colonization in Manchuria

Agriculture in Manchuria and Mongolia. A report of the Agricultural Office
of the South Manchuria Railway Co. published in the *Monthly Supplements*
of the *Manchuria Daily News* (Dairen), for October, December, and February,
1927–1928. [Also reprinted in part in the *Chinese Econ. Journ.*, Vol. 1, Peking,
1927, pp. 1044–1058. Mr. T. Chiba of the Agricultural Office has made other
valuable studies pertaining to agricultural methods in Manchuria, standards
of living, etc., some of which have been published in the *Manchuria Daily News*
(Dairen).]

Chen, Ta. Chinese Migrations, With Special Reference to Labor Conditions.
Bull. U. S. Bur. of Labor Statistics No. 340, Washington, 1923.

Chien, A. P. Fuchinhsien: A Self-Governing Colony in Manchuria. *Chinese
Soc. and Polit. Sci. Rev.*, Vol. 11, Peking, 1927, pp. 456–462.

Davidovich, D. A. (Colonization of Manchuria and Northeastern Mongolia).
Eastern Institute, Vladivostok. [In Russian.]

Futamura, K. Manchurian Settlers in 1927. *South Manchuria Railway Co.
Research Dept. Publ. No. 70*, Dairen, 1927. [The most detailed work available
in Japanese on the statistics of Chinese immigration, routes traveled, dispersion
and settlement in Manchuria.]

Gapanovich, I. I. The Tungus Negidal Tribes of the Amgun Basin. *Manchuria
Monitor*, Harbin, 1927, No. 11, pp. 4–9.

Gorlanov. See Lubimov.

Hoshino, T., edit. Economic History of Manchuria. Bank of Chosen, Seoul,
Korea, 1921.

Hsiao, Chu. Manchuria: A Statistical Survey of Its Resources, Industries,
Trade, Railways, and Immigration, pp. 380–422 in "Problems of the Pacific,
1929: Proceedings of the Third Conference of the Institute of Pacific Relations . . . ," edited by J. B. Condliffe, Chicago, 1930.

Kinney, H. W. Modern Manchuria and the South Manchuria Railway Company. Printed by the *Japan Advertiser Press* (Tokyo) for the S.M.R. Co.,
Dairen, 1928.

Lattimore, Owen. Chinese Colonization in Manchuria. *Geogr. Rev.*, Vol. 22,
1932, pp. 177–195.

Lee, Hoon K. Korean Migrants in Manchuria. *Geogr. Rev.*, Vol. 22, 1932,
pp. 196–204.

Lien-en, Tsao.   The Method of Chinese Colonization in Manchuria.   *Chinese Econ. Journ.*, Vol. 7, Peiping, 1930, pp. 831–852.

Lubimov, A. I., and T. F. Gorlanov.   The Sungari River, Economic Description of Its Landings and Adjoining Districts.   *Manchuria Monitor*, Harbin, 1927, No. 3, pp. 11–17.

Maier, Hans.   Die Mandschurei in Weltpolitik und Weltwirtschaft (in series "Weltwirtschaftliche Vorträge und Abhandlungen," No. 9, edited by Ernst Schultze).   Leipzig, 1930.   [Chapter 3 deals with Chinese colonization of Manchuria.]

Maier, Hans.   Nordmandschurei als Kolonial- und Wirtschaftsgebiet.   Hans Meyer Festschrift, Berlin, 1928, pp. 253–271.

Mallory, W. H.   The Northward Migration of the Chinese.   *Foreign Affairs*, Vol. 7, New York, 1928–29, pp. 72–82.

Manchuria-Mongolia Year Books.   Published in Japanese by the Sino-Japanese Cultural Society and issued through the South Manchuria Railway Company, Dairen.   [Contain materials on population and land utilization for various areas.]

Manchuria Monitor.   Periodical publication of the Chinese Eastern Railway, Harbin.   Printed in Russian and in English sections under same binding and issued recently as a monthly publication.   [Contains valuable articles on agriculture in North Manchuria and the rôle of the Chinese Eastern Railway; citations are made to this work elsewhere in the bibliography.]

Nakajima, S.   Questions Pivoting upon Immigrants into Manchuria.   *Monthly Suppl. of the Manchuria Daily News*, Dairen, February, 1928, p. 5.   [Based on the materials of the South Manchuria Railway, Personnel Bureau of the Labor Department, Dairen, and on detailed study by K. Futamura, cited above.]

North Manchuria and the Chinese Eastern Railway.   xiii and 454 pages.   Economic Bureau of the Chinese Eastern Railway, Harbin, 1924.   [An English translation by T. L. Lilliestrom and A. G. Skerst from the original Russian, published by the same organization in 1922.   An invaluable work on North Manchuria with useful data on colonization.]

Palmer, Morgan.   Colonising in Manchuria.   *China Weekly Rev.*, Vol. 30, Shanghai, 1924, pp. 270–272.

Report on Progress in Manchuria, 1907–1928.   South Manchuria Railway Co., Dairen, 1929.

Report, Second, on Progress in Manchuria, to 1930.   South Manchuria Railway Co., Dairen, 1931.

Research Journal.   Official publication in Japanese of the Research Department of the South Manchuria Railway Co., Dairen.   [Contains materials, among others, on Chinese colonization, as in Vol. 6, No. 2 (Feb. 25, 1926), pp. 77–96; Vol. 7, No. 1 (Jan. 25, 1927), pp. 96–107.]

Schmitthenner, Heinrich.   Der geographische Typus der chinesischen Kolonisation.   *Geogr. Zeitschr.*, Vol. 35, 1929, 526–540.

Shantung Immigrants in Mukden. *Chinese Econ. Journ.*, Vol. 1, Peking, 1927, pp. 802–803.

Simpich, Frederick. Manchuria, Promised Land of Asia. *Natl. Geogr. Mag.*, Vol. 56, 1929, pp. 379–428.

Soolich, Eduard. Das Besiedlungsproblem der Mandschurei. *Zeitschr. für Geopolitik*, Vol. 5, 1928, pp. 854–862.

Ta.   See Chen.

Tsao.   See Lien-en.

Wilm, Paul. The Agricultural Methods of Chinese Colonists in Mongolia. *Chinese Econ. Journ.*, Vol. 1, Peking, 1927, pp. 1023–1043.

Wilm, Paul. Wirtschaftsarten in der Mongolei. *Berichte über Landwirtschaft: Zeitschr. herausg. im Reichministerium für Ernährung- und Landwirtschaft*, Berlin, Vol. 7 (N.S.), 1928, No. 2, pp. 266–313.

Wu, Ching-chao. Chinese Immigration in the Pacific Area. *Chinese Soc. and Polit. Sci. Rev.*, Vol. 12, Peking, 1928, pp. 543–560.

Yashnov, E. E. Kitaiskoye krestyanskoe khozyaistvo v Severnoi Manchzhurii (The Chinese Agriculture of North Manchuria). viii and 525 pp. Economic Bureau of the Chinese Eastern Railway Co., Harbin, 1926. [Also available in Chinese under the title: *Pei Man Nung Yeh*, Harbin, 1928.]

Yashnov, E. E. Kitaiskaya kolonizatsiya Severnoi Manchzhurii i ee perspektivy (Chinese Colonization of North Manchuria and Its Prospects). viii and 291 pp. Economic Bureau of the Chinese Eastern Railway Co., Harbin, 1928. [Contains the findings of Mr. Yashnov after careful study of the subject. A Chinese translation was projected for 1929; no English translation has been made as yet, although the author has set forth his conclusions in English in the publication listed next below. Part I: The General Character and History of Chinese Colonization of Manchuria (including chapters on sources and the history of colonization of North Manchuria); Part II: Colonization Reserve of North Manchuria (including chapters on the following regions: Tsitsihar, Anta, Harbin, Lower Sungari, Petune, Southern Region, Eastern Region, Ussuri, Amur, and Barga).]

Yashnov, E. E. Colonization Prospects in Manchuria. *Manchuria Monitor*, Harbin, 1928, No. 5, pp. 1–7; No. 6, pp. 15–21. [Mr. Yashnov here presents in English his conclusions contained in the original work in Russian: "Chinese Colonization of North Manchuria and Its Prospects," Harbin, 1928.]

Young, C. Walter. Economic Bases for New Railways in Manchuria. *Chinese Econ. Journ.*, Vol. 1, Peking, 1927, pp. 324–335, with original map of economic products and areas of production in Manchuria. [A report to the Chinese Government Bureau of Economic Information (now the Bureau of Industrial and Commercial Information, Ministry of Industry, Commerce, and Labor of the Nationalist Government of the Republic of China). Reprinted in *Far Eastern Rev.*, Vol. 23, 1927, pp. 204–208.]

Young, C. Walter. Chinese Labor Migration to Manchuria. *Chinese Econ. Journ.*, Vol. 1, Peking, 1927, pp. 613–633. [A report to the Chinese Government Bureau of Economic Information, Peking. Contains tables of immigration and emigration, etc. Reprinted in Japanese translation in the *Research Journal* of the South Manchuria Railway Co., Dairen, August, 1927.]

Young, C. Walter. Chinese Colonization in Manchuria: Part I, Motives and Characteristics; Part II, Settlement Zones and Economic Effects (with original map of nine settlement zones). *Far Eastern Rev.*, Vol. 24, 1928, pp. 241–250 and 296–303.

Young, C. Walter. Manchuria, A New Homeland of the Chinese. *Current History* (published by the *New York Times*), Vol. 28, 1928, pp. 529–536.

Young, C. Walter. Chinese Colonization and the Development of Manchuria, pp. 423–465 in "Problems of the Pacific, 1929: Proceedings of the Third Conference of the Institute of Pacific Relations . . . ," edited by J. B. Condliffe, Chicago, 1930. [A "data paper" prepared for the conference. Also printed in pamphlet form.]

THE PIONEER BELTS OF AUSTRALIA

Griffith Taylor

GEOGRAPHICAL CONTROLS

Limits of the Australian Pioneer Belts

A PIONEER belt is a region of recent, of progressing, or of potential settlement." This definition[1] when considered in the broadest sense includes practically the whole of Australia; for only in small areas around the capital cities is the land adequately settled. Even in these small areas the word "adequate" implies only a density of sixteen persons to the square mile (see Fig. 1). The isopleth of one person to the square mile is, however, often adopted in Australia as separating what is close settlement from the inland areas of only moderate settlement. Where the population is greater than one person to the square mile the region may be taken as "having a density that is socially tolerable" and in a sense "economically efficient."

Two further limitations may, however, be briefly discussed. In the first place Bowman lays stress on temperate lands or on such subtropical lands as are cooled by elevation.[2] About 40 per cent of Australia lies between the Tropic of Capricorn and 11° S., and only about 4 per cent of this has an elevation above 2000 feet (Fig. 2). Moreover, only in the Atherton Tableland in northeastern Queensland is there a small tropical plateau of agricultural value, whose climate is ameliorated by virtue of its elevation. The other tropical elevations are situated in regions so dry that no noteworthy settlement is possible. Yet only the actual northern littoral is (in the writer's opinion) greatly handicapped by heat and humidity. In the tropical hinterlands the factors preventing important settlement are not primarily due to their temperature or latitude but depend on the lack of water.

As regards the second limitation there are two large inland areas in Australia where the writer can see nothing to warrant

---

[1] By the Advisory Committee on Pioneer Belts of the Social Science Research Council of New York which formulated the undertaking first proposed and developed by Isaiah Bowman (see his The Scientific Study of Settlement, *Geogr. Rev.*, Vol. 16, 1926, pp. 647–653, and The Pioneer Fringe, *Foreign Affairs*, Vol. 6, 1927–1928, pp. 49–66).

[2] Griffith Taylor: Australian Meteorology, Oxford, 1920, pp. 283–286.

expenditure of time, energy, and money in an attempt to develop them.[3] These have remained uninhabited (so labeled on Fig. 1) in spite of settlement on their borders for thirty years or more. Railways cross these areas in the south and reach to their borders in the west. The overland telegraph has been maintained along their margins since 1872. It is their unattractive features and not their inaccessibility that has prevented these two desert areas from being occupied by man.

Summing up these limitations it may perhaps be considered that in Australia the pioneer belt lies between the population isopleth of one person to the square mile and either the uninhabited or the sparse-pastoral area. The northern littoral from Port Hedland (W.A.) to Cooktown (Q.)[4] should perhaps also be excluded in the terms of the definition referred to at the beginning, for it is both tropical and low-lying.

The economic geographer believes that the distribution of human settlement is almost entirely determined by natural controls. This relation becomes more and more clearly demonstrated as settlement progresses. Australian settlement is now 140 years old, and there is probably no important area in which the economic resources cannot now be fairly well estimated by the scientific student. It is a most interesting problem to ascertain which isopleth or set of isopleths expressing physical conditions most closely agrees with the present-day isopleths of population. It may be well to devote a little time to such an investigation.

If the average annual isotherms be plotted (Fig. 3) it is seen that they show little relation to the "broken crescent" in the east and south where there is a notable population. The isotherms run more or less from west to east, while the population is concentrated in the southeast and southwest corners of the continent.

If the annual isohyets be examined, it is found that the 15-inch isohyet (Fig. 1) agrees fairly well with the boundary of notable settlement in the southern states. But in the tropics there is a large region with a fairly heavy annual rainfall but with practically no population. If, however, the season of rainfall is considered, an isopleth is found that separates populated Australia from the "sparselands" in a remarkably exact fashion. This isopleth is marked "8 mo. each over 1 in. rain" on Figure 1. All to the south or east of this line has one inch of rain (or more) in each of eight

---

[3] Griffith Taylor: Environment and Race, Oxford, 1927, Parts III and IV.

[4] For location of places mentioned in the present article see Figure 6.

months (or more) in the year. It is clear, then, that the region with a somewhat uniform rain indicated by this isopleth is of great importance in determining the distribution of Australian population. Along the north coast there may be equally heavy rain in the year, but it is all concentrated in the three hottest months, and the remainder of the year is dry.

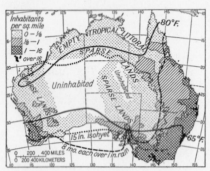

FIG. 1—Relation of population distribution (in 1921) to climate in Australia. Scale of Figs. 1–5, 8, 9, 11, 1 : 75,000,000. Isohyet of 15 inches dotted.

The chief disability of the tropics as experienced in Australia is probably the naturally high humidity in the northern littoral.[5] The regions that have six months with a wet-bulb average over 70° F. are shown in Figure 2; they extend from Port Hedland to Cooktown and also down the east coast to Rockhampton. In view of the fact that there is practically no primary production along the northern littoral (except pearl shelling) it may be ignored as a pioneer belt. But the tropical east coast of Queensland is perhaps the most interesting pioneer belt in the world. Here alone is a fairly large *white* laboring population carrying out all the tropical agriculture, and some little attention may well be given to it. The most important industry in this humid littoral is the growth of sugar cane (Fig. 8). About 273,000 acres are cultivated, almost all in Queensland, and the larger part is in the tropical portion of the state. The supply is adequate for Australian needs, but the industry is rendered possible, I understand, by fixing the price for local consumption at £27 per ton, while any sugar exported is sold at about £11 per ton.

The writer is convinced that there are distinct disabilities affecting white settlement in these humid coast lands, but it is not at all easy to find statistical proof.[6] The birth and death rates are much the same as in the rest of Australia; but the total population in tropical Australia is only about 190,000, of whom about 100,000 live in or near the "sugar coast." There is little doubt that only vigorous people move into tropical Australia, while sickly people

[5] Taylor, Australian Meteorology, Ch. 12.
[6] Taylor, Environment and Race, Ch. 24.

(especially women) tend to leave the tropics. The proportion of males to females is very high, ranging from 167 to 100 in the northwest, to 103 to 100 at Rockhampton. There is a smaller proportion of old women in tropical Queensland than in the rest of Australia, and a larger proportion of young women about twenty-four years old. This probably accounts for the relatively good birth rate.

Huntington states that folk born in Queensland have a higher death rate and a smaller number of children than is the case with settlers born in cooler climates. Sundstroem,[7] as the result of tentative experiments at the Townsville Institute of Tropical Medicine, is satisfied that the basal metabolism is lowered, the blood more alkaline, and the lipoid phosphorus lower in the case of settlers in the vicinity of Townsville

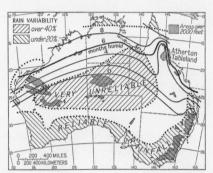

Fig. 2—Climatic discomfort and rain reliability in Australia. The figures on the continuous lines denote the number of months with an average wet-bulb temperature over 70° F. Uplands over 2000 feet in elevation are indicated by close ruling.

(latitude 19° S., average annual temperature 75° F.) as compared with those in temperate lands. Equally interesting indications are suggested by the data collected by Huntington[8] that wharf laborers do 11 per cent more work in winter than in summer in tropical Queensland. Furthermore, he states that there is 5 per cent less work done in a given time in Townsville than in Brisbane and that somewhat similar differences exist between Brisbane and the cooler city of Sydney. There is no doubt that the unusually slack work done by white labor at Darwin has adversely affected trade and industry in that tropical center. Thus Captain Mortimer of the *Marella* reported in 1927 that a full gang at Darwin loaded only 6.7 tons of cargo an hour as compared with 20 tons an hour in Melbourne. It is to be noted, however, that in general only one boat a week calls at Darwin, so that the stevedores perhaps naturally make the most of the available work.

GENERAL TEMPERATURE CONTROL

The control by temperature is relatively unimportant as contrasted with the control by rainfall but deserves some consideration.

[7] E. S. Sundstroem: Tropical Hygiene at Townsville, Melbourne, 1927.
[8] Ellsworth Huntington: West of the Pacific, New York, 1925, pp. 344–345.

In Australia the two temperature "poles" are not north and south, but northwest and southeast (Fig. 3). This arrangement is due to several factors. The region of Marble Bar in the northwestern part of Western Australia experiences hotter conditions in summer than any other part of the continent. To quote an extreme case, in the summer of 1921–1922 the average maximum temperature for three and one-half months was 110° F.[9] On no day was the maximum below 103° F. The writer was in the Marble Bar district around Christmas, 1925, when the summer was unusually dry and the temperature as much as 116°. Since the natural vegetation is strongly xerophytic, the edible mulgas (*Acacia*) and spinifex grass (*Triodia*) had not perished, though much of the native fauna as well as many sheep and cattle had died from lack of water. Here again it was lack of the usual water supply (in wells and water holes), rather than the accompanying heat, that constituted the chief difficulty of the pioneers. This remarkable condition of heat so far from the equator is due to the local pressure control. In summer a permanent low occupies the northwest of the continent, but such is never found in the northeast. Associated with this low is a constant indraft of hot north and northeast winds, which lead to a remarkable "hot loop" in the summer isotherms running from Darwin to Marble Bar (Fig. 3).[10] As a result many of the women and children in these regions move to Perth for the summer. In the rest of the year—as is usual in arid tropical countries—the climate is greatly improved. In central Australia the winter is very attractive, with cool nights (due largely to the absence of cloud and large radiation) and not unpleasant day temperatures. It is of great psychological importance that nearly all tourists, journalists, and politicians visit the hot lands in the winter and pour forth most misleading descriptions of the arid and tropical lands of Australia as a natural consequence. In the wetter northeast the summer temperature is much lower, but the humidity is higher. This type of climate is perhaps even less attractive to the human organism but is approaching optimum conditions for various tropical crops, so that the economic factor here counteracts the temperature factor as regards the pioneer.

In the southeast, at Mount Kosciusko (7328 feet), is the cold temperature pole of Australia. This is almost wholly due to elevation. There are considerable areas from 4000 to 5000 feet above

[9] Taylor, Environment and Race.
[10] Taylor, Australian Meteorology.

the sea near Kosciusko and in eastern Victoria, and here the temperature is reduced 12° to 15° F. below that of the adjacent lowlands. On Kosciusko itself trees grow up to 6000 feet, and there is usually no snow left in autumn. Kiandra, at about 5500 feet, is the highest town in Australia and is based on sparse grazing in the grassy uplands and on a little mining. The Victorian plateaus are also bleak and unoccupied except for sparse grazing.

In the remaining highlands of Australia (excluding Tasmania) the climatic conditions are improved by the cooling due to elevation.[11] Thus on the Blue Plateau west of Sydney there is a large population, based chiefly on tourist traffic, along the railway line (e.g. Katoomba, 10,000) which is primarily due to the cooling consequent on an elevation of some 3000 feet. This is a sterile sandstone plateau for the most part, and hence no agricultural settlement is affected by the lowering of the temperature. The New England Plateau somewhat farther north is between 3000 and 5000 feet elevation. Here are larger stretches of good soils, and agriculture is affected to a greater degree. Potatoes, apples, and allied crops grow here; while British sheep and merino crossbreds are favorably affected by the cooler environment.

GENERAL RAINFALL CONTROL

Australia is eminently the hot-arid continent, for some 66 per cent receives less than 20 inches of rain in a year[12] (Fig. 4). No other continent approaches this proportion except Asia, and here the average temperature is 30° lower, so that the arid control is much less marked.[13]

From the point of view of the pioneer settler many factors beside the total annual supply of rain must be considered. The season of the rain, the reliability of the rain, and the amount removed by evaporation are all very significant in considering the possibilities of settlement in a region. Thus we may instance the following four districts each receiving 15 inches of rain in the year: Roeburne (W.A.), Northam (W.A.), Longreach (Q.), and Nymagee (N.S.W.). Roeburne has so irregular a rainfall that the natural vegetation is almost desertic. Northam receives all of its rain in winter just around the growing period of the wheat plant, hence it is the

[11] Griffith Taylor: The Topography of Australia, *Commonwealth of Australia Year Book No. 20*, Melbourne, 1927, pp. 75–86.
[12] Taylor, Environment and Race.
[13] Griffith Taylor: The Status of the Australian States, *The Australian Geographer*, Vol. 1, Sydney, 1928, pp. 7–28.

center of a great agricultural region. Nymagee is in the uniform-
rain region. Its rain is distributed through the year, and it is only
just on the edge of the agricultural region in the dry-farming and
precarious wheat area. Longreach receives its rain only in the hot
months. It is purely pastoral, but its rain is more reliable than
that at Roeburne, with a corresponding improvement in the prospects of settlement.

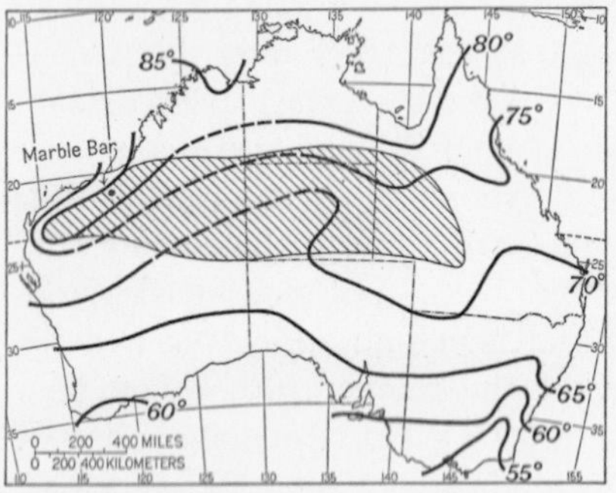

FIG. 3—Average annual temperature (F°).
The ruling indicates the area in which occur hot
spells with an average daily temperature of 90° F.
for ninety consecutive days. (Based on H. A.
Hunt, Griffith Taylor, and E. T. Quayle: The
Climate and Weather of Australia, Commonwealth Bur. of Meteorol., Melbourne, 1913, Figs.
13 and 14.)

We may therefore divide
Australia into various rainfall
regions, based primarily on
amount and season (Fig. 4).
These give the key to the
value of the land for settlement and will show that the
western states are much less
attractive than the smaller
eastern states.

Table I (p. 367) is particularly interesting, for it indicates approximately the
importance of the states as
regards future settlement.
Agriculture at present is en-
tirely confined to the regions shown in columns 2 and 3. The
long drought of the summer-rain region (usually six or eight months
in duration), combined with the poor soils, results in an environment much inferior to those of the uniform-rain and winter-rain
regions. As for the arid region it comprises about 1,378,000 square
miles. In the south I have adopted the 10-inch isohyet as the
boundary. In the north, with an evaporation of 100 inches, the
20-inch isohyet may be adopted. Along the eastern boundary the
arid limit from north to south gradually moves inland from the
20-inch isohyet to the 10-inch isohyet, as shown on the map
(Fig. 4). As will be seen, the natural vegetation has limits that
agree fairly well with this arid boundary.

The second and third columns in the same table may be further
considered. Three states, Western Australia, South Australia,
and Victoria, have large areas with winter rain. These are predominantly given over to wheat. Queensland, New South Wales,
Victoria, and Tasmania have large areas with a fairly uniform rain.
These grow wheat in the cooler drier portions but are well suited

for mixed farming, orchards, dairies, etc., where the rainfall is too heavy for wheat.

It is the mixed kind of agriculture that leads to closer settlement than one-crop wheat farming. The most promising field for the pioneer—as far as rainfall is concerned—would therefore appear to be in Queensland, while New South Wales comes next. Western Australia is at present much less closely settled than New South Wales, but its large areas with an adequate winter-rain régime are rapidly being converted into wheatfields.

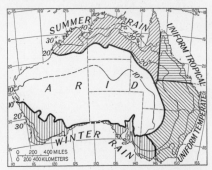

As regards the less important states, it is interesting to compare Victoria with South Australia. The latter is more than four times as large as Victoria but has no chance of rivaling the smaller state; for 311,000 square miles of South Australia are arid and have

Fig. 4—Average annual rainfall in inches (dotted lines) and seasonal rainfall regions (bounded by heavy lines). See Table I for areas of rainfall regions classified by political units and by types of land utilization.

only small value for sparse pastoral occupation. For the same reason Tasmania with 23,000 square miles of humid temperate

TABLE I—RAINFALL REGIONS OF AUSTRALIA

(Areas in thousands of square miles)

	SOME AGRICULTURE		PASTORAL ONLY		TOTAL
	UNIFORM RAIN	WINTER RAIN	SUMMER RAIN	ARID*	
Queensland { Tropical	138	—	173	166	} 670
Queensland { Temperate	193	—	—		
New South Wales . . .	232	—	—	78	310
Western Australia . . .	—	189	299	487	975
Victoria	36	52	—	—	88
South Australia	—	69	—	311	380
Tasmania	23	—	—	—	23
Northern Territory . .	—	—	187	336	523
Total	622	310	659	1378	2969

*Less than 10 inches in the south, gradually rising to 20 inches in the northeast, and less than 20 inches in the north.

land is much more valuable than the 523,000 square miles of the Northern Territory.[14]

One further aspect of rainfall deserves consideration, for it explains the discrepancy in various accounts of arid Australia. In Table II the rainfall in *successive years* at a number of places in the pioneer belt has been tabulated. When one remembers how rapidly xerophytic plants respond to the occasional rainstorm, one should not be surprised at the remarkable difference between the accounts of two visitors to the same place.[15]

TABLE II—MONTHLY RAINFALL IN CONSECUTIVE YEARS

(*in inches*)

PLACE	AVERAGE	CONSECUTIVE YEARS	
Onslow (W. A.)	April. 0.9	1900. . . . 11.0	1901 . . . .0.0
	May 1.5	1900. . . . 10.5	1901 . . . .0.5
Borroloola (N. T.)	March 6.0	1899. . . .29.0	1900 . . . .0.5
	February. . .7.4	1896. . . .21.4	1897 . . . .4.7
Charlotte Waters (S. A.) . .	March 0.7	1908 . . . . 5.0	1909. . . .0.0
	January. . . .0.8	1877 . . . . 9.7	1878 . . . .0.0

NATURAL VEGETATION

A really satisfactory map of the natural vegetation of Australia has not yet appeared. It is obvious that such a map would show more clearly than any other nature's response to the varying environments. Perhaps the best map hitherto published is one recently issued by the Commonwealth Forestry Bureau in Canberra,[16] which in turn is based on research by Diels and by the writer.[17] The present map (Fig. 5) is somewhat simplified but

[14] Taylor, Status of the Australian States.

[15] Taylor, Australian Meteorology, Ch. 16.

[16] Vegetation Map of Australia Compiled by Commonwealth Forestry Bureau, after L. Diels and Griffith Taylor [scale, 1 : 20,000,000,] *in* Third British Empire Forestry Conference, Australia and New Zealand, 1928, Commonwealth Handbook, Canberra, n.d., opp. p. 42.

[17] Griffith Taylor: The Australian Environment (Especially As Controlled by Rainfall), *Commonwealth of Australia Advisory Council of Science and Industry Memoir No. 1*, Melbourne, 1918, *passim*.

Vegetationskarte von Australien, 1 : 27,000,000, *in* L. Diels: Pflanzenwelt von West-Australien (in series: Vegetation der Erde, edited by A. Engler and O. Drude), Leipzig, 1906.

differs considerably in the area allotted to the fixed dunes in the west-center of the continent. The writer has devoted a considerable amount of time to a study of the available reports by explorers and is of the opinion that only near the junction of the three states concerned (26° S. and 129° E.) is there a homogeneous area of *hamada* (rocky plateau free from dunes) large enough to

appear on a generalized map. However, it is in southeast Queensland that the Commonwealth map differs chiefly from earlier maps. Here it indicates savana (open grasslands with only scattered trees) reaching right to the coast in almost all the region between Mackay and Bundaberg. This is of course largely a matter of definition.

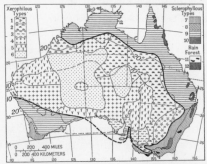

FIG. 5—Natural vegetation. (Sketch map by the author based partly on the maps by Diels and the Commonwealth Forestry Bureau cited in footnotes 16 and 17.) Key to numerals: 1, savana with cypress pine (*Callitris*); 2, savana; 3, mallee (dwarf eucalyptus scrub); 4, mulga (acacia scrub); 5, salt bush steppe; 6, desert (fixed dunes with *Spinifex* and mulga); 7, sclerophyllous forest; 8, sclerophyllous forest, with temperate rain-forest in gullies; 9, savana woodland; 10, high-plateau forest; 11, temperate rain-forest; 12, tropical rain-forest. The heavy line is the major boundary separating the sclerophyllous from the xerophilous types. Lines of mean annual rainfall in inches are dotted.

In the map I have emphasized the chief floral isopleth, viz. the boundary separating sclerophyllous from xerophilous types. It is the line separating the regions more or less covered with eucalyptus from the more arid portions where the acacias are dominant among larger plant forms.

Beginning with true forests, it is by no means generally realized that tropical Australia contains no rain-forests (jungle) large enough to show on the map except from Ingham to Cooktown, with a few smaller patches a little farther north. It is worth emphasizing that the large areas of relatively heavy rainfall (more than 40 inches) in the Cape York Peninsula and the Northern Territory are clothed in the scattered timber known as savana woodland. There is little doubt that during Pleistocene times the tropical rain-forest covered much of the uniform-rain region shown in Figure 4. For instance species of *Flindersia* (leopardwood) are found as far west as Broken Hill. These seem to be survivors of a former rain-forest. The eighty palms so extensively photographed by tourists on the upper Finke basin (west of Alice Springs) are pos-

sibly similar relics. There are no others within several hundred
miles. There are other patches of valuable rain-forest in the warm
temperate region, especially in the northeast of New South Wales.
In cooler temperate regions are analogous jungles where beeches
are perhaps the dominant tree. They occur most largely in Tasmania but are found in Victoria also.

The dense eucalyptus forests occur in the southeast and southwest, where the rainfall is more than 20 inches. The sparser savana
woods characterize the tropical areas with a rainfall of more than
20 inches. The dominant trees are eucalyptus of various species
with *Grevillea, Bauhinia*, etc. None of this latter forest is worth
export, though it is invaluable for local needs. In the southwest
it is of interest to note that a somewhat similar area of savana
woods lies between the 10- and 20-inch isohyets. The greater
reliability of the rain counteracts the heavier rainfall of the northern
littoral—where indeed the evaporation is also very much greater.

As regards all the rest of Australia, it is characterized by savana
(grasslands, indicating marked seasonal rains) or by scrublands,
steppes, and deserts, due to more arid conditions. It is of course
impossible to draw exact boundaries, since the regions merge into
each other. Acacias are ubiquitous—the mulga growing even in
the driest regions (round Lake Eyre) where the rainfall is only
4 inches. In the southeast portion characterized by this xerophilous (drought-resistant) flora is a useful tree, the cypress pine
(*Callitris*). So also along the southern margin of this xerophilous
region are large areas of mallee. This is a dwarf close-set eucalyptus
forming dense thickets some 20 feet high.

Perhaps the chief division in the settled regions is that between
the grasslands and the saltbush. It seems to agree to some extent
with the season of rain. Thus in the northern portion (with summer
rains) Mitchell grass and other grasses are dominant, while saltbush
(*Atriplex*) and bluebush (*Kochia*) are not important. But in the
south the converse is the case, and in certain regions (as north of
the Australian Bight in the Nullarbor Plain) the natural vegetation
consists almost wholly of saltbush. In the western littoral the
mulga region contains much saltbush; while the savana region has
several forms of *Triodia* (or false spinifex) which are eaten by sheep.

Lastly we may consider the great dune areas, which cover over
500,000 square miles. These dunes are usually about 50 feet high
and are very broad. They run more or less east and west and,
since they are now usually fixed by vegetation, seem to indicate

even more arid conditions in the past. Belts of mulga form dense thickets in places, while other scrub trees grow in the hollows. Spinifex (*Triodia*) is also quite common. Large areas of desert waste (the *serir* of the Sahara) are common, while some ground water can usually be obtained in wells, since the rainfall seems to vary from 7 inches in the cooler south to 17 inches in the hot north. This desert environment extends nearly to the Indian Ocean in the northwest. Another large isolated area lies to the east of the overland telegraph line. There are probably fewer than 100 white inhabitants and but few aborigines in these desert areas.

MINERAL RESOURCES

With a few exceptions like Broken Hill, Iron Knob, and Kalgoorlie, metal mining in the long run is perhaps mainly of aid in advertising a country. Few Australian mines[18] have a life beyond thirty years except in the case of coal, and all the coal mines of value are in agricultural country. Among the pioneer belts defined later in this paper, only in the East Queensland region is the pioneer likely to be affected by the development of coal mines. It is of course possible that another "Broken Hill" (with its former population of 30,000) may be discovered in the pre-Mesozoic rocks so widely spread in the pioneer belts. But since probably only about one per cent of the population of Australia dwells in purely metal-mining settlements (excluding Kalgoorlie and Broken Hill) I have not discussed this aspect of pioneering at length.

THE NATURAL REGIONS AND THEIR PROBLEMS

The preceding account of Australia has discussed briefly the major controls that determine present and future settlement. The problems affecting the pioneer may now be determined more precisely. For this purpose it is expedient to subdivide the Commonwealth into a number of more or less homogeneous regions. In Figure 6 about a score of these have been differentiated for the following reasons.

There are three well-marked zones in Australia, an outer *wet* zone, and intermediate *sub-arid* zone, and an inner (or west-central) *arid* zone. Pioneer settlement is primarily concerned with the intermediate zone; but, owing to the sparse settlement in much

[18] Griffith Taylor: Mining and Economic Geology, *in* The Oxford Survey of the British Empire, Vol. 5: Australasia, edited by A. J. Herbertson and O. J. R. Howarth, Oxford, 1914, pp. 216–267.

of the wet zone in Australia, there is still room for more settlers in the wet zone than in the sub-arid "empty" areas. In the writer's opinion there is no likelihood of notable settlement in the large arid region. In the following table A, B_1 and D are subdivisions of the outer wet zone, B_2 is the sub-arid zone, and C is the arid zone. The pioneer belts are B_1 and B_2.

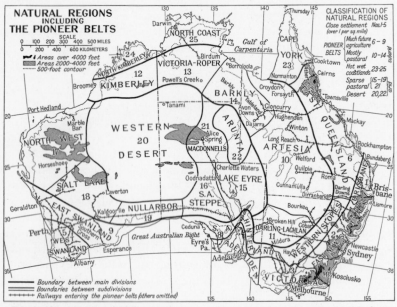

FIG. 6—Natural regions, including those that constitute areas of present and potential pioneer settlement. Scale, 1 : 42,000,000. For physical data relating to each region and for a classification of the regions by climate and by political units, see Table III. Upland areas and 500-foot contour from Orographical Map of Australia, 1 : 4,650,000, Commonwealth Bur. of Meteorol., Melbourne, 1918.

CLOSELY SETTLED REGIONS

I have adopted as a provisional boundary between pioneer belts and adequately settled regions the isopleth of one person to the square mile. Within this region, as stated previously (p. 360), there is settlement that is "socially tolerable and economically efficient," at any rate as far as Australia is concerned. However, since such a density of population is very low and since the writer believes that many millions of future Australians and emigrants will make their homes there, it is proposed to discuss these regions briefly.

In the first place, in this southeastern corner of Australia, topography is a dominant controlling factor, and of hardly any other large area can this be said.[19] The two regions 2 and 3 given in the table below include the two largest cities of Australia. Sydney has more than 1,000,000, and Melbourne nearly 1,000,000 inhab-

TABLE III—CHARACTERISTICS OF THE NATURAL REGIONS OF AUSTRALIA

Zone	Number of Region on Map	Annual Rain in Inches	Annual Temperature F°	Distribution Among the States					
				Q.	N. S. W.	Vic.	S. A.	W. A.	N. T.*
A Moderately close settlement	1	25–60	69	1					
	2	20–50	65		2				
	3	20	58			3			
	4	18	61				4		
	5	20	63					5	
B₁ Wetter zone (agriculture)	6	20–50	70–76	6					
	7	20	65		7				
	8	11	64				8		
	9	12	65					9	
B₂ Sub-arid zone (pastoral)	10	10–25	70–80	10					
	11	12	60–69		11				
	12	20	82					12	
	13	25	82						13
	14	15	80						14
C Arid zone	15	6	67				15		
	16	7	70				16		
	17	8	70–82					17	
	18	9	66					18	
	19	8	63					19	
	20	10	70					20	
	21	10	71						21
	22	8	72						22
D Hot wet coast lands	23	50	80	23					
	24	35	84					24	
	25	50	83						25

(PIONEER BELT label spans the B₁ and B₂ rows)

*Northern Territory is now divided along latitude 20° S. into North Australia and Central Australia.

itants. Hence about one-half of the population of Australia lives in the country shown in the block diagram (Fig. 7). The only well-watered plains in this large area are found in Gippsland, east of Melbourne, and east of the highlands along the middle courses of the Murray, Murrumbidgee, and Lachlan Rivers. These plains receive more than 15 inches of rain, but about 30 per cent

[19] Taylor, Topography of Australia.

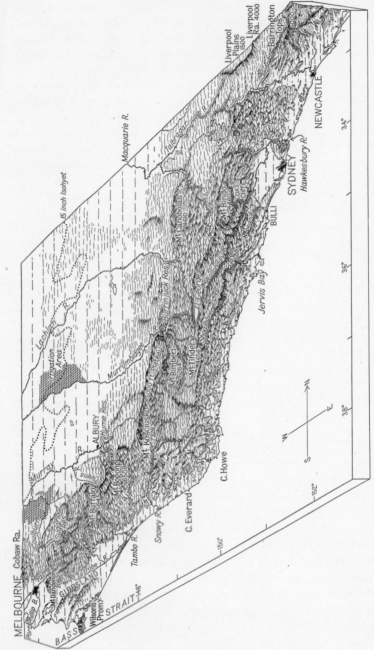

FIG. 7.—Block diagram of the southeastern highlands looking west. (Based on the Sydney, Bodalla, and Melbourne sheets of the International Map of the World, 1 : 1,000,000, and the layer-tint map of New South Wales, 1 : 2,500,000, in the Times Atlas, London, 1922, Pl. 108, the Canberra sheet of the International Map, which covers the area taken from the atlas sheet, not being available at the time.)

of the littoral in New South Wales receiving better rains (e.g. more than 25 inches a year) is too rugged for farming and is still empty after 130 years of settlement. For instance, a great belt of sterile rugged country containing hardly an inhabitant (except where railways cut it) still surrounds the largest city of Australia at a distance of only 50 miles. Obviously a very urgent matter is the adequate contour survey of this most valuable portion of the Commonwealth. This is being carried out at present, and useful maps are being issued in connection with the International Map of the World on the scale of 1:1,000,000. Approximate contours of all the country shown in the diagram are available in this form on the sheets (Sydney, Bodalla, Canberra, and Melbourne) published at Melbourne in 1926–1930 by the Lands and Survey Branch of the Department of Works of the Commonwealth of Australia. It is also the sole region of which any approximate soil maps (by H. I. Jensen) are available.[20]

In this southeast corner are found the chief towns and about 95 per cent of the coal, which occurs chiefly near Newcastle, Bulli, and Morwell (Vic.). It contains the chief dairies, the optimum portion of the wheat belt, and the densest sheep areas. It naturally forms the catchment for the main irrigation schemes. In the diagram the Burrinjuck Reservoir on the middle Murrumbidgee and its irrigated area, some 300 miles down the river, are clearly shown. On the Murray the great Hume Dam is situated just above Albury where the Mitta enters from the south. On the Goulburn (Vic.) is the Sugarloaf Dam, which supplies irrigation areas near the Murray to the northwest.

There is of course no settlement on the bleak Kosciusko Plateau or on the similar Dargo Plateau farther west.[21] It is clear that the topography of Australia, like so many other features of the continent, is arranged to give almost the minimum advantages from the economic point of view.

The northern portion of this closely settled area is of the same type, except that it is considerably warmer. Hence the New England Plateau (with about the same height as the Dargo Plateau in Victoria) is much more favorable for settlement and is largely used for sheep, with some farming. The Queensland portion (around Brisbane) reaches into the sugar belt. The highlands behind Brisbane grow large quantities of wheat, which, however, hardly extends north of the Darling Downs.

[20] H. I. Jensen: Soils of New South Wales, Sydney, 1918.
[21] Taylor, Topography of Australia, pp. 84–85.

The South Australian closely settled region is less rugged, but here again the Flinders Range borders the coast and cuts off rain supplies from the lower Murray. The rainfall is almost wholly in winter—which admirably suits wheat, but means that the pasture has much less value for sheep than in those eastern wheat regions where there is considerable rain in other seasons than winter.

There are much greater possibilities in Western than in South Australia. Although this huge state of nearly 1,000,000 square miles contains about 750,000 square miles of very low economic value, yet the southwest corner (Swanland) is of the same type as the southeast of the continent. It has a heavier rainfall than South Australia and contains valuable forests, which will later give place to close dairy settlement. It would not be unreasonable to class all "Swanland" as a pioneer belt; for, excluding the vicinity of Perth, there are only about 100,000 settlers in the remainder of this large area of fairly well-watered country. In Figure 6 I have indicated that half of Swanland is typical pioneer country, but really only the actual wheat belt (e.g. the more open western part of the "settled" region) is at all closely settled.

THE ARID REGIONS

No geographer will find it difficult to believe that the large area in the center and west of the continent has little to offer the pioneer. Here are two large desert areas without a white settler in more than 500,000 square miles. This is the more remarkable because it has been accessible enough for many decades. The overland telegraph (Adelaide to Darwin) has been maintained since 1872. The Oodnadatta railway has been running since 1891. The East-West railway crosses its southern corner, the Horseshoe and Marble Bar railways reach its western margin. Its northwestern corner nearly reaches the Indian Ocean. Captain Hurley in his recent flight across it describes it as a scene of desolation. We can write it off as of negligible value, except possibly for some ephemeral mining like that at Tanami, Arltunga, etc.

As regards the regions (15–19, 21) of sparse pastoral occupation (which I have been accustomed to refer to as the "sparselands"), their total area, with the deserts (20, 22), is about 1,234,000 square miles. There is a total population of 15,000 settlers,[22] and this has long remained stationary. The Nullarbor region, one of the divi-

---

[22] I exclude such purely mining towns as Kalgoorlie and Broken Hill, which lie right on the boundary of the sparselands.

sions of this arid zone, has a fairly reliable rainfall, but the karst surface handicaps settlement. There are only about 3 per cent of the sheep and 2 per cent of the cattle of the Commonwealth in the huge arid zone (Figs. 9, 10). Any new developments will need vast outlays of capital and will lead to very little addition to the population of Australia. It is of course primarily a question of sinking bores to tap the ground water or of excavating "dams" in clay soils and catching the erratic rainfall. Only in the driest portion, around Lake Eyre—where the fodder is very sparse—is there any large area of proved artesian water. The greater part of the usable sparselands (as distinct from the deserts) has all been leased from the governments, and there is unfortunately no reason to believe that this arid 40 per cent of the Commonwealth will ever be of much importance in the British Empire.

THE HOT COASTLANDS

There is little reason to dwell on these areas. They have no attractions except as ports of entry and contain only three towns, Broome, Darwin, and Thursday Island.[23] A region with an average annual temperature of over 80° F. and with the high wet-bulb shown in Figure 2 can have little attraction for the white settler unless its resources are out of the ordinary. In point of fact the three regions (23–25) are largely formed of an elevated peneplain of sandstone, so that the coasts are rugged and soils poor. Each of the three towns is inhabited chiefly by white government officials and colored folk engaged in pearling or trade. There is practically no productive white settlement, except some hundred miners and perhaps the same number of pastoralists. The writer does not believe that the metalliferous mines so far known will ever lead to noteworthy settlement in the northern coastlands. The iron deposits at Yampi (north of Broome) may be an exception.

PROBLEMS OF THE PIONEER BELTS

The pioneer belts of Australia (Fig. 6) consist of several types of land, which are in general inferior to the closely settled regions but still capable of much greater exploitation, especially in the wetter portions. Probably the rather hot East Queensland Uplands from Cairns to the Darling Downs offer the best inducement to the pioneer. There is a second type comprising the new wheatlands

[23] Griffith Taylor: The Settlement of Tropical Australia, *Geogr. Rev.*, Vol. 8, 1919, pp. 84–115.

on the arid side of the present wheat belt extending from the Darling Downs (Q.) to Eyre's Peninsula (S.A.) and occurring again in the hinterland of Swanland (W.A.). All these areas are more or less capable of agriculture. The third type comprises the main portion of the great Artesian Basin (excluding that round Lake Eyre) and the Darling-Lachlan Plains to the south. This is capable of more intense pastoral occupation, which will lead to considerable settlement. There are also a few valuable irrigation sites on the Lachlan and possibly on the Darling which remain for future development. Lastly there is the belt of cattle country extending from Broome to Cloncurry, where some extension is possible, though it is not likely to lead to much more settlement. If it can be converted in any large degree to sheep country, then its value will be greatly enhanced.

THE AGRICULTURAL PIONEER REGIONS[24]

East Queensland Uplands

Reference to the contours on Figure 6 will show that the Atherton Plateau (some 2500 feet high) is right on the coast at the northern end of this region. It is well watered and is indeed the sole region of that type in tropical Australia. It is still largely covered with fairly heavy forest, but this is giving way to farms. The height reduces the temperature about 7° F., thus making the climate something like that of Brisbane far to the south. It has a great future, for hydro-electric power is available, and such crops as coffee as well as better known subtropical crops grow well. It closely resembles the coffee country of Brazil in environment. Numerous flows of basalt give rise to good soils in many parts.

In East Queensland only along the actual coast is the rainfall over 30 inches in a belt about 30 or 40 miles wide. For the most part this is an embayed and drowned littoral, with low ranges parallel to the coast occupying a good deal of the hinterland. On coastal flats, often due to a slight recent uplift, the tropical jungle has given place to sugar (Fig. 8). This extends in patches all down the littoral from Cairns to Clarence River (N.S.W.). Most districts receiving more than 40 inches contain flourishing sugar-cane plantations. These total about 200,000 acres. In the far north

[24] Griffith Taylor: Agricultural Regions of Australia, *Econ. Geogr.*, Vol. 6, 1930, pp. 109-134 and 213-242, with map, 1:9,000,000.

Italians are tending to outnumber the British, and there is some friction between the two groups. The sugar industry of course exists largely by virtue of the artificial prices paid in Australia for the local produce. About 18,000 acres is given to bananas and pineapples. Obviously this subtropical agriculture can be extended largely as the Commonwealth needs it, but there seems little or no chance of external trade.

Behind the sugar belt is a region where cotton can grow satisfactorily (Fig. 8). At present only between Rockhampton and the Darling Downs is this crop of any note. For some years it made rapid progress with government assistance but declined from 50,000 acres in 1924 to 28,000 acres in 1926. It is a "poor-man's crop" and, like sugar, is also supported by

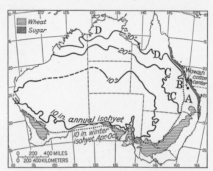

FIG. 8—Chief present agricultural regions. Possible extensions: A, Texas wheat; B, Indian wheat; C, millets; D, cotton. The 20- and 30-inch annual rainfall lines are not drawn east of the 10-inch winter (Apr.-Oct.) isohyet.

government bounties. Wheat is another crop that is grown successfully in the southwest of this region near the Darling Downs. About 150,000 acres are cultivated, but the writer has long pointed out that Texas and Indian wheatlands are homoclimes (similar climates) of the country between the present Queensland wheatlands and the Tropic of Capricorn. The rain is largely summer rain, but here as elsewhere wheat can be grown after the summer rains have fallen. In all the eastern part of this region there is no agriculture, although much of it is a homoclime of parts of Rhodesia and will surely grow millets, kaffir corn, etc., in the future. There is some irrigation commencing in the Dawson valley, where also are valuable coal mines. More coal occurs at Clermont 200 miles northwest of Rockhampton, and small metalliferous deposits are common in the Highlands. There is a coastal railway as far north as Cairns, but only four lines run west across this region to Hughenden, Barcaldine, Roma, and Dirranbandi. This large East Queensland region contains some 200,000 square miles; and in the writer's opinion it offers great inducements to white settlers, though there are of course disabilities due to the hot summers in the northern part.

Western Slopes of New South Wales

This division of the pioneer belt comprises the lowest slopes of the Highlands and in general is about 800 feet above sea level. It consists largely of plains watered by late-mature rivers like the middle Murrumbidgee, the Lachlan, and the upper Macquarie. The center of the wheat belt lies just to the east of the eastern limit of the pioneer belt shown in Figure 6. This region therefore includes the most rapidly changing area of wheat culture. With the spread of dry farming and the development of special breeds of wheat to withstand drought, this western portion of the wheat belt is spreading and producing more bushels to the acre. In the years from 1904 to 1922 the wheat belt has spread from Forbes to Hillston, i.e. right across the present region down the Lachlan River for a distance of 160 miles. In the north of the state the spread to the west has been about 30 miles in the same period. The advance has naturally decreased of late, and the writer does not expect the wheat to spread much beyond the 10-inch winter isohyet shown in Figure 8. As a result of the opening up of new wheatlands in this savana or lightly timbered country, there has been a greater increase of population than in any other part of the state, except perhaps in the subtropical corner (in the northeast) around Lismore. Railways only poorly serve this valuable territory. Seven lines cross it from east to west, e.g. through Moree, Walgett, Coonamble, Nevertire, along the Lachlan, Wyalong, Hay. These lines are about 100 miles apart, so that they by no means constitute a "rail net" (to use Mark Jefferson's term), much less the "rail web" of the completely exploited agricultural regions.

Irrigation is typical in this belt. The Burrinjuck scheme is charted in Figure 7, and the irrigated areas lie in the region under discussion, which has about 15 inches of rain. The farms just west of Narandera support 15,000 people. Much of the first cost has been paid by the government without hope of return, and many soldiers have been settled near the new towns of Griffith and Leeton. About 38,000 acres of fruit, grapes, lucerne, and rice are grown. Further investigation of soils and subsoils is needed before this area can be really satisfactorily settled. A similar scheme on the Lachlan with a large dam at Wyangala has just been approved. The great Hume Dam above Albury on the Murray (see Fig. 7) is being constructed, and many locks and weirs on the same river are approved and will help to develop the southern portion of the region under consideration. Already the cost has amounted to some £5,000,000. There is not much prospect of important irrigation on the smaller rivers. The northern portion is included in the Artesian Basin, which gives water for stock but does not affect agriculture.

Of particular interest is the utilization of the black-soil plains that occupy large areas along the river banks. These are so sticky that they have been cultivated only to a small extent. They tend to dry with very deep cracks but are undoubtedly well suited for maize and other allied crops. The lighter red-soil plains occur at slightly higher levels and are usually easier to work. Obviously a soil survey of all this region is one of the first methods of assisting the pioneer. It is of interest to note how the western wheat limit (see Fig. 8) moves farther from the 10-inch annual rainfall line as one proceeds northward. This western limit is also the boundary between farming and pure pastoral industry, and indeed many farmers in the most arid part of the belt grow wheat on an area one year, feed sheep there the next year, and plow it for fallow the third year. Hence they only obtain a crop once in three years.

Much of this country is rich in minerals, though some of the largest mines like Cobar and Wyalong have become worked out.[25]

South Australian Hinterland

This region has much the same characteristics as the last. Perhaps the chief differences have to do with the rain. It nearly all falls in winter, which suits the wheat plant but does not produce such good natural feed for sheep. Hence the dry boundary of the agricultural region nearly agrees with the outer limit of the arid (or sparse) pastoral lands, and no intermediate region of good stock lands (such as we get in regions 10 and 11) occurs in the south. The northwest corner of Victoria (part of the "Mallee") may be included with South Australia.

The future development of this region is bound up mainly with wheat growing and irrigation. In the so-called "desert" between Adelaide and the Victoria border we find a good example of wrong nomenclature. This region was largely covered with a close-set mallee scrub (of dwarf eucalyptus). The soil was often encumbered with travertine, and there was very little feed for stock. But no geographer, I fancy, would call it "desert," since it has an average

---

[25] Taylor, Mining and Economic Geology, pp. 240–241.

rainfall of 15 inches which is distinctly reliable and a cool climate with low evaporation. I mention this area because a voluminous writer on Australia's resources devotes many pages to an attempt to show that other really arid areas (real deserts) in Australia can be developed as easily. By rolling down the mallee and plowing with superphosphate, economic wheat crops have been grown. Furthermore, by turning in crops of clovers, etc., the soil can be made to produce fodder suitable for sheep rearing.

Hereabouts wheat is grown with a rainfall as low perhaps as anywhere in the world. In the "Upper North" wheat districts of South Australia, an 8-bushel harvest may be secured on a well-distributed 7–8 inch April–November rainfall (*fide* Perkins). Here the total annual rainfall is a little more than 10 inches (Fig. 4). For most of the state a rainfall of 15.5 inches falling between April and October (with 2 inches in the other months) is ideal. Perkins[26] gives the following figures: April-May, 4 inches (seeding rains); June-July, 4.5 inches (winter rains); August-October, 6.0 inches (spring rains); November, 1.0 inch. In this region, only in Eyre's Peninsula is there a rainfall with 17 inches, but here (as in other parts) the farmer is handicapped by salty ground waters in many places. This is a grave disability for his stock, though it does not very directly affect the possible wheat crop. As a consequence the state geologists are carefully investigating the water supply. In the same way the presence of potable waters among many salty bores in the Artesian Basin of the Victorian mallee has determined settlement among the sand hills near Ouyen.

A good deal of irrigation is developing along the lower Murray by pumping water onto rich river flats. At Mildura and Renmark there are 6100 and 4800 settlers respectively, while many smaller settlements occur farther down the river. Communications are better in the eastern part of this region than in the west, for there are a number of lines running north to the Murray. To the northwest of the big river the railways are less frequent. A good deal of this country, however, is rocky, especially in the Flinders and Gawler Ranges.

East Swanland

This large region extends from Geraldton to Esperance and has an area about equal to Victoria. Although the rainfall is low

[26] A. J. Perkins: Report . . . Concerning Climatic Conditions Affecting Wheat Growing in South Australia, *Rept. 17th Meeting Australasian Assn. for the Advancement of Sci.*, *Adelaide Meeting, Aug. 1924*, Adelaide, 1926, pp. 122–137.

(from 10 to 15 inches) it is the most reliable in Australia, and for this reason there are perhaps larger trees here than one would find elsewhere with such a small rainfall. The general rain régime is very like that discussed under South Australia. The 10-inch winter isohyet is not far from the annual 10-inch isohyet (Fig. 8), so that the region is suited for wheat. Indeed this part of Australia has made more progress recently than any other,[27] as the following table shows.

TABLE IV—AREAS UNDER WHEAT IN AUSTRALIA

(millions of acres)

	N. S. W.	VIC.	Q.	S. A.	W. A.	TOTAL
1916–1917 . .	3.3.	3.1	0.2	2.8	1.6	11.5
1926–1927 . .	3.3	2.9	0.1	2.7	2.6	11.7

Around Kellerberrin wheat is grown satisfactorily with a total rainfall of 13 inches. Some wheat is grown nearer Southern Cross, where the rainfall is only 10 inches, but the main crop lies in wetter country to the west. The densest wheat grows to the east of Northam. There is a remarkably empty region between this flourishing wheat district and Esperance, where also the climate is excellent for wheat, though no wheat so far is grown. Clarke describes the country as an upraised peneplain formed of Precambrian rocks.[28] In the south mallee thickets are abundant, and in general the soil is fairly fertile. The predominant trees are eucalypts, Salmon gum in the east and Wandoo gum in the west. The Wandoo region unfortunately is the chief "poison" country in the state, for such plants as *Gastrolobium* and *Oxylobium* are common. These are injurious to stock, and so this country has not yet been occupied. Another drawback, especially in the southeast, is the saltness of the ground water. Hence, in addition to a consideration of the total supply, season, and reliability of the rain, the farmer in these areas has to keep in mind the nature of the ground water and of the feed for his stock.

The absence of railways is a great disability in this region of East Swanland. But no state has pushed on with construction more rapidly than has Western Australia in the adjacent wheat area of West Swanland, where lines run to the east only about 40 miles apart. As shown on the map (Fig. 6) there are two lines running

[27] Taylor, Status of the Australian States.

[28] E. deC. Clarke: Natural Regions in Western Australia, *Journ. Royal Soc. of Western Australia*, Vol. 12, 1925–1926, pp. 117–132.

north and the main transcontinental railway running east across the pioneer belt. From Esperance in the southeast is a short railway that will soon link up with the mining railway from Kalgoorlie to Norseman. There are, however, many salt lakes in this last district, which seem to indicate unfavorable soils.

The Pastoral Pioneer Regions

No fact is more important than that pastoral occupation can support only a relatively meager population. This seems to be particularly true in temperate Australia, where the borders of the agricultural regions have been more or less occupied for a number of years. Australian dry farming seems indeed to occur in hotter and drier lands than, for instance, in the United States. Hence the term "pioneer belt" has a different meaning in these last five divisions from that indicated in the preceding more or less agricultural divisions. In these regions, extending (Fig. 6) from Morgan on the lower Murray in a broad zone round to Broome (W. A.), lies an area whose total population is very meager, about 75,000 in New South Wales, 50,000 in Queensland, 20,000 in South Australia, 1000 in the Northern Territory, and 2000 in Kimberley. Thus this large sub-arid pastoral pioneer belt contains only 2 per cent of the Australian population. In the future this percentage can only become smaller.

The whole problem of pastoral settlement is wrapped up in water supply just as definitely as in the wetter zones. This water may be obtained from three sources. There is firstly the normal rainfall, which in many areas is conserved in large "dams." One typical example is the sheep station of Mutooroo (S. A.) near Broken Hill. This has only 7 inches of rainfall (and is therefore just outside our region) and no springs or creeks. But by spending £100,000, chiefly in excavating "dams," the stations can carry 33 sheep to the square mile, feeding chiefly on saltbush (*Atriplex*). Such outlay is not possible to the pioneer. Secondly, in a considerable portion of the belt there is artesian water. Thirdly, in almost all of it there is normal ground water met with at depths varying from 30 to 300 feet below the surface.[29]

The stock grazed may be either sheep or cattle. In Australia the rough country on the drier side is usually used by cattle. In the south sheep are grazed wherever possible, partly because the

[29] Taylor, Environment and Race.

wool market is much more active than that for beef and partly because Argentina seems able to surpass Australia in most features of the beef trade. But in the hot north sheep do not thrive, and this is the stronghold of the beef cattle.

Darling-Lachlan Region

This is an area of rich soils deposited in a shallow geosyncline but handicapped by a poor and rather unreliable rainfall. Much of it is saltbush country. It is excellent for merino sheep, although the density is much lower than in the wheat belt and intervening districts. The frontages along the Darling River were taken up as early as 1860, and there has been no important unleased grazing land available for many a decade. Since the number of sheep in the state is less now than in 1891, it is obvious that the growth of the sheep industry is not rapid. Improvement in stock rather than increase in numbers is aimed at. The larger sheep stations have all been cut up in recent years, while subdividing into smaller paddocks is general. The rabbit pest, which spread like a blight through the region in the nineties, is now practically under control. King Drought is the chief enemy of the pastoralist—and he is combated by shifting the flocks to distant regions where feed is good. This is usually done by train, but of recent years large motor trolleys have been found of service to save starving sheep.

Only one railway—that to Broken Hill—crosses the region. It is difficult for the scientific mind to understand the folly of politicians spending millions on desert railways like the north-south "white elephant," while railways are so badly needed in the pioneer belts. One hopes that some day the public will listen to the geographer rather than to the booster and political partisan.

Valuable work on the regeneration of the native fodder plants has been carried out near Broken Hill under the guidance of Professor T. G. Osborne. What is needed more than anything else is adequate economic surveys, vegetation surveys, soil and water surveys in the sheep and cattle regions; but very little has been done yet except as regards artesian water. Furthermore, no research can be more valuable than that dealing with the forecasting of drought in these regions.[30]

[30] Griffith Taylor: Climatic Relations between Antarctica and Australia, *in* Problems of Polar Research: A Series of Papers by Thirty-one Authors, *Amer. Geogr. Soc. Special Publ. No. 7*, New York, 1928, pp. 285–299.

Artesia

This area comprises most of the great Artesian Basin except that portion included in the Lake Eyre region (see Fig. 6). There is no agriculture except for small gardens attached to the head stations. These are often irrigated from artesian bores, but one cannot deduce that artesian water can be used on a large scale for agriculture. In the first place the water is always somewhat salty and can generally be used only for a time on the same land. Secondly the artesian water is limited in amount and is not more than is required for the needs of the stock. At the same time in the east of this region it seems likely that some Sudan crops will flourish, for Lake Chad has a similar rain fall and summer temperature, though it is much hotter in winter.

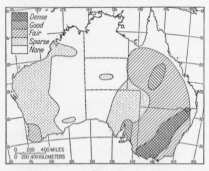

FIG. 9

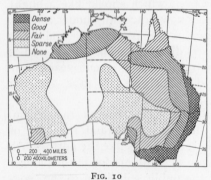

FIG. 10

FIGS. 9–10—Present distribution of sheep (above) and cattle.

The topography consists of vast plains crossed only by insignificant divides between the rivers flowing to the southwest. The soils are largely alluvial, filling in the slight Tertiary hollow of east-central Australia.[31] It is unfortunate as regards agriculture in eastern Australia that the depressions should be arid, while the rugged highlands are well watered. The natural vegetation is savana throughout, and Mitchell grass (*Astrebla*) is a valuable fodder in the northern portion. Thickets of various acacias, such as brigalow, are abundant, especially along the intermittent creeks. In the south where the winter rains are commoner, saltbush is prevalent. As usual, sheep are universal where feed is good, though cattle replace sheep in the hot north and in part in the arid

[31] Taylor, Status of the Australian States.

west. Longreach is especially a center of a great sheep district,
and hereabouts, when any grazing land is made available (by the
government), it is usually allotted by ballot and many hundred
applicants enter.

The outstanding feature of the country is the artesian water
supply, for this is the largest artesian basin in the world.[32] The
total area is about 570,000 square miles, but about one-third of
this lies in the more arid region here
termed the Lake Eyre region.

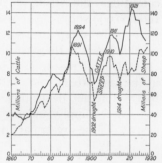

In Queensland in 1880 there were
about 10,000,000 stock. In 1913 there
were 24,000,000, and this increase is
largely due to the supply of artesian
water. Drought years led to sinking
for underground water both here and
in New South Wales. In 1887 the first
deep water supply in Queensland was
obtained at Thurulgoona (near Cun-
namulla). Today there are in the
three states 4577 bores. In Queensland nearly all these are privately
owned, and, of a total of 4000 bores,
about 1000 have been abandoned,
about 1360 are flowing, while about 1776 are subartesian. This

FIG. 11—Growth of the cattle and
sheep industry, 1860–1929. (Based
on graph in *Commonwealth of Australia Year Book No. 20* (for 1927),
p. 625, and statistics for 1926–1929 in
ibid., No. 23 (for 1930), pp. 456 and
459.)

latter term means that the water is derived from a true artesian
basin, but the outflow has been so large that the water level in the
bores has sunk below the surface. Thus, subartesian water is not
to be confused with ordinary ground water obtained in wells,
such as are common in the Barkly Tableland.

The deepest bore, near Blackall in central Queensland, is 7009
feet deep. The largest flow is 1,500,000 gallons a day, from Angle-
dool Bore on the northern border of New South Wales. The
water varies in salinity and becomes more salty in the deeper
western portion of the basin. From 10 to 20 grains of sodium
carbonate to the gallon is usual.

The water is run from the bores into shallow trenches which
often extend for 10 miles across the plains and may be led into
gullies or into water holes. Unfortunately there is a steady diminu-
tion in the flow of many bores. Thus near Moree (N.S.W.) there
was a decrease of 4.7 per cent and near Coonamble of 8.9 per cent

[32] Griffith Taylor: Australia, Physiographic and Economic, 5th edit., Oxford, 1928.

in five years, while in parts of Queensland a decrease of 40 per cent
has been recorded in 15 years. In part this is due to corrosion of
the iron casing, so that the water leaks into porous strata. The
whole matter is being investigated by an artesian commission,
which advises rigid economy in the use of bore waters.

From the graph (Fig. 11) we can see that the pastoral industry
has not grown much since the early nineties but that under present
conditions the stock of Australia (some 12,000,000 cattle and
100,000,000 sheep) have reached a fairly stable condition.[33] There
were more sheep in 1891, and overstocking in part led to the
terrible losses in the great drought of 1902. The next great drought
(1914) found pastoralists better prepared. Cattle have increased
in the last fifteen years but almost wholly in the Northern Territory. Further developments in sheep raising depend largely on
the water supply and on the study of plant, insect, and animal
pests. These are in part discussed in the next section.

Barkly Region

This region consists of a littoral rising gradually to 900 feet
and thence forming fairly level uplands to which the term "tableland" has been erroneously applied. The sole settlement consists of very large cattle or sheep stations. Large areas are necessary, as may be gathered from the amount of land it takes to support
one new settler. Near Camooweal this is stated to comprise about
ten square miles. There is very little surface water in the large
area, but ground water can usually be reached about 200 feet down.
The cost of boring and equipping such a well, however, is more than
£1000. This water will serve cattle within a radius of ten miles
and sheep within five miles. Hence there is no place here for the
pioneer unless he is supplied with several thousand pounds capital.
Development is largely concerned with the substitution of sheep
for cattle, but there are no sheep at present in the Northern Territory (Fig. 9), though Avon Downs carried about 18,000 a few years
ago. Transport difficulties, shearing disabilities, tough or spiny
grasses, lack of shade—all contribute to the difficulties of the sheep
grazier. The hardier cattle are free from many of these disabilities,
but practically no cattle station in the last three regions considered
is paying its way at present. An excellent discussion of the problems of the grazier, illustrated by practical maps, is given by Wynne

[33] *Commonwealth of Australia Year Book No. 20*, Melbourne, 1927, Ch. 16.

Williams.[34] He states that the 20-inch isohyet separates the sour northern grasses from the sweeter grasses of the drier country. There are about 3000 head of cattle near each of the 130 bores. Williams thinks that the drier part of the region may in the future carry one sheep to four acres, which would give 3,000,000 sheep in the elongated suitable tract from Powell's Creek to Boulia.

There is of course no railway through this region, though it is the natural line of entry from the populous southeast to the Northern Territory. For a dozen years the writer has been stressing the overwhelming advantages of this route as compared with that through the central arid country. As regards total amount, seasonal distribution, and reliability of rain; soil, natural vegetation, accessibility, numbers of cattle and sheep, attractions to passengers landing at Darwin—in all of these factors the Barkly route is superior.[35] Yet the Commonwealth has completed the central railway to Alice Springs (for the benefit of a mere 500 settlers in the Macdonnell Ranges), apparently in deference to the prejudices of South Australian politicians.

Victoria-Roper Region

This also is a country devoted wholly to cattle. The rainfall is a little greater and a little more reliable than in the Barkly region. Possibly also the soil is more satisfactory. However, Jensen has studied the soil in this region and states that there is not sufficient water for irrigation and that it would not be a feasible undertaking, since the soil would very soon be rendered too alkaline to produce anything.[36] However, it is possible that small patches of cotton or tobacco could be produced in favorable regions. Nothing can be done in this matter, however, until the better lands of the east are adequately exploited—so that any possible agriculture is a matter of the distant future.

Some of the largest cattle holdings in the world are found in the Victoria River basin, where the Bovril Company has about 10,000 square miles. Originally the cattle were sent to Vestey's meat works at Darwin. This practice, however, has been temporarily abandoned, apparently largely owing to labor troubles as well as to the slump in beef prices. There are no railways in this region,

[34] W. Wynne Williams: The Barkly Tableland of North Australia, *Geogr. Journ.*, Vol. 71, 1928, pp. 61–73.

[35] Taylor, Environment and Race, pp. 284–289.

[36] H. I. Jensen: Tropical Settlement, Brisbane, 1920.

or in the adjacent Kimberley region, in which conditions are similar. While neither of these regions is fully exploited, it should be obvious that they offer fields for wealthy pioneer settlement companies and hold out no inducements to individuals.

Kimberley Region

The writer has separated the southern savana country from the rugged northern portion of the Kimberley area. The latter is hotter and wetter and in the writer's opinion has very little to attract the pioneer, though Easton thinks the forage for stock is better in the north than in the Fitzroy savanas. The extensive alluvials along the Fitzroy River grow abundant grass for cattle; they constitute the chief cattle area in Western Australia. To the south these savanas merge into "pindan" country. This is a scrubby mixture of small eucalypts and other trees (with a little grass) growing in rather reddish soils. This again merges into the sand-ridge desert. Usually there are sufficient water holes or billabongs in the valleys to serve cattle. Some sporadic agriculture near the river may ultimately be possible, though the rainfall of 20 inches is too small for noteworthy crops. An artesian basin extends eastward from Broome, though no bores have been put down, except in Broome, to test its extent. It seems likely that fisheries for food as well as for pearls may become quite important off Kimberley in the future, judging by the results of the Wylie expedition (see the *Australian Geographer*, August, 1928).

SUMMARY

Australia may be divided into twenty-five natural regions, which are classed in five zones. Of these twenty-five there are four in the southeast and one in the southwest which are to be included in the zone of "moderately close settlement." These regions are excluded from the typical pioneer belts. There are also two other zones, the arid zone and the hot wet coastlands (including eight and three regions respectively) that do not properly belong to the pioneer belts, since there is little prospect of notable pioneer development occurring therein. There remain two zones that offer considerable inducements to the pioneer. The first of these is the *wetter pioneer belt* with five regions, where much agricultural development is possible. It extends down the east Queensland coast and thence to the south behind the eastern region of close settlement. In the north the subtropical crops will be largely extended, e.g. sugar and cotton on the coast, millets and maize in the drier inland regions. In the south is the arid wheat belt, where also sheep will doubtless become more numerous as greater development of the sheep "stations" takes place. In Western Australia is a similar hinterland where, however, salty ground water and poisonous native plants in some portions are difficulties to be overcome. Nevertheless, on the whole, the zone with its generally attractive climate is one of the most promising relatively empty portions of the British Empire. Secondly, in the *sub-arid zone*, pioneer settlement of a pastoral nature is possible, but no great addition to the population of Australia is likely in this region except in a few irrigation centers in the extreme east. It is rather an area to be developed by private or chartered companies. As the rest of Australia fills up it is possible that a little cotton or other crops akin to those of the drier Sudan may be grown in this sub-arid zone.[37]

[37] Taylor, Australia, Physiographic and Economic.

HISTORY OF THE PIONEER FRINGES IN AUSTRALIA

STEPHEN H. ROBERTS

TO the geographical historian the story of Australia's development has been one of the continual pushing forward of the fringe of settlement—a struggle with a difficult nature, now flowing on under the influence of a usually exaggerated optimism and now ebbing back before some sharp manifestation of antagonistic natural forces. The ebb and flow were always there, the difficulties of environment and seasons always felt; and yet, after all, the dominant note was in the gradual extension of settlement (Fig. 1).

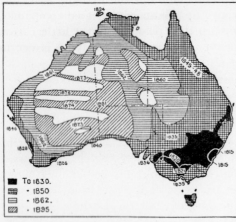

FIG. 1—Progressive exploration and settlement of Australia. Scale, 1 : 68,000,000. (All figures are by the author's brother, F. H. Roberts, and are reproduced from the author's work cited in footnote 1.)

THE STAGE OF COASTAL SETTLEMENT

In the first period occupation was limited to the coast. Then, and for long after, Australia was viewed as a saucer, of which only part of the outer rim was habitable. One lieutenant governor predicted that more than a century would elapse before a blade of wheat was grown, another official of the First Fleet spoke of the land as "so forbidding and hateful as only to merit execration and curses." Settlement was therefore limited to a narrow zone around Sydney. Farms slowly went to the Hawkesbury, then horned stock crossed the Blue Mountains, and, by the end of the twenties of the nineteenth century, with the northern extension to the Hunter River flats and the southern sweep from Bathurst through Argyle and Murray to the sea, the Nineteen Counties set the limits. But that was all. From that time until the dawn of free selection these counties were the officially ordained limits beyond which lands could not be sold and within which all settlement was supposed to be confined.[1]

THE SQUATTING STAGE (MOVE TO THE INTERIOR)

But no rigid frontier laid down in a surveyor's office could conflict with a pioneer belt decreed by nature; and so the stockmen crossed the official limits and, defying officials and blacks and the climate, overran Australia to the outmost fringe of habitability. Such pioneers, who "squatted" where they would, became known as "squatters"—quite a different set of people from their American namesakes. Any grazier on crown lands, rich or poor, was a squatter. When the colony swept into the flood tide of squatting about 1836, the outside men were on the Murrumbidgee in the south and the Macleay in the north; but Australia had no other settlements beyond a coastal embryo around Perth and the quite new posts of Adelaide, Portland, and Melbourne. At this point, with the rise of the unauthorized stockmen, the squatting stage began— in a word, settlement moved from the coast to the interior.[2] The spread of the flocks to the geographical limits had the effect of bringing settlement to the utmost pioneer fringes and started in earnest the struggle with nature. In the late thirties the sheep flowed from the Murrumbidgee to Port Phillip and all over modern Victoria to the verge of the Mallee and Gippsland; and, at the other extreme, the herds left the Macleay for the Darling Downs and even threatened the Burnett. By the end of the forties all the best lands in Australia had gone: Victoria had yielded even its farthest mountain recess or *dumosa* plain; New South Wales was covered out to Menindee and Bourke on the sprawling Darling; the southeastern corner of Queensland was settled to the Burnett; South Australia had grown to Mount Remarkable; and only the west was quiescent. Free laborers and squatting revolutionized the prospects of the land: now came the gold discoveries (1851) and the immigration of small men to usher in the farming period. From 1861, then—from the commencement of free selection—there were two kinds of pioneer fringes, squatting and farming, the one

[1] For full details of every stage of this growth see S. H. Roberts: History of Australian Land Settlement (1788-1920), Melbourne, 1924, especially the footnotes and the bibliography.

[2] This period is extensively dealt with in S. H. Roberts: The Squatting Age in Australia, Melbourne Univ. Press, 1929, especially Ch. 6. See also *idem*, History of Australian Land Settlement, Part III.

concerned mainly with natural difficulties and the other partly affected by environmental conditions but mostly dependent on facilities afforded by governments.

THE PASTORAL PIONEER FRINGES

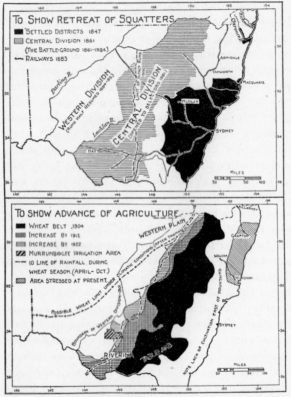

The pastoral aspect may be easily disposed of. With the coming of a large urban and farming influx, the pioneer squatter had to be forced back. Australia, therefore, knew a long struggle when the stockmen who had occupied the land, first on no tenure at all and then by leases, attempted to seize as much as they could in the good regions. According to the degree of their success or failure in this attempt they remained in the good inner lands or were pushed back to the less hospitable parts of the interior.

FIG. 2—The advance of the pioneer fringe in New South Wales, 1847–1922, illustrating the recession of the grazing belt occupied by the "squatter" stockmen (upper figure) as a result of the westward movement of agricultural settlement. Scale, 1 : 20,000,000.

In New South Wales, for example, a constant struggle was fought for the central district (Fig. 2), though simultaneously, to guard their rear, the squatters attempted to stock the Far West—the mulga and saltbush lands, where the sand storm was king. They were soon in touch with the edge of the desert, for the Murray and

Murrumbidgee lands had gone in the forties, and even the Darling to Menindee. Hence, although the first steam paddle boat going up to Canally obviated the 800-mile trip overland in drays, the occupation had to pause, and only a few huge runs could be dotted over the bad country. Victoria was worse off, for there the occupation had gone as far as possible. Indeed, the nature of the country provided insurmountable obstacles in every province except Queensland. South Australia, for instance, was at the edge of the stony desert, and not even the boom of the gold fields could alter this fact. The area occupied might treble in 1853, and people might prate of the new land north of Mount Remarkable: but no one could for long deny the sunburnt, rocky interior. Similarly, in Western Australia the great majority of the lands were useless, and the colony stood still, except for isolated ventures like the stocking of the Murchison and Gascoyne in the fifties. Not till the eighties were the Kimberleys infringed on, and no forward move at all could be discerned. In Queensland, however, the bourn of the squatters of this period, conditions were more hopeful. The sixties saw the boom of the fabled "North Countree," and the streams went out in two directions. North they ran, from the vantage post of 1850 on the Burnett to the Fitzroy, then the Burdekin (1860), and even to the Flinders and the tip of Cape York Peninsula. Still more, the west was favored, especially after the hegira of 1864, and here the rush was romantically tumultuous. The wagons creaked from the Warrego and the Maranoa to the head of the Flinders, the far-flung Barcoo, and right on to Isis Downs, where later the Northern Territory started.

The pioneer fringe of this time was the elastic stop of the last wagon; and every twinkling camp fire, every blue-smoke signal of the receding blacks, marked its forward move. But, this advance over, only the interior desert and the Northern Territory, mysterious and unknown, remained: and, henceforth, the emphasis was not so much on expansion as on consolidating the results achieved and coming to some understanding with the newer race of farming selectors.

The Farming Pioneer Fringes (Selection to 1884)

If the moving wall of pastoral occupation marked the outermost pioneer fringe, there was no less an inner one after 1861—that of the farmer. The Robertson Act of 1861 in New South Wales, by introducing free selection (Fig. 3), marked the dawn of the agricultural revolution in Australia. Hitherto farming had been

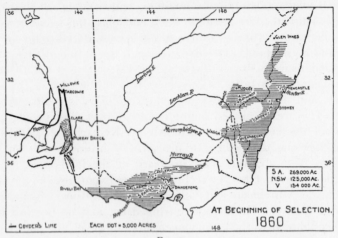

FIG. 3

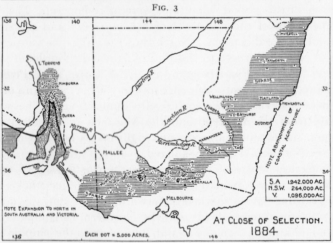

FIG. 4

FIGS. 3–5—Development of wheat lands in New South Wales, Victoria, and South Australia, 1860–1919. Scale of Figures 3 and 4, 1 : 20,000,000; of Figure 5, 1 : 26,-000,000. In Figures 3 and 4 the ruled areas represent the wheat belt. The actual distribution and amount of wheat grown is shown by dots on all three figures, each dot representing 5000 acres. In Figures 3 and 4 Goyder's line, representing the northern limit of the area in South Australia in which agriculture could be carried on successfully by the farming methods in use until the 1890's, is shown as a heavy line.

strangely neglected, so much so that there had been grain imports even in the forties, but now the stage was set for the greatest conflict the continent has had—between the oncoming farmers, who were numerically in the majority, and the receding squatters, who were the first occupiers and who, moreover, still provide the country's staple. Thus, the free-selection laws, though aiding small farmers, by means of their abuse also resulted in much land going to the squatters in freehold. Of the 20,000,000 acres alienated by this

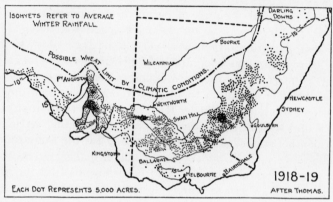

FIG. 5—(For explanation see legend under Figures 3–4.)

means in New South Wales before 1883, for instance, it is difficult to say how much really aided settlement. What is certain is that these years, in all states alike, created perhaps the greatest problem of the future: the best land went to the squatters in perpetuity, so that the newcoming farmers have to pass over the good inner lands that are insufficiently developed and go to the less attractive out-skirts, like the Mallee. Three-quarters of the Riverina went in this way in a few years of the eighties; and, in general, this central period may be called that in which the natural pioneer fringe for the farmers was replaced by an artificial one, farther out, where the struggle was harder.[3]

Though New South Wales suffered most, Victoria, too, lost her western and middle-northern districts (Fig. 6). But, because selec-tion was safeguarded there, especially under the 1869 act, more real settlement took place. Gippsland and the northwest were settled by farmers in the years before 1878, and townships were dotted through these new belts. Cultivation and population increased with selection, so firmly, indeed, that the drought and crisis of the late seventies could be withstood. Queensland did not know

[3] For the evils see Roberts, Land Settlement, pp. 228 et seq.

this struggle, except in the southeastern corner, the Darling Downs, because wheat was possible only in the south and the nature of the country militated against small settlement: hence, the emphasis came to be on small squatters who combined agriculture and pasture and thus erected a new pioneer fringe of their own, that of the aptly named "grazing farmers."

By way of contrast with the eastern states, South Australian conditions provided a simple experiment in pioneer fringes, one in which the stress was all on the natural environment. There, the geographical limitation was very real: the colony's whole history centered on one geographical fact, Goyder's line of rainfall (Figs. 3–4), marking the northern bound of agricultural settlement. Running from Swan Reach to Mount Remarkable, then down to Broughton and up to the Gawler Ranges, this line was astonishingly accurate and was, in effect, an iron band constricting settlement. All of the other states had virgin lands ready for the taking; South Australia alone had a Goyder's line, and, to make matters worse, 60 per cent of the farming land had been alienated by the fifties. Yet the colony has been strikingly agricultural since its first settlement. In 1864, for instance, it grew five times as much wheat per head of population as the others, and ever since 1850 a regular and consolidated advance had been its most striking feature. At times this took the form of an unreasoning boom—in the seventies, for example, when an artificial pioneer fringe (surely one of the most interesting in Australian history!) was set up outside of the wise rain limit. Settlement after 1872 outgrew Goyder's line, especially at the time of Boucaut's forward policy of public works. In 1867 there were no farmers in the north, but the good seasons enticed them on over the sheepwalks of the Burra and the Clare and right up to the Minburra Plains; and the Far West and the southeast were occupied. The doctrine that "rain followed the plow" was in the ascendant, and all believed that a pioneer fringe was an artificial creation. But the grass was a wraith, bred of summer rains and heavy dews, and the rain seemed to have no causal relationship with plows. "Goyder's ghost seems to hover about in the north," said a shrewd German, and the droughts of the eighties pointed the moral; so that the farmers retreated inwards, the new pioneer belt disappeared, and there was no permanent result beyond a striking object lesson and the destruction of many good runs to make bad farms.[4]

[4] Roberts, Land Settlement, Ch. 22, especially pp. 260 *et seq.*

A somewhat similar condition to this obtained in Western Australia, where only the southwest was fit for grain; but the colony was so lethargic until the nineties that this did not matter. Only 58,000 acres were cropped by 1883; free selection had failed; and only the squatters stood aside from the common stagnation.

The Crucial Changes of 1884

Matters stood thus in the middle eighties, when the changes that had been emerging became so obvious that Australia in general entered into quite a new period. The period of the squatters' monopoly had changed to that of the fight with the farmers; now, in turn, this latter merged in the period that still holds—of closer

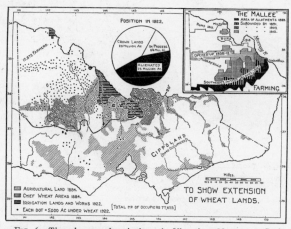

Fig. 6—The advance of agriculture in Victoria, 1884–1922. Scale, 1 : 12,000,000. The progressive occupation of land, 1883–1915, in the Mallee of the northwestern part of the state is shown in the inset.

settlement. The premises in each case had changed, and methods and emphases had to follow suit. The position of every class was metamorphosed.

The squatter, for his part, was forced to transform his methods in every direction. In the sixties the runs were fenced and boundary-riders first appeared; in the next decade freehold entered the squatting world. As a result grazing became more capitalistic, profits dwindled, and lesser men were squeezed out. Previously, 25,000 or 30,000 sheep had made a large squatter; but these holdings could not compare with the huge holdings at the end of the century. At the same time, emphasis had left the fine-wool sheep for the coarser Cheviots, Leicesters, and the much-abused American merinos. Stout combing wool was now in demand, and graziers turned to crossbreeds for their combination of carcass and wool; all of these changes spelled a move outwards to the less rich country.

Nor had the position of the farmer remained unchanged. In 1860 the only agriculture was on the Downs, in central Tasmania, and near Adelaide; but by 1884 farmers had gone to the edge of the South Australian and Victorian Mallee. They had risen to predominance, and hereafter there was a marked consensus of opinion that the stockman had to go to the rougher back country and yield the good land to the small farmer—the "cockatoo" or "cocky" of Australian legend. In a word, the age of closer settlement had come and, with this, a more intensive study of the pioneer fringes.[5]

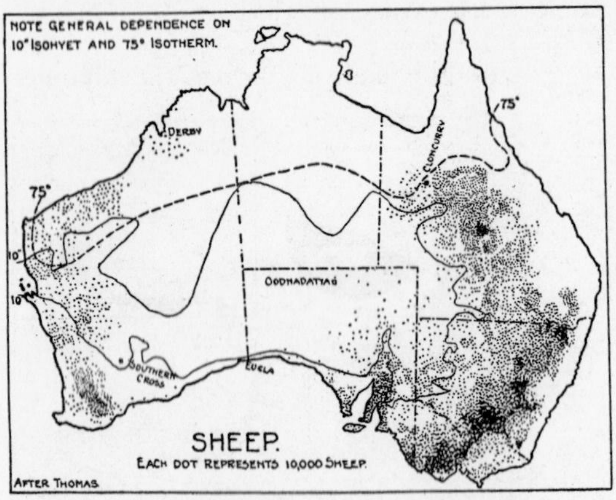

FIG. 7—Present distribution of sheep in Australia. Scale, 1 : 62,000,000. Each dot represents 10,000 sheep. Compare with Figure 9, p. 386, in preceding article.

PIONEER FRINGES IN THE PERIOD OF CLOSER SETTLEMENT

Since then the bifurcation between the squatting and farming pioneer fringes has been much more clearly marked, because now the major issues were solved. The squatters were frankly facing a catastrophe. They were tolerated only in the two outside divisions of New South Wales, and there the mortgaging banks, the kangaroos, the bandicoots, and the rabbits had won. In 1894 there was "barely a ray of hope in the situation," and they were beyond Dubbo in Sturt's heartless desert, the land of rabbits and sand storms, where homesteads were palisaded and buggies could drive over high stockyards. In the nineties the last blows of high rentals and the fall of wool to 8½ pence a pound withdrew these regions from the designation of pioneer fringes and labeled them desolation; and, by 1900, the sheep had dwindled from 16,000,000 to 5,000,000, six million acres had been abandoned, pastoral properties had depreciated from 50 to 80 per cent, and the rabbits were insidiously pushing east. Then came the unprecedentedly severe drought of 1901, and it appeared as if *finis* had been written on the tale of yet another pioneer belt.

[5] Roberts, Land Settlement, Ch. 25.

Somewhat similar events took place in the other colonies. Victoria has had no real squatters since 1884 but only large freehold estates, left idle with sheep in the face of starving agriculture. Interest, therefore, has centered on Queensland and South Australia. The former still remains the country of the large squatter, despite the Labor Government's emphasis on the tableland for smaller settlement. The nineties, here too, saw the crisis of droughts and floods, and occupation stood still. The smaller grazing leases in the west failed to survive the stress, and natural conditions implacably demanded larger men. The program of 1902 was therefore dual—the Burnett for agriculture, with the west

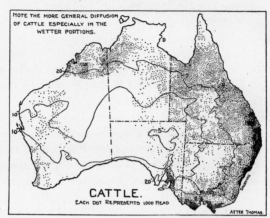

NOTE THE MORE GENERAL DIFFUSION OF CATTLE ESPECIALLY IN THE WETTER PORTIONS.

CATTLE.
EACH DOT REPRESENTS 1000 HEAD
AFTER THOMAS

FIG. 8—Present distribution of cattle in Australia. Scale, 1 : 62,000,000. Each dot represents 1000 head. Compare with Figure 10, p. 386, in preceding article.

and the Gulf of Carpentaria region freed for the squatters. Under such conditions, the graziers gradually recovered, though now there remains the newer menace of the labor demand for subdivision and higher rentals, together with the recurrent emphasis on the tableland. It is the age-old struggle between artificial desires and natural conditions in a pioneer fringe: but such torn interests cannot take away from the hopefulness of Queensland's position. Only six per cent of the land is alienated, and the turn to such new zones as the Burnett depends only on communications and to an even lesser degree, it would appear, on climatic limitations.[6]

This optimism found little reflection in South Australia, where the bill of the eighties had to be met. The squatters had paid too much for their runs at auction, and the result was the paralysis of the nineties. By 1896, 30,000 square miles were abandoned, and no one would look at land, even on the most liberal terms. As against this, however, one fact now stood out: what had been called "exhibitions of squatterphobia" belonged to the past, for

[6] *Ibid.*, pp. 301 *et seq.*

it was seen that it was a national calamity if the stock were driven in from the Gawler Ranges or the Barcoo. The nineties had proved that. But this new orientation seemed too late for the squatters, who had swirled down in the early years of this century to the lowest stage they had yet reached.[7] As a whole, therefore, Australian occupation has been forced back in the forty years since 1890, and now the land has only 75 per cent of the sheep it mustered in 1891—the most striking commentary on the nature of Australia's pioneer fringes, in a pastoral sense!

From the agricultural side, the story is far different. Here, the tone is optimistically progressive, especially in New South Wales and Victoria—the wheat belt (Fig. 5). In the former, homesteads have erected a new pioneer fringe in the east and center (10,000,000 acres had gone by 1911 under the 1894 act!); and lands hitherto useless, like the Pilliga scrub and the famous Dorrigo, have been assailed. In recent years there has been a turn to the Murray and the north coast; and it is estimated that, given railways, the wheat area of the colony can certainly be increased eightfold, and this despite the exodus to the cities and the bad seasons since 1914.[8] The issue is now concerned with railways and research more than anything else: these will permit fruition of the new schemes. In Victoria, in the same years, all the emphasis has been on agriculture (Fig. 6). At first rural life seemed threatened, because in 1898 only 300,000 acres of first- and second-class lands were left and, save for the poor granite plains or the inferior highlands, the only good tracts were in the densely timbered south Gippsland and Otway ranges. But the Mallee (a genuinely new pioneer fringe) has changed all this. A belt of 14,000,000 acres of waterless sandy ridges in the north-west, its strange dwarf gums seemed to stamp the land as fit only for the 120,000 sheep it ran in 1882. But, once it was discovered that the soil was admirable for agriculture, once the German settlers had trekked overland to Warracknabeal and Chaffey had started irrigating Mildura, settlers poured in. Despite the drought 60,000 persons were there by 1898, and its very heart saw experiments in tenant farming. "The Little Desert" round Dimboola fell; and, since then, terms like "the inner Mallee" denote the passing of attention.[9] This region, with Gippsland, is Victoria's safeguard and naturally has absorbed most effort. But, farther south, the

[7] For the position see Report of 1891 Commission on Pastoral Lands (Paper 33 of 1891)—the best *résumé*; also Roberts, Land Settlement, pp. 310 *et seq.*

[8] Report of Select Committee on the Agricultural Industry, N. S. W., 1921.

[9] For the transformation of the Mallee see articles by Kenyon in *Victorian Hist. Mag.*, Vol. 4.

middle west lies athwart the track of settlement, much as it did
sixty years ago. No homesteads may be seen for miles there, and,
when the compulsory repurchase scheme of 1907 broke down, it
seemed as if the west—the fertile region—were destined to remain
a sheepwalk! Irrigation and repurchased estates now absorb
attention, but the west remains as it was.

In South Australia the
position has changed
little: the implication of
Goyder's line remains,
and, though three new
districts (Pinnaroo,
Eyre's Peninsula, and
the southeast) have been
opened up, there has re-
cently been a pause. The
optimism of twenty
years was reversed by
1920: much of the
Mallee land was aban-
doned; to go to the

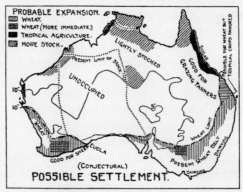

FIG. 9—The areas of possible future settlement in
Australia, showing the use to which the land will probably be put. Scale, 1 : 74,000,000.

coast or the isolated Murray flats was a loss of money as certain
as "flinging it into the deepest part of St. Vincent's Gulf"; and
in all, as an authority declared in 1920, it was recognized that
"the State have erred in the past in regard to their land-settlement
policy in the outside country." The fact Goyder stressed prevents
expansion north; the waterless ridges bar the west; and Pinnaroo
is two-thirds empty. The chronic dearth of land remains the
dominant fact. As contrasted with this, however, Western Australia
offers its atmosphere of "a bold yeomanry"—a constantly en-
croaching pioneer wheat belt. To 1891 only 64,000 acres of wheat
were cropped, and the old stagnation seemed deeply implanted;
but since then, under the impetus of liberal land laws and the forward policy since 1906, a great wheat belt has been built up from
the Murchison to Ravensthorpe, and even the previously despised
"sand-plain" land has been envisaged in the scheme. Land costs
only a third as much as in the eastern states, and plenty remains,
especially in the newer eastern wheat belt. What seems needed
is chiefly facilities and scientific study, as, for instance, of the
poison and mallee lands. But, at least, the future is full of hope.[10]

[10] Royal Commission on Agriculture, W. A., 1916 (Papers 7 and 15 of 1917–1918).

LIMITATIONS OF AND EMPHASIS ON PIONEER FRINGES

Taking Australia as a whole, then, the pastoral industry, after a checkered career, seems confronted by the perennial menaces of nature; and agriculture, though limited by the rainfall, is advancing (Fig. 9). Emphasis is on fighting the climate and pushing out; hence such movements as scientific research, irrigation, and more extensive government aid. The bores of New South Wales and the Northern Territory, such schemes as the Mildura irrigation and the Burrinjuck conservation (1906), and the locking of the Murray (especially after the Commission of 1917 show how the country is considering the problem. But, after all, they show, too, how the problem of the pioneer fringes is only on the threshold of solution. Until 1917, for instance, there was no Interstate Commission for the River Murray, a fact worth volumes of criticism. History reveals the weakness of desultory and isolated actions and no less the need for concerted aid of pioneers; but the lesson is hard to teach in a continent with five state governments, suspicious of any extension of Commonwealth powers. The question of the pioneer fringes thus comes back to science, to government aid, and hence to political conditions.

THE LAND PROBLEM IN TASMANIA

GORDON L. WOOD

PHYSICALLY and politically Tasmania forms a part of the Australian system; and, in considering the problem of land settlement in that country, it is essential to keep these primary relations in the forefront of discussion. Just as, in a geographical sense, the island is a natural region subject to geologic and climatic controls that influence the whole of southeastern Australia, so it is also dominated, in an economic sense, by the policies that regulate the industrial economy of the Commonwealth. In these two facts, somewhat obvious and commonplace though they may be in statement, rather than in any more obscure conditions influencing life and industry, are to be found the key to the outstanding problems connected with rural development in this state. That is not to say that its geographical situation has been without important effects upon the progress of settlement. The outlying situation of the island, its relatively small size, and its distance from the great markets and migration centers of the world have certainly been, to some extent at least, responsible for a slower rate of development than that experienced by the other Australian states. The competition and more insistent claims of much larger and more varied areas in relation to migration and the comparative remoteness of the island have doubtless contributed to the static condition that has characterized settlement in recent years; and, in the adverse situation brought about by the World War, the attraction of immigrants and capital has become increasingly difficult.

HISTORY OF SETTLEMENT TO 1900

The chief phases in the history of Tasmanian settlement can be sketched very briefly. The main tendencies noticeable in the development of New South Wales in the early years are also to be traced in the case of Tasmania. Land grants and leases to both individuals and companies were the first steps in settlement; and they led naturally to the establishment of sheep farming as the mainstay of the colony. Parallel with this development went the extension of agricultural settlement into the country lying behind the two main foci, Hobart and Launceston. The lines taken by

405

this expansion, and their control by the physical conditions in the terrain itself, will be noticed in more detail presently. It will be sufficient at this point to note that in the past Tasmania has filled a more important place in the Australian economy than she does at the present time and that, until the discovery of gold on the mainland, the country was mainly pastoral in outlook. From the fifties to the eighties of last century, however, Tasmania became the chief granary of the continent, and the profitable nature of the trade in farm products with the mainland accelerated and consolidated rural settlement in the island. After 1880 the diminishing demand for the products of Tasmanian farms, due to the growing self-sufficiency of the mainland in agriculture, was compensated by the great mineral discoveries in the island; and for the next thirty years mining absorbed the energies and capital of the community. The initiation and maintenance of great mineral enterprises during this period, and the consequent increase in population, replaced the dwindling interstate markets by one of growing importance at home. But, despite this fact, no great expansion of the occupied area took place during the period, and attempts at "closer settlement," as it now came to be called, were not an outstanding success. Indeed, it may be said that by 1880 most of the accessible country had already been allotted, and later extensions of the occupied area have been mainly under lease and for pastoral purposes. The beginnings of intensive cultivation were to be seen in Tasmania long before the close of the last century, and only those portions of the country that were too rough and too wet for profitable utilization then remained unoccupied.

AMALGAMATION WITH AUSTRALIA

After 1900 a new and very difficult period in the island's history was ushered in by the inauguration of the Commonwealth, of which the state of Tasmania now forms an integral part. Freedom of interstate trade resulted in an invasion of Tasmanian markets by mainland producers, and the intensified competition was felt severely and was not without its effects on the scattered rural population. In the second place, the new system of customs control and the passing of the Navigation Act of 1912 led to a falling away of the direct oversea trade that had proved such a stimulus to the development of the island in the past. Lastly, the influence of the more populous states in the Federal Parliament has not always been exerted in the direction of preserving a just balance between their own interests and those of outlying states with fewer people.

War and Post-War Development

To a detached community organized in the manner thus described the war period brought its own peculiar difficulties. Not the least of these was the increased frequency of interruptions of steamer services, due both to shortage of shipping and to labor troubles on the water front. In addition, this period may be described as one marked by an acute shortage of both public and private capital; and the effect of all these influences on a community of 200,000 people is not difficult to imagine. Private and public financial difficulties have resulted in recent years in persistent unemployment and in a steady loss of people to the mainland. One further influence tending to hold up any expansion of settlement has been the more profitable nature of pastoral, as compared with agricultural, occupations. The rapid increase in the price of wool after 1916 was a potent factor in discouraging closer settlement throughout the Commonwealth, and the effect has been very marked in Tasmania.

Other developments of a different kind were tending to force the industrial life of the island into a different mold after 1910. This new phase turned on the application of the abundant water power available in the island for the generation of electric energy, and in the consequent attraction of this cheap power for great industries is to be found the reason for an increased development of secondary, as distinct from primary, industries. As the population density of the mainland increases this may well prove but the prelude to a great extension of manufacturing which will, by an increased demand for foodstuffs, accelerate the development of many areas that the economist would at present label uneconomic land. In the present situation characterized by minute inquiry into the possibilities of increasing the efficiency of agriculture, by expensive attempts to clear and settle more land on the margin of cultivation, and by loss of the younger and more vigorous portion of the population to the mainland states, the economic geographer finds it difficult to justify the inclusion of Tasmania among the pioneer belts of the world, since at the moment it is not demonstrably a region of either expanding or progressive settlement.

Economic Effect of the Influence of Australia

No study· of Tasmanian settlement, however, could pretend to be complete or accurate which failed to have regard to certain transient influences that have no connection with either the suitability of the country for white settlement or the vigor and enterprise of the inhabitants but which have operated to check development in the last two decades. To ignore these influences in an attempt to weigh the possibilities the island offers for the absorption of further accessions of population would be tantamount to admitting a belief that the country is already closely settled, and such a belief would, of course, be ludicrous.

The first of these considerations has reference to the relatively more attractive conditions of the adjacent mainland for rural settlers. The larger scale of mainland industry, both primary and secondary, the greater concentrations of population to be found there, and the consequent economic attraction of larger and more diversified markets accessible by land transport have constituted a competitive situation in which the resources and organization of the island have so far proved ineffective. In the relatively more powerful attraction of the mainland states for both labor and capital is to be found the chief reason for an arrested agricultural development in Tasmania which can be paralleled in many other more highly developed regions within recent times. The depression of British agriculture and the difficulties of the farmer in certain parts of the United States are due to a similar intense competition with more favorably conditioned areas. The possibilities that demonstrably do exist in Tasmania for both pioneer and closer settlement will not be realized, it is to be expected, until the more attractive areas of the mainland are more densely populated than they are at present. But the process will not, indeed cannot, be rapid.

The second factor operating to an increasing degree to handicap the extension of settlement and to prevent the opening up of new country, the establishment of new industries, and the expansion of old ones is the inclusion of Tasmania in a political system which, by industrial regulation tending to increase the costs of production, has brought the island to the stage of diminishing returns earlier than is the case on the mainland. The imposition of rigid wage standards that are sustained with great difficulty even in the larger states of the Commonwealth represents a crushing disability for the relatively smaller and poorer community. The incidence of industrial and fiscal policies designed for a continental economy and for states richer in both population and material resources renders uneconomic for the island's people much that can be borne by the larger units of the federal system.

In the third place, policies of land settlement that have been put into force in the more extensive areas of the mainland have, by contrast with the smaller chances of gain from agriculture in Tasmania, operated to the disadvantage of the smaller state. Australian settlement has proceeded on the assumption that the settler should be put in the way of becoming a landed proprietor. For the rural entrepreneur—the worker-owner who is the pioneer

TABLE I—STATISTICS OF SETTLEMENT IN TASMANIA

(Total area, 16,800,000 acres)

	1880	1900	1928
Area occupied (millions of acres)	5.9	6.4	9.1
Uninhabited area (millions of acres) . .	10.9	10.4	7.7
Area alienated (per cent of area)	28.7	29.0	37.0
Area leased (per cent of area)	6.2	6.0	17.0
Area unoccupied (per cent of area) . . .	65.1	65.0	46.0
Area under crop (thousands of acres) . .	141.	224.	289.
Area under crop (per cent of area) . . .	.9	1.4	1.7
Population (thousands)	114.8	185.8	215.8
Density per square mile	4.4	7.09	8.23
Density per square mile of occupied land .	12.7	18.6	16.9
Number of cattle (thousands)	127.	165.	213.
Cattle (per cent of Australian)	1.7	1.9	1.8
Number of sheep (millions)	1.8	1.7	1.8
Sheep (per cent of Australian)	2.1	2.4	1.7

to be kept in mind—the broad acres and relatively uniform conditions of the mainland are more attractive than the smaller holdings and less homogeneous conditions to be found in Tasmania. The greater transport difficulties, the scattered and "patchy" nature of the good soil beds, and the greater remoteness from the mainland capitals which are the chief markets for farm products, all these are more suitable to a system comparable to the peasant proprietorship of parts of Europe than to the extensive economy that characterize most new countries. At great disadvantage under present conditions, the more intensive cultivation necessitated by the small available area of arable land in Tasmania has to compete with the cheaper extensive cultivation practiced on the mainland.

Present Status of Settlement

The most accurate presentation of the static condition of settlement in Tasmania at the present time is afforded by a comparison of the statistics connected with the utilization of land since 1880.

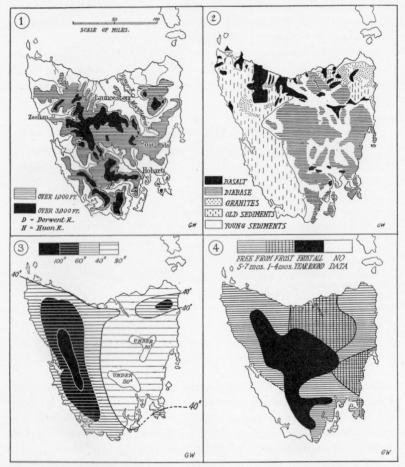

Figs. 1–4—Tasmania, showing (1) relief; (2) geology; (3) mean annual rainfall; (4) duration of frost.   Scale of all figures except Figure 5, 1 : 7,000,000.

These statistics are given in Table I and will serve to show better than much description the true nature of the Tasmanian case.

It should be noticed that, from the standpoint of effective settlement, the progress in the area alienated means very little since it represents an extension of cattle raising and forestry, which involves only a very small number of people engaged in primary pursuits. The most favorable indication revealed by the figures is that representing land under crop or sown to grass, which shows an extension in the last half-century at the rate of about 3000 acres per annum; and, despite the very heavy cost of clearing operations in good soil areas, this may be expected to continue steadily.

Physical and Climatic Controls of Settlement

Settlement in the island is so closely controlled by physical and geological conditions that a brief description of these becomes necessary.

In relief (Fig. 1), the island may be regarded as a great sterile plateau split into three sections by the lowlands associated with the rivers. The Tamar-Macquarie system draining to the north divides the Central Plateau from the northeastern mountain block; and in this wide valley region, with Launceston as its main outlet, settlement is relatively far advanced. Sheep, population, and crop density are here at their greatest. The Derwent and Huon river systems, draining to the southeast, separate the southern portion of the plateau and intersect a great natural forest area. Settlement in this area has been mainly determined by its suitability for fruit growing and forestry, and the chief concentration of population has occurred at its main outlet, the port and capital of Hobart. Cutting back into the Central Plateau is another river system, that of the northwest coastal rivers. Along all these river valleys settlement has pushed back into the interior, and most of the fertile country is already occupied by dairy and sheep farms and orchards. The plateau areas, while scenically grand, are, except on the lower slopes where pasturage for sheep and cattle is to be found, economically useless. Thus about one-third of the entire surface of the state has no significance for the practical purposes of settlement.

The second control to be emphasized is that of climate. Lying in the path of the westerly wind system and open on all sides to oceanic influences, Tasmania is specially suited for white settlement. The industries and occupations carried on in the island indicate a maritime climate with no great extremes of heat or cold. The oceanic effect is shown by the increasing frequency of frosts towards the interior (Fig. 4); but the winter is mild enough for snow to be very unusual in the lowland areas. Regions of similar climate are to be found in France, British Columbia, southern Chile, and the South Island of New Zealand. These places all have a mean annual range, or difference between the average of the hottest and coldest months, of from 10° to 20° Fahrenheit (Fig. 5). The scale of discomfort devised by Griffith Taylor[1] places the ideal white-race climate between 45° and 55° of mean annual wet-bulb temperature; and Tasmanian conditions agree very closely with this test.

It is worthy of note, also, that Tasmania comes well within the cyclonic zone upon which so much stress has been laid by Ellsworth Huntington. A feature of the island's rainfall is thus its association with low-pressure systems moving eastwards. The effect of the rain distribution consequent upon the passage of the lows is most important in its bearing on settlement. In common with most lands in this situation, Tasmania has a pronounced "wet side." Its mountainous western side is, therefore, a region distinguished by a rainfall averaging around 100 inches annually (Fig. 3). The West Coast, as it is termed, is thus too wet for successful agriculture even if other conditions were favorable.

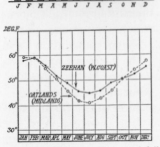

Fig. 5—Mean monthly rainfall (above) and temperature in type areas: rainfall and temperature on the West Coast and in the Midlands, rainfall only in the northeast district.

The Midlands, in contrast to the West Coast, form a rain-shadow area, with a yearly average of about 20 inches; and these conditions are very favorable for sheep raising. The east side is in general a dry region, with a tendency to heavier rainfall in summer than in winter, owing to the influence of moisture-bearing currents from the Pacific.

The areas of heavy rainfall determine the distribution of the forests and their character (Figs. 6–7), although it should be noted that the rainfall is sufficient for tree growth everywhere. Tasmania, in fact, is the one all-forest state in the Commonwealth, and future settlement policies will doubtless be increasingly deter-

[1] For publications of authors cited see the bibliography at the end of the paper.

mined in the light of this fact. The control of the vegetation by rainfall is at once remarkable and significant. In the west and northeast the 50-inch rainfall line marks an entire change in the character of the forest growth. Eucalypts, or gums, are here largely replaced by the evergreen "myrtles," more truly beeches, and the undergrowth attains a density approached only by that of a tropical jungle. As rainfall tapers away to the drier eastern and central regions more open forest conditions, with characteristic species of gums in the main, make their appearance. Thus it will be seen that, in the western rain region, extreme wetness and heavy forest growth are barriers to settlement, and to these must be added the deterrents of poor soils and difficult transport.

The third great physical factor controlling settlement in an emphatic fashion has its origin in the geological conditions (Fig. 2). The unbroken sterility of the rocky plateaus has already been mentioned. An equally rigid control, but in this case by fertility, was imposed in past ages by the great lava flows which, in decomposition, have furnished the most fertile soils in the state. These flows, "frequently weathered to a great depth of chocolate or red-brown soil," according to F. H. Johnstone, occur in a band of contiguous patches of varying extent stretching across the north of the island. These are the areas on which dairy farming and agriculture are firmly established, and a considerable extent of forested country of this type still awaits development. The fertility of the Tertiary sediments around Launceston and Hobart, again, are in marked contrast to the barrenness of the ancient sediments in the west and southwest coast areas.

LAND CLASSIFICATION

Owing to the fact that nothing in the nature of an adequate soil survey has ever been attempted, no scientific classification of Tasmanian lands can be made. Proceeding on the method of trial and error, settlers have roughly allotted the surface of the state to the three main uses of forestry, agriculture, and pasture (Fig. 7); it may be assumed that this division represents fairly accurately the proportion of the occupied land suited to each purpose. Land privately owned comprises 37 per cent of the total area of the island, land held on lease 13 per cent, and unoccupied land 50 per cent. This large proportion of rugged territory is a real barrier to economic development. The occupied land lies roughly in the form of a crescent ranged north, east, and south round the great central mass, and all traffic runs through and not across this zone (Fig. 11). It is estimated that barely 10 per cent of the whole surface is suit-

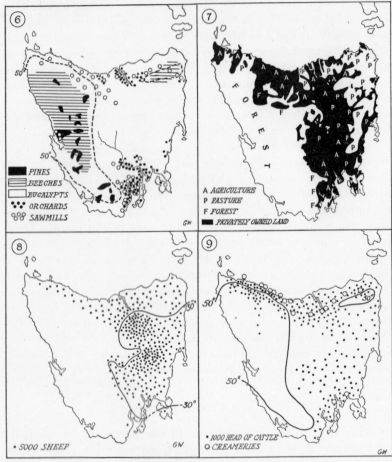

FIGS. 6–9—(6) Forests and orchards; (7) land classification; (8) distribution of sheep; (9) distribution of cattle. On Figures 6 and 9 the 50-inch, on Figure 8 the 30-inch isohyet of mean annual rainfall is shown.

able for some form of agriculture, 40 per cent for sheep or cattle pasture, and 50 per cent for forest or bushland of no economic importance so far as can be foreseen. Much land suitable for agriculture is undoubtedly held at the moment as sheep pasture. High wool prices, rising costs of production, and the uncertainty of mainland markets are responsible for this situation.

The estimate made above is largely guesswork since the material available for reliable classification is scanty and inaccurate. Crown lands available for settlement are classified into first, second, and third class land according to valuation, which largely depends upon accessibility; and this classification is not very helpful when questions of utilization are at issue. After exhaustive inquiry the Com-

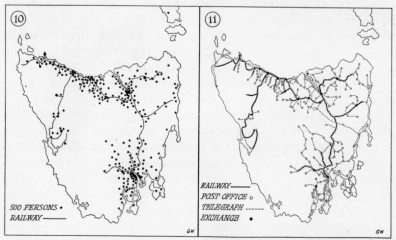

FIGS. 10–11—(10) Distribution of population; (11) communications. Since the telegraph lines run along main roads, the telegraph symbol on Figure 11 also represents the road network.

monwealth Development and Migration Commission is evidently satisfied to plan for better use of existing land rather than for an extension of settlement, which seems to point to an established balance as regards land utilization for forest, farm, and fodder purposes.

THE IMMEDIATE FUTURE FOR SETTLEMENT

The main facts of settlement in Tasmania have now been examined, but the fact must be emphasized that any extension of the agricultural area must be attended by considerable difficulty. "Tasmania now finds itself faced with the problem of diminishing population . . . natural resources fail to provide sufficient income to retain its population. . . . It costs more to grow wheat than on the mainland; the rivers have no wide fertile valleys; the highland country is costly to work; . . . transport has now become the dominating financial burden." The economic position is thus summarized by Professor J. B. Brigden. In the face of adverse physical and economic conditions the state government is making strenuous and persistent efforts to encourage settlement; and the federal government, through the Development and Migration Commission, has recently promoted a series of researches with the object of stimulating agricultural and pastoral industries in the island. One line of attack is to consist of more liberal provision of credit facilities to settlers, and another will be concerned with the application of modern agricultural science to the land problem and with the improvement of farming technique.

Tasmania may, in fact, be regarded as the Vermont of Australia in regard to rural production.   Agriculture is relatively more intense than on the mainland, but the primary producers are lacking in enterprise, unwilling to coöperate, and severely hampered by transport costs, diminishing returns, and defective marketing organization. *Under present economic conditions* it would appear that the optimum population for the island has already been attained, and the pressure of the population upon the resources is already greater than in any other state of the Commonwealth. An extension of manufactures, dependent upon the cheap electrical power which the island offers, will undoubtedly take place where the cost of transport to the mainland of the product is outweighed by the cost of power; and great possibilities for the support of a much larger population turn upon such developments.

In conclusion, it may be said that the areas possessing good soil and rainfall conditions are already, in comparison with mainland states, closely settled. The average potato farm of the northwest would not exceed 100 acres in extent; and holdings, in general, are small. The restrictions imposed by soil and surface conditions upon the employment of machinery and the inadequate use of fertilizers due to the small resources of most Tasmanian farmers are important factors to be considered. All the uneconomic conditions inherent in small-scale industry apply here in the persistent competition with the larger scale of farm practice on the mainland. Fruit growing, on the other hand, is much more progressive and in general more profitable. The main developments in the pastoral industry point in the direction of producing fat lambs for export and towards more effective use of land suited to dairy farming. In addition, many subsidiary industries in conjunction with dairying and orcharding, e.g. the raising of bees, poultry, and pigs, are still a long way from their maximum efficiency. The main hope for any extension of rural settlement in Tasmania, however, lies in the incentive supplied by an increased demand from growing markets on the mainland; and even then it is to be thought that development will be intensive rather than extensive and will be dependent upon many factors that cannot at present be predicted with any certainty.

BIBLIOGRAPHY

Taylor, Griffith. The Australian Environment (Especially As Controlled by Rainfall). *Commonwealth Advisory Council of Science and Industry Memoir No. 1.* Melbourne, 1918.

Taylor, Griffith. The Climatic Control of Australian Production. *Commonwealth Bur. of Meteorol. Bull. No. 11.* Melbourne, 1916.

Huntington, Ellsworth. Civilization and Climate. 1st edit., New Haven, Conn., 1915; 3rd edit., 1924.

Wood, Gordon L. The Tasmanian Environment. 2nd edit. Melbourne, 1929.

Hunt, H. A., Griffith Taylor, and E. T. Quayle. The Climate and Weather of Australia. Commonwealth Bureau of Meteorology, Melbourne, 1913.

Johnstone, F. H. Description of Soils of Tasmania for Wembley Exhibition. London, 1925.

Prescott, J. A. An Inquiry into Tasmanian Soil Conditions. *Journ. Council for Sci. and Indust. Research*, Vol. 1, Melbourne, 1928, pp. 227–232.

Hutchins, Sir D. E. The Forests of Australia, 1922.

Report presented by the Government of Tasmania to the Royal Commission upon Tasmanian disabilities entitled The Case for Tasmania, 1926.

Brigden, J. B. Tasmania, An Economic Sketch. *In* Handbook to Tasmania, pp. 116–135. Australasian Assn. for the Advancement of Sci., Hobart, 1928.

Giblin, L. F. Manufactures. *In* Handbook to Tasmania, pp. 75–81. Australasian Assn. for the Advancement of Sci., Hobart, 1928.

Curtis, H. A. Hydro-Electric Development in Tasmania. *In* Handbook to Tasmania, pp. 69–74. Australasian Assn. for the Advancement of Sci., Hobart, 1928.

Commonwealth of Australia, Development and Migration Commission, Reports on Investigation into Present Position of Tasmania, Melbourne, 1927–29.

Official Year Book of the Commonwealth of Australia. Commonwealth Bureau of Census and Statistics, Melbourne (since 1929, Canberra).

PROBLEMS OF LAND SETTLEMENT IN NEW ZEALAND

J. B. CONDLIFFE

BEGINNING with the arrival at Wellington on January 22, 1840, of the four ships that conveyed the first settlers sent out by the New Zealand Company, the progress of settlement in New Zealand falls into three fairly clear periods. It is of considerable interest to note how economic and geographical factors have provided a framework within which governmental direction has necessarily functioned.[1]

EXPERIMENTATION IN THE FIRST PERIOD OF SETTLEMENT

A week after the company's settlers arrived in Wellington the newly appointed Lieutenant Governor arrived at Auckland. With the advice and assistance of some leading missionaries he negotiated the Treaty of Waitangi, by which the Maori chiefs ceded sovereignty to Queen Victoria and were confirmed in the ownership of their lands. Thenceforth no land could be bought except with the consent of the Crown, and no titles were recognized as valid except where they were based upon crown grants. New Zealand, therefore, offers an example of a land that was opened to systematic colonization less than a century ago and in which the direction of settlement has been under governmental control to an exceptional degree. Successive governments have bought the land from the Maoris, disposed of it to settlers on various forms of tenure, built roads and railways and other public works to open up the country, and in more recent years legislated with the object of encouraging closer settlement.

The first organized settlements were in the central Cook Strait region. Their founders correctly foresaw the future commercial importance of this location. They were also aware that the comparatively dense Maori population of the North Island and the heavy forests of that region betokened a rich soil. In the first decade of settlement, however, these natural advantages were

[1] For a comprehensive survey of New Zealand's economic development see J. B. Condliffe: New Zealand in the Making: A Survey of Economic and Social Development, London and Chicago, 1930.

minimized by a distressing controversy between the settlers and the government, which delayed the quieting of land titles.[2] The Maoris also proved intractable and hostile, while the rugged and heavily forested hinterlands required great capital expenditures before they could be opened up. The first North Island settlers were, therefore, cooped up in restricted areas around two or three ports.[3]

It was some time, moreover, before the true line of economic development became clear. The first settlers exploited the natural resources, such as timber and native flax. They also attempted to reproduce agricultural farming of the English type. Only by painful experience could they learn to develop new forms of farming suitable to the new land. By the end of the first decade of settlement, when the latest Wakefield colonies were planted at Dunedin (1848) and Lyttelton (1850), it was becoming clear that sheep raising by extensive methods, producing an exportable surplus of wool, offered the most profitable line of immediate development.

ESTABLISHMENT OF THE PASTORAL INDUSTRY IN THE SECOND PERIOD

In the second period of development, therefore, from about 1850 to the advent of refrigeration in 1882, the pastoral industry, organized on "extensive" lines, provided the economic basis of development. The eastern plains and rolling foothills of the South Island invited occupation. Their whole area had been purchased from the few Maoris concerned, there were no forests to get rid of, and bullock drays could be driven across the open plains. The system of pastoral leaseholds adapted from Australian experience made access to the land easy and cheap.[4] Many Australian squatters fled from drought and depression in the late forties to take up land in the South Island. When the Australian gold rushes began in 1851 a profitable market was created for the products of New Zealand farming. The benefits of these changes accrued mainly to the South Island settlements. The slower progress of the northern provinces was further checked by the outbreak in the North Island of the second series of Maori wars in 1860. The discovery

[2] The controversy between the Governor and the first settlers is treated in J. C. Beaglehole: Captain Hobson and the New Zealand Company, Northampton, Mass., 1928; A. J. Harrop: England and New Zealand, London, 1926. This controversy was a continuation in the colony of that which in England had so long thwarted the efforts of Edward Gibbon Wakefield to colonize New Zealand.

[3] William Fox: The Six Colonies of New Zealand, London, 1851.

[4] W. P. Reeves: State Experiments in Australia and New Zealand, 2 vols., London, 1902.

of rich gold fields in the South Island in the following decade set the seal upon southern domination. The main stream of economic development and the main stream of immigration flowed into the more accessible and more prosperous and peaceful southern settlements.

When Vogel in 1870 introduced a great borrowing scheme for immigration and public works, 60 per cent of the population lived in the South Island, which naturally appropriated most of the expenditure upon roads and railways and received most of the immigrants. The land boom of the seventies and the severe depression of the eighties and early nineties were worst in the South Island. In Christchurch and Dunedin the urban problems of unemployment, sweating, and social distress were most evident, and in their hinterlands the problem of land monopoly was most acute.[5]

DEVELOPMENT OF SMALL FARMING IN THE THIRD PERIOD

In 1882, however, the first shipment of frozen meat was successfully made from Dunedin to London.[6] A new era was opened up by this innovation, which so greatly widened the colony's export market; but there were considerable difficulties to economic progress. In the first place the geographical frontier still excluded settlers from the rich but inaccessible North Island, there was a tenurial frontier resulting from the aggregation of land in large areas for sheep farming, and to this had been added a financial frontier resulting from the overvaluation and overmortgaging of the land in the boom period. The so-called state-socialist legislation of the nineties was mainly inspired by the necessity of breaking through this situation of land monopoly and of controlling the urban difficulties that had sprung from it. Vigorous measures of taxation, governmental repurchase, loans to small settlers, and leasing of government land broke down the tenurial barrier to settlement. Increasing productivity after refrigeration and the upward turn of world prices in 1895 finally liquidated the results of overvaluation.

More significant than either of these developments, however, was the lifting of the geographical barrier by the opening up of the North Island. The Maori wars were finally ended in 1872, and from 1873 onward legislation facilitated private purchases of Maori lands. The frontier of settlement moved again across the strait to

[5] Reeves, *op. cit.*

[6] J. T. Critchell and J. A. Raymond: A History of the Frozen Meat Trade, London, 1912.

Taranaki and Wellington.   Pioneers took up once more the task
of carving farms out of the forest.   Cattle were run in the virgin
bush until portions of it could be felled and burned.   Catch crops
sown in among the blackened stumps made possible the feeding of as
many as five or six sheep to the acre on this virgin land.   As clearing
progressed and transportation was improved, the land was used for
dairying, which is a development mainly of the twentieth century
and is largely concentrated in the North Island.   With the completion of the North Island main trunk railway in 1908 and the further
development of subsidiary lines and better roads, the frontier moved
north to the western and more recently the northeastern section of
Auckland Province.   These are the characteristic pioneer developments of New Zealand, taken up again after half a century, in
which the main stream of economic progress was deflected to the
extensive sheep-raising economy of the South Island.   The resump-
tion of this characteristic small farming and closer settlement in
the North Island has differentiated New Zealand's development
from the Australian type and has very considerably toned down
the experimental state-socialist legislation of an earlier period.
It is a true case of geographical control of economic and social
progress.

Revival of Maori Agriculture

After the first promising efforts at systematic agriculture under
missionary guidance the Maoris were thrown into a state of dis-
couragement and hostility by the land disputes that caused the
wars of 1843–1848 and 1860–1872.   A Native Land Court was
set up in 1862 to facilitate the purchases of native land, and from
1873 the principle of individualizing native land titles was enforced.
At the same time the Crown's right of preëmption was waived,
and a period of free trade in Maori land set in.   By 1900 the Maoris
had lost most of their ancestral heritage.   Under the system of
individual titles "the right to occupy and cultivate possessed by
their fathers became in their hands an estate which could be sold."
This was the period of decline in Maori population and morale.[7]

From this period the Maoris have emerged with a remnant of

[7] P. H. Buck: The Passing of the Maori, *Trans. and Proc. New Zealand Inst.*, Vol. 55, 1924,
pp. 362–375.
   Report of Commission on Native Land Laws, 1891; Report of Commission on Native Lands and
Native Land Tenure, 1907–1908.
   F. M. Keesing: The Changing Maori, *New Zealand: Maori Ethnol. Research Board Memoirs*,
Vol. 4, Wellington, 1928.

their lands, very unevenly distributed among the tribes. The total area of land remaining to the 60,000 present-day Maoris is 4,400,000 acres, of which 4,200,000 acres are in the North Island. A further area of 1,600,000 acres is leased from native owners.[8] This native land is unevenly distributed, and most of it is in the poorer and less accessible regions of the central and northeastern parts of the North Island. With the exception of a few tribes, the most conspicuous of which is the Ngatiporou inhabiting the northeastern corner behind Gisborne, the Maoris have parted with their best lands and retain only the poorer-placed and less fertile areas.

The last generation, however, has produced a remarkable group of Maori leaders, the most prominent of whom is Sir Apirana Ngata, at present Minister for Native Affairs. His tribe, the Ngatiporou, has retained its good lands and has worked out methods by which the very intricate native holdings have been consolidated into workable farms. The further extraordinary step has been taken of devising coöperative working methods by which holdings are incorporated and worked communally. The adaptation of European methods of rural coöperation and legal incorporation to native customs of communal landholding and group labor is a fascinating example of the regeneration of a native race, all the more interesting because it is essentially due to Maori leadership.

The relations of frontier settlers with the Maoris have ceased to be the important phase of the native land problem. Adequate governmental machinery exists in the Maori Land Boards and the Native Land Court for the amicable and equitable disposal of land by sale. The days of large land sales are, however, past. Most of the land is gone, and, while there remain large uncultivated and unused areas in Maori possession, they are not good land; in any case the Maori tribes are following policies of conservation and even buying back land from the settlers in certain instances. The native land problem is one rather of Maori agriculture, and as such it is proceeding steadily towards solution, guided by very capable Maori leadership and aided by the constructive sympathy of the government. After nearly a century of discouraging contact with European civilization the way seems to be opening for the Maori race to work out successful methods of survival, adaptation, and contribution to the common life of New Zealand.

[8] *New Zealand Official Year-Book for 1928*, Census and Statistics Office, Wellington, 1927, pp. 408 and 427–430.

LAND AVAILABLE FOR SETTLEMENT

The area of crown land available for new settlement in New Zealand is small (Fig. 1). As of March 31, 1927, it was reported as slightly less than 2,750,000 acres. This is a small area compared with the 22,500,000 acres of land still unoccupied, most of which

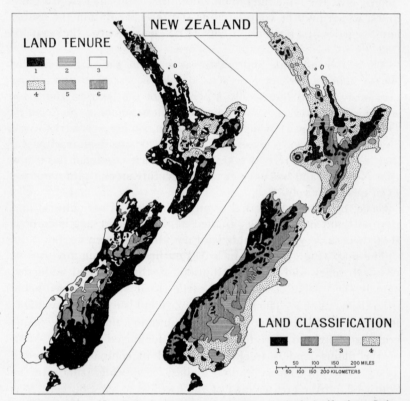

FIGS. 1 and 2—New Zealand, showing (1) land tenure, (2) land classification. Scale, 1 : 15,000,000. (Based on the corresponding maps in the author's work cited in footnote 1.)

Key to numerals on Figure 1: 1, land sold or disposed of by grant; 2, small grazing runs and other leased pastoral lands; 3, crown lands undisposed of; 4, native lands; 5, acquired lands for settlement; 6, national endowment lands.

Key to numerals on Figure 2: 1, forest areas; 2, high and broken land; 3, light pastoral land; 4, agricultural and dairying land.

must be regarded as unsuitable for settlement. The actual extent of land unfit for settlement is variously estimated. One official estimate is less than 4,000,000 acres, 5 per cent of the total area of the Dominion (66,400,000 acres).[9] This ignores the unusable

[9] *Ibid.*, p. 408.

land already in private ownership and occupation and does not deduct land used for forests and similar purposes. In 1927, with a population of more than 1,450,000, the density was estimated as 13.92 per square mile, or "subtracting the area occupied by rivers, lakes, roads, State forests, higher portions of mountain ranges, etc., the remaining area, amounting to about 84,500 square miles, which may be considered as the total inhabitable or usable land, carries a population of 17.02 persons to the square mile."[10]

The latter estimate, optimistic as it is in showing well over 80 per cent of the total area as usable, is less than that given previously, which shows only 5 per cent of the land as "unfit for settlement." Both are at variance with the estimate of the Forestry Department (Fig. 2), which classes 40,700,000 acres as agricultural and pastoral, 12,600,000 as forest land, 10,700,000 as unproductive, and 1,800,000 as rivers, lakes, etc.[11] Such discrepancies show that New Zealand has not yet taken accurate stock of its resources even quantitatively.

Since, however, the actual occupied holding of agricultural and pastoral land in 1922–1923 totaled 44,500,000 acres, it is evident that there is very little usable land not already taken up.[12]

The map (Fig. 3) shows in broad outline the main features of physical relief and the distribution of the principal industry, namely the raising of sheep and cattle (their number is deducible from the symbols). The land of New Zealand is roughly classifiable into plains, hill country, and high mountain ranges. The plains are used more and more for dairying or for mixed farming. Most of the plains land is freehold and held in comparatively small areas. The hill country is used mainly for sheep grazing. In the South Island the greater part of the foothills of the Southern Alps running from Marlborough in the north to Otago and Southland in the south is held on pastoral leasehold in large areas. This is especially true of Otago, where the leasehold area broadens perceptibly. Very little of the North Island is leasehold, and very

[10] *New Zealand Official Year-Book for 1928*, p. 104.

[11] *Ibid.*, p. 477.

[12] *Ibid.*, p. 411.   The holdings were classified as follows in 1922–1923:

	Number	Acres
Agricultural	10,489	2,129,802
Dairying	38,818	6,267,597
Pastoral and other (including unspecified)	36,212	35,255,764

in addition to Maori holdings totaling 805,378 acres.

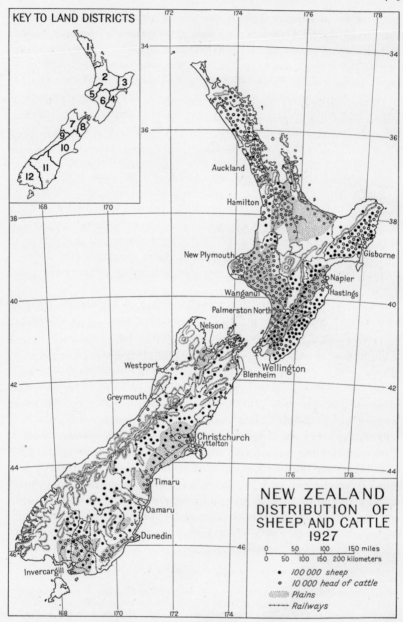

FIG. 3—The broad physical features of New Zealand and the distribution of sheep and cattle in 1927. Scale, 1 : 10,000,000. Key to numbers of Land Districts in inset: 1, North Auckland; 2, Auckland; 3, Gisborne; 4, Hawke's Bay; 5, Taranaki; 6, Wellington; 7, Nelson; 8, Marlborough; 9, Westland; 10, Canterbury; 11, Otago; 12, Southland.

little of the leasehold land in the South Island is being converted into freehold.[13] This fact in itself shows that settlement opportunities are greatest in the North Island.

Closer Settlement the Main Desideratum

Closer settlement and better utilization of the land already taken up are the primary problems of New Zealand pioneering. They depend largely upon the progress made in providing transport facilities. There is a general tendency all over the Dominion towards subdivision and the replacement of large sheep runs by smaller mixed farms or still smaller dairy farms. In the South Island progress is potentially greatest in Southland, where dairying development was rapid until checked by land speculation and premature public works development, and in Nelson, where the completion of the main trunk railway line may open up new areas of pastoral country and also develop coal deposits.

It is in the North Island, however, that pioneering is most profitable. The most obvious areas are those in the railway gaps between Gisborne and Rotorua and between New Plymouth and the main trunk line.[14] There are other areas where special problems have to be faced.[15] In the peninsula north of Auckland the recent completion of the railway has stimulated dairying remarkably. There remain in this area about 1,000,000 acres of kauri-gum land which need liming and treating with superphosphates to bring them into production. In the central plateau there is another great area of light "pumice land" awaiting development.

The main line of progress, however, lies in the development of closer settlement associated with the dairying industry.[16] This is taking place both by the opening up of new areas by railway and road development and by the change over from sheep or cattle raising to the more intensive dairy farming. The problems faced by the settler center round transport. The manufacturing processes of dairying, even when based upon home separation, are

[13] See annual reports of the Department of Lands and Survey, summarized in the *New Zealand Official Year-Books.*

[14] Programme of Railway Improvements and New Works (D-2A, 1924); also Annual Railways Statements (D-2) and Public Works Statements (D-1).

[15] Cf. British Oversea Settlement, Delegation to New Zealand, 1923: Report to the President of the Oversea Settlement Committee from the Delegation Appointed to Inquire into Conditions Affecting British Settlers in New Zealand, Cmd. 2167, H. M. Stationery Office, London, 1924.

[16] Horace Belshaw: Dairying Industry of New Zealand, *Econ. Geogr.*, Vol. 3, 1927, pp. 281–296; Otto Harris: Dairying in New Zealand, *Bull. Geogr. Soc. of Philadelphia*, Vol. 26, 1928, pp. 293–304.

normally carried out in coöperative factories.[17]   Roads are essential.
The problem of isolation of schools and hospitals is dependent
also upon the main problem of transport.

PROBLEMS OF LAND UTILIZATION

If the total area available for settlement is not definitely known,
it is hardly to be expected that there will be accurate detailed
knowledge of the quality of the land.   The section of the Official
Year Book which deals with agricultural and pastoral production
contains the following cheerful but vague statement:[18]   "The soil
covering is varied in character, a considerable portion of it being
of exceptional fertility; but even the poorer soils are largely capable
of profitable utilisation by reason of the comparatively mild and
equable weather conditions."

It is true that, broadly speaking, the climatic barriers to settlement are almost negligible.   No part of the islands has temperatures
that are extreme, and there are no exceptional winds to destroy
crops.   Occasionally in the high foothills of certain parts of the
South Island snow will cause the loss of sheep, but flocks and herds
go unhoused and unclothed and feed on natural pasture all the year
round.   With the exception of a dry pocket in Otago under the lee
of the Southern Alps rainfall is everywhere sufficiently evenly
distributed.   Across the Alps in the forest country of southern
Westland it is very heavy, but dairy farming has pushed into the
valleys in this region.

In the absence as yet of soil surveys it is not possible to write
in any dogmatic way of soil fertility.   There are patches and belts
of light, shingly, or swampy land, including the wandering river
beds.   A considerable area of "pumice country" in the Taupo
district of the North Island, the site of former kauri forests in the
North Auckland peninsula, and abandoned alluvial gold fields on
the west coast of the South Island must all be reckoned with in
calculating the possibilities of future settlement.   Above all, it
must be remembered that large stretches of pastoral grazing land,
especially on the foothills in the South Island, have a thin soil.
In many areas overstocking and in some cases the depredations of
rabbits, which eat away the scanty grass, have facilitated erosion.

[17] Edwin Hall: The Co-operative Movement in New Zealand Agriculture, *Internatl. Rev. of Agric. Economics*, Vol. 71, Rome, 1916, pp. 18–34.

H. L. Russell and T. Macklin: Intensive Dairying in New Zealand and Wisconsin, *Univ. of Wisconsin Agric. Exper. Sta. Bull. 377*, May, 1925.

[18] *New Zealand Official Year-Book for 1928*, p. 438.

It has been calculated that overstocking is adding to the barren lands at the rate of 100,000 acres annually.[19] In parts of the North Island, too, ferns and second growth present a formidable problem, while blackberries and other plant pests have also to be reckoned with. It is clear that in the absence of a systematic inventory of the Dominion's resources mistakes have been made that could easily have been avoided if more scientific knowledge had been available. This has been made apparent in the depression following the post-war boom. Unwise subdivision, overvaluation, the use of land for unsuitable types of farming, and similar errors of judgment might have been lessened if adequate soil and farm-management surveys had been available. The field of investigation in these problems has hardly been touched. Departments of economics in the university colleges are too recent and too ill-equipped to have tackled the problem. In any case, their teaching has been dominated by a rigid external examination system under which all the higher work of the university is still examined in industrial England. There has been excellent geological work, and the Department of Agriculture has rendered yeoman service to the farmer along many scientific lines. The economic and sociological problems of settlement, however, are only now being visualized. The establishment of a new Department of Scientific and Industrial Research is doing much to stimulate governmental and university activity in this field.

The increasing pressure of population, combined with a falling movement of prices, tends now to make the problems of rural economics more obvious and urgent. Table I shows how greatly New Zealand has so far depended upon her natural advantages and especially upon her climate, which is almost ideal for pastoral pursuits.

TABLE I—CLASSIFICATION OF OCCUPIED LAND IN NEW ZEALAND[20]

Cultivated Land	Acres
In grain and pulse crops	600,000
In grasses and clovers (for hay and seed) and green and root crops	1,100,000
In fallow	100,000
In grasses and clovers (not cut for hay or seed) . . . . . ●.	16,600,000
Miscellaneous	200,000
Total cultivated	18,600,000

[19] L. M. Ellis: The Progress of Forestry in New Zealand, Wellington, 1922: "New Zealand possesses 2,500,000 acres of desert wilderness which is being added to at the rate of 100,000 acres per year, producing nothing of value to man or beast, but valuable for the production of forest crops."

[20] New Zealand Official Year-Book for 1928, p. 412.

Unimproved Land

In tussock and other native grasses	14,300,000
In fern, scrub, and second growth	4,200,000
Virgin bush	4,200,000
Barren and unproductive	2,300,000
Total unimproved	25,000,000
Total occupied land	43,600,000

Such a table as this is prima facie evidence that there are still large possibilities for closer settlement in the Dominion; but certain factors of considerable importance enter into the question. Beyond the two sets of problems already raised (the fate of the Maori lands and the need for soil and management surveys) there arise problems of land tenure and of economic and social development.

Problems of Land Tenure

The great bulk of the best land of New Zealand has been taken up by freehold owners. If to the 21,200,000 acres of freehold land are added the 6,000,000 acres held on leaseholds in small areas suitable for mixed or dairy farming, there remains little usable land beyond the 12,500,000 acres held on pastoral and grazing-run leases and the native lands. It is a significant geographical fact that almost all of the pastoral leasehold land lies in the South Island, mainly in Otago (Fig. 1). This is light back-country land, often hilly in character and remote. It is, therefore, largely unsuitable for closer settlement, and very little of it has been turned into freehold. Over wide areas there has been deterioration through overstocking and other forms of predatory farming, and there are expert observers who see in this the main reason why Otago Province should have failed to progress as rapidly as other parts of New Zealand.[21]

The pastoral leases are a legacy from the first period of settlement when they were granted to large runholders who grazed their flocks beyond the limits of the high-priced "company" land. The best of them were turned into freehold on advantageous terms early in New Zealand's history. Those that survive are usually the worse-situated and poorer lands.

Since 1912 the freehold tenure has definitely triumphed, and successive land acts have given the various classes of crown tenants

[21] W. D. Hunt: Land Tenure in New Zealand, Dunedin, 1917.
Cf. also Report of the Southern Pastoral Lands Commission, 1920 (C-15), and Report of Special Committee on the Deterioration of Crown Lands, 1925 (C-15), for similar problems in the North Island.

the option of purchasing their freeholds.[22]   The statistics of land-holding do not show that as great advantage has been taken of this privilege as was expected.   There are evidently fair numbers of small farmers who find crown leaseholds an advantageous form of tenure.   It is broadly true, however, that New Zealand farming is freehold and that its problems are those arising naturally from that tenure.   Speculation in land values, the incidence of land taxes, overmortgaging, too free use of a poorly organized system of rural credit—all these problems have been rendered acute by the recent falling tendency of world prices.

INFLUENCE OF EXTERNAL RELATIONSHIPS: IMMIGRATION

Underlying and to a large extent governing all these domestic factors, of available land, its quality and uses, of tenure and finance, there is the broad general problem of New Zealand's external economic relationships, which are predominantly with Great Britain and which are expressed most obviously in terms of relative prices.   There are two aspects of these external relationships that warrant attention, immigration and the import of capital for the construction of public works.

The population of New Zealand is growing fast.   From 1881 to 1921 the rate of increase shown by quinquennial censuses has been rather more than 12 per cent.[23]   There is a relatively large natural increase, due mainly to a low death rate.   In addition there is a substantial and increasing immigration, almost wholly from Great Britain and the other British dominions.[24]   In the five years 1922–1926 there were 73,493 new immigrants, of whom 95 per cent came from the British Isles.   Against these figures must be set the 26,073 New Zealanders who emigrated in these five years.   Of the new (male) immigrants 23 per cent gave their occupation as agricultural and pastoral, 20 per cent were children under fifteen years, and a slightly smaller number were industrial workers.   Since the ports of oversea arrival and departure are in the North Island and there is a great deal of mobility among all classes of the population in New Zealand, it is impossible to do more than hazard the guess that the bulk of this net immigration remained in the North Island provinces, where economic opportunities are more plentiful.

[22] W. R. Jourdain: Land Legislation and Settlement in New Zealand, Department of Lands and Survey, Wellington, 1925, pp. 155–189.

[23] New Zealand Official Year-Book for 1928, p. 77.

[24] Ibid., pp. 82–94.

Since the last of the Wakefield schemes (1850) there has been no attempt at organized group settlement, such, for example, as Western Australia has had; but there are various agencies at work assisting the immigration of special classes, especially boys and girls who can be trained for rural life. The outstanding institution for this purpose is Flock House, a training farm founded by sheep owners after the war and designed for the reception of young people desirous of entering rural pursuits.[25] It is significant of New Zealand's close connection with Great Britain that special effort should be made to encourage the immigration of "public school" boys. In the same way there is a significant influx of middle-class British families with sufficient capital to take up farming pursuits. The bulk of the assisted immigration, however, consists of working-class people who are nominated by friends or relatives in New Zealand and so secure cheaper passages.[26]

The extent to which new immigrants can be absorbed over brief periods is becoming a matter of debate. The Commonwealth statistician examining the problem for Australia has suggested the possibility of an "absorption" or saturation rate.[27] His statistics tend to show that a surplus of immigrants over and above this rate causes unemployment and a consequent check to immigration. Falling prices in countries that are both borrowers and producers rapidly intensifies the maladjustment caused by too rapid immigration, and it is not surprising, therefore, to find strong protests from the organized urban workers in New Zealand against immigration as a cause of unemployment in recent years. Further sharp falls in the price level in 1928 and 1929 have caused the suspension of assisted immigration.

The absorption of new immigrants, moreover, depends only in part upon the wisdom with which domestic policies of settlement are carried out. These policies could undoubtedly be improved if more accurate knowledge were made available by scientific analysis and survey. But in the long run certain price relationships will prove to be of fundamental importance, and these are largely set by the conditions of world trade in the great staple exports, wool, meat, butter, cheese, and their allied products.

None but a few enthusiasts in the cause of secondary manu-

---

[25] Report cited in footnote 15.

[26] *New Zealand Official Year-Book for 1928*, pp. 89–91.

[27] C. H. Wickens: Australian Population: Its Nature and Growth, *Econ. Record*, Vol. 1, Melbourne, 1925, pp. 1–16. See also Sir James Allen *et al.*, edits.: New Zealand Affairs, Christchurch, 1929, Ch. 6.

factures will concede any great possibilities of industrial development sufficient to absorb large numbers of new immigrants. Urban
and manufacturing industry has more than kept pace with population growth in the period of prosperity based on rising prices. The
market is too small, however, to permit of such industrialization
as Australia has shown in recent years, and the falling price level
since 1921 has hit urban industries at least as hard as the primary
rural pursuits. The relation between export prices and local
costs is an important element in the whole problem, particularly
when the tendency of the general price level is down rather than
up. Readjustment to lower levels is a painful process after a
prolonged period during which speculation has tended to keep
land values and other costs above true productive levels. The
government valuation of occupied land in 1926 was £603,000,000,
of which £341,000,000 was "unimproved" value.[28] This figure
in itself is sufficient to indicate the extent to which prosperity has
been capitalized in land values.

CAPITAL IMPORT

An economic factor of scarcely less importance is the steady
inflow of capital upon which New Zealand has relied in her recent
period of rapid development. Private capital brought in by
immigrants or invested in industry is difficult to measure, but
there is accurate information concerning public borrowings, both
by local bodies and by the national government. The modest
"million a year" of the nineties has swollen to an annual loan of
about £5,000,000 to £10,000,000, and local bodies have also enlarged
their borrowing considerably. At the same time rates of interest
have gone up; and, since price levels have tended to decline, there
is much more discussion concerning the limits within which it is
wise to borrow. Recent investigations, moreover, have tended to
indicate that, while heavy government borrowings continue, the
Dominion has, since 1921, been exporting private capital at the
rate of £2,000,000 annually.[29] Population statistics indicate also
that the rapid rate of increase from 1881 to 1921 has not been
maintained. These facts are indicative of the extent to which a
falling level of world prices checks development in New Zealand.

It is obvious that these economic factors are on the whole dominant in the pioneering problems of New Zealand. Public works

[28] *New Zealand Official Year-Book for 1928*, pp. 659–667.
[29] Allen *et al.*, *op. cit.*, Ch. 8.

built out of loans will normally reduce the farmers' costs of production and at the same time give him transport, power, and more of the amenities of life. This is the primary necessity for further development in the frontier regions of the North Island. If, however, the cost of this capital development should be unduly high it might retard development in the long run. This danger, usually scouted in a young country, is brought appreciably nearer when a sudden turn in the price level drops export prices to lower levels, while fixed charges, such as interest and often wages, and the cost of services, such as transportation and merchandising, remain high.

New Zealand has developed rapidly in the last forty years and is still developing fast. There seems no reason to disbelieve the possibilities of further expansion even under the rather difficult conditions now prevailing because of a falling price level. Such difficult conditions, however, make more evident the wisdom of accurately surveying the Dominion's resources against a background of world economics. Ever since the Wakefield experiments of the forties New Zealand's development has on the whole been orderly and solid; but the experience of the last period of boom and depression in a time of falling prices is in itself sufficient to call for caution in the immediate future.

BIOGRAPHICAL NOTICES CONCERNING
THE AUTHORS

Dr. MACKINTOSH is Sir John A. Macdonald Professor of Political and Economic Science at Queen's University, Kingston (Ontario), Canada. He was one of the Canadian specialists consulted in the formative stages of the group later known as the Canadian Pioneer Problems Committee (see above, p. 7, footnote 10), becoming its Director of Research at the time the Committee was organized (1928). His writings, which deal mainly with Canadian economics and economic geography, include: "Agricultural Coöperation in Western Canada," Toronto, 1924; "Economic Factors in Canadian Nationality" (*Canadian Hist. Rev.*, 1923); "The Canadian Wheat Pools" (*Bull. of the Departments of History and Political and Economic Science*, Queen's University, November, 1925); "The Laurentian Plateau and Canadian Economic Development" (*Econ. Geogr.*, October, 1926); "Canada and Vermont: A Study in Historical Geography" (*Canadian Hist. Rev.*, March, 1927).

Dr. MURCHIE's academic connections have been mainly with the Universities of Manitoba and Minnesota. At the Agricultural College of the former institution he was associate professor of rural economics prior to 1928 and professor of economics and sociology in 1929–1931. In 1928–1929 and again since 1931 he has been at the University of Minnesota, where he now occupies the chair of sociology in the Department of Agriculture. In 1921 he was secretary of the Manitoba Agricultural Survey, in 1926 director of the survey of the unused lands of Manitoba, and in 1927 chairman of the Manitoba Commission on Seasonal Unemployment. As a result of the two last-named activities he has published (jointly with H. C. Grant) "Unused Lands of Manitoba," Manitoba Dept. of Agric. and Immigration, Winnipeg, 1927, and (jointly with W. H. Carter and F. J. Dixon) "Seasonal Unemployment," Manitoba Dept. of Agric. and Immigration, Winnipeg, 1928. Dr. Murchie is chairman of the section of agricultural economics of the Canadian Pioneer Problems Committee.

Professor MARTIN is professor and head of the Department of History at the University of Toronto, having previously occupied the chair of modern history at the University of Manitoba. He has specialized in the history of Canada, especially of the Prairie Provinces. Several of his publications deal with the Red River Settlement, e.g. "Lord Selkirk's Work in Canada," Oxford, 1916; "The Red River Settlement" (in "Canada and Its Provinces," edited by Adam Shortt and A. G. Doughty, Vol. 19), Toronto, 1914. To the volume on Canada of the Cambridge History of the British Empire (Vol. 6, Cambridge, 1930) he contributed two chapters dealing with the history of the Maritime Provinces from 1815 to 1867. In 1928–1929 he was counsel of the Province of Manitoba before the final Natural Resources Commission in the negotiations between the Dominion Government and the Prairie Provinces which culminated in the return to those provinces of the jurisdiction over their natural resources held by the Dominion Government. On this topic Professor Martin has written "The Natural Resources Question," Winnipeg, 1920. Professor Martin is chairman of the historical section of the Canadian Pioneer Problems Committee.

Professor McARTHUR is head of the Department of History at Queen's University, Kingston, Ontario. Among his numerous publications may be mentioned his contributions to the series "Canada and Its Provinces," edited by Adam Shortt and A. G. Doughty, 23 vols., Toronto, 1914–1917, and to Volume 6, on Canada, of the "Cambridge History of the British Empire," Cambridge, 1930. In the former series (Vols. 3, 4, 5) he has written: "The New Régime [1763–1774]"; "Canada under the Quebec Act"; "Lower and Upper Canada, 1791–1812"; "Papineau and French-Canadian Nationalism"; "The Reform Movement in Upper Canada"; "The Canadian Rebellions of 1837"; "Lord Dunham and the Union of the Canadas"; "Constitutional History, 1763–1840"; "History of Public Finance 1763–1867." To the Cambridge History he contributed: "British North America and the American Revolution, 1774–1791"; "British North America under Representative Government, 1791–1812"; "The War of 1812." Professor McArthur is editor of *Queen's Quarterly* and is vice-chairman of the Canadian Pioneer Problems Committee.

Dr. MACGIBBON, chairman of the section on general economics of the Canadian Pioneer Problems Committee until 1929, when he resigned on becoming a member of the Board of Grain Commissioners of Canada, was professor of political economy at Brandon College, Brandon, Man., from 1911 to 1917 and at the University of Alberta from 1919 to 1929. In 1923–1924 he was a member of the Royal Grain Enquiry Commission appointed by the Dominion Government, and in 1930 he was attached as a technical member to the Canadian delegation to the Imperial Conference at London. Among his publications may be mentioned "Railway Rates and the Canadian Railway Commission," Boston, 1917; "The Canadian Grain Trade," Toronto, 1932.

Dr. DAWSON is professor and head of the Department of Sociology at McGill University, Montreal. In 1929, on behalf of the Canadian Pioneer Problems Committee, he made a visit to the Peace River district to study the social structure of its pioneer inhabitants. The present paper is based on that visit. Dr. Dawson is chairman of that Committee's section of sociology. He has written (jointly with W. E. Gettys) "Introduction to Sociology," New York, 1929, and "Population Areas and Physiographic Regions in Canada" (*Amer. Journ. of Sociology*, July, 1927).

Dr. GEORGESON, whose article in the present volume is his last published contribution, died in 1931. A native of Denmark, he came to the United States as a young man and equipped himself for the teaching of agriculture, of which subject he was professor at the Texas State Agricultural and Mechanical College in 1880–1883, at the College of Agriculture of the University of Tokyo, Japan, 1885–1889, and at the Kansas State Agricultural College, 1890–1897. In 1898 he went to Alaska as special agent of the U. S. Department of Agriculture to investigate the agricultural possibilities of the Territory. As a result seven agricultural experiment stations were established in Alaska (see the map on p. 52); of these he was agronomist in charge from 1915 and later director to his retirement in 1928. During his thirty years of work in Alaska he experimented extensively in hybridization and developed a number of hardy grains suited to the northern climate. The results of this work are published in a number of Bulletins and Circulars of the Alaska Agricultural Experiment Stations and in the U. S. Department of Agriculture Yearbooks.

Dr. BAKER is senior agricultural economist in the Bureau of Agricultural Economics of the U. S. Department of Agriculture. His numerous writings deal mainly with the broader aspects of agricultural geography. A synthesis of the conditions revealed by the censuses of 1910, 1920, and 1930 is presented in the three successive versions of "A Graphic Summary of American Agriculture" (jointly with others in the *U. S. Dept. of Agric. Yearbooks* for 1915 and 1921 and *U. S. Dept. of Agric. Misc. Publ. No. 105*, 1931); the topic is treated regionally in "The Agricultural Regions of North America" (in 11 parts, *Econ. Geogr.*, 1926–1932). With V. C. Finch he is the author of "Geography of the World's Agriculture" (1917), an atlas in which the dot method is used to represent distributions, and since 1917 the "Atlas of American Agriculture" has been prepared under his supervision. These various cartographic publications have helped serve as guiding examples in the preparation of the atlas entitled "Agriculture, Climate, and Population of the Prairie Provinces of Canada" (see above, p. 9), recently published by the Dominion Bureau of Statistics, Ottawa, as a result of the coöperative activities of the Canadian Pioneer Problems Committee. As a member of the American Geographical Society's Advisory Committee on Pioneer Problems he acted in a consultative capacity in the formative stages of this publication. Directly bearing on the topic of the present paper Dr. Baker has written on "Agriculture in the Great Plains Region" (*Annals Assn. of Amer. Geogrs.*, Vol. 13, 1923) and "The Spring Wheat Region" (Part 6 of series mentioned above; *Econ. Geogr.*, Vol. 4, 1928). To the *Geographical Review* he has contributed "Land Utilization in the United States: Geographical Aspects of the Problem" (Vol. 13, 1923) and "Population, Food Supply, and American Agriculture" (Vol. 18, 1928).

Mr. PLATT is head of the American Geographical Society's Department of Hispanic American Research. One of the major undertakings of this department is the compilation and publication of a map of Hispanic America from the Rio Grande to Cape Horn on the scale of 1 : 1,000,000, or about 16 miles to the inch (see his description in *Geogr. Rev.*, Vol. 17, 1927), conforming in style of treatment to the International Map of the World being published by various governments. A critical evaluation of the source material used in the preparation of the map is provided in his paper "Surveys in Hispanic America" (*Geogr. Rev.*, Vol. 20, 1930) and in his analytical notes in the four-volume "Catalogue of Maps of Hispanic America" (*Amer. Geogr. Soc. Map of Hispanic America Publs.*, 1930 ff.), both paper and notes being accompanied by a map of Hispanic America showing the extent and character of existing surveys. In the field of political geography Mr. Platt has written "Present Status of International Boundaries in South America" (*Geogr. Rev.*, Vol. 14, 1924) and "A Note on the Political Sovereignty and Administration in the Caribbean" (*ibid.*, Vol. 16, 1926). In 1924 and 1925 he visited most of the countries of South America and gained an insight into some of the problems discussed in the present paper. Later he was associated in planning the Society's Peruvian Expedition of 1927, which visited the settlements in the upper Huallaga, Pachitea, and Perené valleys described in the present article.

Dr. SCHURZ has had wide experience of economic conditions in Latin America. In 1919–1920 he was trade commissioner of the U. S. Department of Commerce in charge of a general economic investigation of Paraguay and Bolivia; from 1920 to 1926 he was commercial attaché at the United States Embassy in Rio de Janeiro; in 1923–1924 he headed the Department of Commerce's crude-rubber survey expedition to the Amazon Valley; in 1926–1927 he was economic adviser to the government of Cuba. He has since been in charge of the Latin-American departments of a number of commercial firms. These activities are reflected in his publications, among which may be mentioned "Paraguay: A Commercial Handbook" and "Bolivia: An Economic Handbook" (*Bur. of Foreign and Domestic Commerce Special Agents Series Nos. 199 and 208*, Washington, 1920 and 1921), "Rubber Production in the Amazon Valley" (joint author; *U. S. Dept. of Commerce Trade Promotion Series No. 23*, Washington, 1925), "The Distribution of Population in the Amazon Valley" (*Geogr. Rev.*, Vol. 15, 1925), "The Manila Galleon and California" (*The Southwestern Hist. Quart.*, Vol. 21, 1917), "Mexico, Peru, and the Manila Galleon" (*Hispanic Amer. Hist. Rev.*, Vol. 1, 1918), the two last a history of Spanish colonial trade and navigation in the Pacific Ocean.

Dr. JONES is professor of geography at the University of Chicago. In 1911–1913 he acted as economic geographer on the Hydrological Commission of the Railway Department of the Argentine Ministry of Public Works that under the direction of Professor Bailey Willis carried out land utilization surveys in northern Patagonia. He extended his field studies of the forms of land occupation to Japan and China in 1916 and to India in 1920. His article "Hokkaido, The Northland of Japan" (*Geogr. Rev.*, Vol. 11, 1921) and the note on "An Isopleth Map of Land under Crops in India" (*ibid.*, Vol. 19, 1929) reflect this work. In the last ten years he has devoted himself especially to developing methods of detailed field surveys of rural and urban areas. On this topic he has written: "Detailed Field Mapping in the Study of the Economic Geography of an Agricultural Area" (with V. C. Finch, *Annals Assn. of Amer. Geogrs.*, Vol. 15, 1925); "A Method of Determining the Degree of Coincidence in Distribution of Agricultural Uses of Land with Slope-Soil-Drainage Complexes" (*Trans. Illinois State Acad. of Sci.*, Vol. 22, 1930); "Field Mapping of Residential Areas in Metropolitan Chicago" (*Annals Assn. of Amer. Geogrs.*, Vol. 21, 1931); "Ratios and Isopleth Maps in Regional Investigation of Agricultural Land Occupance" (*ibid.*, Vol. 20, 1930). With D. S. Whittlesey, Professor Jones is co-author of "An Introduction to Economic Geography" (Chicago, 1925).

Professor WELLINGTON is professor of geography at the University of the Witwatersrand, Johannesburg. He is honorary editor of the *South African Geographical Journal*, to which and to the *South African Journal of Science* he has contributed articles on various aspects of the physical and human geography of the Union of South Africa. These include "The Natural Regions of the Transvaal" (*South African Geogr. Journ.*, Vol. 10, 1927), "The Topographical Features of the Witwatersrand" (*ibid.*, Vol. 7, 1924), "The Vaal-Limpopo Watershed" (*ibid.*, Vol. 12, 1929), "Some Physical Influences in the Human Geography of South Africa" (*South African Journ. of Sci.*, Vol. 26, 1929), "Some Geographical Factors Affecting Agriculture in South Africa" (*South African Geogr. Journ.*, Vol. 6, 1923), and "Land Utilization in South Africa" (*Geogr. Rev.*, Vol. 22, 1932).

Dr. LORAM, a native of Natal, has devoted himself to the cause of negro education. He has successively been inspector of schools and director and superintendent of native education in Natal. In 1920 he was appointed one of the three members of the Native Affairs Commission, the body charged with the formulation of a native policy for South Africa. As such and as a member of the two Phelps Stokes Fund educational commissions and while engaged in making an investigation of native education in Kenya he had opportunities of studying native land and labor conditions in most parts of Africa. On this topic he has written "The Education of the South African Native," New York, 1917. Dr. Loram has on the occasion of repeated visits to the United States given much study to the problems, both rural and urban, of the American negro. Dr. Loram is at present professor of education in the Graduate School of Yale University.

Mrs. TAWSE JOLLIE, whose home has been in Rhodesia since 1915, lives on a farm at Chibuzana, 150 miles from the nearest railway station, Umtali. She was honorary secretary and organizer of the Responsible Government Party in Southern Rhodesia, 1920, and is a member of the Legislative Council of Southern Rhodesia, the first woman to be elected in any British Colonial legislature. She has made a special study of native life and the native question. With her first husband, Archibald Colquhoun, publicist, member of the Pioneer Column, and administrator of Mashonaland, she traveled widely in the Far East, Africa, the United States, and South America. She has written "The Real Rhodesia" (1924). Her recent periodical articles include contributions to the *Geographical Review* ("Southern Rhodesia: A White Man's Country in the Tropics," Vol. 17, 1927) and to *Nada: The Southern Rhodesia Native Affairs Department Annual* ("Uplift in Bantuland," 1930, No. 8).

Mr. DARBY's article is based on a visit to Rhodesia and Nyasaland in 1929 to collect data for the American Geographical Society's studies in pioneer settlement. To the *Geographical Review* (Vol. 21, 1931) he contributed a related article on "Settlement in Northern Rhodesia." Mr. Darby is lecturer in the Honours School of the Department of Geography of Cambridge University. Previously to the present work he has specialized in the historical geography of medieval Europe, in which field he has written a monograph on "The Rôle of the Fenland in English History" and articles on "The Tinplate Migration in the Vale of Neath" (*Geography*, Vol. 15, 1929), "The Architectural Geography of South Britain" (*Sociological Rev.*, Vol. 20, 1928), and "The Tenby Coast: A Local Shore Study" (*Rept. Twelfth Internatl. Geogr. Cong. Held at London and Cambridge, 1928*, 1930).

M. BERNARD is a leading authority on the geography of North Africa. From 1894 to 1900 he was a member of the faculty of the University of Algiers; since 1902 he has been professor of the geography and colonization of North Africa at the University of Paris. His numerous publications on the region of his specialty include: "Les régions naturelles en Algérie," with map in 1 : 2,500,000 (jointly with E. Ficheur, *Ann. de Géogr.*, Vol. 11, 1902); "L'évolution du nomadisme en Algérie" (jointly with N. Lacroix), Algiers, 1906; "Les confins algéro-marocains," Paris, 1911; "Le Maroc," 7th edit., Paris, 1931; "L'Algérie" (both in series: Bibliothèque d'Histoire Contemporaine); "Atlas d'Algérie et de Tunisie" (jointly with R. de Flotte de Roquevaire). He is a member of the Académie des Sciences Coloniales and of the Comité de l'Afrique Française. Before the establishment of the French protectorate he participated in a number of official missions to Morocco and at present is associated with the Commission Interministérielle des Affaires Musulmanes.

Professor VOSHCHININ is professor of colonization in the Department of Geography at the University of Leningrad and professor of emigration and colonization in the Leningrad Agricultural Institute. Before the World War he was a member of the Colonization Commission of the Third Duma, the work of which he dealt with in his "Pereselencheskii vopros v Gosudarstvennoi Dumye III sozyva" (The Colonization Question in the Third Duma), St. Petersburg, 1912. His other publications include: "Na Sibirskom prostorye" (On Siberian Spaciousness), St. Petersburg, 1912, and "Ocherki novago Turkestana" (Sketches of the New Turkestan), St. Petersburg, 1914.

Dr. PRASOLOV's soil investigations, through fieldwork and research, cover the whole territorial extent of the U.·S S. R., both in Europe and in Asia. In 1898–1906 he directed soil survey work in the government of Samara and in 1908–1914 he took part in Professor K. D. Glinka's soil expeditions in Siberia and Turkestan. He is a fellow of the Dokuchaiev Institute of Soils of the Academy of Sciences and a member of the committee on agricultural economics of the People's Commissariat of Agriculture. Among his numerous works may be mentioned: several reports in the series "Materialy dlya otsyenki zemel Samarskoi Gubernii" (Materials for the Evaluation of the Land in Samara Government), Samara, 1904–1911, and in the "Trudy Pochvenno-botanicheskikh Ekspeditsii Pereselencheskago Upravleniya" (Memoirs of the Soil-Botanical Expeditions of the Department of Colonization); "Pochvy Turkestana" (Soils of Turkestan), with soils map in 1 : 4,200,000, Academy of Sciences, Leningrad, 1926; "Soils of the European Part of the U. S. S. R." (Guidebook No. 1 for the Excursion of the Second International Congress of Soil Science, Moscow, 1930); "Yuzhnoe Zabaikale: Pochvenno-geograficheskii ocherk" (Southern Trans-baikalia: Soil-Geographical Sketch), Academy of Sciences, Leningrad, 1927; "Cartography of Soils" (Russian Pedological Investigations No. 6), Academy of Sciences, Leningrad, 1927; the soil maps of European Russia in 1 : 2,520,000 and (under joint editorship with K. D. Glinka) of Asiatic Russia in 1 : 4,200,000 listed above on p. 259; "Vsemirnaya pochvennaya Karta K. D. Glinki" (The World Soil Map of K. D. Glinka), with soil map of the world in 1 : 82,000,000, *Priroda*, Leningrad, 1928, No. 6.

Professor CRESSEY's specialty is the geography of China. On this topic he has written "The Geography of China," 3rd preliminary edit., Shanghai, 1928, and "The Geographic Regions of China" (*Annals Amer. Acad. of Polit. and Soc. Sci.*, November, 1930, and *Proc. Fourth Pacific Sci. Congr.*, Java, 1929, Vol. 2B). Some of his other publications are "The New Map of China" (*Geogr. Rev.*, Vol. 20, 1930), a description, with map, of the new territorial divisions since the revolution of 1911; and "The Geology of Shanghai" (*China Journ.*, Vol. 8–9, 1928). From 1923 to 1929 Professor Cressey was a member of the faculty of Shanghai College. During this period he made several trips to Mongolia, especially to the Ordos and Alashan Deserts in the region of the big bend of the Hwang Ho. Some of the material on which the present article is based was gathered on these field trips. He is at present head of the department of geology and geography at Syracuse University.

Mr. LATTIMORE has spent many years in China and traveled extensively there and in Central Asia. In 1926–1927 he made a journey along one of the old caravan routes from China through Mongolia to Chinese Turkestan. This is described in his "The Desert Road to Turkestan," London, 1928, and *Geogr. Journ.*, Vol. 72, 1928. "High Tartary," Boston, 1930, deals more specifically with Chinese Turkestan on the basis of this journey. In 1929–1930 he carried out work in Manchuria under a fellowship from the Social Science Research Council and with the support of the American Geographical Society. From these have resulted his recent book "Manchuria: Cradle of Conflict," New York, 1932, a historical study of the movements of peoples and the conflict of cultures on the northeastern frontiers of China, and his article on "Chinese Colonization in Manchuria" (*Geogr. Rev.*, Vol. 22, 1932).

Mr. AHNERT, at present resident in Harbin, Manchuria, is a Russian geologist and mining engineer who has long been identified with the geological exploration and investigation of eastern Siberia and the Amur basin region in general. In 1895–1896 he was a member of the geological research committee of the Amur Railway, at that time still a project, and later chief of the expedition to investigate the mineral resources tributary to the right of way of the Chinese Eastern Railway. In 1897–1898 he was a member of the Russian Geographical Society's Manchuria and North Korea expedition, for his work on which he was awarded the Society's Przhevalskii Medal. Associated with the Russian Geological Survey ("Comité Géologique") since 1897, he investigated the gold deposits of the Amur and Yakutsk districts from 1900 to 1913 and subsequently the mineral resources of the South Ussuri region. Stationed in the Far East since 1918, he has been connected with the geological department of the Chinese Eastern Railway since 1920. Among his numerous publications may be mentioned, in addition to those cited on p. 316 above: "Esquisse géologique du Bassin de l'Amour," with hypsometric map in 1 : 1,680,000 (*Publs. du Comité Géologique*, Livraison 17, St. Petersburg 1913); "Voyage à travers la Mandjourie, ' with geological and relief maps in 1 : 840,000 (*Mémoires Soc. Imp. Russ. de Géogr.*, Vol. 35, St. Petersburg, 1904); "What Has Been Done and What Remains To Be Done for the Geological Study of the Russian Far East and Its Mineral Resources" (*Records of the Geol. Committee of the Russian Far East*, Vladivostok, 1926).

Mr. YOUNG has published numerous studies of Manchurian economics and diplomacy and has made field investigations of Chinese labor migrations and the recent tendencies toward permanent colonization by Chinese in Manchuria. He resided in Japan in 1922–1923 and in China in 1925–1927. During these sojourns in the East and also in 1929 and 1930 he visited Manchuria. Mr. Young has been a member of the faculty, in the Department of Political Science, of the University of Minnesota and Johns Hopkins University and professor of international relations at George Washington University. He is at present associated with the Institute of Current World Affairs in New York. In addition to the publications on colonization in Manchuria listed above on pages 358–359 he has written "The International Relations of Manchuria," Chicago, 1929, and "Economic Factors in Manchurian Diplomacy" (*Annals Amer. Acad. of Polit. and Soc. Sci.*, Nov., 1930).

Professor TAYLOR is the leading authority on the geography of Australia. He has long devoted himself to the application of climatology to the problems of settlement and human adaptation to environment in Australia and in the world in general. This aspect of his work is related to his long residence in Australia (1910–1928), during which period he successively occupied the positions of physiographer to the Commonwealth Bureau of Meteorology, instructor in physiography at the University of Melbourne, and professor of geography and head of the department at the University of Sydney. Among his numerous publications in this field may be mentioned: "Australia in Its Physiographic and Economic Aspects (4th edit., London, 1925); "Australian Meteorology" (London, 1920); "The Australian Environment, Especially As Controlled by Rainfall" (Melbourne, 1918); "The Climatic Control of Australian Production" (*Commonwealth Bur. of Meteorol. Bull. No. 11*, 1915); "Geographical Factors Controlling the Settlement of Tropical Australia" (*Queensland Geogr. Journ.*, Vol. 32–33, 1918); "The Distribution of Future White Settlement" (*Geogr. Rev.*, Vol. 12, 1922); "Environment and Race" (London, 1927). Another aspect of Professor Taylor's work deals with the geology and geography of Antarctica, as a result of his association as senior geologist and leader of the western parties with the British Antarctic Expedition of 1910–1913 under Scott. Among the publications in this field may be mentioned: "With Scott: The Silver Lining" (London, 1916); "The Physiography of the McMurdo Sound and Granite Harbour Region" (in scientific reports of the British Antarctic Expedition 1910–1913, London, 1922) and "Climatic Relations between Antarctica and Australia" (in "Problems of Polar Research," *Amer. Geogr. Soc. Special Publ. No. 7*, New York, 1928). Professor Taylor is at present professor of geography at the University of Chicago.

Dr. ROBERTS is Challis Professor of History at the University of Sydney. He was formerly lecturer in modern history at the University of Melbourne. His major publications are: "History of Australian Land Settlement (1788–1920)," Melbourne, 1924; "The Squatting Age in Australia," Melbourne, 1931; "Population Problems of the Pacific," London, 1927; "History of French Colonial Policy," 2 vols., London, 1929. He has also written: "Northern Territory Colonization Schemes," *Rept. of 17th Meeting Australasian Assn. for the Advancement of Sci., Adelaide Meeting 1924*, Adelaide, 1926, and "Racial and Labour Problems" (in "The Australian Mandate for New Guinea: Record of Round Table Discussion"), Victorian Branch of League of Nations Union, Melbourne, 1928.

Dr. WOOD is senior lecturer in economics and economic geography at the University of Melbourne. While previously residing at Hobart he wrote "The Tasmanian Environment: A Human and Economic Geography of Tasmania" (2nd edit., Melbourne, 1929). Among his other publications are "The Pacific Basin" (Oxford, 1930); "Borrowing and Business in Australia" (Oxford, 1930); "The Immigration Problem in Australia" (*Econ. Record*, Nov., 1926); "The Settlement of Northern Australia" (*ibid.*, May, 1926); "Economic Factors in Australian Transport" (*ibid.*, Transport Supplement, 1930); the section on population and economic trends in "Economic Survey of Australia" (constituting the November, 1931, number of the *Annals Amer. Acad. of Polit. and Soc. Sci.*); "Economic Development and Trade" (in "The Australian Mandate for New Guinea: Record of Round Table Discussion"), Victorian Branch of League of Nations Union, Melbourne, 1928.

Professor CONDLIFFE, a native of Melbourne, was professor of economics at Canterbury College, Christchurch, N. Z., from 1920 to 1926. Subsequently he acted as research secretary of the Institute of Pacific Relations with headquarters in Honolulu. After one year (1930–1931) as visiting professor of economics at the University of Michigan he was appointed to the Economic and Financial Section of the League of Nations secretariat at Geneva, where he now resides. His publications deal with the economics and economic history of Australasia and other parts of the Pacific realm and include: "A Short History of New Zealand," Christchurch, 1925; "New Zealand in the Making: A Survey of Economic and Social Development," London and Chicago, 1930; "The Industrial Revolution in the Far East" (*Econ. Record*, Vols. 2 and 3, 1926–1927); "The Economic and Social Movements Underlying Antagonisms in the Pacific," (*Journ. Royal Inst. of Internatl. Affairs*, Vol. 9, 1930). Professor Condliffe also edited the proceedings of the second (Honolulu, 1927) and third (Kyoto, 1929) conferences of the Institute of Pacific Relations, each entitled "Problems of the Pacific" (Chicago, 1928 and 1930).

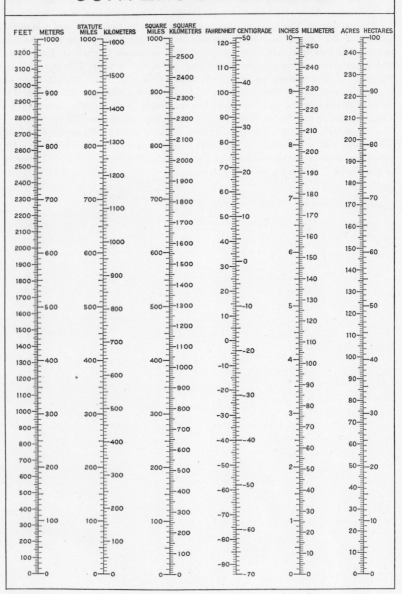

CONVERSION SCALES

INDEX

INDEX

447

ERRATUM
p. 251, line 16 and Table II: *for* rH *read* pH.